Mastering
Voir Dire
and Jury Selection

Gain an Edge in Questioning and Selecting Your Jury

Second Edition

JEFFREY T. FREDERICK, PH.D.

GP | Solo

ABA General Practice, Solo & Small Firm Section

Cover design by Grey Cat Design.

09 08 07 06 05 5 4 3 2

Library of Congress Cataloging-in-Publication Data

Frederick, Jeffrey T.
    Mastering voir dire and jury selection : gaining an edge in
questioning and selecting a jury / by Jeffrey T. Frederick.—2nd ed.
        p. cm.
    Includes bibliographical references and index.
    ISBN 1-59031-434-4
    1. Jury selection—United States. I. American Bar Association.
General Practice, Solo, and Small Firm Section. II. Title.

    KF8979.F73   2004
    347.73'752—dc22

                                                          2004024196

Discounts are available for books ordered in bulk. Special consideration is given to state bars, CLE programs, and other bar-related organizations. Inquire at Book Publishing, ABA Publishing, American Bar Association, 321 N. Clark, Chicago, Illinois 60610.

www.abanet.org

CONTENTS

ACKNOWLEDGMENTS

I wish to thank a number of people who have contributed in many ways to the second edition of this book, in particular, I would like to thank the supportive members of the American Bar Association Press, including executive editors Rick Paszkiet, Jean Iversen, and Holly Wehmeyer, and marketing support from Jill Nuppenau and Katrina Krause. In addition, I would like to thank Elio Martinez for his support in this project.

A number of people contributed supplemental juror questionnaires and/or provided approval for their use in this book. They are listed in alphabetical order: Hon. Carol Bagley Amon, Hon. Linda Baxter, Hon. Roger Beauchesne, Hon. Frederick Block, Hon. Ronald Buckwalter, Hon. Garland Burrell Jr., William Campbell, Esquire, Mr. Richard Cole, Hon. Clarence Cooper, Gregory Cusimano, Esquire, Hon. Raymond Dearie, Hon. Bernice Donald, Hon. Lee Dreyfus, Margorie Fargo, MA, James Fitzgerald, Esquire, Hon. David Folsom, Ms. Cheryl Gallo, Hon. John Gasaway III, Frank Gaziano, Esquire, Hon. Mark Gempeler, Hon. Nancy Gertner, Hon. James Giles, Susan Gill, Esquire, Hon. I. Leo Glasser, Mr. John Gleeson, Barry Gross, Esquire, Mark Harmon, Esquire, Ms. Marcella Harris, Frederick Heblich Jr., Esquire, Robert Heinemann, Hon. Donna Hitchens, Hon. Thomas Hogan, Hon. Edward Hogshire, Hon. H. Russel Holland, Ms. Alisa Hollander, Hon. Orlando Hudson Jr., Hon. Thomas Penfield Jackson, Joseph Kearfott, Esquire, John Keker, Esquire, Mr. Michael Kuntz, William King Jr., Esquire, Hon. Royce Lamberth, Hon. Charles Lamm, Jr., Paul Luvera, Esquire, Hon. Richard Matsch, Hon. Joseph McKinley, Jr., S. Theodore Merritt, Esquire, Mr. Michael Milby, Ms. Jeannette Miller, Hon. Leroy Millette Jr., Hon. Norman Moon, Hon. Henry Morgan Jr., Hon. Michael Mukasey, Hon. Michael Obus, Michael O'Leary, Esquire, Hon. William Parsons, Marla Persky, Esquire, Lisa Phelan, Esquire, Hon. Michael Ponsor, Ms. Jeanne Quinata, Hon. Sylvia Rambo, Hon. William Rhea, Frank Rubino, Esquire, Hon. Alex Saldamando, Hon. Leonard Sand, Hon. Frank Seay, Hon. James Selna, Jonathan Shapiro, Esquire, Andrew Sheldon, Ph.D., J.D., Robert Siedel, Esquire, Hon. J. Robert Stump, Joseph Uberman, Esquire, Hon. Ricardo Urbina, Hon. Stanley Weisberg, William Welch II, Esquire, Hon. Samuel Wilson, James Wyatt III, Esquire, and Gerald Zerkin, Esquire.

Also, special thanks to Jennifer Holden for her assistance in tracking down various supplemental juror questionnaires.

Finally, I would like to acknowledge Dr. Linda Gonder-Frederick. Her continued support and encouragement show the power that is available in committed couples. And a fond farewell with gratitude to a good friend and excellent litigator, Bruce D. Rasmussen, Esquire.

INTRODUCTION

The voir dire and jury selection process is one of the most challenging aspects of a jury trial. It is at this time that lawyers must identify and remove potential jurors who harbor some bias or hold beliefs that would make them less beneficial than others. Success in jury selection requires lawyers to draw upon a number of basic skills. These skills include the ability to:

- operate effectively within the jury selection system in the trial jurisdiction;
- attain the major goals of voir dire (i.e., information gathering, rapport, education, and persuasion);
- identify critical opinions, biases, and experiences of jurors that can influence their decisions;
- encourage jurors to reveal important information about themselves;
- utilize the information about their opinions and feelings that potential jurors communicate through their nonverbal behavior;
- develop and ask the questions on voir dire necessary to uncover desired information;
- capitalize on the information available through the use of juror questionnaires;
- capitalize on methods for handling common situations and problems that arise during voir dire; and
- exercise peremptory challenges and challenges for cause in a manner that removes the least desirable potential jurors.

The goal of this book is to promote the skills needed to be successful in the area of voir dire and jury selection. It is through the sharpening of these skills that lawyers take a major step in improving the chances of a favorable verdict at trial.

We begin our consideration of voir dire and jury selection in Chapter 1 by examining the voir dire situation. What are the major goals of voir dire? How do jurisdictions differ in how voir dire and jury selection are conducted? What is the impact of these differences on how lawyers should approach jury selection?

Chapter 2 examines the story model as a model for juror decisionmaking and the importance of what jurors bring with them to court—the opinions, biases, and experiences that shape how they view and relate to the world around them. We consider the role of stereotypes and jurors' backgrounds and experiences. To more fully understand jurors' viewpoints, we explore the importance of global opinions, i.e., authoritarianism and beliefs in equity; case-specific opinions, i.e., opinions and attitudes that relate to the circumstances and issues in the case; and legal opinions, i.e., views regarding legal principles and procedures.

Chapter 3 considers the information that is gained through understanding the nonverbal communication of potential jurors. We examine the important visual cues pertaining to the body, e.g., movement, posture, orientation, emblems, shrugs, eye contact, and facial expressions. Valuable information is also communicated through auditory cues. Speech disturbances, vocal hesitancy, rising pitch, amount of speech, speed of speech, tone of voice, tense laughter, and word choice provide insights into what jurors are "really" saying.

Chapter 4 turns to preparing for voir dire. In this chapter, we examine the key elements of the preparation process: case analysis and question development. What are the essential aspects to consider when analyzing a case? How do you consider such factors as the strengths and weaknesses of the case, the case theme, and important opinions and personal experiences of jurors? How should questions be asked to meet the various goals of voir dire?

In Chapter 5 we turn to conducting voir dire. This chapter stresses good communication skills and interviewing techniques that facilitate the willingness of jurors to reveal important information about themselves. In addition, we consider key points in structuring the questioning process to maximize juror candor and disclosure. This chapter concludes by addressing the challenges faced in conducting questioning in settings where information is at a premium, i.e., restricted voir dire, group questioning, and judge-conducted voir dire.

We next turn our attention to situations and problems commonly encountered in voir dire and how to make the most of them. Chapter 6 considers two types of problematic jurors, reluctant jurors and difficult jurors, and ways of meeting the challenges they present. In addition, we examine effective methods of handling (a) "negative spiraling," when jurors as a group become less forthcoming on voir dire, (b) the opportunities that "good" potential jurors present, and (c) the effects of pretrial publicity.

Chapter 7 considers the use of juror questionnaires. These questionnaires gather information on the jurors' backgrounds, experiences, and opinions prior to voir dire questioning and serve to supplement the information available on voir dire. In this chapter we discuss how to construct questionnaires to get the most out of their use. Juror questionnaires from the criminal trials of former Lieutenant Colonel Oliver North and Timothy McVeigh, and the civil trial of Exxon Corporation that arose out of the Exxon Valdez oil spill are used, among other juror questionnaires, to illustrate both good and bad points in questionnaire construction. In addition, we consider how to manage the information available through questionnaires, including the use of checklists and computer-assisted information management for complex questionnaires.

Chapter 8 examines how to evaluate jurors. We consider how to integrate the information available regarding jurors (both pretrial and trial information). In addition, we examine the dynamics of jury deliberations, leadership, and the formation of subgroups within the jury. Finally, we consider methods for making a final rating of the favorability of jurors.

Chapter 9 explores selecting a jury. It addresses both challenges for cause and peremptory challenges, along with a discussion of recent developments in the law regarding the prohibition against the discriminatory exercise of peremptory challenges. Finally, we consider strategies for exercising peremptory challenges in the context of the sequential and struck jury methods.

At the end of this book are several appendices for lawyer reference. Appendix I contains the motion for improved voir dire procedures and the court appointment of a jury consultant submitted by the defense in the *Commonwealth of Virginia v. John Allen Muhammad*. Appendix II contains selected opinion questions for criminal trials from the perspectives of both the prosecution and the defense. Appendix III addresses selected opinion questions for civil trials from both plaintiff and defense perspectives. Appendix IV, found on the companion CD, contains the juror questionnaires used in numerous criminal and civil trials. These questionnaires come from such criminal trials as *Colorado v. Kobe Bryant* (sexual assault), *California v. Scott Peterson* (murder), *California v. O.J. Simpson* (murder), *Connecticut v. Michael Skakel* (murder), *United States v. Timothy McVeigh* (domestic terrorism—Oklahoma City bombing), *United States v. Arthur Andersen* (obstruction of justice—Enron scandal), among others, and from civil trials including *In re Exxon Valdez* (Valdez oil spill), *Doe v. Nash* (wrongful termination—AIDS), *In re Visa Check/Mastermoney Antitrust Litigation* (antitrust), *International Paper Co. v. Affiliate FM Insurance Cos.* (bad faith), and *Mildred Valentine v. Dow Corning Corporation et al.* (product liability—breast implant), among others. Each juror questionnaire on the CD is linked to the table of contents for easy reference and accessibility.

This book goes beyond other books on jury selection in its focus on the skills needed to conduct effective voir dire and jury selection. Having a list of questions to ask is only a starting point. Conducting effective voir dire and jury selection requires developing strategies that secure necessary information and adapting to the unique circumstances that lawyers face in their trial jurisdictions. Effective jury selection does not result from memorizing questions from a book. It is a dynamic process that places a premium on knowing what is needed and how to get it.

ABOUT THE AUTHOR

Dr. Jeffrey Frederick is the Director of the Jury Research Services Division of the National Legal Research Group. This division provides research and assistance to attorneys in addressing the problems faced in trying cases before juries. He has assisted attorneys in the application of social science research methods to jury selection and persuasion issues since 1975. He is a member of the American Psychological Association, American Psychology/Law Society, and American Society of Trial Consultants.

He is a nationally recognized speaker and author in the area of jury trials. He has written extensively on the topic of jury trials and trial advocacy, including the book *The Psychology of the American Jury*. He has been part of programs for legal organizations including the Department of Justice, American Bar Association, American Law Institute/American Bar Association, National College of District Attorneys, Florida State Bar Association, District of Columbia Inns of Court, Virginia State Bar Association, Academy of Florida Trial Lawyers, Georgia Institute for Continuing Legal Education, North Carolina Academy of Trial Lawyers, Florida Defense Lawyers' Association, Louisiana Trial Lawyers' Association, New Mexico Bar Association, and University of Virginia Trial Advocacy Institute.

CHAPTER 1

The Voir Dire and
Jury Selection Setting

Objectives

- To understand the goals of voir dire and jury selection.
- To understand the differences between jury selection procedures and their impact on the effectiveness of jury selection.

On January 31, 1989, jury selection began in one of the most publicized criminal cases in recent history, the trial of former Lieutenant Colonel Oliver L. North. Oliver North was charged with twelve criminal counts, including charges of obstructing and lying to Congress; obstructing congressional and presidential inquiries; altering, concealing, and destroying National Security Council documents; and receiving an illegal gratuity. Of more than 210 jurors summoned, more than 120 were removed on the basis of their responses to preliminary questions on a juror questionnaire concerning their exposure to North's immunized testimony before Congress. From the remaining potential jurors, a pool of over forty potential jurors survived the examination by the judge, prosecution, and defense. The final jury consisted of twelve jurors and six alternates.

In terms of its length (approximately six days), the issues raised, and the scope of voir dire, the jury selection process in the Oliver North trial was unusual. Both the prosecution and the defense had to unravel the complexities of this highly publicized scandal and weigh its impact on potential jurors, even though the most-informed potential jurors were excluded early in the process. Despite its unusual nature, however, this case highlights the basic need of every trial lawyer in jury selection: to identify potential jurors who should be removed and seat a jury that is not biased against one's client.

Goals of Jury Selection and Voir Dire

In theory, the goal of jury selection is to select an impartial jury. The attainment of this goal is placed in the hands of the adversary process. The parties attempt to prevent from sitting on the jury potential jurors who they suspect may harbor some bias or prejudice against their client. In essence, jury selection is a filtering process resulting in a jury comprised of those individuals whom the parties and the court fail to remove. A potential juror can be prevented from sitting on the jury through the exercise of one of two types of challenges: challenges for cause and peremptory challenges.

Challenges for cause center on the failure of the potential juror to meet specific statutory qualifications, e.g., residence requirements, or the presence of bias or prejudice. Bias or prejudice on the part of potential jurors can be inferred or actual. Inferred bias refers to the presumption of bias, usually defined by statute, as a result of a relationship between a potential juror and features of the case, e.g., a blood relationship between the potential juror and one of the parties or a financial interest in the outcome of the case. Actual bias is imputed to potential jurors as a result of statements reflecting prejudice or bias made during the questioning process or actual admissions of bias. In the North trial, for example, potential jurors who had been exposed to the immunized testimony or who said they had formed an opinion as to the guilt of the defendant and would be unable to set their opinion aside were removed for cause. As we shall see in Chapter 9, challenges for cause are limited in scope, unlimited in number, and within the discretion of the trial judge.

Lawyers can prevent potential jurors from sitting on the jury through a second method, the exercise of peremptory challenges. Peremptory challenges are those limited challenges whose number is set by statute and varies with the nature of the crime or litigation at issue. Lawyers generally have the freedom to exercise these challenges as they see fit; as we shall see in Chapter 9, however, the peremptory challenge must be exercised in a nondiscriminatory manner in terms of the juror's race, gender, or Hispanic origin.

The four major goals of voir dire:

- *Information gathering:* to elicit critical information from jurors in order to make meaningful use of peremptory challenges and challenges for cause.

- *Rapport:* to establish a positive relationship between the lawyer and jurors that results in more effective voir dire and subsequent persuasion.

- *Education:* to promote jurors' understanding and willingness to adhere to legal principles, juror roles, and the law.

- *Persuasion:* to influence jurors to adopt perspectives on the case beneficial to the lawyer.

The foundation for the exercise of challenges for cause and peremptory challenges is the voir dire, the process of questioning jurors. Voir dire has four major goals: (a) information gathering, (b) rapport, (c) education, and (d) persuasion. We will examine these goals briefly here, returning to them again in Chapter 4.

Information Gathering

The most important goal of voir dire is to gather from potential jurors the information necessary to enable lawyers to intelligently exercise their peremptory challenges and pursue any challenges for cause. Not only is information gathering the most important goal of voir dire, but it is perhaps the only goal of voir dire uniformly recognized as appropriate by the courts. Achievement of this goal is possible only by carefully considering exactly what information is needed, skillfully asking questions that uncover the critical information, and promoting the potential jurors' candor and honesty. Unfortunately, the manner in which voir dire is conducted in many jurisdictions impedes the attainment of the goal of effective information gathering.

Rapport

The second goal of voir dire is to build a positive relationship between the lawyer and jurors. Lawyers establish rapport by treating jurors with respect, showing an interest in the jurors as individuals, making the jurors feel comfortable, and sharing the personal side of themselves. Good rapport with jurors facilitates (a) openness and candor by potential jurors, (b) feelings of friendship toward the lawyer, which increases the persuasiveness of the lawyer, and (c) perceptions of lawyer objectivity, leading to greater trust, which is crucial to the effectiveness of the lawyer's arguments. These benefits lay the groundwork for more effective voir dire and subsequent persuasion at trial.

Education

The third goal of voir dire is education. Jurors arriving for jury service generally are unfamiliar with their new roles and duties and with what will occur at trial. They are also likely to be unfamiliar with legal terminology. Such phrases as "proximate cause" and "preponderance of the evidence" are not in common use outside our courthouses. In addition, many jurors hold opinions contrary to legal principles or standards. For example, opinion polls have repeatedly shown that substantial minorities of the general population (and jury-qualified individuals) tend to presume defendants are guilty and believe that criminal defendants should prove their innocence,[1] and that jurors would disregard the judge's instructions regarding inadmissible evidence.[2]

The need to educate potential jurors is underscored by the fact that failure to provide such education can lead to the jurors' inability to follow the instructions given to the jury by the judge at the end of the trial.

Two basic considerations highlight the need for the education of jurors before they are impaneled on the jury. First, lawyers must determine whether any opinions held by jurors that are contrary to legal principles or the law simply represent misconceptions or misunderstandings of the law or reflect deeply held biases. The latter situation may rise to the level of a challenge for cause or may necessitate the use of a peremptory challenge; the former situation can be corrected by education. Second, jurors process information as the trial unfolds. This processing of information occurs in light of jurors' expectations and beliefs regarding their roles and duties, and the law in the case. If jurors have misconceptions concerning relevant legal principles or the law, their processing of the trial information and their subsequent decisions will reflect these misconceptions.

Timing is a key issue in the education process. Educating jurors as to the law (i.e., judicial instructions) after the evidence is presented can lead jurors to treat the case differently than if they were aware of the relevant law before hearing the evidence.[3] Thus, the appropriate time to acquaint (and educate) jurors with the relevant legal concepts and terminology, decision criteria, trial procedures, and their role as impartial decision-makers is during voir dire. Lawyers and judges foster this educational process by using terms and explanations that jurors can understand, avoiding the often complex and confusing formal legal definitions.

4. Persuasion

The final—and most controversial—goal of voir dire is persuasion. While uniformly condemned by the courts, persuasion during voir dire has not escaped the attention of lawyers. The importance of persuasion during voir dire arises from the nature of the jury selection process itself. Jurors know that the lawyers eventually will be trying to persuade them to adopt their party's position in the case, but they expect these persuasive attempts to be made once the trial "starts," not during the jury selection process. Like the old adage, "forewarned is forearmed," jurors are better able to resist persuasive attempts when they know these attempts are coming. By not expecting a persuasive attempt during voir dire, jurors are susceptible to persuasion. It is for this reason, while perhaps not consciously recognized by lawyers, that persuasion can be effective during voir dire.

The primary goal of persuasion during voir dire is to influence potential jurors to adopt the perspective of the case that the lawyer advocates. By doing so early in the trial process, jurors filter the evidence and arguments made at trial through the lens of the lawyer's viewpoint. This filtering process subsequently makes the opposing lawyer's job that much more difficult.

Voir Dire and Jury Selection Procedures

Achieving the various goals of voir dire and jury selection is no simple task. Success depends on the skills of the lawyers, the practice and laws of the trial jurisdiction, and the latitude of questioning granted by and/or pursued by the judge.[4] All three of these factors vary across jurisdictions. Lawyers have different skill levels when it comes to voir dire. Judges participate and control the voir dire process to differing degrees. And there is considerable variation in the manner in which voir dire and jury selection is conducted from one jurisdiction to the next. It is to this factor that we now turn. The differences in voir dire appear in both the style with which voir dire is conducted and in the method in which peremptory challenges are exercised.

Voir Dire Style

The style of conducting voir dire varies in terms of who asks the questions and how questions are addressed to potential jurors.

WHO EXAMINES. Examination of potential jurors occurs in one of several ways, either solely by the judge (or magistrate), solely by the lawyers, or by a combination of judge/lawyer questioning. In federal courts, a large majority of the judges in criminal and civil trials conduct voir dire examination without oral participation by lawyers. In state courts, the situation is just the opposite, with lawyer- or judge/lawyer-conducted voir dire examination being prevalent.[5]

Who examines the potential jurors is not of minor importance. Because of the high status generally accorded to the judge, voir dire examination conducted by the judge is less likely to yield candid and honest answers by jurors than lawyer- or judge/lawyer-conducted voir dire.[6] Jurors simply are more reluctant to reveal personal, sensitive, or socially unacceptable information or opinions to judges than to lawyers, whom they perceive as closer in social status.

In addition, participation by lawyers in the voir dire process (either through lawyer-conducted or judge/lawyer-conducted voir dire) influences the process in several ways. First, being more knowledgeable about the issues in their cases, lawyers can develop initial and follow-up questions that elicit more valuable information from jurors. Second, questioning by lawyers is more likely to yield the kinds of nonverbal behavior that reflect the jurors' true opinions and feelings. When jurors feel hostile toward or are uncomfortable with a litigant or a lawyer, they are more likely to reveal these feelings nonverbally in response to questioning by the relevant lawyer than to questioning by the judge. Third, the advocacy role of lawyers makes them less likely to accept at face value jurors' assurances that they can be fair and impartial.

HOW QUESTIONS ARE ASKED. There are three methods in which questions are addressed to potential jurors: the individual method, the group method, and the combined method. In the *individual method*, questioning occurs with one juror at a time, generally without other jurors present. The *group method* questions jurors as a collective body, the size of the group ranging from just a few jurors, to a panel equal to the size of the trial jury, on rare occasions, the entire venire. Questions are addressed to the entire group, and, in light of the jurors' answers, the judge may or may not permit individual follow-up questioning.

Impact of voir dire styles:

- *Questioner.* Lawyer or judge/lawyer questioning yields greater juror candor and disclosure than questioning conducted exclusively by the judge.
- *Method of questioning.* The individual method yields more information from jurors than either the combined or the group method, with the latter method being least informative.

The _combined_ method, as the name implies, incorporates the above two methods. Potential jurors are questioned in a group where both individual and group questioning occurs. Questioning of individual jurors is not contingent on the responses made to group-oriented questions but may be pursued at appropriate times.

As with the matter of who conducts the examination, the method of questioning also has an impact on the effectiveness of the voir dire process. The individual method is superior to both the group and the combined methods.[7] The opportunity to tailor questions to each potential juror and his or her responses and the lessened social pressure present when other potential jurors are not in the room leads to a more informative voir dire. In addition, the individual method minimizes the likelihood that other potential jurors will be "tainted" by the answers given by a potential juror, a matter of particular concern in cases involving substantial pretrial publicity or community prejudice against particular litigants. It was for this reason that questioning of potential jurors in the *North* trial took place through the individual method.

Methods of Exercising Peremptory Challenges

The second major variation between jurisdictions centers on the timing of peremptory challenges. There are two basic methods, the sequential method and the struck method.[8]

SEQUENTIAL METHOD. In the sequential method, the exercise of peremptory challenges occurs at some point prior to the examination of all the potential jurors under consideration. With this method, one party is given the opportunity to examine the potential juror(s) first. This party examines the juror(s) and must exercise any peremptory challenges it desires before allowing the second party to conduct its examination. When the individual method of questioning is employed, a potential juror is questioned by one party. At the conclusion of its questioning, the party must exercise a peremptory challenge (provided a challenge for cause is not granted) or accept the juror. If a peremptory challenge is exercised, another potential juror takes the place of

---

How peremptory challenges are exercised:

- *Sequential method:* Challenges or "strikes" are exercised prior to the conclusion of the questioning process.
- *Struck method:* Strikes are exercised at the conclusion of questioning of all jurors being considered.

---

the excused potential juror and the questioning process by the first party begins again. When the first party accepts a potential juror, the second party begins its questioning. At the conclusion of the second party's questioning, this party must decide whether or not to excuse the juror through the exercise of a peremptory challenge. If the potential juror is not excused, the individual becomes a member of the trial jury. If the potential juror is excused, questioning begins with another potential juror. This back-and-forth process continues until both parties are satisfied with the jury or until one or both parties lack the ability to remove potential jurors either through peremptory challenges or challenges for cause.

The process is similar for the group method of questioning. One party questions a group or panel with the resulting exercise of peremptory challenges and questioning of replacement jurors until the panel is acceptable to the party. The second party then questions the panel. The second party proceeds in the same manner as did the first party. Once the panel is acceptable, or no challenges remain, the panel is turned over to the first party for questioning of those potential jurors the first party has yet to question. As with the individual method of questioning, the back-and-forth process continues until neither party can remove potential jurors or the panel is acceptable to both parties.

STRUCK JURY METHOD. The struck jury method differs from the sequential method in a fundamental respect. Both parties question all eligible potential jurors before exercising any peremptory challenges. The questioning process continues until the number of potential jurors who have been questioned and not removed for cause is equal to or, in some cases, greater than the number of trial jurors and alternates needed plus the total number of peremptory challenges available to the parties.

Upon reaching the desired number of "screened" jurors, both parties exercise their peremptory challenges. There are variations in the manner in which the parties exercise these peremptory challenges. In some jurisdictions, the parties alternate in the exercise of their challenges either one or more challenges at a time. Some jurisdictions have the parties exercise their peremptory challenges simultaneously.[9] Those potential jurors remaining after the exercise of the parties' challenges serve as the trial jury, usually including the alternates.

IMPACT OF THE USE OF THESE TWO METHODS. A simple example will illustrate the differences between these methods of exercising peremptory challenges and the resulting impact on the decision-making process of the parties. Suppose a jury of twelve members is to be selected using a group questioning method with each party possessing six peremptory challenges. The process begins by placing twelve potential jurors in the jury box. Under the sequential method, after the first party finishes questioning these potential jurors, the lawyer then decides whom to strike. In making this decision, the lawyer must consider three basic questions. First, which of these potential jurors are least desirable? Second, with the exercise of any peremptory challenge, how likely is it that an even less desirable potential juror will appear in the jury box? Third, if an undesirable potential juror does enter the jury box, can that person be prevented from sitting on the trial jury?

Suppose in our example that the first party decides to exercise three peremptory challenges. Three jurors are removed and three potential jurors are called to fill the empty seats. The first party questions these three new potential jurors. At the conclusion of questioning, the party again must address the three questions raised above. Upon consideration of these three jurors, the party chooses to remove one potential juror. The replacement juror is questioned and, absent any obvious bias, the potential juror is accepted and the panel of twelve jurors is passed to the second party.

The second party questions the panel and, when finished, must consider the same three basic questions faced by the first party. Whom should I remove? Will a less desirable potential juror replace the juror(s) that I have struck? Should an undesirable juror appear in the jury box, will I be able to remove that potential juror? Let us assume that the second party acts in a similar manner as did the first party. The second party exercises three challenges, questions the replacement jurors, and exercises one more challenge before passing the jury back to the first party.

Each side has now exercised four of its six peremptory challenges. We will assume that there are three members of the panel to whom the first party has yet to address any questions. At the conclusion of the questioning of these three potential jurors, the party must decide whether to exercise none, one, or both of its remaining peremptory challenges. This is a complex decision. The party again considers the three fundamental questions, but it does so in light of the fact that whatever is done, the second party can return up to two new jurors. Let us suppose the first party removes one of the three potential jurors and decides that the replacement juror is acceptable.

The second party now considers the last slot on the jury. This party has two peremptory challenges through which to remove any undesirable jurors. If the second party chooses to remove the potential juror under consideration and accepts the replacement juror, it remains for the first party to consider the last slot. It is at this time that both parties face only two of the three fundamental questions, provided challenges for cause are not granted. Is this potential juror undesirable? If the potential juror is removed, will the final juror be even worse?

As can be seen with the sequential method, information is at a premium *and* is always lacking. Lawyers always exercise their challenges without being able to question the replacement potential jurors and, hence, are in the dark. The significance of this situation is apparent when it comes to the exercise of the last peremptory challenge. Lawyers must consider removing a potential juror knowing that if they use the challenge, they cannot remove the replacement juror short of a challenge for cause.

The struck jury method presents a different picture, one involving less uncertainty for the parties. In the present example, the parties screen a total of twenty-four potential jurors excluding those removed for cause (twelve jurors plus six peremptory challenges for each party). Then both parties exercise their peremptory challenges. Barring the simultaneous exercise of peremptory challenges, the parties usually exercise peremptory challenges in rounds where each party has an opportunity to remove a certain number of potential jurors at each round. Should the parties not exercise all their peremptory challenges, if permitted in the trial jurisdiction, the first twelve jurors are usually seated as the trial jury.

Which method is superior? In view of the differences between the sequential and struck methods, a question arises: Is one method superior to the other? The answer is yes. As discussed earlier, the primary goal of voir dire is to gather information that will enable the parties to intelligently exercise their peremptory challenges and to uncover biases that would serve as grounds for a challenge for cause. The sequential method produces a situation where, in jurisdictions allowing some form of lawyer participation in voir dire, the parties do not have access to the same information concerning potential jurors as a result of the stage of the questioning process. In addition, little or no information is available on what kinds of potential jurors may replace excused jurors. The struck jury method is superior because it gives both parties access to the same information before the exercise of any peremptory challenges without depriving the parties of information on replacement jurors.

The importance of the differences between these two methods becomes apparent under several conditions. First, opinions held by potential jurors in the trial community can become polarized through pretrial publicity. When polarization of opinions occurs, the risk that replacement jurors will hold opinions adverse to a party, e.g., belief in the guilt or innocence or liability of a defendant, yet unknown to the parties, increases when the sequential method is used.

Second, the first party to examine a potential juror exercises its peremptory challenges without the benefit of knowing this juror's answers to the opposing party's questions. This informational deficit occurs in terms of both the content of the answers and the nonverbal behavior the juror may have exhibited. Through no fault of the first questioner, sometimes jurors reveal important information to the second questioner simply because further questioning eventually triggers a memory or they become more comfortable with the questioning process. In addition, as we shall see in Chapter

3, the nonverbal behavior of potential jurors is a valuable source of information on the acceptability of potential jurors. With the struck jury method, there is no differential between the parties in availability of information.

Finally, the consequences of the above informational deficits are greatest when the parties are exercising their final peremptory challenge. In this situation, there is a risk that an unacceptable juror (although not revealing, or admitting, a bias sufficient for a challenge for cause) will replace the potential juror excused through the last peremptory challenge. This places the party in a difficult position. When facing an undesirable potential juror, the party either must accept this juror or risk allowing an as yet unknown, even less desirable juror to sit on the trial jury. The struck jury method makes known what kinds of replacement jurors are available.

Thus, through the reduction of uncertainty and the removal of information deficits inherent in the sequential method, the struck jury method is the superior method. In addition, the struck jury method eliminates any procedural advantages gained through the questioning process where one party has a temporary information advantage over the other.[10]

NOTES

1. *See* YANKELOVICH, SKELLEY, WHITE, THE PUBLIC IMAGE OF THE COURTS: A NATIONAL SURVEY OF THE GENERAL PUBLIC, JUDGES, LAWYERS AND COMMUNITY LEADERS (1978) (available at the National Center for State Courts, Williamsburg, Va.). A number of studies conducted by this author and National Legal Research Group, Inc., have consistently shown that substantial minorities of jurors hold beliefs contrary to legal principles (e.g., *see* the report cited in the motion for a change of venue in *United States v Sa'ad El-Amin*, Case No. 3:03CR55). For related findings, *see* BONORA, KRAUSS & ROUNDTREE, JURYWORK: SYSTEMATIC TECHNIQUES (1999).

2. *See* FREDERICK, THE PSYCHOLOGY OF THE AMERICAN JURY (1987), at 139.

3. *See* Kassin & Wrightsman, *On the Requirements of Proof: The Timing of Judicial Instruction and Mock Juror Verdicts*, 37 J. OF PERSONALITY AND SOC. PSYCHOL., 1877–87 (1979).

4. *See* Frederick, *Voir Dire and Peremptory Challenges*, 93 CASE & COM., 18–24 (1988).

5. *See* BERMANT, CONDUCT OF THE VOIR DIRE EXAMINATION: PRACTICES AND OPINIONS OF FEDERAL JUDGES (1977) (available at Federal Judicial Center, Washington, D.C.), and Van Dyke, *Voir Dire: How Should It Be Conducted to Ensure That Our Juries Are Representative and Impartial?* 3 HASTINGS CONST. L.Q. 65–97 (1976).

6. *See* Jones, *Judge-Versus Attorney-Conducted Voir Dire: An Empirical Investigation of Juror Candor*, 11 L. & HUM. BEHAV. 2, 131–146 (1987) and Johnson & Haney, *Felony Voir Dire: An Exploratory Study of its Content and Effect*, 18 L. & HUM. BEHAV. 309 (1994). Jurors are simply less likely to admit bias in response to questioning by the judge than by lawyers. An example of this occurred in a recent death penalty case in which this author was involved (State v. Jerry Layne Rogers, CR No. 83-1440-CF (Fla. 2002)). In this case, the judge asked several questions of jurors in an individual sequestered format concerning their opinions on the death penalty prior to additional questioning by the parties. Eventually, eleven potential jurors were removed for cause after being identified as being unable to follow the law concerning the death penalty. Of these potential jurors, five (45 percent) were identified through questioning by the judge, while the remaining six potential jurors (55 percent) were later identified only as a result of questioning by the parties. Obviously, this finding is disturbing in that some jurors made it through the judge's "net"

based on the judge's questioning. However, it is further disturbing that the six potential jurors who made it through the judge's questioning were later removed for cause based on either (a) the view that the death penalty is the only appropriate sentence for premeditated murder, or (b) the unwillingness to consider mitigating factors in their decisions on the appropriate punishment. In a death penalty case, jurors with such biases are exactly the ones who need to be identified and removed through voir dire.

7. *See* Nietzel & Dillehay, *The Effects of Variations in Voir Dire Procedures in Capital Murder Trials*, 6 L. & Hum. Behav. 1–13 (1982) and Nietzel, Dillehay & Himelein, *Effects of Voir Dire Variations in Capital Trials: A Replication and Extension*, 5 Behav. Sci. & L. 467 (1987). *See also* Johnson & Haney, *Felony Voir Dire: An Exploratory Study of Its Content and Effect*, 18 L. & Hum. Behav. 309 (1994), who found that extensive attorney-conducted voir dire combined with individual sequestered voir dire elicited greater admissions of bias on the part of jurors. Additional support on this issue comes from research showing that a substantial minority of jurors do not reveal critical information in response to questioning in open court but revealed such information either during individual voir dire conducted in the judge's chambers or during post-trial interviews. *See* Mize, *On Better Jury Selection: Spotting Unfavorable Juror Before They Enter the Jury Room*, Ct. Rev. 36, 10 (1999); Mize, *Be Cautious of the Quiet Ones*, Voir Dire, 10, 8 (2003); and Seltzer, Ventuti & Lopes, *Juror Honesty During Voir Dire*, 19 J. Crim. Just. 451 (1991).

8. It should be recognized that lawyers are not given a choice concerning which method will be employed in their cases. However, it is important to be aware of the implications for decision-making that arise from each method. When opportunities for variations in these methods present themselves, e.g., a judge who is willing to change his or her selection methods because of extensive pretrial publicity, knowing what methods are superior will allow the judge to use his or her discretion to make desirable changes. For example, a federal judge in a death penalty case changed the usual procedure of having peremptory challenges exercised after each panel of jurors had been questioned to waiting until a pool of jurors were qualified that equaled the total number of jurors needed (both jurors and alternates) plus the number of peremptory challenges available to both parties (United States v. Aaron Haynes, Criminal No. 01-2-247-D).

9. Some commentators have endorsed the simultaneous or "blind"approach to exercising peremptory challenges as a way of reducing gamesmanship between litigants. *See* Bermant, Jury Selection Procedures in United States District Courts (Federal Judicial Center, 1982). However, this author does not endorse the simultaneous approach. It is rarely the case that the number of potential jurors whom litigants would not want sitting on the jury is limited to the number of their peremptory challenges. Therefore, any benefit of an opponent removing one of a given litigant's "undesirable" jurors simply means that the next most "undesirable" juror will be removed. In this scheme, limiting the effective use of a litigant's peremptory challenges unnecessarily constrains the litigant without serving any higher public policy goal.

10. Given the superiority of the struck jury method, it is often desirable to seek the use of some variant of this method through a pretrial motion. While many judges are reluctant to change familiar systems, even when such changes would not violate relevant jury selection statutes, the benefits secured through the struck jury method are worth pursuing.

CHAPTER 2

Jurors' Backgrounds, Experiences, and Opinions

Objectives

- To understand how jurors construct stories that influence the verdicts they reach.
- To understand how to consider jurors' backgrounds and experiences in jury selection.
- To explore general opinions, e.g., authoritarianism and equity, held by jurors.
- To consider case-specific opinions and legal opinions of jurors.

The most important goal of voir dire is to identify jurors whose viewpoints will influence their verdict and determine how they will interact with their fellow jurors during the course of deliberations. However, before we consider the viewpoints of jurors, it is necessary to examine how jurors arrive at their decisions.

The Story Model

The dominant model for explaining jury decisions is the "story model."[1] The story model proposes that jurors construct "stories" for what happened based on the evidence and arguments and their general knowledge and belief systems. The stories jurors construct are then compared to the potential verdict options presented to them and a match is sought. The result of the matching process in conjunction with the standard of proof then determines the juror's initial verdict choice. This model has proved useful in explaining how jurors process the complex information presented at trial, and it provides guidance in how to present information to jurors. For our purposes, an important feature of the story model is that jurors' knowledge, experiences, opinions, and values influence their preferences for different stories. In essence, the viewpoints that jurors bring with them to court influence their receptiveness to the competing stories or explanations offered by the parties.[2] The lawyer's task is to uncover the jurors' viewpoints through their responses to questions regarding their opinions, beliefs, backgrounds, and experiences as well as through their verbal and nonverbal communication.[3]

The Viewpoints of Jurors

Opinions that jurors hold are shaped by numerous events and experiences in their lives. The jurors' backgrounds (e.g., race, gender, marital status, educational training, religious training, and occupation) and the socialization process exert a strong influence. These backgrounds often influence the experiences jurors have (for example, discrimination in the workplace, being a victim of crime, traumatic events, and military service, among others), which further shape jurors' views. Whether as the result of their backgrounds or other factors, such as having read about discrimination or economic hardships faced by certain small businesses because of lawsuits, or having been a defendant in a lawsuit, jurors' experiences influence their opinions, beliefs, and values. The culmination of these backgrounds and experiences, opinions, beliefs, values, and personality traits creates the view jurors have of themselves and the world around them. It is this total package that jurors bring to trial. Jurors are not simply empty vessels into which lawyers seek to pour information and arguments. Jurors are active information processors who integrate the evidence, arguments, and judicial instructions in light of who they are. In essence, the jurors' viewpoints serve as "filters" through which they process (and in some cases distort) the evidence, arguments, and law in arriving at their decisions.

It is necessary to uncover the backgrounds, experiences, and opinions of jurors that can influence how they will view the case and their subsequent participation in deliberations.[4] In this chapter we will consider five sources of information to help us understand jurors: (a) backgrounds, (b) experiences, (c) global opinions and personality traits, (d) case-specific opinions, and (e) legal opinions. However, before turning to these sources, it is necessary to examine the issue of stereotypes in jury selection.[5]

Stereotypes

Many authors have identified stereotypes of desirable and undesirable jurors. The following are some examples of these stereotypes.

F. Lee Bailey and Henry Rothblatt write concerning physical characteristics of jurors in criminal trials as follows:

> Generally speaking, the heavy, round-faced, jovial-looking person is most desirable. The undesirable juror is quite often the slight, underweight, and delicate type. His features are sharp and fragile, with that lean "Cassius" look. The athletic-looking juror is hard to categorize. Usually he is hard to convince, but once convinced he will go all the way for you.[6]

Murray Sams, Jr., proposing an exception to the stereotype that plaintiffs should desire minorities on their juries, writes:

> Plaintiffs should be very careful about taking a Jewish juror in a medical malpractice case against a doctor. Most Jews want their sons to become doctors ("My son the doctor") and they want their daughters to marry doctors. I have never figured out why, but they do.[7]

Clarence Darrow writes in regard to jury selection in criminal trials:

> An Irishman . . . is emotional, kindly, and sympathetic. If a Presbyterian enters the jury box . . . let him go. He is as cold as the grave. Beware of Lutherans, especially the Scandinavians; they are almost sure to convict.[8]

The above recommendations employ stereotypes in an attempt to predict the verdicts of jurors. However, stereotypes are by their very nature simplistic and, hence, tend to be inaccurate in the long run.

Examining stereotypes more closely reveals a number of problems. First, stereotypes ignore where the crime or litigation is being tried. For example, is it reasonable to assume that ethnic groups (often a basis of jury selection stereotypes) in different regions of the country have the same experiences and degree of identification with their ethnic heritage? That is, do individuals of Swedish, Italian, or Germanic descent residing in Seattle have the same experiences and opinions as their ethnic counterparts in New York City, Omaha, or rural Virginia? Second, stereotypes tend to ignore the type of crime or litigation at issue. Not all crimes or civil suits are the same. Potential jurors who would be desirable for the defendant in a murder case may be undesirable if the defendant is charged with rape (or, for that matter, a murder under a different set of circumstances).

A third problem with stereotypes is that they tend to focus on one characteristic. Jurors are more complex than that. The single-characteristic focus leaves the user with the questions "Which stereotypes, if accurate, are most important to know?" and "What does the possession of several stereotypical characteristics mean in terms of a juror's desirability?" Finally, with the sheer number of characteristics jurors possess, conflicting recommendations arise. For example, as noted by Penrod and Linz, one author contends that young jurors are good for plaintiffs while another author advises that just the opposite is true.[9]

While there are many problems with stereotypes, using stereotypes in jury selection is not inherently bad, deferring for the moment certain public policy considerations. In the absence of detailed information on people, stereotypes form a basis for predicting how people will behave. The first impressions people form of others are a type of stereotyping. Based on little information, people form beliefs about how others will act or what opinions they may hold, filling in what is not known with "stereotypical" information. Jury selection is no different. Lawyers use stereotypes in jury selection. For that matter, social scientists also use stereotypes, although their stereotypes should be based on empirical data.

The key to the issue of stereotypes lies in their use. If there is no information on jurors, stereotypes may be of some limited value. It is important to determine how accurate the underlying assumptions of the stereotypes are, where possible. If a stereotype suggests that certain groups will be hostile or favorable to a party, attempts need to be made to uncover the potential juror's true opinions.[10] Without attempts to verify the applicability of a stereotype to a juror, however, trafficking in stereotypes is risky. For example, in one of the antiwar conspiracy trials in the 1970s,[11] the defense thought a mother of two conscientious objectors would view the defense with favor. As it turned out, she was an adamant holdout for the prosecution. She did not agree with her sons' actions and, hence, did not fit the stereotype that parents of conscientious objectors would have antiwar sympathies.

Backgrounds

The first source of information about jurors is the most basic source: background information. Jurors' backgrounds consist of a variety of information, including such factors as race, gender, occupation, education, and organizational membership. While these factors often play a relatively minor role in the decision-making of jurors,[12] they can have an impact. For example, in one study, the gender of jurors was the most powerful background characteristic in predicting jurors' decisions in sexual harassment cases, with females being more likely to favor the plaintiff while males were more likely to favor the defense.[13] When considering the background of a juror, the lawyer should keep in mind the following question: Does this juror have a viewpoint that is disadvantageous to my client/party? In drawing inferences about the juror's opinions and beliefs based on his or her background, several issues should be considered.

IDENTIFICATION ISSUES. Background characteristics can lead potential jurors to identify with a party, witness(es), or events. Do jurors have backgrounds similar to a party or witness that might lead them to view the party or witness more or less favorably? Would coming from upper socioeconomic status groups lead to pro-business attitudes or an identification with large corporations? These questions and others will shed light on the potential for identification with parties, witnesses, and events.

SURROGATE POTENTIAL. Background characteristics carry the potential to act as a surrogate for critical experiences or opinions. Recognizing the errors inherent in making generalizations, what background characteristics serve as indicators of the potentially greater likelihood that certain jurors have had a critical negative experience or hold a critical negative opinion? For example, many small-business owners oppose punitive damages in general. If the lawyer is unable to investigate satisfactorily the jurors' views on punitive damages, it would not be desirable to ignore this background characteristic.

REFERENCE GROUPS. A special aspect of jurors' backgrounds concerns reference groups.[14] Reference groups are the numerous groups to which people belong, e.g., social, political, religious, economic, occupation related, and demographic. People become members of these groups in a variety of ways. Membership can be voluntary, compulsory, or natural (e.g., age, gender, or race). Reference groups exert a powerful influence on people. They serve as a standard by which we can compare our abilities, beliefs, and values.[15] Membership in religious groups and political organizations, for example, provides individuals with guidelines on appropriate opinions, values, and behaviors, i.e., those opinions, values, and behaviors that lie within the limits of acceptability for group membership.

An additional influence of reference groups is that people tend to accord greater credibility and trust to members of reference groups they value. This carries with it the potential for greater persuasiveness for witnesses who share common group membership with a juror. For example, union membership by a witness will have greater influence with union-supporting jurors than with nonunion (or anti-union) jurors.

This influence of reference groups also extends to jury dynamics. Jurors who share membership in the same reference group (e.g., members of the same fraternal, political, and social organizations or ethnic, gender, and racial groups) can influence each other's positions. In addition, the more relevant the group membership is to the task at hand the greater the influence of common group membership, both between jurors and between jurors and witnesses. For example, fishermen who must address the impact of pollution on fisheries and minorities who consider the impact of discrimination on individuals carry more influence within their respective groups. Also, they can be persuasive with other nongroup member jurors (in some cases acting as "experts" for the jury).

However, there are exceptions to the general influence of group membership. Obviously, one juror simply may disagree with the witness or another juror of the same reference group. Also, jurors may belong to opposing subgroups within the same reference group. For example, jurors who belong to the same general group with relevant task expertise can have different theoretical perspectives or views. When such differences arise, jurors

---

How to evaluate reference groups:

- To what critical reference groups does a juror belong?
- Has the group taken a position on a critical issue (or can a position be inferred)?
- Is the juror committed to the group's position and/or continued group membership?

may give less credence to what the witness or opposing juror says. These differences, particularly between jurors and witnesses, can have important consequences when the juror is the sole member of the jury with some task expertise. An engineer or lawyer on the jury who disagrees with an expert witness can be a very persuasive advocate against the expert witness during jury deliberations. Few of the other jurors are likely to have the knowledge and command of technical details to completely neutralize the "juror expert."

Knowing the reference groups to which potential jurors belong is important for two reasons. First, when the position that a reference group takes on a relevant issue is known, e.g., opposition to capital punishment, opposition to abortion, or support for tort reform, this information can act as a clue to the juror's opinion. Second, there exists the potential for credibility enhancement among reference group members. For example, knowing that a juror and a potential witness attended the same graduate school or are members of the same church provides a clue to how credible the juror will find the witness.

However, knowledge of the potential juror's group membership is not sufficient. It is important to know the level of commitment to and support for the reference group. The greater the commitment, the greater the influence that group membership exerts. The more the juror wants to maintain group membership, the more likely it is that he or she will identify and conform to the stated goals, opinions, and behaviors of the group.

Jurors reveal their commitment to a reference group in a number of ways, including the following:

- Statements of the value the potential juror places on group membership, e.g., "I really enjoy my work at the church"
- Statements reflecting support for the group's goals and objectives, e.g., "I believe we should not use the death penalty" [made by a member of the ACLU]
- Moderate to high levels of participation in the group's activities
- The past or present holding of an office in the organization
- Financial contributions made to the group, if relevant
- Long-time membership in the group
- For busy potential jurors, the desire to participate in more group-related activities if time permitted

All of these factors provide insights into the value jurors place on their group membership and the resulting influence that group membership will have on them.

Experiences

Jurors' past experiences are the second source of information in jury selection. Jurors bring a wealth of experiences with them to trial. These experiences include personal traumas, work- and home-related experiences, exposure to prejudice and discrimination, military service, exposure to the health care and legal systems, and family relationships. Potentially relevant experiences also include exposure to toxic materials, use of consumer products, safety training, familiarity with patents or contracts, and experiences based on exposure to reading materials, television, movies, and the Internet.

Many, if not most, of the jurors' experiences have relatively little or no apparent impact on their lives. However, some of these experiences can exert a distinct influence on their beliefs and behaviors. For example, being the victim of a physical assault such as rape or aggravated assault can change how jurors view defendants charged with such crimes. Other experiences have a cumulative influence. For example, growing up under poor economic conditions can lead jurors to identify more with the "underdog" than with the powerful or wealthy.

A number of issues must be considered when evaluating the experiences that jurors bring with them to trial.

Direct Versus Indirect Experience

Knowing what experiences, whether direct or indirect, potential jurors have had is critical to understanding how jurors will respond to the case. Direct experience refers to the juror's personal exposure to the situation at issue. The juror who has been the victim of a crime has had a direct experience with crime and with how it feels to be a victim. Indirect experience, or nonpersonal exposure to the relevant situation, can arise from several sources. The juror may know someone who has been in a situation similar to that of a party in the case. The juror may have heard or seen accounts of the situation in the news media, entertainment media, on the Internet, or scholarly, literary, or popular press.

The directness of the exposure to relevant situations is important. Jurors with direct experience possess the potential for greater empathy, identification, understanding, and emotional reaction than jurors who have only indirect experience or no experience with the situation. For example, in a wrongful death case involving the death of a mother, a young potential juror whose mother had recently died was a member of the jury venire. The following exchange occurred between this potential juror and the defense counsel:

LAWYER: You mentioned during the questioning by the plaintiff's lawyer that you might have some reservations in serving on this jury?

MR. SMITH: Yes. I really don't think I can be fair in this case. I would have too much sympathy for what the plaintiff is going through. [*At this point, tears well up in the young man's eyes.*]

While direct experiences can have a dramatic impact on the views of jurors, this does not mean that indirect experiences have little impact. Severe injury to a close friend or relative by a drunk driver can have a profound impact on jurors' views of cases where alcohol consumption is an issue. Or even reading materials can have a profound impact on jurors' opinions. For example, consider the following exchange occurring during jury selection in a rape case that eventually resulted in a conviction.

PROSECUTOR: [*Addressing the panel*] Is there any reason that any of you would have any reservations in serving on this jury?

Ms. SMITH: [*Raises her hand*] I am not sure that I can be fair after reading *Against Our Will*. [This is a book written about rape from a feminist perspective. Neither the prosecutor nor the defense lawyer was aware of the nature of this book. I was assisting the prosecutor and recommended that the prosecutor accept and rehabilitate the juror.]

PROSECUTOR: Now, Ms. Smith, would you be able to set aside any opinions you may have formed from what you read and decide this case based solely on the evidence from the witness stand and law as you are instructed by the judge?

Ms. SMITH: Yes, I will do my best.

PROSECUTOR: Thank you.

Evaluating the impact of experiences rests on a number of considerations. The answers to several questions will help to reveal the importance of various experiences in jury selection:

What was the nature of the experience? Exactly what happened or what did the experience involve? If the potential juror was robbed, how was the robbery carried out? A potential juror who is physically assaulted during a robbery will have a different experience than someone who has a wallet stolen from an office desk or locker. If the experience arises from the occupation of the juror, what did the juror do on the job?

How relevant is the experience to the case at hand? The more relevant the experience is, the greater role it will play in the juror's decision-making and during deliberations. Jurors draw upon relevant experiences in their discussions with and attempts to persuade other jurors. Similarity of experiences is a crucial factor in determining their relevance. The more similar the experiences are to events in the case, the more relevant jurors are likely to view them. For example, potential jurors who have been in similar driving conditions as those present in the traffic accident case under consideration are likely to use this experience to evaluate the actions of the parties. Similarity also leads to identification, empathy, and attraction. Potential jurors with experiences similar to those of one of the litigants, e.g., suing or being sued, can lead to identification with that litigant, e.g., the plaintiff or defendant in the lawsuit. For example, consider the following brief exchange concerning a case where an accountant (pro-defense stereotype) was being questioned by the defense in a personal injury case:

DEFENSE ATTORNEY: You raised your hand earlier as to being a plaintiff in a personal injury lawsuit. Would you tell me about this?

JUROR Yes, the case involved an automobile accident that was
(ACCOUNTANT): the fault of the other driver. His insurance company
would not pay for the damages to my car and my medical bills. I sued the insurance company *and you lost."*
(The italics reflect the hostility evidenced by the tone of
the juror's response.)

How did the potential juror react to the experience? Jurors react to experiences differently. One juror may enjoy an experience while another juror
may find the same experience unpleasant. Some jurors may have a positive
view of their military service while other jurors may not. Also, it is possible
that an experience may make an impression on one juror while failing to do
so with another juror.

Did the potential juror change his or her behavior as a result of the experience?
Knowing whether the jurors have changed their behavior after the particular
experience provides valuable information. For example, a rape victim who
subsequently takes a self-defense course and provides counseling at a local
rape crisis center is reacting differently to the rape (although not necessarily
reflecting more or less trauma suffered) than a victim who shows no outward change in her behavior. This difference in reactions also can indicate a
difference in how the two victims may respond as jurors to the crime under
consideration, particularly rape.

How much time has passed since the incident or experience occurred? As time
passes, the impact of the experience often diminishes. For example, the emotional trauma of the death of a loved one is greater during the early stages
of grieving (e.g., the first six to twelve months) than after many years have
passed. A valuable consideration when weighing the impact of time on the
juror's experience is how much the juror can remember about the experience. A vivid memory of the details of an experience that happened a long
time ago indicates the greater impact of the experience. The potential juror's
saying, "I remember it just as if it happened yesterday" or "I can see it clearly
in my mind," gives a clue to the quality of the experience for that person.

How to evaluate jurors' experiences:

- What was the critical experience?
- How relevant is the experience to the present situation?
- What was the juror's reaction to the experience?
- Did the juror change his or her behavior as a result of the experience?
- How much time has passed since the experience occurred?
- What frame of reference will the juror have based on the experience?

Is the experience more or less of a particular quality, e.g., severity or intensity, than the incident under consideration? Jurors' prior experiences act as a frame of reference for how they will view future situations. For example, prior jury service can influence jurors' views of future cases. Two jurors who consider the same case can differ in their view of how serious the crime is if one has considered a more serious crime earlier and the second a less serious one.[16] Other things being equal, facing a severely injured plaintiff in a previous case affects how the jurors view the severity of suffering of a less severely injured plaintiff in a future case.

Does similarity of experience pose a threat to the potential juror? While in general, similarity of experiences promotes empathy for those having the experience, under some circumstances it can promote a backlash reaction. When jurors feel threatened by the experience and cannot cope with this threat, they may react negatively to a person having the same experience. In tobacco liability cases, for example, jurors who smoke may discount the health risks of smoking or place great value on possible contributing health problems of the plaintiff. As a result, these jurors are likely to be unfavorable to plaintiffs in such cases.

Figure 1
Ever Participated in "Risky" Activities?

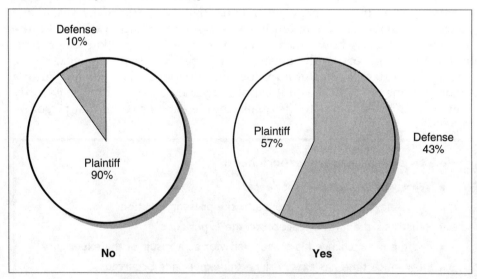

Reprinted with permission of *The Journal.*

Ski Case Example

An example of considering the experiences of jurors can be seen in a ski injury case tried in Virginia where the plaintiff suffered catastrophic injuries while skiing at a ski resort.[17] Our focus group research in this case showed that two types of experiences were important in determining anti-plaintiff biases—the jurors' participation in "risky" activities, in general, and the jurors' skill level or skiing experience. As shown in Figure 1, those potential jurors who engaged in risky activities (e.g., sky diving, bungee jumping, and motorcycle riding) were less favorable to the plaintiff, with only 57 percent returning verdicts for the plaintiff as compared to 90 percent plaintiff's verdicts from those who had not engaged in risky activities.

In addition, as shown in Figure 2, the more experience that jurors had with skiing (as reflected in their reported level of expertise) the less favorable they were to the plaintiff. What was of particular interest was the finding that it was not just whether the potential juror had skied before, but his or her having a level of expertise beyond the beginning level that was most important, with verdicts for the plaintiff decreasing from 88 percent for those without ski experience to 56 percent for those with an intermediate level of skiing expertise. Both of these experiences were important in the jury selection in that case.

Figure 2
Verdicts as a Function of Ski Experience

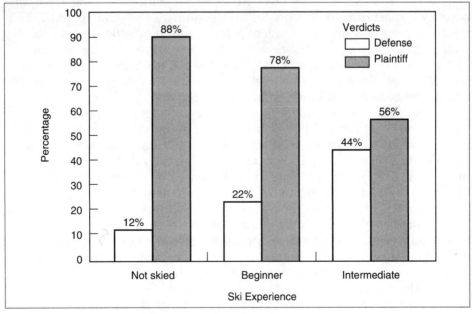

Reprinted with permission of *The Journal*.

Global Opinions and Personality Traits

A third source of insight into jurors' viewpoints concerns global or general opinions and personality traits. A number of global opinions and personality traits are useful to consider and we will examine two such characteristics here—authoritarianism and beliefs in equity.[18] However, it is important to realize that in general, global opinions and personality traits do not predict specific actions of jurors with great accuracy. Because of their necessarily general focus, they tend to predict general patterns of behavior but can fall short of the mark in predicting specific verdicts. Even with this shortcoming, global opinions and personality traits are useful in assisting lawyers in jury selection.

Authoritarianism

For almost three decades, the personality trait most frequently considered in jury selection has been authoritarianism[19]—that is, an indication of antidemocratic or prefascistic tendencies in a person. While contemporary researchers do not endorse the psychoanalytic roots of authoritarianism, the nine-component model of the authoritarian personality provides a glimpse of this kind of person. The components of the model are (a) *conventionalism*—the adoption and support of middle-class norms and values; (b) *authoritarian submission*—acquiescence or submission to the desires or orders of authority figures; (c) *authoritarian aggression*—the desire to punish violators of norms or social values; (d) *anti-intraception*—opposition to imaginative, creative, or subjective ideas or behaviors; (e) *superstition and stereotype*—adherence to stereotypes and prejudice, e.g., anti-Semitism and racism; (f) *power and toughness*—identification with power figures and "being tough"; (g) *destructiveness and cynicism*—feelings of hostility toward others; (h) *projection*—the view that others have the same feelings, opinions, and perspective on the world as oneself; and (i) *sex*—an exaggerated concern with sexual behavior and the sexual "goings on" around them.

These elements of the authoritarian personality offer some useful insights into what kind of people authoritarians are. Authoritarians tend to be politically conservative, racist, rigid, highly punitive, and acquiescent to authority figures.[20] Authoritarian jurors in criminal trials are conviction prone, more punitive, more likely to be influenced by expert testimony, more influenced by character evidence, and more lenient in their verdicts for offenders who are *similar* to themselves.[21]

The important implication for criminal trials is that authoritarian jurors, in general, tend to be favorable to the prosecution. These individuals are the backbone of a pro-prosecution jury. Authoritarian jurors respond well to the fact that prosecutors represent the legitimate authority of the state and society, an authority that endeavors to punish violators of the law (i.e., those who break societal norms and rules). The people associated with the prosecution often include police and law enforcement personnel. The fact that their jobs serve to enforce the laws and to protect society enhances the prosecutor's position in the eyes of authoritarians. In addition, authoritarian jurors view criminal defendants unfavorably. The defendants are charged with breaking laws and are often from a lower socioeconomic status group than many of the jurors (and hence dissimilar to these jurors). In many cases, criminal defendants are social nonconformists or minorities, a feature that taps into prejudices held by authoritarians. These factors combine to produce a situation where, in general, authoritarians are favorable to the prosecution.

An example of the use of authoritarianism in jury selection can be drawn for the trial of Joan Little.[22] Joan Little, a young black woman, was incarcerated in the Beaufort County Jail in Washington, North Carolina. On August 27, 1974, she escaped from jail. On that day, authorities found the dead body of the white male night jailer, Clarence Alligood, in her locked cell. The body had multiple ice pick wounds in the neck, head, and body. The jailer was naked from the waist down with semen on one of his legs. Joan Little maintained that she had killed her jailer in the process of fending off a sexual assault.

A number of issues in the case highlighted the need to know which jurors were authoritarian. These issues included racial prejudice, i.e., a black assailant and a white victim; sexual assault, i.e., Ms. Little claimed she was fending off a sexual assault; the backgrounds of the principals, i.e., Ms. Little was incarcerated for breaking and entering at the time when Mr. Alligood was a law enforcement officer (night jailer) and a family man; and prisoners' rights, i.e., the right of prisoners to be protected from physical or sexual abuse at the hands of their jailers. In examining these issues, it became apparent that authoritarian jurors would not be sympathetic to the defense. The resulting jury selection strategy produced a significantly less authoritarian trial jury than the overall jury pool. After seventy-five minutes of deliberations, the trial jury acquitted Ms. Little.[23]

While authoritarian jurors tend to lean toward the government in criminal cases, they are not always desirable for the prosecution. Lawyers should not blindly follow the stereotype that authoritarians make undesirable jurors for criminal defendants. As the nine-component model of authoritarianism illustrates, the construct is complex. It is necessary to consider these complexities to determine whether authoritarians are either desirable or undesirable (or, as with many civil cases, an irrelevant consideration in the case).

There are a number of exceptions to the pro-prosecution orientation of the authoritarian juror. For example, cases involving "crimes of obedience" such as the Oliver North case gain a sympathetic ear with authoritarians. Mr. North's claim that he was following the President's desires to supply support to the Nicaraguan contras would strike a responsive chord with authoritarian jurors. In addition, his claim to be following the directions and wishes of his immediate superior that the operations involving the sale of arms to Iran and other contra-related activities be kept secret would generate more sympathy for Mr. North than for the government prosecutors.

Cases involving allegations of misconduct by law enforcement personnel, e.g., excessive force or police brutality, are likely to enlist authoritarians' sympathy for the criminal defendant, in the absence of other compelling issues. Authoritarians are likely to be receptive to claims by law enforcement personnel that they were responding to the level of force necessary in the situation at hand. The fact that the defendants are police officers and the potential for other police to testify in favor of these defendants would play into authoritarian sympathies. Also, authoritarians and law enforcement personnel are likely to have similar conservative views on law enforcement. This similarity in views (and resulting identification) enhances the testimony of law enforcement personnel. Of no minor importance is the fact that the alleged victim is likely to be someone who is thought to have broken the law, a fact that does not escape the attention of the authoritarian juror.

Finally, authoritarians tend to be favorable to criminal defendants in certain racially motivated crimes against minorities (where racial prejudice becomes a factor) and in certain sexual assault cases. On this latter point, authoritarians tend to hold opinions unsympathetic to rape victims in intraracial sexual assaults. Particularly when issues of consent or the rape victim placing herself in a risky or unconventional situation arise, authoritarian males, and many authoritarian females, are desirable for the defense. In the above instances prosecutors who rely on broad pro-prosecution authoritarian stereotypes may exercise their peremptory challenges in a counterproductive manner.

Questions that tap into the authoritarian personality construct are necessary to determine the degree of authoritarianism of potential jurors. Agreement with such traditional questions as "Do you believe that obedience and respect for authority are the most important virtues children should learn?" and "Do you believe that it is best to give the police vast and unlimited power and authority to maintain law and order?" reflect authoritarianism.[24] In most jurisdictions, these types of general questions often are not acceptable to the court. Questions that reflect authoritarianism in the legal context are of more practical value. Such questions include:

"Would you believe the word of a policeman over other witnesses?"

"Do you believe that if the prosecution goes to the trouble of bringing someone to trial, the person is probably guilty?"

What to consider when using general opinions in jury selection:

- Is the opinion dimension (e.g., authoritarianism or equity beliefs) relevant?
- How will jurors possessing the characteristic respond to the circumstances of the case?
- What questions will uncover the jurors' opinions?
- What questions will be allowed by the court?

"Do you believe that a criminal defendant should be required to testify in his own defense?"[25]

Lawyers can develop relevant questions that relate to authoritarianism by considering the different aspects of the criminal case. Beliefs concerning the insanity defense, support for capital punishment, whether or not the defendant will testify, and the actions of law enforcement personnel would be important areas to consider, where appropriate. While these areas may not directly tap into the authoritarian personality construct, they can provide valuable "proxy" information on authoritarianism.

Equity

A second important area of general attitudes is beliefs concerning fairness in relationships. One theory that addresses fairness in relationships is equity theory.[26] Equity theory concerns people's views of the fairness of what parties contribute to and receive from a relationship. A common thread in equity formulations is that people dislike inequity. When people believe a relationship is inequitable, they are motivated to restore equity to the relationship.

In jury selection, it is important to recognize the task that jurors face and its relation to fairness in relationships or equity. Concerns over the equitable nature of the relationship between the parties are present in both criminal and civil contexts, although these concerns are more salient in the civil area.

In the criminal area, jurors evaluate whether the defendant committed the crime(s) charged. Thus, jurors must examine the relationship, if any, between the defendant and the victim. While jurors' concerns for equity often are present, it is important to recognize the impact of the constraints the law imposes. As a rule, jurors are not told that they act as the conscience of the community and hence can acquit an otherwise guilty defendant if fairness requires it—what is referred to as jury nullification.[27] As such, there are strong pressures on jurors to follow the law and to resist equity considerations in cases where their views of what is fair and what violates the law conflict, unless fairness issues are extreme.

In the civil area, equity concerns are particularly important. Jurors consider the relationship between the plaintiff and the defendant and resolve any inequity that exists. Unlike the criminal area, where the verdict applies only to the defendant, jurors in a civil proceeding, to some degree, control what happens to both plaintiffs and defendants. That is, the monetary award given the plaintiff is, at least theoretically, at the expense of the defendant. For example, if the defendant in a libel case is found liable, jurors restore equity to the relationship between the parties by having the defendant monetarily compensate the plaintiff for his or her losses (both tangible and intangible). If the defendant is not found liable, or though liable occurred it has not significantly damaged the plaintiff's reputation, the required action against the defendant reflects these findings.

Two points emerge when considering equity in jury selection. First, it is important to establish how jurors feel about the situation they face. For example, do jurors feel that certain actions by a rape victim, e.g., accompanying the defendant to his apartment, mean she consented or in some way contributed to or assumed the risk of what happened? Or, do jurors feel that the fact that a woman goes to the defendant's apartment is not a legitimate "contribution" and does not imply consent to sexual relations with the defendant?

The value jurors place on various "contributions" made and the "outcomes" the parties receive will affect their views of the fairness or equitableness of the relationship. In the rape case example, jurors who believe the presence of the woman in the defendant's apartment implies consent or indicates assumption of risk would be favorable to the defense. In a libel case, a juror who feels that a person's reputation is of great importance would be likely to place a greater monetary value on the damage to the plaintiff's reputation than would a juror who views a person's reputation as being of less importance.

The second point concerning jury selection relates to the value different jurors place on equity in relationships.[28] When issues of equity or fairness are salient, jurors who place a higher value on equity may respond differently than those with a lesser concern for equity. A number of questions should be helpful in evaluating jurors' concerns for equity. The following questions consider several issues for plaintiffs and defendants in a personal injury context.

Plaintiff:[29] The plaintiff wants to ensure that jurors place a high value on fairness, that they would compensate victims (restore equity), and they would not let the magnitude of money damages at issue limit their views on compensation.

"Do you believe that every effort should be made to compensate victims of an accident?"

"Do you believe that victims of accidents should be compensated to the full extent the law will allow?"

"How important do you believe it is that victims are compensated when they have been injured in accidents?"

"How do you feel about providing monetary compensation to victims of accidents?"

"How would you feel about returning a substantial monetary award to the plaintiff?"

"Would you have any reservations in awarding substantial money damages in this case, if the facts and the law supported such a finding?"

Defendant: The defendant wants to ensure that jurors are not simply compensation oriented. They need to make sure that jurors will consider fairness for all the parties (i.e., evaluation of both sides of the equity "equation").

"Do you believe that just because a plaintiff files a lawsuit that he or she is entitled to money damages?"

"Do you believe that all injured people deserve to be compensated, even if that means that a defendant who is not negligent pays the award?"

"How do you think you would feel if you found that the defendant was not negligent and, therefore, the plaintiff was not entitled to any compensation whatsoever from the defendant?"

"Would you have any reservations in awarding the plaintiff zero or no money damages if the plaintiff fails to prove that the defendant was negligent?"

"Do you feel that justice would be done if you found that the defendant is not negligent and, hence, that the plaintiff is not entitled to money damages?"

Case-Specific Opinions

The final source of information concerns case-specific opinions. Case-specific opinions differ from general opinions and personality traits in that, as the label implies, these opinions directly relate to the specific features of the case, e.g., the theme, the parties, potential witnesses, evidence, arguments, and standards of conduct by the parties. The value of case-specific questions is that they are better predictors of the jurors' actions than are general opinions because they are more directly connected to the decisions jurors will make.[30] For example, in a rape case where consent is an issue, it is useful to know how authoritarian a potential juror is. However, it is more important to know whether the juror views a woman as having implicitly given her consent to having sex when she accompanies a man to his apartment or bedroom.

Questions to help identify important case-specific opinions:

- What is the theme of the case?
- What are the major issues in the case?
- Was there any pretrial publicity?
- What are the case's strengths and weaknesses?
- Which witnesses will testify?
- What important arguments will be raised?
- What facts or circumstances must be addressed or defused on voir dire?

Identifying potentially useful case-specific opinions results from a thorough analysis of the case. This analysis addresses the following questions:

- What is the theme of the case?
- What are the major issues in the case, both legal and emotional?
- What pretrial publicity, if any, has surfaced concerning the case, and what is the content of the publicity?
- What are the strengths and weaknesses of the case?
- Who will testify at trial?
- What are the key arguments for both sides of the case?
- Will voir dire questioning need to defuse the potential negative impact of certain facts?
- Is there anything unusual about the circumstances of the case that requires exploring them with the jurors, e.g., a large man with a gun claiming self-defense in the shooting of a smaller, unarmed man?

Important case-specific opinions arise in all cases. In civil cases, particularly personal injury cases, pursuit of the jurors' views concerning the "lawsuit crisis," tort reform, and jury awards is important.[31]

> "Have you heard, seen, or read anything about what has been called the "lawsuit crisis" (or tort reform or money awards by juries)? What do you think about this?"

> "How many of you feel that there are simply too many lawsuits today?"

> "How many of you feel that people today are too eager to file lawsuits?"

> "How many of you feel that jury awards are becoming too high?"

In breach of contract cases, the jurors' views on contracts, their concern for fairness in contracts, their support for strict adherence to contract terms versus the intent of the contract, and their views on the responsibilities of signatories to the contract are potential areas for inquiry. The following questions are examples of issues of interest:

> "Could you tell me a little about your views on contracts?"

> "Do you believe that parties should follow the contract terms no matter what the consequences?"

> "Which do you think is more important, that the parties follow the exact terms of a contract or that the intent of the contract is achieved?"

> "What do you think are some of the obligations or duties of those who sign a contract?"

> "Are there any situations where you feel that a party should not be required to fulfill the terms of a contract?"

"What would be examples of those situations?"

"Have you heard the expression 'a person's word is his bond'? What does this expression mean to you?"

In medical negligence cases, questions concerning lawsuits against doctors, quality-of-care issues, the patient's duties in the doctor-patient relationship, and compensation issues are often important. Relevant questions for the plaintiff or defense would include some of the following:

PLAINTIFF: How do you feel about lawsuits brought by patients against their doctors?

PLAINTIFF: Do you believe that patients have a right to expect quality care from their doctors?

DEFENSE: How do you feel about a situation where a patient withholds information from his doctor?

DEFENSE: Do you believe that because the plaintiff is injured she deserves some money from the defendant?

PLAINTIFF: If the evidence and the law in this case were to support a finding of damages in excess of $1 million, would you have any reservations in awarding such a figure? How would you feel about returning a substantial damage award if you were a juror in this case?

In cases where the plaintiffs are injured while involved in "risky activities," it would be important to ask whether jurors feel that those involved in risky activities should not complain if they get hurt. More specifically, as shown in Figure 3, in the ski case described earlier, it was important to know whether the jurors supported the opinion that skiers should not complain if they are hurt when they accidentally run off the ski trail. Fifty percent of the jurors who believed that skiers should not complain under these circumstances rendered verdicts for the defense, while only 5 percent of the jurors who were either neutral or disagreed with the statement decided the case for the defense.

In a criminal case, case-specific opinions of interest may address the impact of pretrial publicity, the believability of eyewitness testimony, and the government's use of "sting" operations or immunized testimony. The following are some illustrative questions:

"Have you heard anything on the radio or seen anything in the newspaper or on television or the Internet concerning this case [be explicit with the case description]?"

"Tell me a little about what you recall from hearing the radio reports, reading the newspaper, or seeing reports on television or the Internet."

"Based on what you have heard and discussed with your friends and coworkers, have you formed any impressions of what went on? What are these impressions?"

DEFENSE: Do you believe that under certain circumstances, an eye-witness's memory of what happened may not be accurate? Can you tell me what you think might be some of the circumstances where an eyewitness may make honest mistakes in what he or she remembers about what happened?

PROSECUTION: How do you feel about the use of "sting" operations to catch those involved in criminal activity?

Finally, an important set of case-specific attitudes concerns philosophies on punishment, particularly capital punishment. One of the most consistent findings in psychological research on juries is that jurors who oppose the death penalty are less conviction prone than are jurors who favor the use of the death penalty.[32] In addition, those jurors that the death qualification process excludes are more due process oriented and less oriented toward crime control than death-qualified jurors.[33] Death-qualified jurors are more receptive to aggravating circumstances and are less likely to endorse certain types of mitigating circumstances (i.e., nonstatutory mitigators).[34]

Determining jurors' attitudes toward the death penalty is a primary consideration in capital punishment cases. This determination must go beyond whether or not the potential juror satisfies the death qualification hurdle of *Wainwright v. Witt*[35]—that their views on the death penalty would prevent or

Figure 3
Skiers Should Not Complain If Hurt Running Off Slope

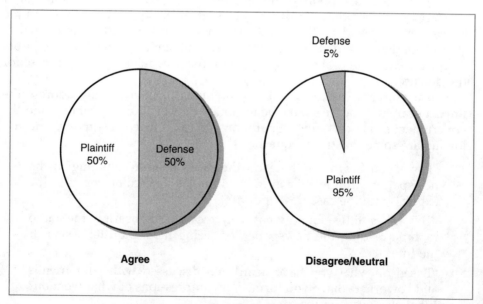

Reprinted with permission of *The Journal*.

substantially impair the implementation of their duties. Questions that further elaborate the jurors' beliefs on the death penalty are as follows:

"Do you favor the death penalty for anyone who deliberately kills another person?"

"Are you in favor of the death penalty for [specify appropriate case, e.g., premeditated murder]?"

[If in favor of the death penalty] "Can you tell me why you favor the death penalty?" or "What are the main reasons you support the death penalty?"

"Do you consider yourself to be a strong supporter of the death penalty for [premeditated murder]?"

"If a person is convicted of first-degree murder, do you feel that he should receive the death penalty?"

"Do you believe in an 'eye-for-an-eye' in cases of [premeditated murder]—that is [if a person premeditates the killing of another person], he should pay for it with his life?"

"Do you believe that everyone who [commits a premeditated murder], no matter what the circumstances, should be sentenced to death?"[36]

Legal Opinions

As mentioned in the previous chapter, a large minority of the population has opinions that conflict with various laws and legal principles of our justice system.[37] Therefore, it is important to explore with potential jurors their understanding and opinions concerning key legal principles and laws. When exploring the potential jurors' legal opinions, it is necessary to determine whether any misconceptions discovered are the result of a simple misunderstanding or reflect a deeper, entrenched belief. This latter situation can result in a potential juror's rejecting the court's instructions and following his or her own view of what the law should be. Uncovering the potential jurors' views on legal issues is achieved through systematic exploration on voir dire. Any education of jurors necessary to ensure that jurors understand and follow the appropriate legal standards should occur once jurors reveal their legal attitudes.

How to uncover the jurors' views on legal issues:

- Identify those legal opinions that are relevant.
- Do not tell jurors what the appropriate legal opinions or positions are.
- Have jurors describe their positions and associated beliefs.

Whether in criminal or civil trials, knowing the jurors' views on the relevant legal principles and laws is crucial. In the criminal area, it is necessary to explore the potential jurors' opinions concerning the prosecution's burden of proof, level or standard of proof/doubt, presumption of innocence, and the defendant's right not to testify. For example, questions from the defense perspective that explore jurors' opinions regarding the defendant's testimony would include the following:

"Would you expect that someone accused of a crime would naturally want to tell his or her side of the story?"

"How would you feel about a defendant who chose not to take the stand at trial? Would you tend to believe that he or she was trying to hide something?"

Notice that the above questions do not tell the jurors that the defendant does not have to take the stand. They explore the potential jurors' reactions to a defendant who exercises his or her right not to take the stand—without explicitly stating what the defendant's rights are.

The prosecution may be interested in the jurors' views on the appropriateness and value of circumstantial evidence as reflected in the following:

In a trial, there are two ways to prove a given fact. The first way is by direct evidence. Direct evidence proves a fact by itself, e.g., an eyewitness's statements or someone's fingerprints on an object. The second way to prove a given fact is by circumstantial evidence. Circumstantial evidence involves a collection of facts that leads you to conclude that another fact occurred, e.g., if you wake up one morning and snow is on the ground, where previously no snow had been, you would conclude that it snowed sometime during the night. Now, in this case, there will not be any direct evidence that the defendant murdered [the victim]; the case relies on circumstantial evidence. Would you tell me how you feel about considering only circumstantial evidence in deciding whether the defendant murdered [the victim]?

In civil cases, areas of concern are the potential jurors' opinions regarding the burden of proof, the level or standard of proof/doubt, the appropriateness of certain elements of compensatory damages (e.g., pain and suffering or loss of consortium), and punitive damages.

Some questions by the plaintiff would be as follows:

"Would any of you have any reservations in returning a verdict against a doctor/company/defendant for negligence?"

(In medical negligence cases)"Would you have any reservations in returning a verdict in favor of the plaintiff in a case involving the doctor's failure to diagnose a serious illness?"

"Would you have any reservations in filing a lawsuit against a doctor/company/driver if you felt that you were hurt as a result of their negligence?"

"How many of you would not have any reservations in deciding a case against the defendant if the plaintiff showed that it was more likely than not that the defendant was negligent?"

"How many of you feel that providing compensation for damages such as pain and suffering is any less important than compensation for such economic damages as lost wages or medical expenses?"

"How many of you feel that you really cannot compensate someone for the loss of a loved one and, therefore, such compensation should not be given?"

"The damages in this case are substantial (or are in excess of $1 million). Would any of you have any reservations in awarding this total figure ($1 million) if you found the defendant to be negligent?"

"How many of you feel that given the size of the damages in the case something more than a preponderance of the evidence would be needed in order to find in favor of the plaintiff?"

"How many of you have heard or read anything about punitive damages from the media or discussions with family, friends, or colleagues?"

"How do you feel about the awarding of punitive damages?"

"How many of you feel that punitive damages should not be used to punish corporations for wrongdoing?"

"Does anyone feel that punitive damages do more harm than good?"

"Would you have any reservations in awarding potentially substantial punitive damages if the law and the facts supported such a finding?"

Defense questions might address the following:

"How many of you feel that because a lawsuit is filed, the plaintiff probably deserves something?"

"How many of you feel, for whatever reason, that a money award for any emotional suffering of someone (for "x") should necessarily be a large sum of money?"

"How many of you feel that given your views about life, you would tend to initially accept the damages figures (for "x") claimed by the plaintiff as being appropriate?"

"How many of you feel that when it comes to awarding money damages (should damages be awarded) it is worse to award too little than to award too much?"

"Would the fact that the plaintiff has claimed more than $1 million in damages leave you with the impression that the plaintiff deserves something?"

"Would you have any reservations in awarding *no* money damages if the plaintiff fails to prove the case?"

"How many of you feel that punitive damages serve a valuable role in punishing corporations for wrongdoing?"

"Does anyone feel that punitive damages are appropriate in this case just because the plaintiff makes a claim for them?"

Notes

1. *See* Hastie, Penrod, & Pennington, Inside The Jury (1983) and Pennington & Hastie, Inside the Juror (1994).

2. *See* Huntley & Costanzo, *Sexual Harassment Stories: Testing the Story-mediated Model of Juror Decision-making in Civil Litigation,* 27 L. & Hum. Behav. 29 (2003).

3. The next chapter addresses this last feature, verbal and nonverbal communication. For an additional discussion of jury selection, *see* Frederick, *Tips for Understanding and Identifying Juror Bias,* The Journal 2 (1999).

4. Chapter 8 considers the topic of jury deliberations in detail.

5. The Supreme Court has ruled that peremptory challenges cannot be used in a discriminatory manner based on stereotypes concerning the race, Hispanic origin and gender of jurors. *See* Batson v. Kentucky, 476 U.S. 79 (1986); Hernandez v. New York, 500 U.S. 352 (1991); and J.E.B. v. Alabama *ex rel.* T.B., 511 U.S. 127 (1994). *See* Chapter 9 for a further discussion of this topic.

6. *See* Bailey & Rothblatt, Fundamentals of Criminal Advocacy (1974) at 284–85.

7. *See* Sams, *Persuasion in the Voir Dire: The Plaintiff's Approach,* in Persuasion: The Key to Damages 3 (G. Holmes ed., 1969).

8. As cited in Pavalon, *Jury Selection Theories: Art? Science? Guessing Game?* Trial 31 (1987).

9. See Penrod & Linz, *Voir Dire: Uses and Abuses,* in The Impact of Social Psychology on Procedural Justice 135 (M. Kaplan ed., 1986).

10. Gathering information regarding the assumptions of stereotypes brings up the concern some lawyers express that uncovering a juror's opinions will help the opponent. That is, exploration of jurors' opinions may alert the opposing party to the presence of desirable and undesirable jurors. In practice, however, I have seen enough jurors who are found to differ from their "stereotype" that, in most cases, the risk posed by the failure to accurately gauge a potential juror's true desirability outweighs the risk of revealing potentially desirable jurors to the opponent.

11. *See* Schulman, Shaver, Colman, Emrich, & Christie, *Recipe for a Jury,* Psychol. Today 33–44, 79–84 (1973).

12. *See* Goodman, Loftus & Greene, *Matters of Money: Voir Dire in Civil Cases,* Forensic Rep., 3, 303–29.

13. *See* Huntley & Costanzo, *supra* note 2.

14. *See* Frederick, The Psychology of the American Jury 168 (1987).

15. *See* Festinger, *A Theory of Social Comparison,* 7 Hum. Rel., 117–40 (1954).

16. *See* research cited in a discussion of contrast effects and the issue of joinder, Frederick, *supra* note 14, at 264–68.

17. See Hoar v. Great Eastern Resort Management, Inc., 256 Va 374 (1997). It has been attributed to be the first case in Virginia where a ski resort has been held liable for injuries sustained while the plaintiff was skiing. The jury awarded $6.2 million in compensatory damages. *See* Frederick, *supra* note 3 for a further discussion. Figures 1, 2, and 3 that are included in this chapter are reprinted with permission of the *Journal.*

18. Other global opinions can be relevant depending on the circumstances of the case, e.g., racism. For a consideration of some other global opinions, *see* Bonora, Krauss & Roundtree, Jurywork: Systematic Techniques (1999).

19. *See* ADORNO, FENKEL-BRUNSWICK, LEVINSON, & SANFORD, THE AUTHORITARIAN PERSONALITY (1950). For a discussion of the authoritarian personality and a review of relevant research, *see* FREDERICK, *supra* note 14, at 82–89.

20. For a critical summary of the research, *see* BROWN, SOCIAL PSYCHOLOGY (1965).

21. *See* studies cited in FREDERICK, *supra* note 14.

22. For an in-depth discussion of this trial, *see* McConahay, Mullin & Frederick, *The Uses of Social Science in Trials with Political and Racial Overtones: The Trial of Joan Little*, 41 LAW & CONTEMP. PROB. 205–29 (1977).

23. While the verdict was favorable for the defense and consistent with the selection criteria, it is not possible to further evaluate the usefulness of the authoritarian construct in this case since the verdict was unanimous on the first ballot.

24. *See* ADORNO ET AL., *supra* note 19.

25. For questions that address authoritarianism in the legal context, *see* Kravitz, Cutler & Brock, *Reliability and Validity of the Original and Revised Legal Attitudes Questionnaire*, 17 L. & HUM. BEHAV. 661–77 (1993). Additional questions that reflect authoritarianism and related constructs can be found in ROBINSON & SHAVER, MEASURES OF SOCIAL PSYCHOLOGICAL ATTITUDES (1969). *See also* Jurow, *New Data on the Effect of a Death Qualified Jury on the Guilt Determination Process*, 84 HARV. L. REV. 567 apps. B through E (1971).

26. The roots of equity theory can be traced to Aristotle's discussion of the concept of distributive justice. *See* THE WORKS OF ARISTOTLE (W. Ross trans. 1966). For a detailed discussion of how equity theory relates to juries, *see* FREDERICK, *supra* note 14, at 89–98.

27. *See* Horowitz & Willging, *Changing Views of Jury Power: The Nullification Debate, 1787–1988*, 15 L. & HUM. BEHAV. 165–82 (1991).

28. Individual differences in jurors' preferences for equity in relationships have not been sufficiently investigated at this time to the point of developing the necessary opinion scales. *See* Frederick, *Jury Behavior: Equity Considerations in Student and Juror Decisions*, paper presented at the annual meeting of the American Psychology Law Society, Cambridge, Massachusetts, October 1981, for a discussion of research indicating that individual differences in preferences for equity in relationships could predict verdict preferences of jurors in a civil case.

29. These questions have been shortened to reflect the opinion of interest and may need to be adapted to meet the requirements of the particular trial.

30. For support for superiority of case-specific questions over general opinion questions and demographics, *see* Goodman, Loftus & Greene, *Matters of Money: Voir Dire in Civil Cases*, FORENSIC REP. 3, 303 (1990) and HANS, BUSINESS ON TRIAL: THE CIVIL JURY AND CORPORATE RESPONSIBILITY (2000).

31. *See* HANS, *id.*

32. *See* Cowan, Thompson, & Ellsworth, *The Effects of Death Qualification on Jurors' Predisposition to Convict and on the Quality of Deliberations*, 8 L. & HUM. BEHAV. 53–80 (1984). *See also* a discussion of capital punishment research and the Supreme Court's rejection of it in Lockhart v. McCree, 106 S. Ct. 1758 (1986), and Thompson, *Death Qualification After* Wainwright v. Witt *and* Lockhart v. McCree, 13 L. & HUM. BEHAV. 185–215 (1989).

33. *See* Fitzgerald & Ellsworth, *Due Process v. Crime Control: Death Qualification and Jury Attitudes*, 8 L. & HUM. BEHAV. 31–51 (1984). It is also important to note that the death qualification process itself increases potential jurors' views of the likelihood of the defendant's guilt. *See* Haney, *On the Selection of Capital Juries: The Biasing Effects of the Process Effect*, 8 L. & HUM. BEHAV. 121–32 (1984) and Haney, Hurtado & Vega, *"Modern" Death Qualification: New Data on its Biasing Effects*, 18 L. & HUM. BEHAV. 619–633 (1994).

34. Butler & Moran, *The Role of Death Qualification in Venireperson's Evaluations of Aggravating and Mitigating Circumstances in Capital Trials*, 16 L. & Hum. Behav. 175 (2002). Earlier research found that excludable jurors are more receptive to mitigating than aggravating circumstances (under Witherspoon v. Illinois, 1968). *See* Luginbuhl & Middendorf, *Death Penalty Beliefs and Jurors' Responses to Aggravating and Mitigating Circumstances in Capital Trials*, 12 L. & Hum. Behav. 263–281.

35. Wainwright v. Witt, 105 S. Ct. 844 (1985).

36. It is often necessary to remind jurors that premeditated or deliberate murder does not include self-defense or the accidental killing of another. Additional death penalty questions can be found in Appendix II. *See also* Cowan et al. *supra* note 32, and Bonora et al. *supra* note 18.

37. *See* survey findings cited in footnote 1, Chapter 1.

CHAPTER 3

Understanding Jurors' Nonverbal Communication

Objectives

- To explore how jurors reveal their opinions and biases in their nonverbal behaviors.
- To understand the importance of deviations from normal patterns of communication.
- To develop strategies for utilizing nonverbal communication in jury selection.

To evaluate potential jurors' opinions and biases, it is important to be aware of what jurors are telling us beyond the answers they give to questions posed during the course of voir dire. As we shall see in Chapter 5, the way that voir dire is normally conducted inhibits candor and openness on the part of potential jurors. In addition, there is evidence that potential jurors may seek to deceive lawyers through their answers to questions posed to them.[1] Thus, while the jury selection process places a premium on the information jurors provide, strict reliance on the content of jurors' answers may not reveal the jurors' true feelings and opinions.

Types of Nonverbal Communication

One of the most important ways people communicate has nothing to do with the content of what they say, especially when it comes to their opinions and emotions. Studies have shown that from 60 to 65 percent of people's total communication occurs through what are termed nonverbal behaviors.[2] This type of communication consists of *kinesic behaviors* (nonlinguistic body motions) and *paralinguistic behaviors* (noncontent aspects of speech).[3] Considerable attention has been paid to the presence of anxiety in nonverbal communication, particularly in detecting when someone is lying.[4] When people are anxious because of sensitivity to the subject matter, general nervousness, or a wish to deceive, they can reveal or "leak" their anxiety (and other feelings) through a variety of kinesic and paralinguistic behaviors. Lawyers can uncover the underlying opinions, feelings, and biases of potential jurors during the jury selection process by paying attention to the information contained in non-verbal communication.

Nonverbal indicators of what jurors are feeling or when they are evading the truth are of two types: visual cues (i.e., what we see) and auditory cues (i.e., what we hear). Several points should be kept in mind when considering visual and auditory cues. First, there is no Pinocchio effect (i.e., the fictional character Pinocchio's nose growing longer when he told a lie). No single cue or behavior is universally associated with lying. Second, although we will consider these cues separately for the purposes of explanation, in reality the behavior of jurors is rarely this simple. Nonverbal cues usually occur in clusters or combinations of cues that provide the overall meaning to the behavior. Therefore, it is impor-tant not to fall victim to simplistic one-clue/behavior interpretations of the nonverbal communication of potential jurors at any given time.

Third, jurors may exhibit individual behaviors or a cluster of behaviors for a variety of reasons. For example, when potential jurors fold their arms, it may reflect animosity toward what is being said or it may simply mean the air conditioning has made them cold. Careful attention to the whole process is necessary in order to glean useful information about potential jurors' true feelings.

Fourth, in considering what to look for in the jurors' nonverbal commu-nication, it is necessary to start at the beginning. That is, we must consider the normal pattern of the jurors' nonverbal behavior. How do jurors act sim-ply as a function of their being in the voir dire situation? Observing jurors at the beginning of voir dire provides a critical comparison point or baseline for evaluating their subsequent actions. Does the juror's behavior change in response to what is happening on voir dire (who is asking the questions or what topic is being addressed)? For example, does the juror show signs of nervousness or agitation throughout the questioning or only when the topic of race relations or tort reform is discussed? Is the juror more open and talk-ative with one lawyer than with another?

Finally, it is important to understand that nervousness and deliberate deception may not produce the same responses within the same individual. Jurors may reveal outward signs of nervousness (e.g., increased blinking or lack of eye contact) in sensitive topic areas, but, when it comes to specifically expressing an opinion on the topic that is misleading or a lie, they may exert greater control over their nonverbal communication (e.g., maintaining higher levels of eye contact). This latter activity can arise from stereotypes concern-ing successful deception held by jurors, e.g., that lack of eye contact is asso-ciated with lying.

The key to understanding jurors' answers lies in deviations or breakdowns in their typical behavior. It is through the information these breakdowns provide and the overall patterns or clusters of jurors' behaviors that lawyers can better understand what the jurors are really saying.

Visual Cues: What We See

The first category of cues comprises what is seen in the potential juror's behavior, such as movements, posture, and facial expressions. Seven types of cues are important:

- Body movement
- Body posture
- Body orientation
- Inadvertent Emblems
- Shrugs
- Eye contact
- Facial expressions

Body Movement

In general, the more movement the potential juror exhibits, the greater the anxiety. These movements can involve the entire body (e.g., shifting body postures) or more limited parts of the body (e.g., wringing hands or tapping fingers). Gross movements such as repeatedly shifting the body's weight ("fidgeting" or "squirming") reflect anxiety or nervousness on the juror's part, the traditional reaction to being placed on "the hot seat."

More subtle body movements relate to actions that dissipate the nervous energy or arousal produced by anxiety—rubbing the hands together and squeezing them at the same time, strumming the fingers repeatedly on a chair arm or tapping them on a book, newspaper, or other object. Strumming and tapping movements, however, can also reflect impatience. While not necessarily an indicator of deception, these body movements often suggest unfavorable reactions to the lawyer asking the questions. Twisting an object such as a tissue, necklace, bracelet, watchband, or ring with the hand is often analogous to hand wringing and is a more subtle sign of anxiety.

Other signs of anxiety are what are termed "adaptive" movements,[5] such as scratching one's head, pulling or twirling one's hair, or briefly touching one's face. Grooming can also reflect anxiety. Anxious potential jurors can be seen brushing their hair back with one hand or quickly shaking the head so that their hair falls in place. This anxious grooming can also lead potential jurors to "pick" at their clothing, removing lint, or they may "straighten" their clothing (dresses, coats, shirts, or ties).

Not all of these movements indicate anxiety. For example, scratching of the head also may reflect uncertainty, particularly if the head is tilted at an angle while the scratching occurs. While wringing the hands reflects anxiety, rubbing the palms together in a back-and-forth motion can indicate confidence or anticipation of something desirable. Steepling the hands, where the hands are placed palms together with the fingers pointed skyward, indicates confidence in one's position or in what one is saying. In addition, expressive gestures that complement what is being said generally indicate a greater degree of comfort or involvement in the process. These cues or behaviors should not be mistaken for anxious reactions on the part of potential jurors.

Body Posture

This cue combines two sources of information, body rigidity and gestures. In general, the more rigid the body posture of a potential juror, the greater the anxiety the juror is experiencing. Signs of rigidity include an erect, stiff posture and the tightening of muscles. Tightening of the muscles in the hands and fingers can produce the appearance of "white knuckles" when anxious potential jurors grasp the arms of their chairs or clasp their hands in their laps. More subtle signs of anxiety occur with the tightening of smaller muscle groups in the body, particularly the face. For example, in jury selection for a medical negligence case against a hospital, questioning of a hospital administrator on the issues of hospital liability and size of damage awards led to a subtle but informative nonverbal response. Although his answers were not overtly anti-plaintiff, his jaw muscles tightened whenever liability and damage award issues were addressed. When questioning returned to less sensitive areas, his jaw muscles relaxed.

Rigidity is also apparent when normal head and body movements do not occur during the course of voir dire questioning. This lack of movement can manifest itself in crossed arms, crossed legs, and legs crossed at the ankles. However, it is important to consider the above cues in light of other features of the potential jurors' nonverbal communication. For example,

Visual Cues to Anxiety and Deception	
Source	*Examples of Behaviors*
Body Movement	Shifting postures, wringing hands, repetitive movements, or "adaptive movements"
Body Posture	Greater rigidity and less head and body movement
Body Orientation	Closed orientation, folded arms, crossed legs, or leaning away from speaker
Inadvertent Emblems	Nested fist in the crook of the elbow or clenched hand on leg
Shrugs	Presence of shoulder shrugs
Eye Contact	Less eye contact and greater blinking; exceptions: hostility and cultural norms of reduced eye contact
Facial Expressions	Frowning, skeptical expressions, detached or fixed smiles

Adapted with permission of *Virginia Lawyer.*

H-105   20th 6 St.

crossed arms with a genuine smile indicate comfort, not anxiety or resistance. Crossed legs with a slight kicking motion can reflect boredom or impatience. Placing the hands in pockets, particularly with the fists balled up, reflects anxiety and sometimes even hidden hostility.

Various gestures can also provide information on potential jurors' feelings.[6] Placing fingers in front of the mouth can indicate reluctance or the holding back of the juror's true feelings. Placing a hand in front of the mouth can reflect a lack of confidence or embarrassment at what the potential juror is saying. Jurors who tilt their heads may be evaluating what is being asked or questioning the statement being made (enhanced by the juror's pursed lips). An open hand to the throat can indicate a need to protect oneself from an anxiety-provoking situation, topic, or person, such as the criminal defendant.

A final aspect of body posture concerns the concept of "mirroring."[7] Mirroring refers to the degree that individuals adopt the body postures and mannerisms of those around them (or those of a speaker). Mirroring usually indicates agreement or a positive response to what is being said or identification with the person who is saying it. Potential jurors may mirror the postures or mannerisms of lawyers or other jurors with whom they identify or toward whom they have positive feelings. Mirroring among jurors is useful when considering the development of cliques or relationships that may form in the jury. Potential jurors mirroring each other are revealing potential bonds that may form if they serve together on the jury.

Body Orientation

A third cue concerns the orientation of the potential juror's body to the lawyer. Body orientation refers to the relationship of the front of the listener's body to the speaker. Open orientation can be seen in the "squaring" of the listener's body to the speaker. An open orientation by a juror generally shows lack of anxiety, positive feelings toward the speaker, or agreement with the speaker or his or her position. In a basic sense, an open orientation leaves the vulnerable parts of the body exposed, a position people are reluctant to take in the presence of someone (or something) that makes them feel uncomfortable. Thus, the degree to which the body is angled away from the speaker, as when the shoulder is turned toward the lawyer or party, reflects the "closed" nature of the relationship or resistance to the speaker or his or her position. This closed orientation can be particularly informative when it reflects an ongoing orientation toward one party or the other.

A related feature of orientation involves whether parts of the body are brought together to close off or "protect" the body. Crossing of the arms or legs can combine with orientation to reflect a further closing off to the lawyer. Jurors who cross their arms in this manner reveal their resistance or even hostility toward the lawyer or party to which it is directed.

Like mirroring, body orientation can provide information about potential relationships within the jury. How jurors associate in the hallways, lunch rooms, and the jury box during the course of jury selection provides glimpses of the relationships between jurors. Several jurors may stand together in a small group with the outlying members turning their bodies in toward the center of the group, reflecting the "closed" nature of the group. This exclusivity is particularly telling when other potential jurors are standing near the group, yet are not included in it. The orientation of jurors also can reveal relationships in the jury box. When several potential jurors tend to turn toward one another, other jurors can be left "outside," with their bodies oriented either straight ahead or away from these potential jurors.

Finally, leaning forward or away from the speaker can reveal the degree of interest in the lawyer or the position advocated. Generally, jurors who lean forward reveal their interest, attention, or receptiveness, but this is not necessarily a positive sign for the lawyer. A hostile potential juror, whose forward lean indicates attention to the lawyer or party, reflects a more combative interest, not the presence of any positive feelings. Leaning away by jurors, on the other hand, generally indicates less interest or less receptivity. This latter cue also may reflect comfort with what is being said or the fact that a decision has been reached. In either case there is a decrease in the jurors's need to be vigilant or attentive.

Inadvertent Emblems

Emblems are gestures that can be made in place of a word. The nodding of the head (yes) or the cupping of the hand behind the ear (speak up/I can't hear) communicates the intent of the person without the use of words. Like "slips of the tongue" there can be "slips of gestures" or "leaks of emblems."[8] A key to detecting information contained in the leakage of emblems is that it is exhibited outside the normal presentation area (and oftentimes is present only in partial form). For example, an emblem or gesture such as a clenched or shaking fist is often made in front and away from the body and is a sign of hostility or anger. Generally, such emblems are inappropriate for expression during voir dire questioning. However, a clenched fist tucked in the crook of the elbow is not so obvious, yet can still be emblematic of the jurors' true hostile feelings.

Shrugs

Shrugging the shoulders while answering a question indicates a lack of confidence arising from anxiety (as a result of deception), embarrassment, or uncertainty. Shrugs can be the juror's way of qualifying an answer. Potential jurors who shrug when answering a question about the defendant's presumed innocence or awards for pain and suffering are telling lawyers that they are not sure or do not agree with what they are saying. This information is important to know in evaluating the desirability of these jurors. A shrug may indicate the juror's lack of commitment to what is being said. Under these circumstances, potential jurors are telling lawyers that while they may verbally agree, this agreement may have no impact on their decisions. Finally, shrugs can also indicate indifference about an issue, as in the case of a juror who shrugs when noting that police may sometimes go too far in subduing potential lawbreakers.

Eye Contact

The willingness or ability of potential jurors to make and maintain eye contact during questioning can be a measure of the anxiety they feel. If there is anxiety or tension in the interaction between the lawyer and potential jurors, this tension will build up over time. As the tension rises, potential jurors will respond by breaking eye contact (through either averting the eyes or blinking). When eye contact is broken, the tension level temporarily decreases and the jurors can then resume eye contact with the lawyer. If anxiety is not present, potential jurors can maintain a moderate to high level of eye contact with the lawyer or party in the interaction. The same is true when the potential juror has positive feelings toward the lawyer or party or is interested in what the lawyer has to say. However, when the potential juror is anxious (possibly as a result of being deceptive), breaks in the normal pattern of eye contact occur, with potential jurors averting their eyes at critical times or blinking more often.

Knowing the relationship between eye contact and anxiety allows lawyers to consider several useful questions. Do potential jurors maintain eye contact with the lawyer or party when they give their answers, or do they avert their eyes at critical times? For example, when potential jurors are asked how they feel about rendering a million-dollar judgment against the defendant, do they say, "I wouldn't have any reservations about rendering a million-dollar verdict [averting eyes] against the defendant [re-establishing eye contact]"? Or in the case of a criminal defendant possibly not taking the stand to testify, do jurors say "I would not hold it against the defendant [averting eyes] if he chose not to testify [re-establishing eye contact] in his own defense"? Averting the eyes at the last part of the answer reveals the juror's anxiety. Do potential jurors increase their blinking in response to questions concerning certain opinions or when a particular lawyer asks the questions? Are potential jurors able to maintain eye contact throughout the questioning process? A potential juror's failure to maintain eye contact could mean that the juror would not be a desirable choice for the examiner.

Three exceptions to the relationship between eye contact and anxiety should be kept in mind. First, although steady eye contact is usually an indication of juror ease or interest, an increase in eye contact can reflect hostility. This phenomenon is captured by the expression "know your enemy" (e.g., "I don't like you and I am keeping my eye on you"). Second, an increase in eye contact has also been associated with attempts to deceive or hide one's true feelings.[9] As such, when jurors choose to lie or mislead and believe that a steady gaze would make them appear more truthful, they may increase their eye contact. Third, cultures differ in their view of the appropriate levels of eye contact. For example, potential jurors of Hispanic and Asian backgrounds may exhibit lower levels of eye contact, which simply reflects their cultures' views. These exceptions highlight the need to consider all nonverbal and verbal cues together in order to evaluate potential jurors' feelings and opinions.

Facial Expressions

Probably the cue that people rely upon most in their interactions with others is facial expressions. Frowning, smiling, looks of concern, or skeptical or incredulous expressions can reveal feelings about a situation or person. The problem with facial expressions is that over the course of socialization, people learn to control their facial expressions more than other aspects of nonverbal communication. Potential jurors may smile or exhibit signs of interest even when their feelings are inconsistent with these expressions. However, unless a potential juror is particularly adept at controlling or manipulating nonverbal communication, inconsistencies between feelings and outward appearances will leak out. Leakage occurs in two areas: aspects of the facial expressions themselves and inconsistencies with other body cues.

The facial expressions of the potential juror can betray underlying "hidden" feelings in several ways. First, the potential juror may exhibit what are termed "microexpressions."[10] Microexpressions are very short or fleeting expressions, measured in terms of milliseconds. Microexpressions often are inconsistent. For example, when the facial expression of someone who is not happy but is smiling is filmed in slow motion, microexpressions may show a grimace, belying the dominant smiling expression. Unfortunately, microexpressions are unlikely to be seen and responded to on a conscious level. However, microexpressions do influence us on a subconscious level. They can be important sources of lawyers' "gut" feelings about jurors, where lawyers have a positive or negative reaction to a juror yet cannot give an objective reason for this feeling.[11]

A second way potential jurors can betray their true feelings is through the quality of the facial expression itself. While there are no hard-and-fast rules for lie detection, a fixed smile, one that lasts longer than is appropriate for the situation, can reveal deception. Jurors often use smiles to mask other feelings. The fixed smile appears to linger, where the genuine smile naturally disappears as the situation or feeling changes. This fixed smile can reveal the degree of control the juror is exercising, with the "controlled" face giving the appearance of unemotionality or composure when the juror should be reacting to the situation. For example, when a lawyer inadvertently embarrasses a hostile juror, the juror may adopt a fixed smile to cover his or her hostile reaction to the lawyer.

In addition, a nongenuine facial expression is often asymmetric, not involving the whole face as a genuine expression normally does. The "crooked smile" is such an expression. In a crooked smile, the lips turn up in a smile on one side while the lips on the other side remain horizontal or turn slightly down, in a frown or grimace.

Finally, leakage occurs through the jurors' other nonverbal body cues. This leakage occurs when a facial expression communicates some desired effect but the body cues send a conflicting message. For example, potential jurors may verbally express a willingness to treat a party fairly and the facial expression may appear neutral or positive. However, the body cues may reflect resistance or anxiety, with crossed arms and a closed orientation. As will be discussed later, the degree of consistency of nonverbal cues is a major factor in uncovering a jurors' true feelings.

One type of potential juror highlights the above discussion of facial expressions. The "smiling" juror wears a smile during the voir dire questioning by the lawyer, giving the impression that the juror is receptive to or feels positive toward the lawyer or party. However, this juror is really hostile or in some other way unfavorable. Once selected, this juror smiles at the lawyer during the trial, continuing to foster the impression that the juror is favorable. When the jury returns a verdict against the client, the smiling juror continues to smile (and only later is revealed as having opposed the client's case).

The key to detecting the smiling juror lies in examining the consistency of his or her nonverbal cues. Are there wrinkles or crow's-feet at the outside corners of the juror's eyes that should accompany genuine smiling? Is there a softness to the eyes that is associated with positive feeling or are they hard, as would be consistent with the expression "eyes that looked daggers"? Is the smile asymmetrical (e.g., one side of the smile lifts up while the other side of the smile stays relatively flat or points downward)? Is the smile consistent with other nonverbal cues, e.g., body orientation and postures? Always beware of the potential juror who smiles but angles his or her body away and maintains a rigid posture!

Auditory Cues: What We Hear

The second category of cues focuses on what we hear, i.e., auditory cues. There are eight auditory cues that can indicate the presence of anxiety or deception:

- Speech disturbances
- Vocal hesitancy
- Rising pitch
- Amount of speech
- Speed of speech
- Tone of voice
- Tense laughter
- Word choice

As mentioned earlier, most of these cues reflect a deviation or breakdown in the potential juror's normal patterns of behavior, in this case, speech. It is risky to underestimate the importance of the auditory cues! They may be more valuable for detecting deception than visual cues are.[12]

Speech Disturbances

Disruptions in the juror's normal pattern of speech can reflect anxiety. The frequency of disruptions in the potential juror's answers increases as the level of anxiety rises. These disruptions take the form of breaks in the potential juror's answers with "um's," "uh's," or "er's." For example, differing levels of anxiety in response to the question "Do you think that you could return a verdict of no money damages, if the evidence and the law supported such a finding?" are reflected in the following two potential answers given by a juror:

"I think that I could return a verdict of no money to the plaintiff." [undisrupted answer]

"I think, uh, that I could return, uh, a verdict of no money to the, er, plaintiff." [disrupted answer]

The presence of disruptions in the latter answer reflects greater anxiety over what the potential juror is saying than the former. Speech disruptions also can occur with the repetition of words within the juror's answer, such as "I think that I [slight pause] I could return a verdict of no money damages. . . ."

Finally, disruptions or nonfluencies in the potential juror's speech can appear in the use of unfinished sentences and the interruption of sentences. Failure to complete sentences can reflect anxiety. For example, when the answer is intended to be "I think I can be fair to the defendant," the anxious juror may respond with "I think I can be . . ." breaking off before "fair to the defendant." Disruptions can also appear when jurors begin a sentence, stop, and start a new sentence, as in the answer "I think I–Fairness is important." The key to understanding the importance of the incomplete sentence or switching to a new sentence lies in how the juror ends the answer. It is the avoidance of certain words or the trailing off of the incomplete answer that should alert the lawyer to potential problems.

Vocal Hesitancy

Vocal hesitancies are pauses that occur in the juror's answers. Vocal hesitancies occur more frequently as the anxiety level of the potential juror rises. Pauses can also occur during deception when more cognitive resources are needed to construct and monitor the lie.[13] These pauses can occur at the beginning of the answer; for example, "[pause] I wouldn't have any reservations about awarding punitive damages." As with speech disruptions, pauses or breaks can occur during the course of the answer or sentence such as, "I wouldn't have any reservations [pause] in awarding punitive damages." In either case, it is important to hear what vocal hesitancies are communicating about the juror's real feelings.

Finally, vocal hesitancies can reflect censoring on the part of jurors. Some questions require that jurors give more than a minimal amount of thought to their answers. During these times of contemplation, jurors may reflect not only on their true feelings but also on what answer would make them look good. For example, when questioned about his or her view of a criminal defendant not taking the witness stand, a juror who pauses before saying, "I guess that's his right" may be reluctant to express the opinion that such a scenario would indicate guilt.

Rising Pitch

The level of the juror's pitch also can reflect anxiety. Anxiety can cause the muscles in the throat to tighten, resulting in speech that is higher in pitch. Noting when a rise in pitch in the juror's answers occurs in response to different topic areas can reveal those areas that cause greater anxiety. The dramatic example of this cue occurs when the juror utters an answer to an anxiety-producing question with a short, high-pitched squeak of "yes" or "no." Rising tone also may reflect uncertainty in the answer given. In this case, while the statement itself is declaratory in nature, the rising tone toward the end of the statement reveals the juror's lack of confidence in what he or she has said.

Amount of Speech

The presence of positive feelings toward the lawyer or an expectation of social approval from the lawyer can reveal itself in the amount of speech the juror provides. When jurors feel positive toward a lawyer they are more willing to talk with this lawyer. The same applies to those jurors who seek approval from (i.e., want to be liked by) the particular lawyer or party. When jurors do not like a lawyer or party, their willingness to talk or provide full and candid answers in response to the lawyer's questioning decreases. Thus, talkativeness can reveal important information about how the jurors feel about the parties in the case.

It is also useful to pay particular attention to the potential juror's willingness to provide full answers or to reveal information beyond what lawyers request in their questions. Lawyers should be leery of potential jurors who give brief answers to their questions (or certain topic areas) yet give detailed answers in response to questioning by the opposing lawyer. In fact, this differential in responsiveness can reach the point where potential jurors actually interrupt the questioning of other jurors by a favored lawyer in order to volunteer information or their opinions on the topic.

There is a qualification to the general rule that talkativeness reflects positive feelings. This exception addresses the content of the juror's answers. Answers that provide irrelevant information or are evasive can indicate deception or anxiety. A juror who feels anxious or is trying to deceive the lawyer may use irrelevant information as a screen. The juror's goal is to tell the lawyer something to satisfy the need to provide an answer yet at the same time not reveal the juror's true feelings. For example, when a juror is asked about his or her ability to treat the defendant fairly, a direct answer would be, "I would treat Mr. Jones fairly," while an evasive answer would be, "I think everyone would agree that fairness is important." Note that in the latter answer, the juror specifically avoids revealing how he or she feels toward the defendant. This may be a simple oversight, or it may reflect the juror's desire not to reveal his or her true feelings. Further questioning (or consideration of past answers) is necessary to properly evaluate which is present in the answer, oversight or evasion. Consider the following exchange that occurred during the *North* jury selection.

PROSECUTOR: . . . Is there any other reason that it would be difficult for you to serve as a juror?

JUROR: No.

PROSECUTOR: Sometimes people have religious beliefs that make it hard for them to be a juror. Do you have any beliefs that come from your religious ideas or philosophical ideas that would make it hard?

JUROR: Well, I am a Christian but, you know, I believe in the truth, because the truth is God's friend. *(Notice how the juror fails to answer the question.)*

PROSECUTOR: Okay. And if the truth, as you understood it, and the law as you heard it from the judge—

JUROR: Yes.

PROSECUTOR: —led to a decision that required you to vote Colonel North guilty, you could do that, if that's the way you honestly believed it?

JUROR: No, I couldn't do that, because, you know, I wasn't there and I don't know if he did it. Say, if I would vote guilty, you know, people's life [sic] is precious and I would be taking his life, in a sense, and I couldn't vote guilty.

PROSECUTOR: No matter what you heard in the courtroom?

JUROR: Right.

PROSECUTOR: You still couldn't vote guilty?

JUROR: No.

PROSECUTOR: I appreciate your candor very much. Thank you, ma'am.

JUROR: Thank you, sir.

COURT: Thank you very much. You are excused.

As will be discussed in Chapter 5, failure to detect the irrelevant answer can have potentially disastrous consequences.

Speed of Speech

How fast the juror's answer is given, once the answer is initiated, is another cue to anxiety. Jurors may rush their answers when they feel anxious about them. By speaking faster, jurors reduce the duration of their anxiety.

Tone of Voice

The tone of the juror's voice can be an important cue to deception and negative feelings. This cue appears to be more accurate in detecting deception than the visual cues considered earlier.[14] A cold and condescending tone of voice generally indicates deception (and aloofness or potentially negative opinions, such as animosity). Thus, it is critical to treat with extreme caution the potential juror who answers in a cold and condescending tone of voice during questioning by the lawyer.

Tense Laughter

Laughter has long been recognized as a tension release. Jurors can reveal their tension through the quality of the laugh itself and the appropriateness of laughter for the situation. The tense laugh is often too loud for the situation. While laughter may be appropriate, the volume of tense laughter is higher than that of normal laughter. In addition, jurors may abbreviate or cut short tense laughter. This occurs when the juror does not intend to laugh or realizes that laughter is inappropriate. The juror then abruptly cuts off the laugh.

Finally, it is possible to identify tense laughter by noting the appropriateness of laughter for the voir dire situation. Laughter that occurs during the discussion of sensitive topics is inappropriate and likely a result of anxiety on the part of the juror.

Auditory Cues to Anxiety and Deception

Source	Examples of Behaviors
Speech Disturbances	Nonfluencies, "um's," "er's," and word repetition
Vocal Hesitancy	Pauses before and during answers
Pitch	Rising pitch
Amount of Speech	Lesser amounts of speech; exception: irrelevant or evasive speech
Speed of Speech	Rapid speech
Tone of Voice	Cold, condescending tone
Tense Laughter	Inappropriate laughter or higher than normal volume of laughter
Word Choice	Greater psychological distancing (e.g., "them" v. "African-Americans") and use of negation conjunctions

Adapted with permission of *Virginia Lawyer.*

An example will highlight the nature of tense laughter. In a medical negligence suit against a doctor in a small community, one potential juror was a patient of the defendant doctor. The juror asserted that she could be fair during the questioning by the plaintiff's lawyer. However, tense laughter gave her away. When asked about her ability to be fair, given her status as a patient of the defendant, she responded, "Yes, I could be fair, heh! heh!" She was later asked if she would have any reservations about returning a verdict in excess of $1 million if the evidence and law supported such a finding. She responded, "No, heh! heh!" This laughter was not sarcastic but was obviously inappropriate for the situation. The distress felt by the potential juror at the possibility of serving on the jury was apparent from her other nonverbal communication. The anxiety became so intense that she unconsciously broke the tension by laughing—a laugh that sounded more like a bark than a laugh.

Word Choice

Unlike the previous cues, the final cue in the auditory area concerns the content of the jurors' responses. The words jurors choose to communicate their answers can be very informative. The choice of words can reflect a psychological distance the jurors impose between themselves and the objects about which they are speaking. The presence of psychological distancing can indicate negative feelings or anxiety on the part of jurors. For example, jurors who refer to the plaintiff as "she" or "the plaintiff" are placing more psychological distance between themselves and the plaintiff than are jurors who use the plaintiff's name. Psychological distancing can also reflect the presence of prejudice against certain groups. Jurors who refer to African-Americans as "them" or "those kind of people" as compared to "Blacks" or "African-Americans" are revealing their prejudice or feelings of anxiety.

The directness or indirectness of the communication also reflects psychological distancing. A juror who has negative feelings or is not being truthful may say, for example, "Overall, I don't have any really bad feelings toward them [Acme Corporation]" when he or she might be thinking that Acme Corporation has done a lousy job with safety management.

An additional consideration in word choice lies in the style of speech that potential jurors use.[15] Jurors who use a nonassertive or "powerless" speech style are less persuasive and are viewed in less favorable terms than those who use a powerful speech style. Characteristics of powerless speech include hedges (e.g., "I think," "I believe," or "kind of"), intensifiers (e.g., "so," "too," or "very"), hesitations (e.g., "you know," "uh," "well," or pauses), polite or overly formal diction (e.g., "sir," "please," or "thank you"), and an interrogative tone (i.e., the rise in intonation or pitch associated with questioning, even in declarative contexts).

Speech style is relevant to our consideration of potential jurors' communication in two ways. First, several features of powerless speech encompass some of the cues discussed above, indicating that powerless speech also can reflect deception or anxiety. Second, in terms of jury selection, potential jurors who use a powerless speech are likely to be less persuasive in conveying their views than those who use a powerful style of speech. Thus, speech style can provide valuable information as to the likely influence (and potential leadership role) jurors will have during the deliberation process.

Two points remain concerning word choice. First, using the negation conjunction "but" to connect two statements can serve to invalidate the first statement. For example, a juror might say in response to a question, "I could be fair, but I did read in the paper that the defendant admitted killing the victim." This statement carries with it the high probability that the potential juror really does not believe the first part of the answer ("I could be fair") and is letting the lawyer know this by adding the second statement ("but I did read in the paper that the defendant admitted killing the victim").

Second, asking questions that require jurors to put their answers in their own words will facilitate the evaluation of the jurors' choice of words. Open-ended questions are questions that do not restrict the answers available to the juror, such as, "How do you feel about the use of capital punishment for premeditated murder?" Note that this question does not provide an obvious answer for the juror. Questions that restrict jurors' answers are referred to as closed-ended questions, such as, "Do you believe in the use of capital punishment for premeditated murder?" The value of the open-ended question lies in the information the jurors provide when they express their opinions and feelings in their own words.

How to Evaluate Jurors' Nonverbal Communication

Up to this point, the various visual and auditory cues have been considered separately. However, the proper evaluation of potential jurors' behaviors involves incorporating all available information. In practice, capitalizing on these cues does not require additional time but simply a sensitivity to what information is available.

The key concept for evaluation of the nonverbal cues lies in consistency. It is necessary to attend to patterns or clusters (representing consistency of cues) of nonverbal communication—that is, how do the cues work in concert to present a picture of what the juror is really doing (e.g., concealing the truth) or feeling? The presence of inconsistency among the cues raises a red flag indicating that something is afoot. Particular attention should then be given to discovering what actually is happening.

Establish a Baseline

Considering the overall pattern of the jurors' behaviors in the process of voir dire is essential in evaluating the verbal and nonverbal communication of jurors. As mentioned earlier in this chapter, the first step in this process is to establish a comparison point or baseline of anxiety or nervousness that the jurors are experiencing in the jury selection process. Anxiety does not exist

---

How to evaluate jurors' nonverbal communication:

- Establish a baseline or comparison point
- Evaluate changes or deviations in the jurors' responses
- Look for patterns and inconsistencies in behavior
- Be aware of who the jurors look to for answers in uncertain situations
- Observe jurors at all times

---

in a vacuum. Jurors may show signs of anxiety or nervousness simply because they are being asked questions in court.

By establishing a baseline of activity or anxiety, lawyers can interpret subsequent changes in behavior within the context of the jurors' typical behavior. The best way to establish this baseline is to observe the jurors' nonverbal communication while they answer questions concerning their backgrounds. These questions produce the least anxiety. Thus, the beginning of voir dire should, and usually does, contain simple, nonsensitive questions of this sort. The pattern of the jurors' responses will reveal how anxious they are at being part of the voir dire process and their overall pattern of nonverbal behavior.

Evaluate Change in Jurors' Responses

After establishing the baseline of anxiety and activity patterns for jurors, evaluations are made in light of how the jurors' subsequent behaviors change. Particular attention is paid to changes occurring as a function of who asks the questions and what topics are being addressed. For example, do potential jurors start to withdraw from the lawyer as the area of questioning shifts from issues of worker safety or pain and suffering to issues relating to punitive damages or contributory negligence? Also, noting any changes in the jurors' nonverbal communication when different lawyers conduct their examination is important. Do the potential jurors respond differently when the prosecutor, plaintiff's lawyer, defense lawyer, or judge asks the questions? Finally, does the juror's nonverbal behavior differ from that of the other jurors? For example, does this juror shift nervously in his or her seat when discussing race relations while other jurors answer without such nervous behavior?

Notice Patterns and Inconsistencies

Since there is no Pinocchio effect, it is necessary to look at the clusters of nonverbal behaviors of jurors. Such clusters of behaviors may be good or bad depending on the context in which the behaviors occur. However, it is also important to notice when patterns of behavior conflict not only with what is being said, but with other clusters of nonverbal behavior. For example, the juror smiles, looks you straight in the eye, and says that he would treat your client fairly, but the juror's body is leaning away from you and toward your opponent and his arms are folded across his chest.

Watch Jurors' Sources of Support

Beyond changes in the jurors' behavior, it is necessary to evaluate where jurors turn for support in uncertain situations. There is considerable uncertainty in the voir dire situation. It is important to note who jurors look to for support or clarification when they become confused by questions or are unsure of their answers. Do jurors continue to make eye contact with the lawyer asking the questions—in essence, seeking clarification or assistance from this lawyer? Do jurors look to the lawyer for the opposing party? Do they look to the judge or to their fellow jurors? Their responses in the face of uncertainty may indicate where these jurors will turn for answers or support when questions arise during the course of trial. Potential jurors who look to the opposing counsel for answers or support should be removed, where possible.

Observe Jurors at All Times

While much of the previous discussion has focused on the jurors' reactions to the questions posed to them, information is available at other times as well. Alert lawyers can capitalize on these occasions. First, observe the potential jurors' reactions to both the questions posed to other jurors and the subsequent answers. Jurors will often nod in agreement, show skeptical or critical facial expressions, or give other nonverbal indicators of their own opinions and feelings in response to the voir dire of their fellow jurors.

Second, observe the reactions of potential jurors while these jurors are in the spectators' section of the courtroom. Jurors are less likely to feel as though they are in a fishbowl when they are in the spectators' section rather than the jury box. As a result, jurors tend not to inhibit their nonverbal reactions when they are in the spectators' section. Judges often provide a brief description of the case while the potential jurors are congregated en masse in the spectators' section. Desirable and undesirable potential jurors can reveal themselves through their positive or negative nonverbal communication in response to these introductory remarks. For example, jurors may adopt a sympathetic, concerned expression or a hostile posture when looking at the plaintiff or defendant during the judge's introductory remarks. In some cases, potential jurors may react more dramatically as when a juror cries in the spectator section upon hearing a description of the case.

Third, particular attention should be paid to jurors when the court or lawyers introduce the parties to the dispute. It is important to note the direction of the jurors' gazes and the reactions of jurors during the introduction of the parties. It is natural for jurors to direct their gaze toward the party being introduced. However, some jurors may refuse to look at the party or fail to meet the returning gaze of the party at this time. Inability to make eye contact or to direct their gaze at the party can reveal the juror's negative reactions to the party. In addition, jurors often can be seen with sympathetic, concerned, or even hostile expressions on their faces. All of these reactions add to the information lawyers collect regarding the desirability of potential jurors.

Finally, it is helpful to observe potential jurors during breaks, while in the hallways, or at lunch counters. As mentioned in the discussion of body orientation cues, potential jurors can reveal the relationships present or being formed through their interactions with one another. To whom do jurors talk? With whom do jurors eat? Is deference being shown to certain jurors by other jurors? Which juror or jurors appear to be leading the interactions or making decisions among the jurors? These observations can provide valuable information on how the jury will act as a group and the leadership potential of various jurors.

Notes

1. *See* Broeder, *Voir Dire Examinations: An Empirical Study*, 38 S. Cal. L. Rev. 503–28 (1965); Mize, *On Better Jury Selection: Spotting Unfavorable Jurors Before They Enter the Jury Room*, Ct. Rev. 36, 10 (1999); Mize, *Be Cautious of the Quiet Ones*, Voir Dire, 10, 8 (2003); Seltzer, Ventuti & Lopes, *Juror Honesty During Voir Dire*, 19 J. Crim. Just. 451 (1991); and Vidmar, *Case Studies of Pre- and Midtrial Prejudice in Criminal and Civil Litigation*, 26 L. & Hum. Behav. 73 (2002).

2. *See* studies cited in footnote 27 from *Judge's Nonverbal Behavior in Jury Trials: A Threat to Judicial Impartiality*, Va. L. Rev. (1975).

3. For reviews of the area of verbal and nonverbal communication, *see* Frederick, The Psychology of the American Jury (1987); Ekman, Telling Lies: Clues to Deceit in the Marketplace, Marriage, and Politics (1992); Zuckerman, DePaulo, & Rosenthal, *Verbal and Nonverbal Communication of Deception*, in 14 Advances in Experimental Social Psychology 1–60 (L. Berkowitz ed., 1982); Mehrabian, Nonverbal Communication (1972). For its relation to trial practice in general, *see* Aron, Fast, & Klein, Trial Communication Skills (1991); as it relates to jury selection, *see* Dimitrius & Mazzarella, Reading People: How to Understand People and Predict Their Behavior—Anytime, Anyplace (1999); Frederick, *Jury Behavior: A Psychologist Examines Jury Selection*, 5 Ohio N.U. L. Rev. 571–85 (1978); Frederick, *Jurors' Verbal and Nonverbal Communication: What Attorneys Should Look for During Jury Selection*, 39 Va. L. Rev., 24–27 (1990); Suggs & Sales, *Using Communication Cues to Evaluate Prospective Jurors During Voir Dire*, 20 Ariz. L. Rev. 629–42 (1978); and judge's behavior, *see* *Judge's Nonverbal Behavior in Jury Trials: A Threat to Judicial Impartiality*, Va. L. Rev. (1975).

4. For example, *see* Zuckerman et al., *id.*

5. *See* Hocking & Leathers, Nonverbal Indication of Deception: A New Theoretical Perspective, 47 *Communication Monographs* 119–31 (1980).

6. For a related discussion, *see* Aron et al., *supra* note 3.

7. For additional discussions of mirroring, *see* Bonora, Krauss & Roundtree, Jury Work: Systematic Techniques (1999), and Aron et al., *supra* note 3.

8. For a further discussion, *see* Ekman, *supra* note 3.

9. Mann, Vrij & Bull, *Suspects, Lies, and Videotape: An Analysis of Authentic High-Stake Liars*, 26 L. & HUM. BEHAV. 365 (2002).

10. *See* Haggard & Issacs, *Micromomentary Facial Expressions as Indicator of Ego Mechanisms in Psychotherapy*, in GOTTSCHALK & AUERBACH, METHODS OF RESEARCH IN PSYCHOTHERAPY (1966). *See also* ARON ET AL., *supra* note 3.

11. A note of caution is needed when considering "gut" reactions. It is always important to ask yourself the questions: Why am I reacting to the potential juror in this manner?" and "What is it about this potential juror that is either good or bad for my client?" Focusing on the answers to these questions helps separate a truly insightful gut reaction from the more generic positive or negative feelings toward a potential juror. The latter reaction may reflect more on one's personal likes and dislikes rather than on whether the potential juror holds opinions and values that are beneficial to the client.

12. There appears to be a hierarchy of accuracy among cues to deception. Speech cues have the greatest accuracy, followed by body cues, with lowest accuracy being associated with facial expressions. *See* Zuckerman et al., *supra* note 3.

13. *See* Mann et al., *supra* note 9.

14. *See* Zuckerman et al., *supra* note 3.

15. For a summary of research on speech styles, *see* O'Barr & Lind, *Ethnography and Experimentation: Partners in Legal Research*, in THE TRIAL PROCESS, vol. 2 of PERSPECTIVES IN LAW AND PSYCHOLOGY 181–207 (B. Sales ed., 1981).

CHAPTER 4

Preparing for Voir Dire

Objectives

- To understand how to use case analysis in preparing for voir dire.
- To develop voir dire questions that achieve the four major goals of voir dire.

A key to successful voir dire and jury selection is preparation. This means taking the time necessary to develop questions and strategies that will make maximal use of what is available on voir dire. Ideally, the development of voir dire is an evolutionary process. It starts in discovery, where notes about witnesses are taken and the eventual framework of the case develops, and culminates when lawyers finalize their voir dire questions in the days immediately preceding trial.[1] There are two basic steps in the preparation of the voir dire for trial, case analysis and question development.

Case Analysis

The first step in preparing for voir dire is to conduct an in-depth analysis of the case. This analysis considers:

- The strengths and weaknesses of the case
- The theme of the case
- The nature and extent of pretrial publicity
- Important opinions and attitudes of jurors
- Important experiences and reference groups of jurors
- Potential grounds for challenges for cause
- A statement of contentions
- Opposing counsel's important voir dire topics and questions

Through case analysis (and becoming familiar with local voir dire procedures), a clearer picture emerges of how to achieve the goals of voir dire and which jurors to prevent from sitting on the jury (either through a challenge for cause or a peremptory challenge).

The Strengths and Weaknesses of the Case

The case analysis starts with an examination of the strengths and weaknesses of the case. A number of elements combine to reveal the strengths and weaknesses of the case. These elements include evidence and arguments, the credibility and persuasiveness of witnesses, the characteristics and credibility of the parties, the nature of the law and judicial instructions, and the lawyers' personalities. A listing of the strengths and weaknesses results from addressing the case as a whole, anticipating the opponent's evidence and arguments along with one's own.

A good voir dire emphasizes the strengths and defuses the weaknesses of the client's case. Determining how jurors react to these strengths and weaknesses is crucial. It is important to discuss the evidence in the case that provides an advantage to the client. Asking jurors if they would ignore certain pieces of physical evidence or if they have any problems with such evidence can emphasize the strengths of one's case. For example, a prosecutor may ask,

> "There will be tape recordings introduced at trial that reflect the conversations of the defendant in this case [concerning a particular aspect of this case]. How do you feel about using tape recordings of conversations in a trial like this?"

or

> "Would you have any reservations about considering this evidence in arriving at a decision concerning the guilt or innocence of the defendant?"

Strengths also appear as a function of the opponent's weaknesses. For example, in certain entrapment cases and organized crime cases, the prosecution often must put witnesses on the stand who have been involved in criminal activity. The defense should attack this weakness, addressing the lack of credibility of these witnesses on voir dire. Questions such as the following are helpful:

> "Do you believe that criminals might try to pressure a person into illegal activity, if it means more money being paid to the criminal or less jail time for the criminal?"

> "Do you believe that criminals might lie in order to get a better deal with the government?"

> "How do you feel about witnesses who testify as a result of receiving money or special treatment by the government in terms of their willingness to tell the truth?"

Like the strengths of the case, the weaknesses need to be addressed. Addressing the weaknesses is often more important than addressing the strengths. It is crucial to evaluate how jurors will react to the weaknesses of the case. Defusing a weakness further advances the client's cause. However, if a weakness in the client's case will influence a potential juror, use of a peremptory challenge or, if possible, a challenge for cause may be in order. For example, if a weakness in the defendant's case stems from the presence of an adverse eyewitness, the defense needs to address this point. Exploration of the reliability of eyewitness testimony in the eyes of jurors is crucial. Jurors who recognize that people who witness a violent crime may be mistaken in their identification of the assailant would be desirable. Jurors who doubt the fallibility of eyewitness identification under these circumstances would be undesirable.

Finally, it is possible to take a strong point for the opponent and use it to one's own advantage. This situation arises when the opponent has some evidence (e.g., a "day-in-the-life" videotape) that arouses juror sympathy for the opponent or promotes a negative emotional reaction against the client. Explaining or possibly showing such evidence to potential jurors during voir dire can produce several benefits. First, it allows the lawyer to determine whether any jurors would be biased as a result of this evidence and, hence, subject to a challenge for cause. Second, with less extreme juror reactions, a heightened sensitivity or lack of sensitivity to this evidence may reveal a candidate for a peremptory challenge. Third, the context in which the lawyer presents the evidence can serve to defuse some of the negative reactions of jurors and even desensitize jurors to the evidence.

However, caution is necessary when using this approach. Particularly with defendants, it is a risky approach to use in situations where issues of liability or guilt are potentially favorable to the client and where showing the biasing evidence can produce a high level of bias in all jurors. Care should be taken not to prejudice the jury against the client. It is possible for the jurors' emotional reactions to color their interpretation of the liability evidence before the groundwork can be laid to defuse this adverse reaction.

The Theme of the Case

Crucial for success at trial is identifying a persuasive theme of the case. A theme provides jurors with a framework for processing the evidence, arguments, and judicial instructions they will receive. Developing questions that reveal the potential jurors' receptivity to the party's theme is important. If jurors reject the theme, the task of persuasion becomes difficult indeed. For example, if the plaintiff's theme of the case is that severely injured persons should be given sufficient compensation to enable them to stay at home rather than being placed in an institution, potential jurors who reject this theme are undesirable for the plaintiff. Uncovering this fact enables the lawyer to shape a more receptive jury by removing those jurors who react most negatively to the theme.

The Nature and Extent of Pretrial Publicity

Most cases have little or no pretrial publicity. However, in those cases where there is pretrial publicity, it is important to consider the potential impact of this information. Social science research on pretrial publicity has shown that it does influence jurors' decision-making.[2] Of critical importance is that research also indicates that jurors often do not recognize and/or admit bias produced by pretrial publicity. One study found that only 26 percent of those jurors exposed to damaging pretrial publicity recognized their biases, while the remaining supposedly "neutral" jurors who were exposed to damaging pretrial publicity still convicted the defendant at a 2-to-1 rate as compared to jurors not exposed to such publicity.[3] Later studies have supported this finding.[4] Similar results concerning the "hollowness" of assertions by respondents that they can be "fair and impartial" have been found in surveys and public opinion polling.[5]

When an incident or case has attracted media attention or when other relevant cases (e.g., the McDonald's coffee-spilling case) have been publicized in the trial jurisdiction, jurors' views may be affected by this coverage. Thus, it is necessary to ask about the jurors' exposure to such publicity and to assess what impact this exposure has had on their views.

Important Opinions and Attitudes of Jurors

Construct a list of important opinions and beliefs of jurors. In Chapter 2, we discussed various global, case-specific, and legal opinions that can be important. It is helpful to examine all three areas of opinions and beliefs and make as detailed a list as possible. At this stage of analysis, it is better not to restrict consideration of the potentially important opinions and beliefs.

Depending upon the case, it may be important to know the jurors' opinions on victim compensation, corporate responsibility, worker safety, business practices, contract disputes, the lawsuit (insurance) crisis, damages, eyewitness testimony, presumption of innocence, burden of proof, authoritarianism, capital punishment, or equity or fairness in relationships. The

---

Basic elements of case analysis:

- Determine the strengths and weaknesses of the case.
- Identify the best theme.
- Analyze the nature and extent of pretrial publicity.
- Identify important opinions and beliefs of jurors.
- Establish likely important experiences and reference groups of jurors.
- Determine potential grounds for cause.
- Develop a statement of contentions.
- Anticipate your opponent's important voir dire topics and questions.

importance of making an expansive list cannot be overemphasized. Engaging in this process will help focus attention on the subtleties of the case.

Considering the full range of opinions enables lawyers to:

- anticipate and pursue additional opinions when given an opportunity to do so, i.e., in follow-up questioning;
- develop questions not included in the past; and
- uncover life experiences that tap into critical opinions that the lawyer may not be able to pursue, e.g., security guard experiences or other occupations associated with higher levels of authoritarianism.

After constructing the "long list" of opinions and beliefs, it is necessary to pare it down to a shorter list reflecting the most important opinion questions that the court will allow.

Important Experiences and Reference Groups of Jurors[6]

The case analysis also examines life experiences and reference groups that could be important. This examination considers the circumstances of the case, potential witnesses, and the parties involved in the case. Important areas of inquiry often include occupation and employment experiences; accidents and traumatic events; hobbies; various social, volunteer, or religious activities; marital and family status; education; prior jury service; military service; exposure to pretrial publicity; leadership experience; and involvement/contact with the court system or litigation. It is helpful to develop a list that reflects the life experiences of jurors that may influence their beliefs and subsequent decision-making and actions during deliberations. The list also includes membership in various reference groups that may influence jurors' beliefs.

Developing the list of experiences and reference groups reveals similarities between potential jurors and the people who will be witnesses, parties, and lawyers in the trial. We tend to like people who are similar to ourselves and to perceive them as more credible—and hence more persuasive.[7] Witnesses, parties, and lawyers can be more persuasive with a jury when they share some salient or relevant characteristic with jurors. For example, the judgments of jurors have been found to benefit defendants who are of the same race as the jurors as compared to defendants facing racially dissimilar jurors.[8]

An important practical benefit of listing important experiences and reference groups appears in the logistics for exercising peremptory challenges in many jurisdictions. Peremptory challenges often are exercised under time pressures that either are actually present (e.g., judge or juror impatience with the jury selection process) or are subjective in nature (e.g., the lawyer wanting to proceed with trial). These time pressures can lead to the failure to properly evaluate the importance of various experiences or reference groups. Considering the importance of juror characteristics prior to trial, when the "pressure cooker" atmosphere is absent, produces a more systematic and effective jury selection.

Potential Grounds for Challenges for Cause

Advance consideration of potential biases on the part of jurors is necessary to reveal those jurors who warrant exclusion through a challenge for cause.[9] The preceding two areas of analysis (opinions and attitudes of jurors, and their experiences and reference groups) serve as the basis for this analysis. It is important to establish what answers by jurors will serve as "red flags" for juror bias. Consideration of these answers should include not only what might reflect bias but also what key phrases from appropriate statutes are necessary to support challenges for cause. Asking the following question will help to bring into focus important areas of concern: "What answers regarding the jurors' opinions, experiences, and membership in reference groups are likely to reflect a bias against my client or the inability of jurors to discharge their duties?" The following are sample areas.

Answers of concern

RELIGIOUS AFFILIATION:	"I would not be able to render a verdict because it is not my place to judge someone"; or "My church/synagogue forbids taking a life."
PRETRIAL PUBLICITY:	"(I have seen news reports about the case on television and) I think the defendant is guilty"; "I think that the government should not try to get people to commit crimes"; or "I heard that the defendant had confessed to the crime [inadmissible confession]."
CIVIL DAMAGES:	"I do not believe that money should be given for pain and suffering"; "I believe that the plaintiff should get money for what she has suffered, no matter who's at fault"; or "I would not be able to place a money value on these damages—I just couldn't do it."

Approaching each topic area in the above manner highlights potential problem answers. By considering these answers in advance, lawyers know what the critical answers are and how to elicit these opinions from jurors, if present.

Statement of Contentions

The analysis of the case also helps in developing a statement of contentions. This is a statement of what the case is about from the party's perspective. Often, the statement is short, consisting of a few sentences describing the party's contentions in the dispute. Occasionally, the statement of contentions can consist of a five- to ten-minute or longer description.[10] Following is an example of a fairly short statement of contentions by the defendant in a lawsuit against a municipality for the maintenance of an unreasonably dangerous street:

> "This case arose out of the incident where three university students drove down Clover Road on a Saturday night, October 20th, a little after 9:30 p.m. Instead of

turning into the entrance of Clover Apartments, the driver continued to drive beyond the end of the road and into a creek where the driver and passengers, including the plaintiff, drowned. We contend that the driver failed to attend to the road and drove off the curve. The driver should have stopped his car when he noticed that he was off the road."

The above statement of contentions sets out the defendant's major points in the case. There are two major advantages of the use of a statement of contentions. First, the statement gives potential jurors a context from which to answer the questions that will be asked on voir dire. The jurors know what the case is about and, therefore, can respond to questions in a more meaningful manner. Second, the statement allows lawyers their first opportunity (depending on the type of introduction the judge may have made) to see how the potential jurors may respond to their case. Careful attention is paid to the potential jurors' nonverbal communication to evaluate how each of the jurors reacts to what is said.

Opposing Counsel's Important Voir Dire Topics and Questions

The final consideration in case analysis centers on what topics the lawyer expects the opposing party to address on voir dire. It is not sufficient that parties address what traditionally are "their" areas of inquiry. It is important to consider the opponent's areas of inquiry for two reasons. First, an opportunity exists to blunt the impact of the opponent's questioning. For example, both parties in a personal injury case need to address the issue of damages. The plaintiff often needs to address a juror's willingness to render a substantial award, if appropriate. The defense needs to address the juror's willingness to award no damages, if appropriate. The following illustrates both parties addressing their issue along with anticipating their opponent's treatment of this issue.

PLAINTIFF: If you were to be a juror in this case and the evidence and law supported a verdict of over $1 million in damages, would you be willing to award over $1 million to the plaintiff? Would you have any reservations about doing so? Would you agree with me that if we did not show you the defendant was liable no damages would be warranted? That is, would you judge this case on the merits, awarding substantial money damages only where allowed by the law?

DEFENSE: The plaintiff may ask you (or has asked others in the panel) if you (they) could return an award in excess of $1 million. My question to you is, would you be willing to return a verdict of zero or no money damages if the plaintiff fails to prove that [the defendant] is liable? Would you have any reservations about doing so? Do you feel that just because the plaintiff has filed a lawsuit asking for $1 million the plaintiff deserves something?

There is a second benefit to anticipating the opponent's questions. In many jurisdictions, particularly those that employ the sequential jury selection method discussed in Chapter 1, once a party has examined the jurors, the opposing party examines the jurors. When the jurors are turned over to the opposing party, the judge may not allow the original party to pursue any new information that the opposing party uncovers, especially when the new information does not appear to support a challenge for cause. Thus, by not covering all topic areas with the jurors, the original questioner exercises peremptory challenges without benefit of valuable information.

Question Development

The second step in preparing for voir dire centers on the development of the questions to ask potential jurors. The case analysis discussed above forms the framework for developing these questions. The pursuit of the four goals of voir dire (as outlined in Chapter 1) influences the form and content of these questions. For example, the way lawyers phrase questions affects the willingness of jurors to reveal information about themselves (information gathering), fosters an open, positive relationship with jurors (rapport), informs or educates jurors as to standards and rules (education), and influences opinions and beliefs (persuasion). While these goals are treated separately here, in practice they are not so independent. Voir dire is a social interaction between lawyers and jurors (and between the judge and jurors and among the jurors themselves). There is a natural give-and-take quality to the interaction. This feature of voir dire often blurs the distinctions between the various goals. It is the task of lawyers to know what they intend to achieve through this interaction and to take advantage of the opportunities that present themselves during the questioning process.

It is important to recognize the practical limits of voir dire in terms of the four goals and the relative importance of these goals. There is a hierarchy of importance to the pursuit of the various goals of voir dire. Information gathering is first and foremost. Rapport is second and, to a large degree, is interrelated with information gathering. Education ranks third. Finally, persuasion is the last goal. This hierarchy should always be kept in mind when developing voir dire questions.

Information Gathering

As the primary goal of voir dire is information gathering, questions need to foster a willingness on the part of jurors to reveal information about themselves. Several aspects of how questions are phrased influence information gathering: closed-ended versus open-ended questions, questions that lead to socially desirable responses, question variation, follow-up questions, and question flexibility.

OPEN-ENDED QUESTIONS. A major distinction in the phrasing of questions is the use of open-ended versus closed-ended questions. As mentioned in the previous chapter, closed-ended questions are questions that restrict the jurors' answers to a few implied or specified responses.[11] Examples of closed-ended questions are as follows:

"Do you believe that patients should be able to sue their doctors over the treatment they receive?"

"Do you believe that defendants in criminal trials who do not testify in their own defense are probably guilty?"

"Do you agree or disagree with the law that allows for monetary damages designed to punish a defendant?"

Each of these questions restricts the answers to either an implied "yes" or "no" response or a specified "agree" or "disagree" response (with the potential of an "I don't know" or "maybe" response).

Open-ended questions do not restrict the jurors' responses and, in fact, require the jurors to develop their own answers to the questions. Open-ended questions are often prefaced with phrases such as:

"What do you think/feel/believe . . .?"

"Why?" or "Why do you think/feel/believe . . .?"

"How do you feel about . . .?"

"Tell me about . . .?"

"When do you feel/think/believe . . .?"

"In what way . . .?"

Converting the above closed-ended questions to open-ended questions can be accomplished as follows:

"How do you feel about patients suing their doctors over the treatment they receive?"

"What would your impression be of defendants who do not testify in their own defense?"

"What do you think about the law that allows for monetary damages designed to punish a defendant?"

Open-ended questions offer several advantages over closed-ended questions. First, open-ended questions provide lawyers with more information. Jurors must express their opinions in their own words. The result is a richer answer in terms of what is said and how it is said (i.e., both verbal and nonverbal communication).[12] Second, the answers to open-ended questions provide greater direction for further exploration of the jurors' opinions. The lawyer has a better idea of what needs to be followed up and what does not. Finally, open-ended questions do not let jurors "off the hook." Jurors may answer various questions in an inconsistent or contradictory manner. With an open-ended question, it is very easy to ask the juror to explain the discrepancy. The following interchange illustrates this capability.

LAWYER: You mentioned that railroads are responsible for ensuring the safety of the public at crossings and you also said that

JUROR: the public needs to be careful at crossings on private land. Would you tell me (or explain) a little more about your feelings in this area?

Yes. As a rule, I believe that railroads are responsible for safety at their crossings. However, I believe than when the public uses a crossing on private property, the public needs to be particularly careful in using such a crossing because the railroads really do not expect a high volume of traffic there.

QUESTIONS THAT LEAD TO SOCIALLY DESIRABLE RESPONSES. A second consideration in developing questions to elicit information from jurors concerns the problem of what are termed socially desirable responses. Socially desirable responses are not the jurors' true opinions. They are answers that reflect what they think the lawyer wants to hear or would foster a positive image of the juror. Obviously, the problem with socially desirable responses in jury selection is that they hide the jurors' true feelings or thought processes.

Again, the phrasing of questions influences the likelihood of jurors giving socially desirable answers. Socially desirable responses are more frequent when the "acceptable" answer is obvious or is implied by the question itself. Closed-ended questions are particularly susceptible to such responses. An example of closed-ended questions likely to elicit a socially desirable response are:

"Do you have any biases against big corporations?"

"Would you be fair?"

"You would follow the judge's instructions on this matter, wouldn't you?"

The first question alerts the jurors to the correct answer by the word "bias." Most people know it is not acceptable to be biased or prejudiced. The latter two questions are likely to yield affirmative responses that also may not reflect the jurors' true feelings. The first of these questions requires that the jurors admit that they cannot be fair—a position jurors are not likely to

---

How to use questions to get the jurors to reveal information about themselves:

- Use open-ended questions.
- Avoid questions that lead to socially desirable answers.
- Vary the questions asked to jurors.
- Prepare useful follow-up questions in advance.
- Be flexible in phrasing questions to get the information you want.

either recognize or, if recognized, admit. The last question tells the jurors what the right answer is through its form, "You would . . ., wouldn't you?"

QUESTION VARIATION. A common problem that arises during voir dire, particularly lengthy voir dire, is that potential jurors hear the questions lawyers ask and the answers given by other jurors numerous times before the questions are finally addressed to them. This situation can produce several negative consequences.[13] First, jurors become bored with the examination process. Second, as voir dire progresses, jurors will tend to give superficial answers. Third, jurors questioned later will tend to conform to the answers of previous jurors. Finally, when the phrasing of questions yields a consistent pattern of responding (e.g., agreement or disagreement with closed-ended questions), jurors may adopt what is termed a "response set." That is, after a series of questions yields a consistent response of "yes," there will be a tendency to answer "yes" to the next question, even if the juror does not totally agree with the answer. Thus, the answer reflects the *pattern* of the responses, not the real views of the juror.

Lawyers can prevent the above problems by developing multiple questions or a pool of questions for the various topic areas. This pool of questions will include several questions that elicit the same critical opinions/information. These questions should be varied in their form, using both open-ended and closed-ended formats. In addition, the questions should vary in their "direction." For example, using "should not" instead of "should" changes a question's direction, e.g., "Do you believe that corporations should/should not be responsible for the actions of their employees?"

By varying the questions in terms of which questions are asked to jurors, the form the question takes, and the direction of the question, lawyers keep the jurors' attention and force them to think about the answers they give. The result is greater juror involvement in the questioning process, which in turn yields a more informative voir dire.[14]

FOLLOW-UP QUESTIONS. Considering the possible answers jurors may give and how to follow up on these answers will maximize the usefulness of the information jurors provide. The most important benefit of follow-up questions is that they clarify the information given by further refining the juror's answers. Examples of follow-up questions are:

"In what way?"

"Why is that?"

"Do you feel [whatever was expressed] applies to this defendant?"

Considering the potential answers that jurors may give to questions will help in the development of effective follow-up questions. Not only will such preparation produce more fruitful follow-up questions, but lawyers can anticipate and defuse potentially problematic situations with jurors. For example, biased jurors may give strident and unfavorable answers to questions; e.g., "I don't think you should make the plaintiff rich by giving him the money from punitive damages." Upon hearing this answer other jurors turn their attention to the lawyer to see how he or she responds. If lawyers are caught off guard and stumble with their responses (e.g., "Well, that's the way the law is"), the jurors may view the lawyers as not being confident in their cases. However, anticipating problematic answers and responding in a confident manner minimizes any negative impact of the juror's answer. For example, a more confident response would be, "Punitive damages are not designed to make the plaintiff rich but to punish the defendant for willful and wanton actions that injured the plaintiff. Your answer seems to indicate some reservations concerning punitive damages. Let's talk about this. . . ."

FLEXIBILITY. The last component of developing questions is flexibility in their phrasing. When lawyers cannot ask the desired questions, they know less about jurors. Getting the most information possible requires being flexible in the phrasing of questions. Adjustments must be made in those situations where the judge does not allow certain ways of phrasing questions. For example, after asking several questions with the phrase, "What are your feelings concerning . . ." or "Do you have any feelings about . . .," the opponent may object to the use of the term "feelings." If the judge sustains the objection, it is still possible to rephrase the question to obtain the necessary information. For example, in the above situation, the judge may allow the phrase "preconceived notions" in place of "feelings." Being flexible and rephrasing the question will minimize the loss of information on the jurors' feelings when jurors have heard the previous questions and understand that "preconceived notions" really means "feelings."

Rapport

Establishing rapport with jurors is the second goal of voir dire.[15] By establishing rapport with jurors, lawyers enhance the favorable impression they are making on the jurors and increase the jurors' willingness to disclose information on voir dire. Lawyers promote positive rapport when they:

- treat jurors as individuals;
- show an interest in what jurors are saying;
- treat jurors with respect; and
- make jurors feel comfortable during questioning.

The results of good rapport are a more revealing voir dire and greater persuasion potential for the lawyer as the trial unfolds.

The major determiner of positive rapport is the nature of the interaction process between the lawyer and jurors. The way the questions are phrased plays a key role in this process. There is a close relationship between information gathering and rapport. Many of the considerations relevant to information gathering apply here. Questions that encourage jurors to express themselves facilitate rapport. Open-ended questions are particularly important, as they provide opportunities for jurors to talk with lawyers.

People tend to enjoy talking about themselves when someone will listen and appreciate what they are saying. Developing questions like the following allows jurors to talk about themselves and fosters rapport:

"What do you do at [their job]?"

"It sounds like an interesting job. What do you like most about what you do?"

"What do you like to do in your free time?"

"Would you tell me a little about your children, how old they are, [marital status (if appropriate)], and [their employment status]?"

It is important to phrase questions in a nonjudgmental manner. Sometimes questions on voir dire sound as though the juror is taking a test. When this happens, jurors can become defensive, and rapport suffers. The following questions illustrate the differences between judgmental (or evaluative) and nonjudgmental questions:

Judgmental ("test") questions

"Are you employed?"

"Did you go to college?"

"Did you vote in the last election?"

Nonjudgmental questions

"What is your employment status?"

"What is your educational background?" or "How many years did you go to school?"

"Did you have an opportunity to vote in the last election?"

Also, questions that show empathy for what jurors are going through foster rapport with jurors. Using an introductory phrase or sentence is often helpful. For example, "I realize that it has been a long day of questioning/sitting/waiting around. However, I need to ask you these additional questions ..." and "I am sorry to hear of your mother's illness. Are you responsible for taking care of her?"

Keys to establishing rapport with jurors:

- Treat jurors as individuals.
- Show interest in what jurors say.
- Always treat jurors with respect.
- Make jurors feel comfortable during questioning.
- Have jurors talk about themselves.
- Do not ask "test-like" questions.
- Show empathy.

Seeking to develop good rapport with jurors will help in achieving all the goals of voir dire. Using questions that encourage jurors to talk establishes the groundwork for good rapport.

Education

During the course of voir dire, jurors need to be made aware of and understand critical issues and legal principles. It is important that jurors understand what their task is before the evidence and arguments in the case are presented. Such advance knowledge allows jurors to process more efficiently the information they encounter at trial. Education is distinguished from persuasion in that the questioner does not encourage jurors to adopt a particular perspective on the case that favors one party. The questioning is simply to promote an understanding of the issues or legal principles that will be important in the case.

Ideally, education goes hand-in-hand with information gathering. Initial voir dire questioning seeks to uncover the jurors' opinions that relate to critical legal issues without directly informing the jurors what the law is on these issues. In this way, jurors reveal their beliefs concerning these legal issues without being influenced by what the law requires. After uncovering the jurors' relevant opinions, lawyers' discussion of these beliefs can occur in the context of the critical legal issues or principles. Through the questioning process, the questioner seeks to have jurors understand why and how they are to apply the law in the case. Finally, a commitment is sought from jurors to follow the critical legal principle(s) in the case.

The following exchange illustrates how a plaintiff's lawyer would educate a juror on the issue of a corporation's responsibility for the actions of its employees.

LAWYER:	Mrs. Jones, do you work outside the home?
JUROR:	Yes. I am a sales clerk for an office supply store.
LAWYER:	What kind of work do you do as a sales clerk?
JUROR:	I take orders for various kinds of office supplies from my customers.
LAWYER:	I suspect that on occasion a problem with an order may arise. When that happens, what do you do?
JUROR:	Well, if it is one of my customers, it's my responsibility to make things right.

How to educate jurors:

- Uncover jurors' beliefs related to the critical legal opinions.
- Explain and discuss specific legal issues or principles.
- Seek a commitment from jurors to adhere to the critical legal principles.

LAWYER:	I see that you feel responsible for what you do on the job. How do you feel about corporations, in terms of any responsibilities they might have for what their employees do on the job?
JUROR:	I guess I really haven't thought too much about it. I suppose that corporations should have some responsibility for what their workers do.
LAWYER:	What kind of responsibility would that be?
JUROR:	I feel that when employers hire someone, they should be responsible for what this person does on the job. You know, like if I make a mistake with an order. I am responsible because I did it, but my company is responsible because they hired me in the first place.
LAWYER:	What if a worker makes a mistake that damages someone else's property? How do you feel about that?
JUROR:	I think that the corporation should pay for the damage.
LAWYER:	Given your feelings in this area, would you have any reservations concerning the law that says that corporations are responsible for the actions of their employees while they are on the job?
JUROR:	None whatsoever.
LAWYER:	If you were to serve on this jury, would you promise to follow the judge's instructions and hold the defendant corporation liable for the actions of its employees while they are on the job?
JUROR:	Yes, I would do that.

The above exchange illustrates an approach for educating the potential juror. However, such an open exchange is not always possible. In some jurisdictions, lawyers may be able to pursue the critical issue or legal principle only in a summary question format, if at all. For example, "According to the law, corporations are responsible for the actions of their employees while they are on the job. Do you have any reservations concerning this law? Would you have any reservations in following this law?" In such a situation, it is important to recognize that while jurors are being informed and, to some degree, educated about the legal principle, the jurors' true feelings on the law are not likely to surface.

Persuasion

The last goal of voir dire is persuasion. Persuasion differs from education in that an attempt is being made to influence, even if only to a subtle degree, the perspectives of potential jurors. This influence results from the interaction between the lawyer and the jurors. The opportunity for persuasion in the voir dire process derives from three elements. First, potential jurors are attentive listeners at this time. In order to respond to the questions asked, jurors must keep a relatively high level of attention. Second, and most important, jurors are not expecting lawyers to try to persuade them at this time. Jurors expect persuasion when the trial actually begins. They do not expect persuasive attempts at this "preliminary" stage of trial. The jurors' failure to anticipate a persuasive attempt means that their persuasion defenses are not in a state of readiness. Therefore, persuasive attempts are likely to be more successful at this stage of the proceedings.[16] Third, this is part of an interactive process under control of the lawyer (and the judge). The lawyer controls what will be addressed and the tone/phrasing of the questions.

A number of the features of question development can foster persuasion. Seven features are considered here.

STATEMENT OF CONTENTIONS. The presentation of the case to jurors in a statement of contentions can initiate the persuasion process. We noted earlier that the statement of contentions forms the context from which jurors answer subsequent questions. However, this statement also can advance the party's perspective on the case. As such, the statement promotes the persuasion process. A statement of contentions that highlights the strengths of the party's case (e.g., the existence of a signed contract) and seeks to defuse its weaknesses (e.g., portraying an eyewitness as not having a clear view of the event) fosters persuasion. Careful consideration is given to selecting words and phrases that convey the desired psychological impact. For example, labeling someone who stops to help at the scene of an accident a Good Samaritan promotes a positive view of that person. Also, in the Iran-contra trials, considerable attention was given to the description of the Nicaraguan contras. The government labeled them "contra rebels." The defense chose to call them "freedom fighters."

LEGAL DEFINITIONS. A problem with legal definitions and instructions that the court delivers is that often they tend to confuse jurors.[17] It is this confusion that becomes the point of attack in persuasion. Development of clear, yet advantageous, explanations of legal concepts or terms is a key part of the persuasion process. The questioner encourages jurors to "plug in" the favorable definition and use it throughout the trial. When jurors do so, the opposing party's persuasive task becomes more difficult. The following explanations of preponderance of evidence offered by lawyers for the plaintiff and the defense illustrate this point:

> PLAINTIFF: In this case, the plaintiff need *only show* by a preponderance of the evidence that the defendant doctor was negligent in his treatment of Mrs. Smith. Preponderance of the evidence is a legal term that simply means more likely than not, a simple tipping of balancing scales [*gesturing with hand movements*]. That is, we need only show that it is more likely than not that the defendant doctor was negligent in his treatment of Mrs. Smith [*again, illustrating the tipping of the scales*].

DEFENDANT: The plaintiff in this case has the burden of *proving* by the preponderance of the evidence that Dr. Jones was negligent. That is, the plaintiff *must prove* by the *greater weight or preponderance of the evidence* that what Dr. Jones did when he was caring for the plaintiff constituted negligence.

The major difference between the above two explanations of preponderance of the evidence is the subjective impression of what the term means. The plaintiff uses "only show," "more likely than not," and hand gestures to reflect the minimum burden placed on the plaintiff. The defendant seeks to raise the perception of the level of proof needed by using "must prove," "greater weight," and "preponderance" to foster an impression of a relatively high standard.

ISSUE FOCUS. Focusing the jurors' attention on the important issues in the case from the client's perspective fosters persuasion. Lawyers use this approach in tandem with information gathering to uncover the jurors' opinions and influence their perspective on the case. That is, after gathering the information, the questioner frames a question that portrays the client's position in a favorable light. For example, when a medical negligence case involves a prior medical condition, the defense lawyer may ask: "We contend that the plaintiff was injured years ago and that this injury is the cause of her problems today. Do you think that Dr. Jones should have to pay damages to compensate the plaintiff for problems that were caused by an injury the plaintiff suffered years before ever seeing Dr. Jones?"

Contrasting the lawyer's position with that of the opponent in a favorable manner facilitates persuasion. For example, when a severely injured plaintiff requires constant or periodic medical attention, the plaintiff's lawyer may ask: "Should the defendant be found liable in this case, do you feel that it is important to provide sufficient money compensation to allow [the plaintiff] to stay at home as compared to being kept in an institution?" This question offers two alternatives for the fate of the plaintiff: staying at home versus being placed in an institution. Most people feel that staying at home (where possible) is preferable to being kept in an institution. Thus, the jurors' attention is focused on the fate of the plaintiff and their endorsement of the plaintiff's desired outcome.

WORD CHOICE. The words lawyers choose in phrasing their questions are important in the persuasion process. Different words produce different impressions of events. Describing a collision between two vehicles as one vehicle having "bumped" or "smashed" into the other vehicle affects the impression of the speed of the vehicle on impact. "Bumped" implies a lower speed at impact than does "smashed."[18] Earlier we discussed the lawyer's choice of words in connection with the statement of contentions and explaining key legal terms. However, consideration of what words or phrases to use is important in all aspects of voir dire. Referring to the client by name (e.g.,

---

Basic elements in persuasion on voir dire:

- Develop a beneficial statement of contentions.
- Define legal concepts in a beneficial manner.
- Focus attention on desirable issues.
- Use words and phrases that promote the client's case.
- Strengthen jurors' commitment to desired opinions/positions.
- Capitalize on psychological reactance.
- Sincerely compliment jurors.

John Smith) or by title (e.g., defendant or plaintiff or client) affects the jurors' view of the nature of the relationship between the lawyer and the client. Using the client's name implies a more personal relationship.

Consideration of critical words or phrases is not limited to client labels. Persuasion through word choice applies to all aspects of the case. Referring to an aborted fetus as a "fetus" versus an "unborn baby" affects the emotional reactions of jurors. Referring to "side letters" in real estate transactions as "side agreements" versus "under-the-table deals" affects the perceived legitimacy of the transactions. Describing the grounding of an oil tanker as an "avoidable grounding" as compared to an "accident" reflects different views of the culpability of the crew and ship owners regarding the incident. Being consistent in the use of psychologically beneficial words and phrases in the questions asked (and in the remainder of the trial as well) is necessary to achieving any persuasive benefits from word choice.

COMMITMENT. Commitments that jurors make also affect persuasion. Commitment refers to how strongly jurors hold a particular belief or opinion.[19] The stronger the commitment to beliefs or opinions, the less willing jurors are to change them. Commitment to a position or opinion can be strengthened by (a) expressing the opinion publicly; (b) taking action on the basis of one's opinion; (c) adopting the position or opinion as a result of free choice, not coercion; and (d) showing the interrelationship of the opinion to other highly valued opinions.

Increasing the jurors' commitment to favorable opinions during voir dire fosters persuasion (or increased resistance to the opponent's position). This process takes several forms based on the above contributors to commitment. The following example illustrates methods for capitalizing on the above contributions in order to increase the jurors' commitment to rendering a verdict of no money damages if no liability is found.

Increasing commitment through the public expression of the desired opinion would be as follows:

LAWYER: If you were a juror in this case, would you be willing to render a verdict of no damages if you find that Federal Express [defendant] is not liable?

JUROR: Yes.

LAWYER: Would you promise the Court and Mr. Smith [the company representative] that you will return a verdict of no damages unless you find that Federal Express is liable?

JUROR: Yes, I will.

Increasing commitment through actions taken on the basis of the juror's opinion (in this case highlighting the juror's relevant prior actions) is accomplished by the following:

LAWYER: In your past experience as owner of your business, have you ever been in a situation where someone asked for something that the person didn't really deserve? For example, perhaps an employee asked for a raise but you felt the employee really didn't deserve one.

JUROR: Yes.

LAWYER: Without mentioning any names, what did you do in that situation?

JUROR: I told him that I would not approve the raise. I also told him why I would not do so.

LAWYER: How did you feel about not giving the employee the raise?

JUROR: Well, I would have liked to give him the raise but it just wouldn't have been right.

Holding the desired opinion as a result of free choice, not coercion, would be reinforced as follows:

LAWYER: You have said that it would not be right to give something to someone when they do not deserve it. And in a similar way, you have said that you do not feel that Federal Express should be required to pay money damages if the accident was not the fault of Federal Express. Is this something that you feel strongly about?

JUROR: Yes, it is.

LAWYER: And you would hold this opinion, no matter who is here talking with you or who might be parties in this case?

JUROR: Of course.

Showing the interrelatedness of the desired opinion to other highly valued opinions is accomplished as follows:

LAWYER: There is no dispute that the plaintiff has been injured. Some people may feel that she should be given something just because she has been injured. You have said that only if Federal Express is liable would you feel that money damages are appropriate. Why do you think that it is important that Federal Express pay money damages only if it is indeed liable—even when it means that the plaintiff would receive no money compensation?

JUROR: [States reasons for supporting his or her position—e.g., sense of fairness, awareness of his or her responsibility as a juror]

LAWYER: [Restating these reasons and adding others, if appropriate] So, you see that what we are talking about is not simply an empty rule, but it is an important part of your duty as a juror in our system of justice. If you were chosen as a juror, would you take on this duty and discharge it to the best of your ability?

JUROR: Yes, I would.

One final note concerning commitments. Commitments do not act as talismans. Simply having jurors commit to desired opinions or positions does not ensure that they will keep their "promises." Commitment produces a resistance to change as a function of the strength of the commitment. Jurors will and do go back on their promises when sufficient persuasive pressures are present.

PSYCHOLOGICAL REACTANCE. Persuasion can occur through the phenomenon of psychological reactance.[20] Psychological reactance refers to how people respond when they feel their freedoms are in jeopardy. According to the theory, when people feel that their freedom of choice or behavior is being threatened or eliminated, they are motivated to restore the threatened or lost freedom. The classic challenge, "Don't cross that line," is an invitation to psychological reactance. It will produce a strong desire for the person challenged to cross the line.

Psychological reactance is likely to arise during voir dire when jurors feel that one of the lawyers is compromising their freedom to decide the case. If jurors feel that a lawyer is misleading them (hence compromising their freedom to decide the case appropriately), they will react negatively toward the offending lawyer—with potentially negative consequences for the offending lawyer's client.

Psychological reactance can appear when the issue of sympathy arises in personal injury cases. Suppose the plaintiff's lawyer fails to address the issue of sympathy, choosing instead to focus on a sympathetic discussion of injuries/damages. The defense may try to instill psychological reactance against the plaintiff by addressing the issue of sympathy. However, the defense couches the topic in a manner implying that the plaintiff was trying to mislead the jury:

DEFENSE   Obviously, the plaintiff has been seriously injured. We all
LAWYER: feel sympathy for him in this situation. That is a normal reaction. However, in the plaintiff's lawyer's discussions

> with you, he/she failed to mention that if you serve as a juror in this case, the judge will instruct you that sympathy should not be a factor in your decision. That is, the law specifically says that sympathy is not an appropriate consideration in your decision. If you sat as a juror, would you set aside any feelings of sympathy and try this case solely on the facts and the law?

In the above approach, the defense portrays the plaintiff's lawyer as withholding something from the jurors. The defense reveals to the jurors that feelings of sympathy are not an appropriate consideration in their decision. In addition, the defense hopes the jurors will think that any positive feelings or empathy they may have for the plaintiff are also inappropriate.

The plaintiff's lawyer must respond to this situation, lest psychological reactance remain against the plaintiff. However, the response should not be, "The plaintiff is not here today seeking sympathy. He has received a great deal of sympathy from his friends and loved ones." Such a response is defensive and confirms the implication by the defense lawyer that the plaintiff's lawyer was trying to mislead the jurors. In addition, the defense lawyer's attempt to label as inappropriate any positive feelings toward the plaintiff remains intact.

To counteract this situation, the lawyer for the plaintiff should let the jurors know that they are not expected to remove their feelings. More important, the law requires that they consider what has happened (e.g., financial, physical, and emotional suffering) to the plaintiff. The following shows what can be done to use psychological reactance to the plaintiff's advantage and to reestablish the bond of positive feelings toward the plaintiff.

PLAINTIFF'S LAWYER: The defense talked with you [or other jurors] about sympathy and said that you are to remove any sympathy you may have for the plaintiff. What he/she failed to mention was that if you should decide that the defendant is liable, you are to consider the true value of what has happened to John Smith. What he has gone through—his physical suffering, his financial losses, his loss of society and comfort, and his loss of the ability to do things that you and I take for granted. Would you promise John that you won't check your feelings at the door and that you will take into account all the factors that the law says are appropriate?

A final note about psychological reactance. It is a volatile tool. If jurors think that lawyers are trying to manipulate them, a negative backlash is likely to occur. This applies to the use of psychological reactance as a tool and to other attempts to persuade them in general as well.

INGRATIATION. The final aspect of persuasion is ingratiation.[21] Ingratiation refers to complimenting or rewarding people in the hope that they will treat the ingratiator or his or her request more favorably. In voir dire, lawyers may compliment jurors with the hope that the jurors will view them more positively. To the degree that jurors do not suspect this ulterior motive, ingratiation can be effective. Complimenting the attentiveness, candor, or honesty of jurors tends to produce positive feelings toward the lawyer, provided the lawyer's sincerity is not suspect.

The ultimate ingratiation technique in voir dire is "grandstanding." Grandstanding refers to the approach of making a short speech to the jurors at the beginning of voir dire. In the speech, the lawyer states a belief that all of the jurors present are unbiased and honest and, subsequently, there is no need to ask any questions. This speech is concluded with the grand gesture of not exercising any peremptory challenges.

While the grandstanding approach compliments the jurors and conveys confidence in the case, there are two serious risks in this approach. First, grandstanding precludes the lawyer from doing what is necessary to detect and reject potential jurors who are undesirable for the client. Second, grandstanding makes it difficult for the lawyer to participate later in the voir dire questioning process when the opposing counsel's questions and exercise of peremptory challenges leaves jurors in the box who are undesirable to the grandstander. An attempt to reenter the voir dire process at that point may cause the lawyer to lose credibility in the jurors' eyes. After all, why would a lawyer want to participate further in voir dire if it was true that there was no need to question or remove any of these "unbiased" jurors? The answer is often to the disadvantage of the grandstander.

NOTES

1. There are other aspects of jury selection that will not be considered here. These aspects involve sources of information on potential jurors gathered outside the voir dire process. These sources of information include (a) investigation of potential jurors through private investigations, Internet searches, and community networks, (b) public opinion polling (what are termed community or juror surveys), and (c) refinement of voir dire questioning (both in the questions selected and in lawyer practice) arising from trial simulations and mock jury selections. A brief discussion of these aspects of voir dire is considered in Chapter 8. For an in-depth discussion of these topics, *see* FREDERICK, THE PSYCHOLOGY OF THE AMERICAN JURY (1987), BLUE & SAGINAW, JURY SELECTION: STRATEGY AND SCIENCE (1990), and BONORA, KRAUSS & ROUNDTREE, JURYWORK: SYSTEMATIC TECHNIQUES (1999).

2. *See* Bornstein, Whisenhunt, Nemeth & Dunaway, *Pretrial Publicity and Civil Cases: A Two Way Street?* L. & HUM. BEHAV. 26, 3 (2002); Moran & Cutler, *The Impact of Prejudicial Pretrial Publicity*, 21 J. APPLIED SOC. PSYCHOL. 345 (1991); Robbennolt & Studebaker, *News Media Reporting on Civil Litigation and Its Influence on Civil Justice Decision Making*, L. & HUM. BEHAV. 27, 5 (2003); Studebaker & Penrod, *Pretrial Publicity: The Media, the Law and Common Sense*, 3 PSYCHOL., PUB. POL'Y & L. 428 (1997); Sue, Smith & Gilbert, *Biasing Effects of Pretrial Publicity on Judicial Decisions*, 2 J. CRIM. JUST. 163 (1974); and Vidmar, *Case Studies of Pre- and Midtrial Prejudice in Criminal and Civil Litigation*, 26 L. & HUM. BEHAV. 19 (2002).

3. Sue, Smith & Pedroza, *Authoritarianism, Pretrial Publicity and Awareness of Bias in Simulated Jurors*, 37 PSYCHOL. REP. 1299 (1975).

4. Ogloff & Vidmar, *The Impact of Pretrial Publicity on Jurors: A Study to Compare the Relative Effects of Television and Print Media in a Child Sex Abuse Case*, 18 L. & HUM. BEHAV. 507 (1994).

5. *See* Vidmar, *Case Studies of Pre- and Midtrial Prejudice in Criminal and Civil Litigation*, 26 L. & HUM. BEHAV. 73 (2002). A number of studies conducted by this author and National Legal Research Group, Inc., have consistently shown that jurors' preconceptions of guilt for a defendant as a result of pretrial publicity are not related to their subsequent assertions of their ability to be fair and impartial (e.g., *see* the report cited in the motion for a change of venue in *United States v Sa'ad El-Amin*, Case No. 3:03CR55). For related findings, *see* BONORA, KRAUSS & ROUNDTREE, *supra* note 1.

6. *See* the discussion of experiences and reference groups in Chapter 2.

7. *See* research cited in FREDERICK, *supra* note 1.

8. *See* Ugwuegbu, *Racial and Evidential Factors in Juror Attributions of Legal Responsibility*, 15 J. EXPERIMENTAL SOC. PSYCHOL. 133–46 (1979). However, similarity is not always a benefit. In some instances similarity can produce a negative reaction in the similar individual. When jurors are faced with a victim who is similar to themselves and feel greatly threatened by what has happened to the victim, they may blame the victim for what happened. This blaming process reduces the perceived threat to jurors because the bad event happened to someone who in some way "deserved" it. *See* a discussion of this phenomenon in connection with the need to believe in a just world in Lerner, *The Desire for Justice and Reaction to Victims*, in ALTRUISM AND HELPING BEHAVIOR 205–29 (J. Macaulay & L. Berkowitz, eds., 1970).

9. *See* Chapter 1 and Chapter 9 for additional discussions of challenges for cause.

10. *See* a description contained in BLUE & SAGINAW, *supra* note 1. Some jurisdictions have allowed short "mini-opening" statements to be made before voir dire questioning begins.

11. *See* Chapter 3 for a discussion of the value of open-ended questions in relation to the verbal and nonverbal communication of jurors.

12. Research comparing the use of open-ended (nondirective style) questions and closed-ended (directive style) questions has shown that conducting voir dire using open-ended questions led to more self-disclosing on the part of jurors and a greater willingness by jurors to admit problems with their ability to follow the law. *See* Middendorf & Luginbuhl, *The Value of a Nondirective Voir Dire Style in Jury Selection*, 22 CRIM. JUST. & BEHAV. 129–151 (1995).

13. For a further discussion of these problems, *see* FREDERICK (1987), *supra* note 1.

14. Obviously, concerns over question variation should not lead to the omission of certain questions for fear of boredom. It is important to strive to gain the same information from all jurors. However, it often requires some creativity and flexibility to uncover all the information needed from all the jurors.

15. *See* A. GINGER, JURY SELECTION IN CRIMINAL TRIALS (1980).

16. For a detailed discussion of persuasion in jury trials, *see* Chapter 6 in FREDERICK, THE PSYCHOLOGY OF THE AMERICAN JURY (1987). For a more general review of persuasion, *see* COGNITIVE RESPONSES IN PERSUASION (R. Petty, T. Ostrom, & T. Brock eds., 1981).

17. Research indicates that comprehension levels of jury instructions are disappointingly low, with averages of 50 percent comprehension or less; *see* ELWORK, SALES, & ALFINI, MAKING JURY INSTRUCTIONS UNDERSTANDABLE (1982).

18. *See* Loftus, *Reconstructive Memory Processes in Eyewitness Testimony*, in THE TRIAL PROCESS, vol. 2 of PERSPECTIVES IN LAW & PSYCHOLOGY 115–44 (B. Sales ed., 1981).

19. For a discussion of commitment in jury selection, *see* FREDERICK, *supra* note 1, and Blunk & Sales, *Persuasion During Voir Dire*, in PSYCHOLOGY IN THE LEGAL PROCESS

39–58 (B. Sales ed., 1977). For a general discussion of commitment, *see* McGuire, *The Nature of Attitudes and Attitude Change*, in 3 THE HANDBOOK OF SOCIAL PSYCHOLOGY 136–314 (G. Lindzey & E. Aronson eds., 1969).

20. *See* generally Brehm, *Responses to Loss of Freedom: A Theory of Psychological Reactance*, in CONTEMPORARY TOPICS IN SOCIAL PSYCHOLOGY 53–78 (J. Thibaut, J. Spence, & R. Carlson, eds. 1976).

21. *See* E. JONES, INGRATIATION (1964).

CHAPTER 5

Conducting Voir Dire

Objectives

- To explore communication skills that facilitate lawyers' effectiveness in conducting voir dire.
- To develop techniques that improve juror candor on voir dire.
- To understand the importance of flexibility on voir dire.
- To explore the basic organization of the voir dire.
- To develop effective methods for addressing reduced information settings found in voir dire.

Voir dire is a social interaction between lawyers, judges, and jurors. There is a give-and-take process basic to voir dire. To achieve the goals of voir dire requires great skill and attention to the process by lawyers. One fact should always be kept in mind. The primary goal of voir dire is to gather information from the jurors about their backgrounds, experiences, opinions, and beliefs. The remaining goals of education, rapport, and persuasion are secondary to discovering jurors' likely opinions, biases, and perspectives, and what role they will play in deliberations.

This chapter focuses on the task of conducting effective voir dire.[1] Before we consider ways of conducting voir dire more effectively, however, it is necessary to address the obstacles faced in conducting voir dire.

Obstacles to Effective Voir Dire

Conducting a successful and informative voir dire is complicated by several factors:

- *Formal setting.* The formal physical environment of the courtroom and the behavior and roles of the court personnel can intimidate many jurors, thus inhibiting their full participation in voir dire.

- *Subordinate position.* Jurors are reluctant to be candid because they are in a subordinate position, not allowed to speak unless they have been given permission to do so.
- *Brief examination.* The short duration of the questioning of any individual jurors minimizes their openness.
- *Public disclosures.* The answers that jurors give (some of which may concern very personal information) usually are made in open court, which lessens their willingness to answer honestly.[2]
- *Failure to recognize/admit bias.* Whether as a result of evaluation apprehension or failure to recognize potentially biasing experiences or opinions, jurors often do not admit bias, particularly as a result of pretrial publicity.[3]
- *Evaluation apprehension.* Jurors are often reluctant to answer candidly because of their concerns over what others might think of them.[4]
- *Group questioning.* The fact that the questioning of jurors often occurs in groups ranging from several jurors to twenty or more jurors leads to conformity to the opinions and behaviors expressed in these groups.
- *Lack of lawyer questioning.* In many federal courts, and in those state courts emulating the federal system, judge-conducted questioning dominates. The lack of lawyer participation in the questioning process hampers the ability to uncover important information about jurors.[5]

Whether through one or a number of the above obstacles, researchers have found that candor and disclosure of information on the part of jurors is less than ideal.[6] The task of conducting effective voir dire requires that lawyers take advantage of social interaction skills and capitalize on the structuring of the voir dire questioning to maximize juror candor and disclosure during voir dire.

Social Interaction Skills

Getting the information needed from potential jurors requires (a) good communication skills on the part of lawyers and (b) the use of techniques that encourage maximum participation by jurors.

Communication Skills

Seven basic communication skills will encourage jurors to be more open with lawyers on voir dire.[7] These skills are fundamental in achieving the goals of information gathering and rapport development.

PERSPECTIVE. How lawyers view the voir dire process plays a major role in the experience that jurors have on voir dire. The lawyers' perspective affects how they interact both verbally and nonverbally with jurors. Lawyers can approach the voir dire process as an interrogation, job interview, or as a conversation.

Seven basic communication skills:

- Use a conversational style of questioning.
- Show empathy.
- Express sincerity and interest in what jurors are saying.
- Maintain a warm and friendly attitude.
- Be supportive.
- Capitalize on juror identification through similarity.
- Listen to jurors.

The interrogation perspective is the antithesis of what is desired on voir dire. Approaching voir dire in this manner rapidly destroys the possibility for open and candid answers from jurors. Jurors react in a guarded and defensive manner, closing off any open and candid communication. The job interview approach (i.e., "we are looking for fair and impartial jurors and need to know if you would qualify to serve") also defeats the goal of securing accurate information from jurors given the pressure to be a "good" job candidate. However, by viewing the voir dire process as a conversation with the jurors, lawyers foster a more open and relaxed atmosphere. Jurors respond to this climate with a greater willingness to share their experiences and opinions. The resulting conversation may be with one juror or with a number of jurors at one time. The key feature is the tone of the questioning set by the lawyer.

EMPATHY. Jurors face a potentially uncomfortable and threatening situation in voir dire. Showing empathy for what jurors face is important. Acknowledging the discomfort of jurors and being supportive are important when jurors appear nervous or are having difficulty answering questions. The following statements are helpful in showing empathy with what the juror is going through.

"We all understand that it's difficult to talk here in the courtroom. If there is anything I can do to make it easier, just let me know."

"I realize that some of my questions may be difficult to answer."

"I know that we usually do not think about these issues, but in this case it is important that we do so."

Being empathetic toward jurors will encourage them to do the hard work necessary to answer difficult questions.

SINCERITY AND INTEREST. Jurors are more likely to be forthcoming about their opinions and experiences when lawyers are sincere in the questions they ask and express interest in what the jurors have to say. Failing to show an interest in what the jurors are saying closes the door to juror honesty and candor. The verbal and nonverbal communication of lawyers plays a key role in the jurors' willingness to answer questions candidly. Avoid shuffling papers, continually looking down at notes, or searching through note cards for the next question while the jurors are speaking. These actions communicate that what jurors have to say is not important. Also, simply reading a list of questions or interrupting the jurors during their answers will cause the communication process to break down.

Showing an interest in what the jurors are saying is a key component in breaking down the barriers to juror disclosure and rapport. Facing the juror squarely with an open and relaxed posture, maintaining a moderate to high level of eye contact, and removing obstructions between the lawyer and the juror facilitates open communication. When sitting at a table, moving books to the side or even moving around to the side of the table will foster open communication in voir dire.

WARMTH. Maintaining a warm and friendly attitude with jurors is important. Jurors like lawyers who are pleasant and are willing to share aspects of their personal lives with them. Smiling where appropriate and maintaining an open and relaxed posture facilitates a positive impression. Being cold and aloof increases the "distance" between the lawyer and jurors, placing an additional obstacle to juror disclosure.

SUPPORT. It is important to minimize any feelings of intimidation, threat, or embarrassment that jurors may experience. When a juror appears confused by a question, accept responsibility for being unclear or having asked a confusing question. Taking this approach will minimize the possibility that jurors will react in a defensive manner when misunderstandings occur in the questioning process.

In addition, being critical of jurors' answers can embarrass them. For example, consider the following exchange between a juror and the prosecutor:

PROSECUTOR: Have you ever been in a situation where you had to listen to witnesses, even if it was watching a TV show, where you had to listen to witnesses and make up your mind about who was right and who was wrong?

JUROR: Yes. Sometimes at night I watch People's Court, Divorce Court.

PROSECUTOR: Do you like those shows?

JUROR: Yes, I enjoy them.

PROSECUTOR: I think they are boring, but some people just—they seem to be getting more and more popular.

The above example illustrates a situation that could embarrass a juror. The potential for embarrassing jurors necessitates a cautious approach to comments made to jurors. Juror embarrassment can produce a negative reaction by the juror being questioned or by other jurors hearing the comment. Further, it erodes rapport with and positive regard for the questioner.

IDENTIFICATION. Capitalizing on potential similarities between lawyers and jurors is helpful in voir dire. Jurors tend to like lawyers who are similar to them and they will be more open in their answers to these lawyers. This bonding or identification process by jurors can be enhanced by drawing attention to potential similarities such as common hobbies, activities, past experiences, or geographical identification. For example, the following comments highlight several potential similarities:

LAWYER:	[Military service] I see you served in the Marines. Were you based in Camp Lejeune?
JUROR:	Yes.
LAWYER:	I was there in 1974. Was [Name] still the camp commander when you were there?
JUROR:	Yes, he was still there last time I heard.

. . .

LAWYER:	[College] You mentioned that you went to State College. That was before the clock tower was repaired, wasn't it?
JUROR:	Yes.
LAWYER:	I remember a lot of us were late to class because of that clock.
JUROR:	It sure did trick a lot of us.

. . . .

LAWYER:	[Geographical identification] I see that you live over near the new shopping center. I grew up over there. Were you there when it still was the all-night drive-in theater?
JUROR:	Yes.

Taking advantage of common experiences like these will encourage jurors to be more candid and honest with the questioning lawyer.

LISTENING. One of the most important communication skills is listening. The skill of listening involves paying close attention to, showing interest in, and hearing exactly what jurors are saying. Where possible, it is helpful to have someone besides the lawyer record the jurors' responses in detail so that lawyers can devote their attention to their interaction with the jurors. The greater attention paid to jurors results in an increase in their participation in the voir dire process. When jurors feel that only superficial attention is being paid to them, they will respond with superficial answers.

A critical feature of listening is hearing what is being said. On the surface, this seems obvious, but real listening is a rare and valuable skill. Examples of common failures in listening include attributing the wrong marital status to a juror and using the wrong name when referring to a juror. Neither of these errors puts the lawyer in a positive light. However, more significant failures in listening occur. It is possible to miss a subtle qualification in the juror's answer (e.g., "Yes, I guess," indicating some reservation). Also, it is possible to assume what the answer will be and thus ignore the juror's actual (opposite) answer. Consider the following example:

PLAINTIFF: Sir, you are a psychologist, is that right?

JUROR: Yes.

PLAINTIFF: Do you feel that a woman who has been raped has suffered something more than physical trauma—that is, she has suffered emotional trauma as well?

JUROR: No.

PLAINTIFF: Thank you. My next question . . . [Because the juror was a psychologist, the lawyer assumed that the answer would be "yes" and continued to the next question. Fortunately, this error in listening was caught and brought to the attention of the lawyer. The original question was asked again, eliciting the same answer and allowing the lawyer to pursue needed follow-up questions.]

An additional component of listening is detecting "irrelevant speech" on the part of jurors. As discussed in Chapter 3, irrelevant speech is used by jurors to provide a response without actually answering the question. Revisiting the *North* voir dire questioning example below, we see how the prosecutor's persistent questioning headed off a serious problem with this juror.

PROSECUTOR: . . . Is there any other reason that it would be difficult for you to serve as a juror?

JUROR: No.

PROSECUTOR: Sometimes people have religious beliefs that make it hard for them to be a juror. Do you have any beliefs that come from your religious ideas or philosophical ideas that would make it hard?

JUROR: Well, I am a Christian but, you know, I believe in the truth, because the truth is God's friend. *[Irrelevant answer]*

PROSECUTOR: Okay. And if the truth, as you understood it, and the law as you heard it from the judge—

JUROR: Yes.

PROSECUTOR: —led to a decision that required you to vote Colonel North guilty, you could do that, if that's the way you honestly believed it?

JUROR: No, I couldn't do that, because, you know, I wasn't there and I don't know if he did it. Say, if I would vote guilty, you know, people's life is [sic] precious and I would be taking his life, in a sense, and I couldn't vote guilty.

PROSECUTOR: No matter what you heard in the courtroom?

JUROR: Right.

PROSECUTOR: You still couldn't vote guilty?

JUROR: No.

PROSECUTOR: I appreciate your candor very much. Thank you, ma'am.

JUROR: Thank you, sir.

COURT: Thank you very much. You are excused.

These latter problems may not be commonplace. However, when they occur, potentially disastrous consequences can arise in jury selection.

Interview Techniques

In addition to good communication skills, three techniques increase the jurors' willingness to provide information to lawyers and, in some cases, they facilitate persuasion. These techniques are disclosure reciprocity, positive reinforcement, and modeling.[8]

DISCLOSURE RECIPROCITY. Disclosure reciprocity refers to the tendency of people to respond in kind to disclosures made by others. When people reveal something about themselves to us, we tend to respond by revealing something about ourselves to them. In voir dire, lawyers can foster disclosure reciprocity by revealing aspects about themselves.

> "I am going to ask you a number of questions about your background and experiences in a minute and I think that it is only fair to tell you a little about myself. I work with the law firm of Smith and Smith. I am married and have one child and my wife teaches social studies at City High School."

Such disclosures encourage jurors to tell something about themselves. However, it is important to reveal only noncontroversial information. Disclosing information that is inappropriate (too intimate) or that jurors may view in a negative light (e.g., political party affiliation) can short-circuit the process of disclosure reciprocity.

POSITIVE REINFORCEMENT. Positive reinforcement is providing a reward or reinforcement for desired actions by jurors so that the likelihood of those actions being repeated in the future will increase.[9] Two sources of reinforcement are available to lawyers, verbal and nonverbal reinforcement. Comments such as "yes," "thank you," "I appreciate your thoughtfulness," "good," "I see," or "uh-huh" in response to jurors' answers serve to verbally reinforce

---

Three ways lawyers can increase jurors' willingness to disclose information:

- *Disclosure reciprocity.* Provide jurors with limited noncontroversial information about yourself.

- *Positive reinforcement.* Provide positive verbal and nonverbal reinforcement for desired answers or behaviors of jurors.

- *Modeling.* Use models (either the lawyer or other jurors) to show jurors what are desired behaviors or answers.

jurors for what they have said. Lawyers may use smiling, an open and for-ward-leaning body posture, and facial expressions of interest and attention as nonverbal reinforcement for the jurors' answers.

Positive reinforcement can be employed to achieve three of the four goals of voir dire: information gathering, rapport, and persuasion. Positive reinforcement increases the willingness of jurors to reveal information about themselves, thereby facilitating information disclosure and rapport. When jurors are open and forthcoming with information, lawyers can facilitate fur-ther disclosures by providing positive reinforcement for these actions. Lawyer-juror rapport likewise increases through the positive experience jurors have as a result of receiving positive reinforcement.

In the case of persuasion, it is important to reinforce jurors for express-ing desirable opinions so that they will hold these opinions more strongly, use them in their decision-making, and be more likely to express them dur-ing the course of jury deliberations. This process is fairly simple. The lawyer provides positive reinforcement to potential jurors when they express desir-able opinions. In this manner, positive verbal and nonverbal reinforcement serves to foster the endorsement and expression of positive attitudes on the part of jurors.

MODELING. The third interview technique that fosters attainment of the goals of voir dire is modeling. Modeling is a form of learning called "obser-vational learning," where learning occurs by watching the behaviors of oth-ers and noting the consequences of their actions.[10] Modeling in the voir dire process is important because jurors often are unsure about what they are supposed to do in this situation. In addition, they are unsure about what are appropriate opinions and beliefs to hold regarding many areas of the voir dire questioning. As a result, jurors will turn to those around them for an indication of what is appropriate. The potential models available are lawyers, judges, and their fellow jurors.

Modeling can foster disclosure on the part of jurors and, to some degree, persuasion. In voir dire, lawyers want to capitalize on the presence of models in the courtroom who are open and candid. Lawyers and judges serve as models of the desired behavior when they reveal information about them-selves. Jurors themselves serve as powerful models for other jurors. Given the uncertainty that jurors have regarding voir dire, they pay close attention to what other jurors are doing and saying. When one juror is candid and forth-coming in his or her answers, this juror serves as a good model for the other jurors. Exposure to these good models will encourage jurors to be open and honest in their answers to the lawyers' questions. Similarly, exposure to mod-els exhibiting undesirable behavior (e.g., lack of candor or minimal participa-tion during voir dire) can make these undesirable behaviors more prevalent among jurors.

Modeling also can foster persuasion on voir dire. A juror who expresses opinions favorable to the client and is subsequently treated in a positive manner by the lawyer serves as a positive model for other jurors. This positive (good) model can lead to the strengthening of desired opinions held by other jurors and to other jurors adopting or being more receptive to desirable opinions.

Structuring the Voir Dire

Development of an effective voir dire relies on several basic elements in how voir dire questioning is conducted. These elements are (a) flexibility, (b) the organization of voir dire, and (c) the use of effective group questioning techniques.

Flexibility

Given that voir dire is by its very nature a social interaction, a key to conducting effective voir dire is flexibility. This flexibility is in terms of:

- when to address various topics,
- how to phrase questions,
- developing new topics/questions, and
- responding to the opponent's questions.

ADDRESSING TOPICS. There is no fixed order for when to address various topics on voir dire. While it is important to consider when it is best to explore certain topics or opinions, as discussed in the previous chapter, always asking questions in the same order can lead jurors to give superficial answers. Varying the placement of the questions or topics in the overall structure of voir dire can reduce this problem. For example, inquiry into worker safety issues can occur when considering general opinion questions or when discussing the jurors' occupations.

HOW TO PHRASE QUESTIONS. Flexibility also applies to the phrasing of questions. While open-ended questions are extremely useful, in practice only a small proportion of voir dire questions can be of this type.[11] It is important to use open-ended questions wisely and to capitalize on new opportunities for their use. In addition, the wording of the question itself may need to change as a result of what the court allows and the answers given by jurors. In the latter instance, ways of rephrasing questions to make the desired points more effectively with subsequent potential jurors can surface in light of the answers given by jurors appearing earlier in voir dire.

DEVELOPING NEW TOPICS/QUESTIONS. When jurors reveal issues of concern, capitalize on them. As voir dire questioning progresses, the jurors' answers can indicate new areas worthy of investigation. For example, if some jurors make a distinction between public and private lands in terms of defendant liability in railroad crossing accidents, then it is necessary to pursue this issue with all possible jurors. Failure to do so may allow unfavorable jurors to go undetected.

Areas where lawyers need to be flexible when conducting voir dire:

- The placement of topics or questions.

- The phrasing of questions.

- The development of new topic areas and questions.

- The response to the opponent's questions.

RESPONDING TO THE OPPONENT'S QUESTIONS. It is important to respond not only to new issues jurors raise but to the opponent's questions as well. When the opposing lawyer raises important issues or questions not previously considered, the original party benefits by addressing these issues or questions in subsequent questioning. This may mean asking the same or slightly adapted questions to previously unquestioned or "new" jurors, as is often the case with background information. It also may mean counteracting any adverse persuasion by rephrasing questions to promote a more desirable perspective. Not responding to an important area or question raised by the opponent gives an unnecessary advantage to the opponent.

Organization of Voir Dire

While flexibility is valuable in conducting voir dire, it is possible to apply a basic structure to voir dire topics that promotes collecting the information in an organized fashion. This structure consists of:

- the introduction,
- knowledge of relevant entities,
- background information/relevant experiences,
- pretrial publicity issues,
- statement of contentions,
- opinions and beliefs,
- legal opinions and beliefs,
- jury behavior issues, and
- closing issues.

INTRODUCTION. Ideally, lawyers want to take a conversational approach to the voir dire process. This approach starts by introducing jurors to the voir dire process. The objectives of this introduction are to acquaint jurors with the voir dire process and what is desired from them and to make jurors feel comfortable. It is important to stress the positive nature of voir dire. It is not enough to simply state that voir dire means "to speak the truth" and then proceed to ask questions of the jurors. Jurors need to know that voir dire is conducted in order to seat an impartial jury. Voir dire is the only opportunity the lawyers have to get to know the jurors. The goal is not to pry into the jurors' lives but to seek information to help determine who might be best suited to serve on the jury. The following illustrates this approach to introducing voir dire:

> "Ladies and gentlemen, my name is Joe Smith, and I represent Mrs. Jane Jones, the plaintiff [or defendant] in this lawsuit. As was mentioned by the judge, this part of the trial is called the voir dire. *Voir dire* is an Old French phrase that means "to speak the truth." It is a time when we lawyers will be asking you a number of questions about your backgrounds, experiences, and opinions. These questions are not designed to pry. They serve a very important function in the jury selection process. They give us an opportunity to get to know you. More important, the questions may cover areas that might be sensitive to some of you, perhaps as a result of some past experience. Should this occur we will have an opportunity to explore those experiences with you. This will make sure that there is nothing that might interfere with your ability to feel comfortable sitting on this jury.
>
> "The judge mentioned that it is important that you be candid, open, and honest in your answers. The goal of jury selection is to select a jury that is impartial to both sides in the case. It is by your being forthright and candid in your answers that we can ensure that such a jury is achieved."

The introduction is the time when lawyers can take advantage of self-disclosure and modeling. By telling a little about themselves, they encourage juror openness through reciprocity and the (nonpersuasive) modeling of what the jurors should do on voir dire.

KNOWLEDGE OF RELEVANT ENTITIES. The next step in the voir dire process addresses the jurors' knowledge of the various people or entities who will play a role in the trial. This step is often taken in conjunction with the general introduction. Lawyers introduce themselves, the parties (particularly one's own client), lawyers for the opposing side (if necessary), and related personnel. This introduction shows the jurors who the significant personnel are in case any juror knows one or more of these individuals or has any personal, social, or business relationships with them.

Particular attention is paid to any nonverbal reactions made by jurors in response to either party in the case. Directing the jurors' attention to one's client through a hand gesture (e.g., touching the client's shoulder) is helpful. While the jurors' attention is directed to the client, the lawyer observes the reactions of jurors. In addition, the list of potential witnesses for both sides is read to the jurors to see if they have any personal, social, or business relationship with any of these individuals.

BACKGROUND INFORMATION/RELEVANT EXPERIENCES. After considering the parties, witnesses, and other personnel, it is time to inquire into the backgrounds of jurors. This inquiry consists of gathering basic information from the jurors, e.g., occupation, education, marital status, length of residence in the community, hobbies, experience with lawsuits, and significant positive or negative experiences. The case analysis forms the basis for developing questions that address important background characteristics and experiences.

The background-oriented nature of the questions provides important information on jurors' lives and experiences. Also, these questions give lawyers an opportunity to establish rapport. As such, the questions should not be phrased in a manner that could prove embarrassing to jurors. For example, the question "Do you have a job?" could embarrass an unemployed or laid-off worker. Phrasing the question in an open-ended manner reduces the potential for embarrassment, e.g., "What is your employment status at this time?"

Background questions that encourage jurors to "open up" to lawyers and allow jurors to become comfortable with speaking in the courtroom are beneficial. The following questions illustrate this approach:

"Tell me a little bit about what you do at work."

"You said that you went to college. What did you study at college?"

"What courses did you enjoy?"

"What did you find enjoyable about these courses?"

Encouraging jurors to talk about themselves not only reveals important information but also increases juror candor and openness in later questioning.

Finally, as discussed in Chapter 3, having jurors discuss their backgrounds serves as a baseline for determining their overall level of anxiety or nervousness in the voir dire setting. This baseline is used to evaluate changes in their verbal and nonverbal behavior when they later are asked to consider important topics and opinions.

PRETRIAL PUBLICITY ISSUES. The presence of pretrial publicity regarding the case or the incident that spawned the case needs to be addressed early in voir dire. A description of the case or incident serves as a starting point. This description is not a statement of contentions. It covers the appropriate information available through the media. The statement should be brief. The goal at this point is not to provide jurors with "new" information but to find out what jurors remember.

Key components in the organization of voir dire:

- Introduction
- Knowledge of parties or entities
- Background information and relevant experiences
- Impact of pretrial publicity
- Statement of contentions
- Relevant opinions and beliefs
- Issues relating to the jurors' roles and duties
- Closing issues

After the case has been described, questioning turns to the jurors' awareness and knowledge of the case or event and any impressions or opinions they may have formed. The following are examples of questions that could be used:

"Have you heard anything on the radio or seen anything in the newspaper, on television, or on the Internet concerning this [case or event]?"

"Tell me a little about what you recall from having read, seen, or heard about this case."

"Based on what you have seen and heard and discussed with your friends and coworkers, did you form/have any impressions of what occurred?"

"What were/are these impressions?"

Jurors' answers to these questions will indicate the appropriate avenue of questioning regarding any preconceptions of guilt or liability or other area of importance.

Placing the pretrial publicity section at this point in the voir dire is not always desirable. Cases that are highly publicized or controversial, or where a substantial bias exists in the community, may require investigation of pretrial publicity issues at an earlier point in the questioning process. Early questioning regarding pretrial publicity can prevent wasting court time on jurors who exhibit sufficient bias for their removal through a challenge for cause.

STATEMENT OF CONTENTIONS. A statement of contentions is the next item on the voir dire agenda. The statement of contentions presents the case from the party's perspective, e.g., a case of self-defense not murder. The statement of contentions is not bound by what has been reported in the media. It contains a basic summary of the case and the assertions of the party. The statement can be a sentence or two or it can be much longer, depending upon what the court will allow.

The statement of contentions serves as a context for subsequent questioning on voir dire. It provides the jurors with an understanding of why lawyers are asking various questions. Lawyers benefit by paying close attention to the jurors' nonverbal behavior while the statement is being made. Jurors often reveal their initial reactions to the party's assertions during the delivery of the statement. As we saw in the previous chapter, this statement also contains persuasive potential when lawyers choose psychologically beneficial words and phrases.

OPINIONS AND BELIEFS. After the statement of contentions comes the examination of the various opinions and beliefs that are important in determining juror desirability. There are several considerations when addressing important opinions and beliefs. First, the primary goal of voir dire is information gathering. As such, it is important to uncover the jurors' opinions first before any attempts are made to educate or persuade jurors.

Second, when investigating opinions and beliefs, address less sensitive or less difficult topics first. Give jurors an opportunity to feel comfortable answering opinion questions before venturing into sensitive areas. For example, in a wrongful death case, for jurors who have personally experienced the loss of a family member, the loss suffered by the deceased's surviving family members is a more sensitive area than issues of worker safety. Therefore, it is better to consider these more sensitive wrongful death issues later in voir dire.

Third, within topic areas, address the less sensitive or less difficult questions before advancing to more difficult questions. For example, it is helpful to begin with less difficult or sensitive questions when discussing the views of jurors regarding the impact of a mother's death on her surviving children. For example:

"Is your mother living?"

"How often do you see your mother?"

"Do you recall what kinds of things you and your mother did together when you were a child?" [Probe for guidance, emotional support, help in school, and like activities.]

After these questions, it is easier for jurors to answer a question regarding what the loss of a mother would mean to her children.

"Could you tell me what you feel would be some of the most important losses that a child would suffer when his mother is killed?"

Fourth, it is important to address with specificity the key opinions at issue in the case. For example, in death penalty cases it is important to address whether jurors would consider aggravating and mitigating factors in an intentional murder case in their decision as to the appropriate punishment for such a crime. Consider the following examination of a juror in a death penalty case in terms of the need to be specific—to the point of specifying the exact details of the crime at issue.

COURT: All right. Would your feelings about the death penalty in any way prevent you or substantially impair you from performing your duties as a juror under your oath and under my instructions in either phase of the case?

VENIREMAN: No.

COURT: Would your feelings, just so—I want to make sure, would your feelings about the death penalty either prevent or make it very hard for you to consider all mitigating evidence and all the aggravating evidence before deciding whether to impose the death penalty?

VENIREMAN: Sorry. You lost me there. Repeat again.

COURT: Would you consider all of the mitigating evidence and all of the aggravating evidence before you decided to impose the death penalty or not?

VENIREMAN: Certainly.

COURT: All right.

[*Prosecutor*]

MR. NOVAK: Good evening. If I could ask you. If we were in a situation where the guilt phase is concluded and one or more of the defendants have been found guilty of murder in further-ance of the drug trafficking offense, and therefore that necessitated the second phase, penalty phase, where, as the Judge told you, the government would have an oppor-tunity to present to you evidence as aggravating factors, basically why it is the government believes the defendant should receive the death penalty, of course then the defen-dants, they have the opportunity, if they choose to do so, to introduce their own evidence in mitigation, reasons why they believe the death penalty should not be imposed. Would you consider the testimony introduced by the government and the defense prior to deciding whether the death penalty is appropriate in that case, or would you automatically find in favor of the death penalty without regard to the aggravating or mitigating evidence?

VENIREMAN: I would consider both options, both sides.

MR. NOVAK: Before you made a final decision?

VENIREMAN: Before the final decision was made.

MR. NOVAK: Thank you.

THE COURT: Any questions?

[*Defense attorney*]

MR. ZERKIN: Yes, Your Honor. Good afternoon, ma'am. I notice on the questionnaire you were born in Clay County, Mississippi. Is that where you were raised?

VENIREMAN: Raised in Monroe, the next county over, right.

MR. ZERKIN: The specific capital crime that four of the defendants are charged with is a knowing, intentional, unlawful murder in furtherance of a conspiracy to distribute crack cocaine. If you found one or more of the defendants guilty of that specific charge, do you believe that, regardless of the aggravating or mitigating circumstances, for that crime the only appropriate punishment would be death?

VENIREMAN: Read the crime.

MR. ZERKIN: The crime?

VENIREMAN: The charge.

THE COURT: Read the whole question again.

MR. ZERKIN: I will do that. If the jury found one of the defendants, one or more of them, guilty of the following crime: A know-ing, intentional, and unlawful murder in furtherance of a conspiracy to distribute crack cocaine—that is the crime— would you then, regardless of the aggravating or mitigating circumstances, believe that the death penalty was the only appropriate punishment for that crime?

VENIREMAN: I think I would have to vote for the death penalty if it was a knowing crime, based on my religious beliefs, yes.

MR. ZERKIN: Okay. That is based on religious beliefs?

VENIREMAN: Right.

MR. ZERKIN: So for the crime that is at issue here, you would believe that that would be the only appropriate punishment, am I correct?

VENIREMAN: Right.

MR. ZERKIN: Thank you.

THE COURT: Any questions?

MR. NOVAK: Could I ask another? Ma'am, I think—I want to understand, because I think your answer to my question and answer—

VENIREMAN: He explained it to me I think a little better. He read the whole thing there, and I understood more about what the question was when he read it. I am having a little problem with aggravating and mitigating here, so I—what he said, the whole crime—I can answer my question from that.

MR. NOVAK: That is fine. Let me ask you one question. Again, aggravating factors are the evidence that the government would put forward as to why the government believes that death is the appropriate sentence for the defendant. Mitigating is evidence that the defendants may elect if they want to introduce as to why they say it is not appropriate, the death penalty. My question to you originally was this: If the defendant is convicted of the crime that Mr. Zerkin just described, that is, of an intentional, knowingly, unlawfully killing someone in furtherance of a drug punishment, they are convicted of that then we get to the second phase where there is this issue about the government putting on aggravating factors, and defense, if they want to, can put on mitigating evidence. My question to you is: Would you consider the aggravating and mitigating factors before making your decision, or as I understand what you said to Mr. Zerkin was, that you would automatically sentence them to death without any regard to the aggravating or mitigating evidence.

. . .

VENIREMAN: Based on my religious beliefs, if it was a knowing crime, committed by someone who knew what they were doing, I would vote for the death penalty.

MR. NOVAK: Thank you.

THE COURT: You may step outside for just a moment.

[Venireman withdrew.]

MR. NOVAK: Move to strike.
THE COURT: You agree she should be?
Mr. Zerkin: Yes.

[Juror excused for cause.]

Fifth, cover all the topic areas with all the jurors. Where possible, avoid skipping topic areas with different jurors. Information is lost when lawyers skip topic areas or questions with certain jurors.

The question of skipping questions with jurors arises most frequently when addressing favorable jurors, unfavorable jurors, and nonassertive jurors. In some situations questioning certain jurors in detail is not desirable. This is the case with extremely favorable or extremely unfavorable jurors. Lawyers may not want to risk exposing very favorable jurors to a challenge for cause by the opponent.[12] However, it is important to cover all topics with favorable jurors to ensure that there are no "chinks" in the jurors' favorability. With particularly unfavorable jurors, it is possible to skip certain areas in anticipation of using a peremptory challenge (under the assumption that a successful challenge for cause with this juror is not possible) so that these jurors do not act as spokespersons for the opponent's views.[13]

The case for skipping questions is less compelling with nonassertive jurors. These jurors are likely to be potential followers, not leaders on the jury. However, cutting short voir dire questioning with these jurors can lead to the failure to discover critical information concerning their opinions and experiences that reveals their favorable or unfavorable nature as it relates to the case. The overall favorability of all jurors must be established in order to make intelligent decisions on how peremptory challenges are to be used. In addition, it is desirable to develop rapport with all the jurors, not just a selected few. Jurors neglected on voir dire are likely to feel unimportant or ignored.

Finally, asking about opinions and beliefs of jurors can often yield unusual or unfavorable responses. The lawyer's reactions to the answers and the choice of follow-up questions in these situations are very important. Follow-up questions to unfavorable or unusual answers given by jurors can convey confidence or lack of confidence in one's case. Jurors look to the lawyers to see how they react to what an unfavorable juror says. Jurors may view lawyers as lacking confidence in their case when they become flustered in the face of an unusual or unfavorable response by a juror. For example, a plaintiff's lawyer who is uneasy about the lawsuit (insurance) "crisis" issue communicates this fact to the jurors in the following interaction:

LAWYER: How do you feel about the right of people to sue when they are injured as a result of someone else's negligence?
JUROR: I think that people are too willing to sue others just as a way of making money—people just seem to be greedy these days.
LAWYER: Ah—It's the law—you see, that people do have that right?
JUROR: I guess they do.

In the above interaction, jurors are likely to see the lawyer as being defensive, perhaps reflecting uncertainty in the strength of the plaintiff's case. However, a different follow-up approach by the lawyer would yield a more positive, confident impression.

JUROR: I think that people are too willing to sue others just as a way of making money—people just seem to be greedy these days.

LAWYER: I can appreciate your concern. People shouldn't treat law-suits lightly. Do you feel that Mrs. Smith [the plaintiff] or myself is seeking anything but a just verdict in this case?

JUROR: No.

LAWYER: If you were injured by someone who was negligent, would you feel that you were being greedy by choosing to sue the negligent party?

JUROR: No, indeed.

LAWYER: So, how do you feel about lawsuits for personal injury?

JUROR: I think they should sue if they have been wrongly hurt.

While the plaintiff's lawyer may eventually remove this juror, the appropriate use of follow-up questions prevents the jury from viewing the plaintiff's case as being weak or unjustified.

LEGAL OPINIONS AND BELIEFS. Consideration of the jurors' opinions regarding the law and legal principles is best delayed until information on the jurors' other opinions has been gathered. Discussing legal opinions early in questioning can serve to reveal to jurors what the socially desirable answers or opinions are. It is important that lawyers uncover the jurors' untainted opinions that bear on legal principles or the law. Thus, it is better to address topics such as the burden of proof, a defendant's right not to testify, multiple defendants, multiple charges, negligence, liability, and damages later in the questioning. Not only will lawyers know what the jurors' general opinions are, but this knowledge will shape the discussion of legal opinions in terms of the goals of information gathering, education, and persuasion.

JURY BEHAVIOR ISSUES. It is important to address issues that directly relate to how jurors are to discharge their duties. The logical place to consider these issues is after a discussion of the legal opinions and issues, near the end of voir dire questioning. Relevant duties include following the law, participating in deliberations, using their own judgment, listening to their fellow jurors, and not changing a verdict unless convinced by the evidence. Lawyers can use a variety of questions to elicit the jurors' views of their duties. However, education becomes a major emphasis in this area. It is critical that jurors understand and commit to discharging those duties that are favorable to the lawyer's case.

For example, in the criminal area, prosecutors will concentrate on the jurors' (a) ability to follow the law, (b) willingness to judge others, and

(c) ability to work together to arrive at a unanimous verdict. Illustrative questions include the following:

"If you sat on the jury in this case, would you have any reservations about returning a verdict of guilty against the defendant, if the evidence proved beyond a reasonable doubt that the defendant was guilty of first-degree murder?"

"Do you have any religious or ethical beliefs that would make it difficult for you to judge someone?"

"If you sat as a juror, you would be required to judge the defendant and return a verdict of guilty if the evidence proved the defendant to be guilty. Would you have any reservations about returning a guilty verdict if the evidence proved the defendant to be guilty? How would you feel about returning a guilty verdict?"

"The verdict of guilty requires a unanimous decision among the jurors. If you sat as a juror in this case, would you be willing to go over the evidence in the case, listen to your fellow jurors' views, and work with them in arriving at a decision in this case?"

Criminal defense lawyers would address such areas as (a) the willingness to return a not guilty verdict, (b) the unanimous decision requirement, (c) perceptions of a hung jury, and (d) the willingness of jurors to stand by their opinions. The following questions are illustrative of these areas:

"If you sat as a juror in this case, would you have any reservations in returning a not guilty verdict if the prosecution failed to prove beyond a reasonable doubt that Mr. Smith [the defendant] committed the crimes charged?"

"Would you feel in not returning a conviction that your job was somewhat incomplete or a failure?"

"A verdict of guilty must be unanimous—that is, all the jurors must agree with any verdict of guilty. If you sat as a juror, would you respect each juror's opinion and work to see that the final verdict reflects the views of all members of the jury?"

"If you sat on the jury and your fellow jurors were unable to agree on the verdict—what we call a hung jury—how would you feel about that?"

"Would you feel a sense of failure or incompleteness in not being able to agree on a verdict?"

"Would you feel like you didn't do your job as jurors?"

"If you believed by what you heard and saw in court that the prosecution had failed to prove beyond a reasonable doubt that Mr. Smith was guilty, would you be willing to stand by your decision no matter if other jurors felt a different way?"

"Would you feel that it is important that you stand by your opinion? Why is that?"

In the civil area, plaintiff's lawyers will concentrate on issues such as (a) sympathy, (b) the jurors' willingness to render a verdict of liability, (c) the jurors' willingness to render a verdict on damages, and (d) working together to reach a verdict. Sample questions in these areas are the following:

"The judge will instruct you that you should not base your decision on liability of the defendant on sympathy. Mr. Smith [the plaintiff] has not come here today seeking sympathy. However, when you consider the issue of damages, you will need to come to grips with exactly what has happened—how this [tragedy] has changed his life. If you sat as a member of this jury, would you be able to consider this and not feel that you are supposed to 'close your eyes to these facts?' Would you have any reservations in doing so?"

"If you were selected as a juror in this case would you be able to follow the law and find the defendant liable [negligent] if the evidence supported such a finding?"

"In your role as a juror, should you find that the defendant is liable (was negligent), would you award the full amount of damages allowed by law? Would you have any reservations in doing so?"

"If you sat as a juror in this case, would you be willing to go over the evidence in the case, listen to your fellow jurors' views, and work with them in coming to a decision in this case?"

The civil defendant would likely concentrate on issues similar to those addressed by the plaintiff but from a different perspective. Some of the issues would be (a) sympathy, (b) the finding of no liability/negligence, (c) returning a verdict of no money damages, (d) waiting until the deliberations before making a decision, and (e) the jurors' willingness to stand by their opinions.

"If you are a juror in this case, the judge will instruct you that your decision is not supposed to be based on sympathy for one party or the other. Would you have any reservations in deciding this case strictly on the evidence and the law in this case and not on any sympathy you may feel for either party?"

"Would you have any reservations in rendering a verdict in favor of the defendant, if the plaintiff failed to prove that the defendant was negligent [liable]?"

"If you sat as a juror in this case, would you be willing to render a verdict of no money damages for the plaintiff should the plaintiff fail to prove that the defendant was negligent [liable]?"

"In this case the plaintiff presents evidence first and the defense presents its evidence last. As a member of the jury in this case, you would be required not to come to a decision in this case until after all the evidence and arguments have been presented and the judge has given you his/her instructions on the law. Would you have any problems in waiting to form an opinion until this time?"

"As a juror you would be required to fight the tendency people have to make up their minds as soon as possible. Would you be able to do so in this case? Do you see why it is important to fight this tendency? Why?"

"If you believed by what you heard and saw in court that the plaintiff had failed to prove by a preponderance of the evidence that Mr. Smith [the defendant] was negligent, would you be willing to stand by your decision no matter how the other jurors felt?"

"Would you feel that it is important that you stand by your opinion? Why is that?"

Hardship issues that would interfere with discharging the duties of jurors, such as the length of the trial, relevant medical and physical conditions, and problems with sequestration, are appropriate for consideration at this time. If problems are likely to arise, however, it is useful to consider hardship issues earlier in the questioning process. Examples of hardship-related questions are:

"This trial is likely to last for X days/weeks. Is there any reason why you would not be able to sit as a member of this jury and give your full attention to this matter?"

"Do you have any problems with your hearing or vision that would make it difficult for you to serve as a juror in this case?"

"Do you have a medical condition or are you taking any medication that may interfere with your ability to concentrate or attend all sessions during this trial?"

"As I said earlier, this trial is likely to last for X days/weeks. During this time, you will be sequestered. That means that you will be staying at a hotel during the trial and will be unable to go home or be with your family or friends except when allowed by the judge. Would this cause you any undue hardship or cause you not to be able to sit as a member of this jury and give your full attention to this matter?"

CLOSING ISSUES. In closing the voir dire examination, it is important to focus on two issues: undiscovered problems and fairness. Even after all the questioning by the lawyers, certain biasing experiences that jurors have had may remain undiscovered. This situation can result from the failure to ask a particular question (perhaps pertaining to an unusual experience or unusual reaction to a common experience). In addition, undiscovered biases may arise with jurors who had reservations near the beginning of voir dire but were reluctant to admit them at the time. When a well-conducted voir dire produces an atmosphere of openness and candor, these undiscovered problems can surface in response to a summary question at the conclusion of voir dire:

"We have discussed a number of things over the course of our questions and you have been very candid with me about your views.

However, there are oftentimes questions that were not asked that relate to past experiences that you may have had or opinions that you may hold that would cause you to lean one way or the other. In view of this, I would like to ask you the following questions:

(1) Is there anything that has come to mind during the course of questioning (by anyone) that you have not had a chance to tell us about? If so, now is the time to do so.

(2) If you were at either one of these tables, would there be any reason why you would not want yourself as a juror in this case? That is, at this time, would you feel uncomfortable being at either table and having someone like yourself as a juror?"

While the common response to these questions is "no," some jurors will respond with "yes." These types of questions give lawyers a final opportunity to uncover potential bias or prejudice that would otherwise remain unspoken, and possibly undetected.

Finally, conclude voir dire with a discussion of fairness. Such a discussion enhances lawyer credibility and, again, allows jurors an opportunity to reveal any reservations that they might have in serving on the jury. The following question illustrates this point.

"This is a very serious case. Do you feel that there is any reason that you could not be fair to both sides in this case?"

Fairness should always be discussed in the context of how jurors should treat all parties in the case. Failure to do so can lead to the opponent trying to instill psychological reactance by implying in subsequent questioning that the original lawyer wants "fairness" only for his or her client.

Reduced Information Settings

A number of situations arise that act to reduce what lawyers can learn about jurors during voir dire. Three of these situations are prominent: (a) restrictions on the content of voir dire questioning, (b) group-conducted questioning, and (c) judge-conducted questioning.

Restricted Content

One of the ways that the information available from jurors is reduced is through the court's restricting the content of the voir dire. Potentially valuable information is lost when questioning is prohibited on important topics. Three approaches can be helpful when facing a restricted content situation.

REQUEST EXPANDED VOIR DIRE. In anticipation of restrictions being placed on the questions or topic areas addressed during voir dire, a pretrial motion should be filed outlining the need to address important topics. This motion should include examples of the questions to be asked and, where available, citations indicating support for making the requested inquiries.[14] It is often

---

Responding to restrictions on the content of voir dire questioning:

- Seek greater latitude in voir dire questioning.
- Request the use of a juror questionnaire.
- Set priorities for the information being sought.

---

useful to combine this motion with requests for other changes in the voir dire procedure, such as a request for attorney-conducted questioning.

USE JUROR QUESTIONNAIRES. The second approach is requesting the use of a juror questionnaire to expand the information obtained during jury selection. Juror questionnaires gather information concerning the jurors' backgrounds, relevant experiences, and, on occasion, opinions. Some courts mail juror questionnaires to jurors with instructions for their completion and return, while other courts have jurors complete these questionnaires upon arrival for jury service. In either case, the jurors' answers are made available to all parties prior to the questioning of these jurors on voir dire. Juror questionnaires have the potential for reducing the overall time spent questioning jurors in court, increasing juror candor, and expanding the information available to lawyers. We will consider the topic of juror questionnaires in detail in Chapter 7.

SET PRIORITIES. When faced with a restricted voir dire situation it is helpful to establish priorities for questions designed to collect information. The most valuable information comes from properly phrased questions addressing the case-specific, and sometimes general, opinions of jurors. The next most valuable information comes from the jurors' case-relevant experiences. While potentially useful, basic demographic information is often the least valuable.

While the above hierarchy serves as a general guideline, it is important to be aware that the content of voir dire that is most often restricted concerns the opinions of jurors. As such, when opinion information is restricted, case-relevant experiences of jurors take on greater importance. Therefore, when allocating limited voir dire time/questions, case-relevant experiences should be given a high priority.

Group Questioning Techniques

This chapter has focused on lawyers conducting the questioning of individual jurors during voir dire. Such questioning could be in an individual context, outside the presence of other jurors, or in a group context, with other jurors present. However, many jurisdictions conduct voir dire questioning either entirely or partly in a group format. In this situation, questions are addressed to the entire trial venire or some smaller portion, e.g., a group of three to twelve jurors.

Seven ways to improve group questioning:

- Get jurors involved early.
- Keep jurors participating.
- Don't let jurors hide.
- Offer jurors a second chance to respond.
- Lead up to sensitive questions.
- Avoid the socially desirable response bias.
- Ask the "last chance" questions.

Questioning in the group format produces less information than questioning on an individual basis.[15] When faced with group questioning, it is important to request in a pretrial motion that all or part of the questioning of jurors be conducted through individual questioning. This motion should spell out the need for juror candor, which is inhibited by the group questioning process; the areas where juror bias may arise; why these areas are best addressed through questions directed to individual jurors; and how individual questioning could be conducted efficiently given the logistics of the courtroom environment.[16]

Given the prevalence of group questioning, the issue remains: What can be done to encourage jurors to reveal information about themselves when they are questioned in a group? There are seven approaches that can increase information disclosure: getting jurors involved early, keeping jurors participating, not letting jurors hide, offering jurors a second chance to respond, leading up to sensitive questions, avoiding the socially desirable response bias, and asking the "last chance" questions. Employing these approaches in conjunction with the principles of good communication skills and interview techniques fosters maximum participation by jurors.

GET JURORS INVOLVED EARLY. A key to being effective in group questioning is having jurors participate early in the voir dire questioning. There are two major methods for accomplishing this task.

Initial hand raising. Asking questions in a group situation often requires jurors to raise their hands in order to give their answers. Lawyers can promote the jurors' willingness to participate in this process by having all the jurors raise their hands at once near the beginning of voir dire. Jurors often are shy or uncomfortable about raising their hands in a group. Giving all the jurors an opportunity to raise their hands near the beginning of voir dire will reduce their reluctance to raise their hands in response to later questioning. Lawyers can accomplish this as follows:

"I will be asking a number of questions today that will require you to raise your hands from time to time. I have found that raising hands for the first time in a group like this is usually the most difficult. So, let's everyone raise our hands at this time and get this over with."

It is also possible to accomplish this task in a less obvious fashion by asking a question for which everyone would answer affirmatively. For example, jurors could be asked a question that relates to a qualification for jury service. "How many of you have lived in this county/city [jurisdiction] for the past two years?" All jurors should answer affirmatively. In this case, you are not actually concerned with their answer (unless a juror does not qualify for jury service) but just the fact that all jurors will have the opportunity to raise their hands.

Initial background summary. A second method for having jurors participate in the process early is to have each juror in the group give a brief summary of his or her background. For example, consider the following approach:

LAWYER: I would like to start out with each of you having an opportunity to tell us a little about yourself. We would like to know your name, your marital status, educational background, occupation, and any hobbies or activities that you enjoy in your spare time. We will start out with juror number one. Could you tell us your name, marital status, your educational background, what you do either in terms of your job or working at home, and what you like to do in your spare time?"

The initial background summary should be short so that jurors can remember all the items of information requested and it should be tailored to fit the case. When necessary, jurors should be given supportive prompts for information inadvertently omitted. The goal is to help jurors take the first steps in feeling more comfortable speaking in the group and to uncover useful background information.

The above approaches break the ice with jurors and lead to their fuller participation in the voir dire process.

KEEP JURORS PARTICIPATING. Once voir dire questioning begins it is imperative that jurors keep participating. However, two features of the way group questioning is normally conducted operate to minimize participation. These features are (a) phrasing questions in a minority response pattern and (b) posing questions to the group as a whole. The impact of these features is often seen at times when it is most troublesome—near the middle to the end of voir dire where questioning into important opinion areas is typically conducted. Two approaches can be employed to help counteract the tendency for participation to drop off as voir dire continues.

Majority response questions. The way questions are phrased influences participation in the process by jurors. Whether the majority of jurors will raise their hands or not is a result of the phrasing of the questions. For example, asking the panel of jurors: "How many of you have been a victim of a crime whether you reported it or not?" is likely to yield a minority of jurors who raise their hands. Phrasing questions in such a manner is efficient in gathering critical information (and in decreasing note-taking demands). However, when the phrasing of most, if not all, of the questions is such that only a minority qualify to raise their hands, jurors tend to become accustomed to not raising their hands. Adoption of this tendency—what is called a "response set"—is counterproductive to gaining information from jurors. Phrasing questions so that the majority response varies between raising and not raising hands prevents jurors from adopting such a response set and keeps them paying attention to the questions being asked. The effectiveness of this approach is maximized when a few majority response questions are judiciously placed throughout the voir dire questioning process.

An additional advantage to phrasing questions so that the majority will raise their hands is that the lawyer can spot the reluctance of some jurors to raise their hands. Jurors who raise their hands more slowly may be revealing their qualified support or even disagreement with the question. In this situation, jurors respond to the majority of jurors raising their hands (indicating the socially desirable answer) but their hesitation can be telling.

Springboard method. A second approach to encourage continued participation in group voir dire is to ask a question of one juror and use his or her answer as a "springboard" to question the rest of the group. The subsequent questioning can be in the form directing the original question to several other jurors or to the group as a whole, or asking jurors their opinion in light of the answer given by the original juror. By varying which juror acts as the springboard, jurors are given more opportunities to speak on their own and face a more interesting voir dire process, both of which lead to greater overall participation in the questioning process.

DON'T LET JURORS HIDE. While an affirmative response may not always require a show of hands, some jurors will refrain from raising their hands out of a reluctance to participate in voir dire. As a result, it is sometimes necessary to pursue questions with those who do not raise their hands in order to ensure that critical information is obtained from all of the jurors. Asking jurors follow-up questions, even when they do not raise their hands, lets them know that they cannot hide. This approach is particularly effective in combination with the majority response questioning approach. In this manner, lawyers encourage participation by all jurors, even those who are initially reluctant to answer.

OFFER JURORS A SECOND CHANCE TO RESPOND. Oftentimes the raising of hands in group questioning is quickly followed by the additional questioning of those jurors who raised their hands. Sometimes jurors who should have raised their hands do not respond because they are reluctant to do so or are unsure if they qualify to respond. Some jurors who do not raise their hands initially may respond after they hear the follow-up questioning of the jurors who originally raised their hands. When only a few jurors respond, use this situation as a second opportunity to ask the question. Giving jurors a second chance to participate will encourage reluctant jurors and it will also allow jurors who simply took too much time in arriving at their answer an opportunity to respond. The following example illustrates this approach.

LAWYER: How many of you have had an unsatisfactory experience with a contractor?

[One juror raises his hand.]

JUROR: When I was buying a new house a few years ago, I had a dispute with the contractor over some of the furnishings.

LAWYER: How was it eventually resolved?

JUROR: The contractor changed the furnishings to meet what was written in the contract.

LAWYER: Have any of you had an experience like Mr. Jones's [the juror]?

[*Other jurors raise their hands.*]

Giving jurors another opportunity to respond to a question is particularly important when one or a few jurors give unfavorable answers to a critical question. Failure to take full advantage of this approach could lead to an unfavorable juror not being subject to a challenge for cause or, worse yet, not being identified as a potential candidate for a peremptory challenge.

LEAD UP TO SENSITIVE QUESTIONS. It is particularly important in group questioning to begin with noncontroversial questions before proceeding to more sensitive topics. Such a progression allows jurors more time to think about their true feelings as questioning progresses, and it also fosters continued candor by jurors by keeping them in the habit of answering questions. For example, jurors with biases favoring law enforcement in an excessive force case may not reveal their biases when faced early in voir dire with the question "How many would have any reservations in awarding money damages to a plaintiff in a lawsuit brought against a police officer over an alleged excessive use of force in making an arrest?" Biased jurors are more likely to admit their biases when the final critical question is delayed until questioning first covers such topics as (a) their contacts with law enforcement, (b) their satisfaction with the experiences they have had with law enforcement personnel, (c) their beliefs about the appropriate use of force by police, and (d) their beliefs as to whether law enforcement personnel are being given the appropriate credit for the jobs that they do.

AVOID THE SOCIALLY DESIRABLE RESPONSE BIAS. As discussed in the previous chapter, the phrasing of questions can affect the degree of candor exhibited by jurors. Using phrases that give jurors a clue as to the socially desirable or "correct" answer increases the chances that jurors will respond with what they think is a socially acceptable answer, regardless of their true feelings.

Therefore, avoid such wording as "Do you have any biases . . .", "Do you understand the law that says . . .", and "Would you follow the law . . .". Group questioning only serves to increase the pressure to respond in socially acceptable ways and, as such, even greater care should be taken to minimize this potential bias.

ASK THE LAST CHANCE QUESTIONS. We considered closing questions earlier in this chapter as the last chance to uncover critical information about jurors. While such questions are important in individual questioning, they are even more important in group questioning. Given the potential for jurors to have missed opportunities to answer questions during group voir dire, either as a result of reluctance or uncertainty, asking jurors the "last chance" or closing questions is the last line of defense in group questioning.

Judge-Conducted Voir Dire

The final situation that reduces the ability to learn about jurors arises when the judge conducts the entire voir dire examination of jurors.[17] Lawyers can take several steps to maximize judge-conducted voir dire.

SUBMIT QUESTIONS IN ADVANCE. In anticipation of trial, determine how the judge normally conducts the questioning process. Armed with this knowledge, develop and submit in advance of trial a list of questions for the judge to ask. Judges often request that the parties submit voir dire questions to them. Even if unsolicited, it is important to submit these questions. Where possible, phrase questions in a manner that is consistent with the judge's pattern of questioning, provided such phrasing does not diminish the value of these questions. Judges are more likely to ask questions that are phrased in a familiar—and acceptable—manner.

PHRASE QUESTIONS IN THE DESIRED FORM. It is important to phrase the questions in the exact form in which they are to be asked. Careful attention to the

---

What to do when faced with judge-conducted voir dire:

- Request at least some attorney-conducted questioning.
- Submit questions in advance.
- Phrase questions exactly as they are to be asked.
- Support the need to ask desired questions.
- Don't unnecessarily restrict the scope of questions.
- Provide follow-up questions.
- Work with the judge to develop questions.

wording of the question ensures that the information desired is the information obtained. If necessary, explain the need to ask a question in its present form.

The questions also should be in the proper form for the voir dire situation. Judges may refuse to ask a question because it is not in the proper form. For example, the judge may exclude questions suitable for individual questioning because the jurors will be questioned in a group. Alternatively, the judge may decide to rephrase a question that is not suitable in its present form. As a result, the question may not be exactly what the lawyer desires, thus potentially reducing the value of the jurors' answers.

DEFEND YOUR QUESTIONS. It is important to be prepared to explain and argue, if necessary, the importance of asking any given question. Judges may fail to understand the need to ask a certain question or may view a question as reflecting an attempt to "try the case" during jury selection. Failure to adequately explain the need for the question can prevent judges from seeing the importance and appropriateness of the question, leading to the exclusion of otherwise useful questions. Therefore, it is necessary to demonstrate that the reason for asking particular questions (e.g., views on medical negligence, circumstantial evidence, or the use of sting operations) centers on the ability of jurors to discharge their duties and not on any attempt to seek a commitment to a particular verdict.

DO NOT UNNECESSARILY RESTRICT THE SCOPE OF THE QUESTIONS. It is important that the questions asked by the judge are not worded in a way that will exclude valuable information. For example, in many criminal cases, it is important to know whether the juror has been a victim of a crime. In some federal jurisdictions jurors are asked:

"Has any member of the panel ever been involved in a criminal matter in any court that concerned yourself, any member of your family, or a close friend either as a defendant, a witness, or a victim?"

Unfortunately, the above question restricts the jurors' frame of reference to a matter involving the courts. Many jurors are victims of crimes that either go unreported or do not ever proceed to court. These jurors may not reveal their history of being a victim of a crime in this situation. A more useful question regarding victim status would be:

"Has any member of the panel, or any member of your family, or a close friend, ever been a victim of a crime, whether the crime was reported or not?"

It is also possible to increase the likelihood that useful information would be uncovered by not restricting certain sensitive questions solely to the juror's own experience. In some situations, jurors may be reluctant to admit that they have done something that carries a social stigma. For example, a juror may be reluctant to admit to having been arrested in the past. Expanding the scope of questions concerning sensitive areas is often helpful. Asking jurors if they or any members of their family have been arrested will increase the likelihood that the relevant jurors will answer this question truthfully, particularly if they are told that any follow-up will be addressed at side bar out of the hearing of their fellow jurors.

PROVIDE APPROPRIATE FOLLOW-UP QUESTIONS. Follow-up questions are necessary to ensure that the desired information is uncovered. For example, consider the following questions from a product liability case involving flammable contact cement:

> "Have any of you or your close family members ever worked for a business or company where flammable or extremely flammable materials were used or manufactured?
> a. If so, what safety precautions did you/they take?
> b. What safety precautions did the company take?"

> "Have you or a close family member ever worked where explosion-proof fans or equipment were used?
> a. If so, do you remember whether the products used were labeled?
> b. Do you remember whether the product labels said 'DANGER' or 'WARNING'"?

Providing the follow-up questions increases the chances of obtaining useful information. In addition, providing follow-up questions encourages the judge to seek additional information given certain answers. Finally, providing follow-up questions can also serve to alert the judge to the value of follow-up questions with answers not previously addressed or with questions for which he or she has not traditionally sought follow-up information.

BE FLEXIBLE. Finally, some flexibility is necessary in developing questions. It is sometimes possible to work with the judge to develop questions that address areas of concern when he or she initially refuses to ask a certain question. Provided that the judge sees the importance of the area of inquiry, being flexible in the development of questions can yield information that would otherwise remain unknown.

NOTES

1. For other discussions of voir dire, see BALL, DAVID BALL ON DAMAGES: A PLAINTIFF'S ATTORNEY'S GUIDE FOR PERSONAL INJURY AND WRONGFUL DEATH CASES (2001); BLUE & SAGINAW, JURY SELECTION: STRATEGY AND SCIENCE (1990); Frederick, *Effective Voir Dire: From the Mouths of Jurors*, TRIAL 66–70 (Aug. 1988); FREDERICK, THE PSYCHOLOGY OF THE AMERICAN JURY (1987); BONORA, KRAUSS & ROUNDTREE, JURYWORK: SYSTEMATIC TECHNIQUES (1999); and Penrod & Linz, *Voir Dire: Uses and Abuses*, in THE IMPACT OF SOCIAL PSYCHOLOGY ON PROCEDURAL JUSTICE 135 (M. Kaplan ed., 1986).

2. See Mize, *On Better Jury Selection: Spotting Unfavorable Juror Before They Enter the Jury Room*, CT. REV., 36, 10 (1999); Mize, *Be Cautious of the Quiet Ones*, VOIR DIRE, 10, 8 (2003); and Seltzer, Ventuti & Lopes, *Juror Honesty During Voir Dire*, 19 J. CRIM. JUST. 451 (1991).

3. *See* Sue, Smith & Pedroza *Authoritarianism, Pretrial Publicity and Awareness of Bias in Simulated Jurors*, 37 PSYCHOL. REP. 1299 (1975); Moran & Cutler, *The Impact of Prejudicial Pretrial Publicity*, 21 J. APPLIED SOC. PSYCHOL. 345 (1991); and Ogloff & Vidmar, *The Impact of Pretrial Publicity on Jurors: A Study to Compare the Relative Effects of Television and Print Media in a Child Sex Abuse Case*, 18 L. & HUM. BEHAV. 507 (1994). For additional discussion of the biasing effects of pretrial publicity, *see* Bornstein, Whisenhunt, Nemeth & Dunaway, *Pretrial Publicity and Civil Cases: A Two Way Street?* L. & HUM. BEHAV. 26, 3 (2002); Robbennolt & Studebaker, *News Media Reporting on Civil Litigation and Its Influence on Civil Justice Decision Making*, L. & HUM. BEHAV., 27, 5 (2003); Studebaker & Penrod, *Pretrial Publicity: The Media, the Law and Common Sense*, 3 PSYCHOL., PUB. POL'Y & L. 428 (1997); Sue, Smith & Gilbert, *Biasing Effects of Pretrial Publicity on Judicial Decisions*, 2 J. CRIM. JUST. 163 (1974); and Vidmar, *Case Studies of Pre- and Midtrial Prejudice in Criminal and Civil Litigation*, 26 L. & HUM. BEHAV. 73 (2002). In addition, a number of studies conducted by this author and National Legal Research Group, Inc., have consistently shown that jurors' self-reports of being fair and impartial are not related to their views on whether a particular defendant is guilty. That is, jurors who (as a result of pretrial publicity) believe the defendant is guilty are statistically just as likely to say that they can be fair as those who have been unaffected by the publicity (e.g., *see* the report cited in the motion for a change of venue in *United States v. Sa'ad El-Amin*, Case No. 3:03CR55).

4. *See* Marshall & Smith, *The Effects of Demand Characteristics, Evaluation Anxiety, and Expectancy on Juror Honesty During Voir Dire*, 120 J. PSYCHOL. 205 (1986). *See generally* Chaikin & Derlega, *Self-Disclosure*, CONTEMPORARY TOPICS IN SOCIAL PSYCHOLOGY (Thibaut & Carson eds., 1976) and Suggs & Sales, *Juror Self-Disclosure in Voir Dire: A Social Science Analysis*, 56 Indiana L.J. 245 (1981).

5. *See* Jones, *Judge- Versus Attorney-Conducted Voir Dire: An Empirical Investigation of Juror Candor*, 11 L. & HUM. BEHAV., 2, 131 (1987).

6. *See* Broeder, *Voir Dire Examinations: An Empirical Study*, 38 S. CAL. L. REV. 503 (1965); Mize, *supra*, note 2; Seltzer, Ventuti & Lopes, *supra*, note 2; and Vidmar, *supra* note 3. Unfortunately, beyond general lack of candor and evaluation apprehension, there are times when jurors seek to be on the jury in order to pursue an agenda. Such an agenda-seeking juror was seen in the jury selection in *Commonwealth of Virginia v. Thomas*, where a potential juror who was qualified was eventually removed prior to being seated on the jury as a result of coworkers coming forward and advising the court that the juror told them that he knew Thomas was guilty and he was going to "fry the bastard" if he made it on the jury. Commonwealth of Virginia v. Jeffrey Allen Thomas, 263 Va. 216, 559 S.E.2d 652 (2002). This juror had assured the court that he could be fair and impartial, which the court took to be "sincere" and "honest." This incident also serves as an indication of the challenges faced in assessing the honesty of jurors based on their demeanor and verbal assurances.

7. In some situations, e.g., confronting a hostile juror, lawyers may deviate from the skills discussed here. However, absent such special circumstances, the main goal of voir dire is to have jurors open up and reveal important information to lawyers.

8. *See* FREDERICK (1987), *supra* note 1.

9. *See generally* LEARNING PROCESSES (M. Marx ed., 1969).

10. *See generally* BANDURA, PRINCIPLES OF BEHAVIOR MODIFICATION (1969).

11. For a discussion of the value of using open-ended questions (nondirective style of questioning) in uncovering grounds for challenges for cause, *see* Middendorf & Luginbuhl, *The Value of a Nondirective Voir Dire Style in Jury Selection*, CRIM. JUST. & BEHAV. 22, 2,129 (1995).

12. The questioning of favorable and unfavorable jurors is considered again in Chapter 6.

13. For a qualification of this position, *see* the discussion of the discriminatory use of peremptory challenges in Chapter 9. Consistency in questioning of all jurors is one potential consideration in evaluating whether a peremptory challenge has been exercised in a nondiscriminatory manner. It is important to note that those opinions that the unfavorable juror might express are exactly the type of information that would form an appropriate reason for exercising a peremptory challenge. Any decision to avoid questioning a potential juror in certain areas of voir dire should also consider the implications for facing the assertion that a challenge was exercised based on the juror's race, gender, or Hispanic origin.

14. *See* BONORA, KRAUSS & ROUNDTREE, *supra* note 1, for citations supporting the exploration of various topics during voir dire.

15. *See* the discussion of the implications of various voir dire procedures in Chapter 1.

16. Appendix 1 contains the motion for improvements in voir dire procedures, including a request for the court appointment of a jury consultant, submitted by the defense in *Commonwealth of Virginia v. John Allen Muhammad,* Criminal Case 54362–54365. *See* BONORA, KRAUSS & ROUNDTREE, *supra* note 1, for an excellent discussion of motions in support of individual questioning of jurors along with sample motions.

17. As discussed in Chapter 1, judge-conducted voir dire has been shown to yield less information from jurors than attorney-conducted voir dire. As such, a pretrial motion should be made requesting that lawyers be allowed to conduct some, if not most, of the voir dire questioning. It is useful to include in this motion a discussion of what areas of potential bias need to be examined and how attorney-conducted voir dire would be the best way of doing so. Even if the motion is denied, it serves to provide an opportunity to increase the sensitivity of the judge to particular problem areas in voir dire.

CHAPTER 6

Common Situations and Problems in Voir Dire

Objectives

- To explore problems and situations that arise in conducting voir dire.
- To develop skills that enable lawyers to overcome problems and capitalize on opportunities present in voir dire.

The social interaction that is voir dire combines the judge, lawyers, jurors, and circumstances of the case to produce a unique event. However, there are a number of situations and problems that arise in the questioning process. This chapter explores some of the more common of these and considers ways of taking advantage of the opportunities for conducting effective voir dire.[1]

Five situations and problems will be considered: (a) reluctant jurors, (b) difficult jurors, (c) negative spiraling, (d) good jurors, and (e) pretrial publicity.

Reluctant Jurors

As has been stressed earlier, jurors often find questioning in the voir dire process an intimidating experience. Some jurors are particularly affected by the process. They are nervous about speaking in public and reluctant to participate. They appear hesitant and reserved. Worried about the evaluations being made of them, these jurors participate in the process as little as possible. Their answers are brief. Single-word answers such as "yes" or "no" are common. Hedging an answer in the form "I guess," "I'm not sure," or "Maybe" and failing to take a position—saying "I don't know"—also are characteristic.

What should lawyers do when they encounter the reluctant juror? Should they leave this juror and proceed with the questioning of other jurors? No! Reluctant jurors cannot be ignored. Two dangers await those who do not explore the opinions and experiences of reluctant jurors. First, abandoning questioning of the reluctant juror leaves lawyers with little to no knowledge concerning this juror's opinions and biases. Just because a juror is reluctant to express his or her opinions or beliefs in open court does not mean that the juror has no unfavorable opinions. This juror can render an adverse verdict just as easily as any other juror.

Second, reluctant jurors serve as a potential model for other jurors. Remember, jurors watch to see what other jurors do or say on voir dire. Other jurors see a "bad" model when the questioning of reluctant jurors concludes without their having to provide the information requested: "See, it's not necessary to answer the questions fully. The lawyer will just go on to the next juror."

Encouraging Reluctant Jurors

What can be done to break down the barriers that the reluctant juror erects? There are several skills that lawyers can bring to bear to encourage the reluctant juror to be more forthcoming.

SHOW EMPATHY. Show empathy for what the reluctant jurors are going through. Expressing an understanding for the difficulty of the situation and an appreciation for their efforts in being open and candid will help reluctant jurors to open up:

> "I realize that this situation is unusual and one that can make people feel a little uncomfortable." *or*

> "This issue is something that we usually don't think about. The answer may be difficult to put into words and I appreciate your willingness to answer my questions." [Then proceed with the question.]

Complete the empathetic response by listening carefully to their answers and showing an interest in what they have to say.

RETURN TO THE COMFORT ZONE. It is important to not simply proceed with further questioning in the face of less informative answers from reluctant jurors. Defer important questions until these jurors are more open. Return to areas of questioning where the reluctant jurors feel more comfortable. The jurors' family life and what they do on the job often are areas where they feel more comfortable talking.

> "You mentioned that you have several children. Tell me a little about them, their ages, marital status, and occupations, if any." *or*

> "You said that you work over at [business/employer]. Can you tell me a little about what you do there?"

Let the jurors become comfortable in talking (again). When these jurors feel more comfortable, questioning can return to the more important areas with a greater chance for more open and honest answers.

USE DISCLOSURE RECIPROCITY. In situations where lawyers have not already told a little about themselves, take the opportunity to do so. These disclosures can be about the lawyers' background or similar experiences. Where appropriate, lawyers can further the disclosure process by revealing their own nervousness in this situation. With a nervous juror, such a disclosure can be particularly helpful in fostering rapport and openness. Remember, when lawyers tell about themselves, jurors are more likely to tell about themselves in return.

EMPOWER THE JUROR. Sometimes reluctant jurors (and other jurors as well) feel they are not "qualified" to answer an important opinion question or to do something that they may be required to do. They may feel unsure about what losses a child would suffer by losing his or her mother. They may feel unsure about deciding the guilt of a criminal defendant. When faced with the ultimate question, they feel uncomfortable about their ability to answer it.

Under these circumstances, it is necessary to empower reluctant jurors to answer the question. Make sure the jurors know there are no right or wrong answers. Also, help the jurors draw upon their own experiences to see that their opinions are valid or that they are "qualified" to perform their task as jurors. For example, the following approach would help empower a juror who is hesitant about rendering a verdict against the prosecution in a highly publicized criminal case.

JUROR: I am not sure I can really decide a case like this. It's a pretty difficult thing to decide.
DEFENSE LAWYER: Have you ever had to make a tough decision at work or at home—a decision that would disappoint someone?
JUROR: Yes, I guess. At work, I had to fire someone last year. You know, it was a tough decision because he had a family and all. However, it just had to be done.
DEFENSE LAWYER: I see—so you did not take the easy way out but made a tough choice. Now in this situation, could you render a decision of not guilty if the prosecution failed to

---

Tips for handling the reluctant juror:

- Be empathetic.
- Return to the comfort zone.
- Use disclosure reciprocity.
- Empower the juror.
- Reinforce the juror for opening up.

> prove beyond a reasonable doubt that Mr. Smith is guilty—knowing that the prosecutor would be disappointed?

JUROR: I think I can.

USE POSITIVE REINFORCEMENT. Finally, be sure to reinforce reluctant jurors when they open up. Provide positive verbal reinforcement such as "Thank you" and "I appreciate your telling me this" for their answers. In addition, use nonverbal reinforcers such as leaning the body forward, nodding, and smiling to help break down the barrier behind which reluctant jurors hide.

Difficult Jurors

Difficult jurors are those who do not like certain lawyers or their clients. These jurors also may be biased in favor of the opposing party. Comments from difficult jurors often reflect these biases:

"I don't think that you should make plaintiffs rich."

"This kind of case shouldn't be in court."

"Corporations shouldn't be held responsible for the actions of their employees—I would be ruined."

"I don't think I could be fair to the defendant."

What should be done when jurors make these kinds of statements? Should the lawyer argue with the juror? Should a peremptory challenge be exercised immediately, if possible? Should a request be made for a challenge for cause?

Lawyers are in a potentially awkward position when they face difficult jurors. It is important not to allow these jurors to infect the other jurors with their pro-opponent responses or have these jurors act as spokespeople for the opposition. However, by the same token, arguing with the difficult juror can inhibit other jurors from giving candid answers. Worse yet, other jurors may react negatively to the lawyer who argues or in some other way treats one of their colleagues on the jury badly—however difficult the juror may be.

What is done with the difficult juror depends on a number of factors:

- *How many peremptory challenges are available?* The more peremptory challenges available, the better able the lawyer is to remove difficult jurors by exercising peremptory challenges.
- *How willing is the judge to grant challenges for cause?* The greater latitude the judge gives for challenges for cause, the more likely it is the difficult juror can be removed in this fashion.
- *What is the distribution of opinions in the jury venire?* How bad is what this juror says compared to what the other jurors have said? Sometimes it is not possible to prevent all difficult jurors from sitting on the jury.
- *How are the other jurors reacting to what the difficult juror says?* Whether the other jurors react in a favorable, neutral, or unfavorable manner influences what should be done with this juror.

■ *When are peremptory challenges exercised in the trial jurisdiction?* Under the struck jury method the exercise of peremptory challenges occurs at the end of voir dire. In the sequential method, challenges can be exercised at some point prior to completion of questioning with all the jurors. Thus, the point at which the difficult juror can be removed is affected by when peremptory challenges can be exercised.[2]

A key to dealing with difficult jurors is anticipating these jurors. Look for early warning signs of the difficult juror. These signs are present when the juror (a) exhibits unfavorable nonverbal communication during the court's introductory remarks and/or during the initial questioning on voir dire; (b) possesses unfavorable background characteristics and/or past experiences, such as undesirable occupations or unfavorable personal experiences; (c) voices slightly unfavorable opinions during the initial stages of questioning; (d) wears certain styles of dress or brings objects into the courtroom that indicate potential identification with the opposition, such as conservative- or liberal-oriented reading material or political campaign buttons; and (e) associates or is friendly with "known" undesirable jurors. Paying attention to these early warning signs allows lawyers to anticipate difficult potential jurors and, thus, be more effective in dealing with them.

Dealing with Difficult Jurors

There are three basic options available for dealing with the difficult juror: (a) remove the juror through a peremptory challenge, (b) rehabilitate the juror, or (c) seek a challenge for cause.

EXERCISING A PEREMPTORY CHALLENGE. Once the lawyer decides to remove a difficult juror through a peremptory challenge, the question of when to do so remains. Strictly speaking, the question is moot in the struck jury method, since the exercise of all peremptory challenges occurs upon completion of the voir dire examination. In variants of the sequential method, however, timing of the use of peremptory challenges is an important issue. Assuming

---

Early warning signs of difficult jurors:

■ Unfavorable nonverbal communication during the judge's introductory remarks and/or during the initial voir dire questioning

■ Possession of unfavorable ("red flag") background characteristics and experiences

■ Initial slightly unfavorable opinions

■ Identification with the opposition as reflected in the jurors' attire or objects they bring to court

■ Association with "known" undesirable jurors

a jurisdiction that allows for the exercise of peremptory challenges prior to the examination of all jurors, should lawyers remove the difficult juror after receiving a series of unfavorable answers? No, not before considering the reactions of the other jurors to the difficult juror. Often, jurors will show a positive, negative, or neutral reaction to what the difficult juror says. The nature of this reaction determines the best timing for the use of the peremptory challenge.

Suppose that the court is very restrictive in allowing challenges for cause and, after weighing the necessary factors, the lawyer decides to excuse the difficult juror through a peremptory challenge. When the answers of the difficult juror elicit a negative reaction from the other jurors, remove the difficult juror at this time. The other jurors will understand why the difficult juror is being removed and will appreciate the lawyer's doing so. Some of the jurors may even look over at the lawyer in recognition of the fact that the lawyer has saved them from having to deal with the "bad" juror.

When other jurors do not respond negatively to the difficult juror, wait until later to remove this juror. Ask a few innocuous questions of this juror and proceed to questioning of the other jurors. Do not give the difficult juror an opportunity to expound upon his or her opinions, unless a challenge for cause is an option. At the conclusion of questioning of the jurors under consideration, exercise all appropriate peremptory challenges at one time. This strategy will draw less attention to the difficult juror.

How to deal with difficult jurors:

- Exercising a peremptory challenge
  - If other jurors react negatively to the juror, strike as soon as possible, otherwise wait.
- Rehabilitation of jurors
  - Uncover the basis for the undesirable opinion.
  - Differentiate it from the present situation.
  - Remind jurors of their duties.
  - Secure a commitment to be fair.
- Challenging for cause
  - Start inquiry slowly.
  - Reinforce jurors' candor and honesty.
  - Summarize jurors' position(s).
  - Reinforce the strength of their opinions.
  - Relate bias to the inability to discharge duty as jurors in the present case, not on inability to be fair.

REHABILITATION. In some situations it may not be possible to remove a difficult juror. The answers that some difficult jurors give do not qualify them for a challenge for cause. In addition, these answers may not be as bad as those answers given by other, even less acceptable, jurors. When left with no recourse but to accept the juror, rehabilitation becomes the goal of the interaction. Rehabilitation centers on getting difficult jurors to either change their opinions (which is difficult) or set aside their negative opinions in this case. There are several steps in rehabilitating jurors:

- *Uncover the basis for the jurors' undesirable opinions.* To develop an appropriate strategy for rehabilitation, it is necessary to know why the jurors hold their opinions.
- *Differentiate the past experience/opinion from the present circumstances.* Show jurors how the basis for their opinion does not apply in the present situation.
- *Remind jurors of their responsibilities as jurors.* Promote rehabilitation by focusing the jurors' attention on the role and duties of jurors requiring them to be fair and to base their decisions on what occurs at trial.
- *Secure a commitment to be fair.* Have jurors pledge in open court to decide the case based upon the facts and the law, not upon some personal experience.

The following example illustrates these steps:

JUROR: I don't like medical negligence suits against doctors.

Uncovering the basis for the opinion:

LAWYER: Why is that?
JUROR: Well, my doctor has always provided me with excellent medical treatment. So, I guess I kind of see things his way.

Differentiating the past opinion:

LAWYER: Well, I'm glad to hear that your doctor has treated you well. Your doctor's treatment of you aside, do you think that other doctors may make errors in treating their patients?
JUROR: Well, yes.
LAWYER: So, you see that just because your own doctor has treated you well doesn't mean that other doctors might not do something wrong?
JUROR: Yes, that's true.

Focusing on the juror's duties and securing a commitment:

LAWYER: Now, this is a very important case to both parties. Can you, and would you, pledge to Mr. Smith [the plaintiff] and the court that should you be selected as a juror you will follow your duty as a juror and base your decision on

	the facts as presented on the witness stand and not on any past experience or prior opinions you might have about doctors being sued for medical negligence?
JUROR:	I will do my best.
LAWYER:	I know you will. Do you have any reservations in your mind about being able to follow the judge's instructions and decide this case solely on the evidence given in this trial?
JUROR:	No.
LAWYER:	Thank you.

CHALLENGES FOR CAUSE. The final option is the challenge for cause. The difficult jurors have shown through their answers that there is potential for bias or an inability to discharge the duties required of jurors. Or there is the tactical decision to pursue a challenge for cause because there are too few (or no) peremptory challenges remaining to remove all difficult jurors.

Challenges for cause should not be treated lightly. A challenge for cause should be made when there exists good reason to expect that the juror will reveal the requisite bias. Keep in mind that the questioning necessary to secure a challenge for cause can make the juror uncomfortable and even make some jurors angry. Inability to remove a juror who has been antagonized by such questioning can have tragic consequences for the client.

Recognizing the potential for bias early in the voir dire is crucial. Understanding the law and the judge's past actions concerning challenges for cause will shape the approach to these challenges. The case analysis should identify potential "red flags." Remember, bias can result from positive opinions and experiences as well as from negative opinions and experiences. The following are some potential red flag areas:[3]

- *Exposure to pretrial publicity.* This includes both inadmissible evidence and opinions formed as a result of exposure to pretrial publicity and/or discussion with members of the community.
- *Relationship with parties, counsel, employees of parties or law firms, or witnesses.* These relationships include personal, social, and business relationships.
- *Exposure to the justice system.* This category includes experiences with prior jury service, contact with the criminal justice system or law enforcement personnel, or being a party in a lawsuit that has produced potential bias.
- *Biasing personal experiences.* Experiences such as being a victim of a crime or experiences (particularly negative ones) with a product, corporation, governmental entity, HMO, or physician, among others, can produce bias against a party.
- *Biasing opinions.* The jurors' views on the criminal justice system, responsibilities of litigants, appropriateness of types and elements of damage awards, lawsuits, and sexual harassment, among other issues, can reflect bias.

- *Bias against the party.* Perceptions of a party may reflect bias. Favorable or unfavorable perceptions may be general in nature (e.g., classes of defendants, pro-/anti-government, pro-/anti-corporations, pro-/anti-criminal defendants) or specific to a party (e.g., negative opinions regarding a particular corporation).
- *Inability to discharge their duties as jurors.* The inability of jurors to perform their duties includes the inability to render a verdict (e.g., unwillingness to judge others), expecting defendants to prove their innocence or lack of liability, demanding that the party with the burden of proof provide more evidence than the law requires, and the inability to perform case-specific duties (e.g., unwillingness to render punitive damages where appropriate).
- *Hardship.* Hardships involved in serving on the case, such as poor health, providing care for others, or financial difficulties, can serve as grounds for cause.

It is helpful at the beginning of voir dire to "give jurors a way out" for revealing their potentially biased opinions. Let them know they may have opinions because of past experiences that would make it best for them not to sit on the case, stressing at the same time that there is nothing wrong with this—it's not a failure on their parts. Because of their experiences, however, it would be better that they be considered for a different jury. In this way, the lawyer encourages the jurors to be candid, a feature essential for success in challenges for cause.

When pursuing a challenge for cause, start slowly. The initial answers that jurors give rarely reveal their more extreme opinions and biases. For this reason, a series of questions is often necessary to promote juror candor and uncover sufficient grounds for cause.

One of the most common mistakes made is to move for a challenge for cause prematurely. The juror gives an answer reflecting some degree of bias and a request is immediately made for a challenge for cause. In response to this request, the judge discusses with the juror his or her duty to follow the law. In this interaction with the judge, it is highly unlikely that the juror will admit that he or she will not follow the judge's instructions (even when the juror possesses a significant bias). The lawyer may subsequently question the juror further, but the chances of having the juror admit bias have been significantly reduced.

In the initial stages of developing grounds for a challenge for cause, open-ended questions are useful for uncovering potential areas of bias. As questioning progresses, both open-ended and closed-ended questions are used. As the questioning nears an end, however, closed-ended questions can bring the bias into focus.

Reinforce jurors for their candor and honesty. To be successful in a challenge for cause, the court must recognize that the juror is in some way biased. Reinforcing the juror for candor and honesty increases the likelihood that the juror will reveal these biases.

Summarize the juror's position while progressing through the questioning process. When pursuing more than one area, summarize the juror's negative opinion before proceeding to additional areas. Leading questions are helpful at this point. Use leading questions to summarize the critical, biased opinion that the juror subsequently endorses. Reinforce the strongly held nature of the critical belief or opinion. Sometimes the juror has had a personal experience that results in the juror holding a critical opinion or bias. Being a victim of a crime or being sued can lead to negative opinions of criminal defendants or plaintiffs, respectively. Use the jurors' experiences to reinforce the strength of their opinions. Have the jurors admit that having had the relevant personal experience is important to the views that they hold.

Also, the length of time that the juror has held the opinion can reinforce the strength of the opinion. When jurors have had the experience recently, highlight how such a recent occurrence would naturally make it fresh in their minds. For critical experiences that occurred a long time ago, reinforce the fact that the opinion is one the juror has held for a long time and is thus strongly held.

In addition, critical opinions of jurors can arise as a result of certain ethical or religious beliefs (e.g., not wanting to judge others). Discussing with the jurors their involvement with their religious community or commitment to religious or ethical training reinforces these opinions. Again, the focus is on reinforcing the strength with which the critical opinion is held by the juror.

The final question before making a motion for a challenge for cause should summarize the relevant points of bias and relate them to the inability of the jurors to discharge their duty. Do not focus on the jurors' willingness to be fair. In general, people do not want to admit in public, or sometimes even to themselves, that they cannot be fair. A question such as, "Would you be fair to my client?" is likely to produce the socially desirable response of "Of course I can be fair." In light of this tendency, give jurors the opportunity to show the judge how they would not follow the law and discharge their duties as jurors. For example, the jurors may expect a higher standard of proof, require a party to prove something that is not necessary, or ignore some legal principle or standard. In any of these events, the jurors are indicating that they would not follow the law.

To illustrate some of these points, consider the following exchange:

LAWYER: Do you own your own business?
JUROR: Yes, I do.
LAWYER: How long have you owned your business?
JUROR: For fifteen years.
LAWYER: How do you feel about whether a corporation should be financially responsible for the actions of its employees?
JUROR: Oh, I don't think they should. If that was the case, I'd be ruined.
LAWYER: It sounds to me like you have a strong opinion that a corporation should not be responsible for its employees' actions. Is that correct?
JUROR: Yes. That's correct.

LAWYER:	Based on this opinion, do you think that in order to find the defendant liable you would expect the plaintiff to provide more evidence than would otherwise be required?
JUROR:	I would say so. Yes.
LAWYER:	Now, it's important that you tell us how you feel, and I appreciate your being so honest. Would it be fair to say that even though the judge would instruct you differently, you would still hold the plaintiff to a higher burden of proof? That is, you would require the plaintiff to present more evidence to convince you of the defendant's liability?
JUROR:	Yes.
LAWYER:	Your honor, I would like to request a challenge for cause.

Often, the pursuit of a challenge for cause does not end here. The judge, or the opposing party, may question the juror on the matter. As a result of this questioning, the juror may retreat from the previous position. The object for the lawyer seeking the challenge for cause is to bring out the critical bias again.

Jurors must be led to restate their biased opinion. Using leading questions that incorporate the jurors' previous answers is often necessary. Encourage the jurors to reiterate their former answers. Reinforce the jurors for their previous honesty and candor. After all, their honesty in revealing their opinions is what the court desires. Also, let them know that holding such an opinion is not unusual or "bad." Communicate to jurors that while they would try their best not to let biases interfere, strong opinions are difficult to ignore.

Let us return to the difficult juror to see how such an exchange might go:

JUDGE:	Mr. Jones, now I will instruct you that if you sat on the jury, it is your duty to try this case based on the evidence from the witness stand and the law as I give it to you. Would you be able to follow my instructions and be a fair and impartial juror?
JUROR:	Yes.
JUDGE:	Counsel, you may continue your questioning.
LAWYER:	Thank you. Mr. Jones, I would like to follow up with a few questions. I appreciate your being so candid in your answers. Now, you're an owner of a small business. And running such a business is difficult. As a result of your circumstances, you said that you feel that corporations should not be responsible for the actions of their employees. Isn't that correct?
JUROR:	Yes.
LAWYER:	Would you tell me a little more about your feelings on this matter?
JUROR:	I have a number of employees and I can't be around all of them all the time to make sure that mistakes aren't made. If something serious goes wrong, I know I would be in real financial trouble.

LAWYER: I see. So you can personally identify with the defendant here?

JUROR: Yes, I can.

LAWYER: So when you say you don't believe that corporations should be responsible for their employees' actions, this comes from a strong sense of identity with the defendant?

JUROR: Yes, I would say so.

LAWYER: As you mentioned earlier, this kind of strong feeling that you have would lead you to naturally expect the plaintiff to provide you with more evidence than would otherwise be required in finding the defendant liable?

JUROR: To be honest, yes.

LAWYER: I appreciate your being honest. Now, jurors are called for a variety of cases. And you have been called for this one. Sometimes because of past experiences that we have had or strong feelings, it simply would be best for some jurors to serve on some cases and perhaps not on others. There is nothing wrong with the juror, it is just that a different case would be more suitable. You have been very candid about your opinion regarding corporate responsibility for employees' actions. Do you feel that you would have reservations about serving on this case and being able to set aside your strong feelings on this matter?

JUROR: Let me put it a different way. I just wouldn't feel right sitting here knowing that I might have to punish this company because of a mistake that an employee may have made. It strikes too close to home.

JUDGE: You realize that your business will not be affected by what happens in this case, don't you?

JUROR: Yes, I do. But I still would not feel right about holding the company responsible when it's the employee who makes the mistake.

LAWYER: Judge, I would renew my motion.

JUDGE: Mr. Smith, you may step down.

When pursuing a challenge for cause, be confident. It is important not to reveal to the other jurors any fear or uneasiness about what the difficult juror is saying. Jurors will be watching to see how the questioner responds. Signs of discomfort may diminish jurors' views of the strength of the case.

Negative Spiraling

When the pattern of answers that jurors give reflects less willingness to give open and candid answers as questioning continues, lawyers have hit a negative spiral. Negative spiraling often arises when lawyers begin to address sensitive opinion areas. It also occurs when lack of variation in the style of questioning fosters "mindlessness."[4] For example, posing an identical question to a series of jurors can produce negative spiraling. If the lawyer asks one juror (juror 1) for an opinion and then asks jurors 2, 3, 4, and 5: "How do you feel about that?," juror 5 is likely to respond with "I agree with what juror 1 said."

Jurors also pick up key phrases from the answers of other jurors, subsequently reducing what lawyers find out about their true opinions. For example, when juror 2 says, "I have no preconceived opinions on that," a light may go on in the other jurors' heads: "Hey, that sounds like the kind of answer I should give in court. I'll bet that's what the judge expects to hear." Adopting this phrase, they may answer subsequent questioning all too frequently with, "I don't have any preconceived opinions about that."

Breaking the Negative Spiral

Negative spiraling is the antithesis of what is desired on voir dire. Several steps are available to break the negative spiral: (a) treat jurors as reluctant jurors, (b) use positive modeling, (c) capitalize on breaks in the process, and (d) use untainted jurors.

TREAT JURORS AS RELUCTANT. The first step in combating a negative spiral is to identify the situation early. Treat the jurors as reluctant jurors. Use the tools for encouraging openness in reluctant jurors: show empathy, return to the comfort zone, use disclosure reciprocity, empower the jurors, and reinforce jurors for giving open answers. Breaking the negative spiral early through the use of these tools is the best strategy for achieving continued juror candor.

USE POSITIVE MODELING. Modeling is an important tool in breaking negative spirals. Find and develop one or more positive juror models in the panel for use in counteracting negative spiraling. Return to them when necessary to show other jurors how they should respond to the questions. Ask several questions to which the juror can give open and detailed answers. Then, proceed with the questioning of the other jurors. The other jurors will be more likely to give more fruitful answers.

CAPITALIZE ON BREAKS. Use recesses to help break the "code of silence" that develops in a negative spiral. When jurors are in a negative spiral and a recess is imminent, take advantage of it. Do not proceed with important questions. If possible, ask basic background questions until it is time for the recess. After the recess, inquiry into more important areas can be undertaken with a jury that is refreshed. Important questions will not have been "wasted" and the jurors will be more willing to consider them.

USE UNTAINTED JURORS. Jurors who have not been exposed to negative spiraling can be used to counteract its effects. Because these jurors are "untainted" by prior answers to questions, they are less likely to adopt the same unresponsive pattern of answers of previous jurors. Untainted jurors

---

How to break negative spirals:

- Treat jurors as reluctant.
  - — Show empathy.
  - — Return to the comfort zone.
  - — Use disclosure reciprocity.
  - — Empower jurors.
  - — Reinforce jurors for openness.
- Use positive modeling to show desired openness.
- Capitalize on breaks in the process to break the "code of silence."
- Use untainted jurors.

---

are often available when new panels of jurors are brought into the courtroom. Use them to break the spiral of uninformative answers.

An example of this approach occurred during the morning questioning of a jury panel when one of the jurors answered a question with, "I'll have to wait and see the evidence." This response spread like wildfire through the panel, leading other jurors to adopt the same pat phrase. After the lunch break, a potential juror who had missed the morning session entered the courtroom. The judge, annoyed by the juror's prior absence, placed him in an empty seat in the jury box. In an effort to break the negative spiral, the untainted juror was questioned. Under the guise of bringing the juror "up to speed" with the other jurors, all the questions were posed to him. His answers were open and honest. After that, the negative spiral was broken and the phrase "I'll have to wait and see the evidence" was not used again.

Good Jurors[5]

While a great deal of attention has been paid to handling difficult jurors, good jurors should not be ignored. Good jurors often receive minimal attention on voir dire for fear that interacting with them will alert the opponent to their presence on the panel. This concern, though valid, is often moot. Most good jurors become known to both sides through their answers in court. This is the case when jurors give extremely favorable answers to questions on voir dire. Although opposing counsel may subsequently remove them, failing to use good jurors to best advantage during voir dire eliminates an important opportunity.

Using Good Jurors During Voir Dire

Good jurors provide benefits beyond the possibility of serving on the jury. The key is to take advantage of these jurors. Several opportunities are available: (a) positive modeling, (b) education, (c) commitment, and (d) sealing.

POSITIVE MODELING. Positive models serve a valuable function in voir dire. As such, identify potential positive models (in terms of both "expressiveness" and favorability of answers) early. Develop the positive model through positive reinforcement. Once identified and developed, use positive models to help other jurors open up by having these models express themselves openly in response to your questions.

Good jurors can also counteract the effects of negative models. When jurors become less informative in their answers, as is the case of negative spirals, return to questioning the positive model as soon as possible in order to reestablish open communication with the jurors.

Use good jurors to model favorable positions or opinions. Questioning of good jurors that reveals favorable opinions can influence the opinions of other jurors. As such, modeling of favorable opinions is very useful. It is particularly useful in counteracting unfavorable comments made by other jurors.

EDUCATION. Good jurors can educate other jurors on important issues. Often good jurors have had personal experiences that make them "good." For example, having been mistaken for someone else, knowing someone who was unfairly treated by law enforcement, being in an accident and not remembering what happened, having been sexually harassed at work, or having been unjustly sued are personal experiences that make for good jurors for certain parties. Discussing these experiences with good jurors educates the remaining jurors on important issues in the case.

COMMITMENT. The benefits of having good jurors discuss their opinions and experiences are not limited to their impact on other jurors. By having good jurors express themselves in the courtroom, their commitment to their opinions increases. As commitment increases, there is a greater reluctance on the part of these jurors to go against their previously stated opinions.

An additional benefit to having good jurors state their views in the courtroom is that these jurors will become more comfortable expressing themselves. The greater willingness of good jurors to express themselves is a

---

Techniques for using good jurors effectively:

- Have good jurors act as positive models.
- Have good jurors educate other jurors on important issues or opinions.
- Prepare good jurors for deliberations by reinforcing their commitment to desired opinions.
- "Seal" good jurors so they are not easily removed via a challenge for cause.

distinct advantage should they sit on the jury. Lawyers want good jurors to be committed to their positive views and willing to express these views during deliberations.

SEALING. Before turning the jurors over to the opponent, "seal" the good jurors—that is, have them state publicly that they would be fair, thereby reducing the likelihood that the opponent will be able to remove them by a challenge for cause.

In some situations, the opponent may not be able to remove a good juror through a peremptory challenge. Perhaps the opponent is out of peremptory challenges or is more concerned with other jurors. In either event, it is important to prevent the unnecessary removal of any good jurors by a challenge for cause. The following exchange illustrates the sealing of a good juror:

LAWYER: Now, Mrs. Smith, you are a fair person, aren't you?
JUROR: I'd like to think so.
LAWYER: If you sat as a juror in this case, would you be fair to both sides?
JUROR: Yes, I would be fair to both sides.
LAWYER: When the judge instructs you as to the law in this case, would you be able to follow these instructions?
JUROR: Yes, I would.
LAWYER: Would you have any reservations about following the judge's instructions to be fair in this case?
JUROR: None whatsoever.

After going through such a series of questions, good jurors will not be an easy target for a challenge for cause.

Pretrial Publicity

Whether in large cities or rural areas, jurors' lives are touched by the media. Jurors who watch news programs and talk shows, read the print media, read the news on the Internet, and listen to the radio news and call-in programs are exposed to information that relates to many cases. The impact of this flood of information can lead to subtle and not so subtle biases that potential jurors often do not recognize.[6]

When extensive pretrial publicity occurs, it is necessary to uncover what information and opinions jurors associate with the case.[7] To uncover this information, jurors must be encouraged to talk. However, getting jurors to talk is no simple task. Jurors tend to minimize or downplay their exposure, awareness of relevant information, and opinion formation arising from pretrial publicity. Some jurors are defensive about their ability to recall information encountered in the media or through discussions with their friends and acquaintances. Other jurors may feel, as a result of questioning by the judge or the parties, that they should not have read, watched, or listened to the media coverage of events. Many jurors formed opinions at the time they were exposed to the media coverage but feel that, as jurors, they "are not supposed to have any opinions." All of these factors contribute to jurors' lack of candor about their exposure to pretrial publicity and the opinions formed as a result.

Conducting Questioning on Pretrial Publicity

Several techniques are available to enhance the ability and willingness of jurors to discuss what they remember and the opinions they have formed as a result of exposure to pretrial publicity. These techniques are: (a) refresh jurors' memories, (b) acknowledge appropriateness of exposure, (c) encourage disclosure, and (d) validate opinion formation.

REFRESH JURORS' MEMORIES. Often pretrial publicity occurs at the time of the original event and tapers off as time passes. There may be a short burst of publicity within a few days of trial. Because of the timing of pretrial publicity, refreshing the memories of jurors for what they encountered enables them to recall more readily what they have been exposed to and any opinions they may have formed.

Two approaches refresh jurors' memories in terms of content or context. Discussing the content of the pretrial publicity with jurors helps them recall what they have read or heard. In using the content approach, lawyers present brief descriptions of what appeared in the media. It may be as brief as mentioning that there were several reports in the media about the event. The content of publicity may be considered in greater detail. However, care is needed when going into detail regarding the content of the publicity. While careful probing about what the jurors have heard is necessary, it is important to avoid biasing or tainting jurors by exposing them to "new" information.

The content approach is particularly problematic when media accounts include information that is inadmissible at trial, e.g., mistaken reports that the defendant exercised his Fifth Amendment rights or that the defendant failed a polygraph test. Disclosure of this critical information taints all jurors who hear it. Under these circumstances, determining whether the juror has been exposed to the source of the inadmissible information (e.g., listened to

---

Techniques for uncovering the impact of pretrial publicity:

- Refresh the jurors' memories (via either content and/or context).
- Let jurors know it is appropriate for them to have been exposed to media coverage.
- Encourage jurors to disclose what they know.
- Let jurors know that it is natural to have formed opinions in light of their exposure.

the news broadcast at the critical time) may be sufficient to have the juror removed for cause, but not always.

The second approach refreshes the memories of jurors by addressing pretrial publicity in the context in which it occurred. The context approach has jurors recall what they were doing at the time of the pretrial publicity. Inquiry into the media-relevant habits of jurors, such as their television news viewing habits now and at the time of the publicity and what they were doing around the date of the publicity (e.g., working, on a holiday schedule, or on vacation), enables the jurors to visualize their lives at the time. The result is a greater ability to remember the pretrial publicity and any impressions and opinions they formed.

ACKNOWLEDGE APPROPRIATENESS OF EXPOSURE. It is important to stress the appropriateness of the jurors' exposure to pretrial publicity. Sometimes jurors feel that they should not have paid attention to the event. When jurors feel this way, they may try to hide the extent of their exposure. They may say that they did not see the publicity or that they paid little attention to it. Jurors are more forthcoming with what they remember if they know that being exposed to the publicity was not wrong on their part. In discussing both content and context aspects of publicity, let the jurors know that people often cannot help noticing prominent headlines in the newspaper and that keeping up with current events is a natural thing to do. After all, the jurors did not know they would be called later for jury service. Showing acceptance of the jurors' exposure to pretrial publicity will lead to their being more candid about what they remember.

ENCOURAGE DISCLOSURE. Encourage jurors to say what comes to mind when they try to recall what they have heard or seen about the event. Do not treat the recall of pretrial publicity as if jurors were taking a test. Show empathy for their having to try to recall what they may have heard or seen months or even years ago. Use phrases that prompt the jurors to respond. Phrases such as, "Do you remember anything else?" or "You mentioned that the gun was left at the scene. Do you recall anything else?" encourage jurors to tell more. However, a phrase such as, "Is that all?" serves to discourage jurors from answering by communicating the possibility that the jurors are "failing" a test.

Always reinforce jurors for disclosing what they recall. Use verbal and nonverbal reinforcement to encourage juror openness. Where possible, compliment jurors on their ability to recall information. These compliments will lead jurors to disclose any further information they recall.

VALIDATE OPINION FORMATION. Finally, jurors should be told that there is nothing wrong with forming opinions about the event as a result of their exposure to pretrial publicity. By validating people's natural tendency to form opinions based on what they encounter, jurors are more likely to reveal these opinions. The lawyer might say:

"You know, it's a part of being human to form impressions or opinions about what we read in the newspaper or watch on television.

When you were reading about this incident, what impressions did you have (or what went through your mind at the time)?" *or*

"Having seen so much in the newspapers, it's only natural to form some impression about what happened. Would you tell me a little about what impressions you had at the time?"

It is often better to start with the term "impressions" rather than "opinions." Using this term allows hesitant jurors to reveal their opinions without seeming to be judgmental. As jurors reveal more of their "impressions," lawyers can discuss them with the jurors in terms of opinions (e.g., "So, based on what you read in the newspapers, it was your opinion that . . ."). After the jurors reveal their impressions/opinions, be sure to reinforce them for their disclosures. Once the opinion is out, the decision can be made whether to pursue a challenge for cause or attempt to defuse the unfavorable opinion.

Case Example: Pretrial Publicity and the Case of Oliver North

The following is an example of questioning regarding pretrial publicity in the trial of Lieutenant Colonel Oliver North. The goal of this particular questioning was to determine whether the juror had been exposed to any of the immunized testimony that Colonel North had given before Congress. Whether the juror had formed an opinion regarding the case was not the point of this particular examination.

COURT: . . . I gather you are a salesperson, and you follow the news on television?

JUROR: Yes.

COURT: And you don't remember reading or seeing anything about this case?

JUROR: I've seen it, but I didn't read it.

COURT: You've seen it but you don't believe it?

JUROR: I said I've seen it but I didn't read it.

COURT: But you've seen something about the case?

JUROR: Yes.

COURT: On television, I take it?

JUROR: Yes.

COURT: And you say that you certainly saw something about Oliver North on television?

JUROR: Yes.

COURT: But as far as you can recall, you didn't see or read any of his testimony before the congressional committee?

JUROR: No, I didn't.

. . .

COURT: Would you tell me, just in your own words, as best you can, what you know, in your mind, feel you've heard or seen or learned about Lieutenant Colonel Oliver North,

	from the television you've seen and anything else that has come to your attention. Just in your own words, what do you remember?
JUROR:	Well, I've heard them talking about it, but really I don't know that much about politics so I really, you know, don't understand all the things that's going on.
COURT:	What do you remember?
JUROR:	Well, I was just knowing that they was saying that he was one of the witnesses for this contra thing, the trial that was going on.

[Note: The juror is resistant to telling what she "knows" and seeks to minimizes what she "knows."]

COURT:	Did anything you heard give you a bad impression about him, an unfavorable impression about him?
JUROR:	No.
COURT:	Counsel may examine, if you wish.

. . .

[Defense questioning]

COUNSEL:	Good morning, [Juror]. How are you?
JUROR:	I'm fine.
COUNSEL:	My name is Brendan Sullivan and I represent Colonel North. I'm sorry to intrude on you by asking questions, but that's the only way we know to proceed to get a fair jury. You understand that, right?
JUROR:	Yes.

. . .

COUNSEL:	Now let me ask you a couple of questions here. You were down here yesterday for the first day of jury selection, correct?
JUROR:	Yes.
COUNSEL:	And you filled out the questionnaire but didn't have a chance to come in because time just ran out, right?
JUROR:	Yes.
COUNSEL:	Okay. Now, you learned from the questionnaire that the case was about Colonel North, correct?
JUROR:	Yes.
COUNSEL:	And when you went home last night, there were stories about Colonel North and the jury selection all over the TV. Did you see any of those?
JUROR:	No, I didn't, because I went out to the store and by the time I got back the news was gone.
COUNSEL:	I see. So you didn't see any TV news programs at all last night?

JUROR:	No, I didn't.
COUNSEL:	Did you see any this morning?
JUROR:	No.
COUNSEL:	Did you take a look at the newspaper this morning at all?
JUROR:	No, I haven't seen the paper.
COUNSEL:	So you've seen no newspapers today?
JUROR:	No.
COUNSEL:	Okay. Now, you indicate that the way you get most of the news is through the TV, is that right?
JUROR:	Yes, when I watch it.
COUNSEL:	And your hours up there at Sears on [location] are what? Do you work right up until the 9:00 closing time?
JUROR:	Not every day.

. . .

COUNSEL:	I see. Now, I want to take you back a little bit to the summer before last. It is sometimes easy to remember something if you focus on what you were doing at a certain time of the year. The 4th of July, the summer before last, the summer of 1987, do you tend to do something with family, a cookout or anything around the 4th of July weekend so you will know where you were last 4th of July, two 4th of July's ago?
JUROR:	Yes, we usually have a cookout.

[Note: Defense counsel is refreshing the juror's memory via the context approach.]

COUNSEL:	You have a cookout with the family?
JUROR:	Yes.
COUNSEL:	After the 4th of July, two summers ago, in that week, for four days Colonel North testified on television all day long on all the channels. Did you happen to catch any of that at all?
JUROR:	No, because I was working.
COUNSEL:	I see. Now I know up at Sears on the basement level, as I remember, there are about 100 TV's on in that store every hour of the day. Am I right about that?
JUROR:	Yes.

[Note: Defense counsel continues with the context approach.]

COUNSEL:	And it almost makes you dizzy to go by it, as I recall. Am I right about that?
JUROR:	Yes.
COUNSEL:	What floor do you work on there?
JUROR:	I work on the basement floor. It's where I can maybe basically hear the TV's but I don't really see them.

. . .

COUNSEL: And Colonel North, during that week right after the 4th
of July, was on the TV every day. Do you remember
that?

JUROR: Yes.

COUNSEL: And after that four days of testimony, he testified two
more days the next week. They had him up there six days
altogether testifying in uniform. Do you remember the
general sight of him?

JUROR: I had seen him like passing through, but just to stop and
listen, no.

COUNSEL: Did you hear some of the words some of the time up
there?

JUROR: Not very clear.

COUNSEL: I see. Did some of the other workers talk about it, talk
about what Colonel North said on TV?

JUROR: I've heard them speaking about it, but like I'm saying I'm
really not into politics so I didn't pay it any attention.

COUNSEL: Right. Do you know whether there were some particularly
dramatic moments on the TV that people were talking
about at that time?

Well, let me ask you this: The allegations in this case, for
example, are alleging that Colonel North was shredding
documents or destroying government documents.

JUROR: I heard something like that, yes, spoken about.

[*Note: Defense counsel incorporates refreshing the juror's memory via the content
approach into his questioning.*]

COUNSEL: You would have heard something like that in that week
when the TV's were on?

JUROR: Yes.

COUNSEL: All right. And the allegations in this case refer to allegations that Colonel North lied to Congress about some
things. Do you remember anything like that on the TV, just
vaguely? I know you can't remember exactly. No one can.
I don't remember what I had for lunch.

JUROR: Uh-huh.

[*Note: Defense counsel encourages the juror to disclose information through showing empathy for the juror.*]

COUNSEL: Do you follow me there? Something generally on the TV
about that?

JUROR: Somewhat.

COUNSEL: Now, in addition, [Juror], and I appreciate your candor on
this, do you also get a chance to look at the *Washington
Post* once in a while?

[*Note: Defense counsel reinforces the juror for being candid.*]

JUROR: Sometimes, but not that much, not to really read, you know, about it.

COUNSEL: Not at work anyway? It's a busy store, isn't it?

JUROR: Yes.

COUNSEL: Always someone waiting to be helped. Do you get the *Washington Post* delivered to your home?

JUROR: Well, my husband he usually picks it up, but usually when I look at it is mostly like the Metro section. The front page, I don't really look at.

COUNSEL: Now, that particular two weeks still back there during the time when all the TV's were on at Sears, virtually the top half of the papers were about Colonel North. There were headlines about an inch thick describing his testimony up there on the Hill. Would it be fair to say that you probably glanced at those headlines?

JUROR: Just enough to know that it was, you know, speaking about him.

. . .

COUNSEL: Thank you very much for letting me ask these questions.

COURT: I was not clear about two of your answers from Mr. Sullivan. You say you heard something about lying to Congress and something about destroying documents, right?

JUROR: Yes. I heard it but I wasn't—like I wasn't clear on it, you know. I didn't really sit down and just listen to it.

COURT: What I'm trying to find out is, did you hear it over TV in relation to Colonel North's testimony or did you hear it because somebody spoke to you about it or told you about it?

JUROR: It was just like if I—when I go to lunch, sometimes they have the TV on, where I go in to get a drink or something like that, and just be up there talking, but just to sit down and watch it or listen to it, I didn't do that.

COURT: Well, what do you mean then you heard about it if you didn't listen to it? You must have heard something. What did you hear, the best you can recall it?

JUROR: Well, like I said, they were talking about, you know, him shredding the papers, the documents, and things that he did while he was in the service.

[*Note: Compare this more detailed response to the responses given to the initial questioning by the judge.*]

COURT: Thank you very much.

[Prosecution]

COUNSEL: Could I ask one question of [Juror]?

COURT: Yes, certainly.

COUNSEL: [Juror], when you heard people talking about shredding documents, was Colonel North on TV or was this a news show that you were watching?

JUROR: It was just like, you know, the news, when they have the news on, like the 6:00 news or the 11:00 news.

COUNSEL: I've committed the crime that lawyers do all the time. I said one question. I have one more.
Were the people talking about what the charges were against Colonel North? Is that what you heard when you heard something about lying or shredding?

JUROR: It was something like that. I'm not really clear on it.

COUNSEL: It wasn't Colonel North talking about any of those things?

JUROR: No.

[*Note: The prosecutor has the juror attribute her exposure to general news programs, not the congressional hearings.*]

COUNSEL: That's all I have. Thank you, Your Honor.

COURT: Mr. Keker?

COUNSEL: No objection, Your Honor. We believe there is no problem.

. . .

[Questioning by defense counsel]

COUNSEL: Your Honor, if I could just clarify a little bit. I don't know if you've had the benefit of being in that Sears store.

COURT: I have. I apparently haven't shopped it as much as you, but I have been there.

COUNSEL: Well, in this particular store I bet there are 100 TV's going.

COURT: I know. Very confusing.

COUNSEL: They are across that wall. And it is very confusing. . . . The problem was this: the TV was on there every day for six days, and it is virtually impossible—

COURT: Along with the chatter of different programs. They are not all on the same program, are they?

COUNSEL: Sometimes they are.

COURT: Sometimes they are all on the same program, usually, probably the same program.

COUNSEL: Your Honor, every network that week was Colonel North.

COURT: Well, you have been presenting a picture as though you couldn't pick up the front page and find any story other than North or there wasn't room enough for anything other than a headline.

COUNSEL: No.

COURT: Or anything but the headline. It wasn't quite that bad, was it?

COUNSEL: I thought it was.

COURT: This lady said she didn't look at the front page. Very sensible lady. Do you object to this juror?

Counsel:	Yes, Your Honor.
Court:	On what grounds?
Counsel:	On the grounds that she saw Colonel North actually testifying, and I believe the record, notwithstanding the last questions, is that she saw and heard him testifying about the shredding. I don't think we could ever be certain that's not the case. I believe that to be the record.
Court:	I believe that, too. She is excused.

Notes

1. *See* also Frederick, *Effective Voir Dire: From the Mouths of Jurors,* TRIAL 66–70 (Aug. 1988).

2. *See* Chapters 3 and 9 for discussions of the struck versus sequential method of exercising peremptory challenges.

3. For a good discussion of challenges for cause, *see* BONORA, KRAUSS & ROUNDTREE, JURYWORK: SYSTEMATIC TECHNIQUES (1999).

4. *See* Chapters 4 and 5 for discussions of problems associated with phrasing questions and asking questions on voir dire.

5. The phrase "good jurors" refers to those jurors who, for whatever reason, are favorable to the party in the case. Obviously, good jurors are in the eye of the beholder.

6. For a discussion of the impact of pretrial publicity, *see* Bornstein, Whisenhunt, Nemeth & Dunaway, *Pretrial Publicity and Civil Cases: A Two Way Street?* L. & HUM. BEHAV. 26, 3 (2002); FREDERICK, THE PSYCHOLOGY OF THE AMERICAN JURY (1987); Moran & Cutler, *The Impact of Prejudicial Pretrial Publicity,* 21 J. APPLIED SOC. PSYCHOL. 345 (1991); Ogloff & Vidmar, *The Impact of Pretrial Publicity on Jurors: A Study to Compare the Relative Effects of Television and Print Media in a Child Sex Abuse Case,* 18 L. & HUM. BEHAV 507 (1994); Robbennolt & Studebaker, *News Media Reporting on Civil Litigation and Its Influence on Civil Justice Decision Making,* L. & HUM. BEHAV. 27, 5 (2003); Studebaker & Penrod, *Pretrial Publicity: The Media, the Law and Common Sense,* 3 PSYCHOL., PUB. POL'Y & L. 428 (1997); Sue, Smith & Gilbert, *Biasing Effects of Pretrial Publicity on Judicial Decisions,* 2 J. CRIM. JUST. 163 (1974); Sue, Smith & Pedroza *Authoritarianism, Pretrial Publicity and Awareness of Bias in Simulated Jurors,* 37 PSYCHOL. REP. 1299 (1975); and Vidmar, *Case Studies of Pre- and Midtrial Prejudice in Criminal and Civil Litigation,* 26 L. & HUM. BEHAV. 73 (2002). *See* also the brief discussions of pretrial publicity in Chapters 4 and 5.

7. In questioning jurors regarding pretrial publicity, it is important to develop methods for questioning that will not "taint" the other jurors. Appropriate methods are questioning jurors exposed to pretrial publicity on an individual basis in the judge's chambers or in open court, with all other jurors sequestered. However, the practice of questioning all "exposed" jurors at one time (with unexposed jurors absent) risks tainting exposed but otherwise acceptable jurors.

CHAPTER 7

Juror Questionnaires

Objectives

- To explore the basics of juror questionnaires and their construction.
- To understand the benefits of using juror questionnaires.

A major challenge faced during the jury selection process is to gather useful information about potential jurors so that lawyers may intelligently exercise peremptory challenges and uncover grounds for challenges for cause. The problem, however, is that voir dire as conducted in federal courts and many state courts impedes the discovery of important information about jurors. Particularly in federal courts, voir dire is limited in (a) what questions can be asked; (b) who asks the questions; (c) how much time is allotted for the questioning process; and (d) the opportunity for individual questioning of jurors. Using juror questionnaires can lessen problems that arise under the restrictive voir dire conditions present in many courts.

One tool for lessening the problems caused by restrictive voir dire conditions is the supplemental juror questionnaire. This questionnaire is designed to supplement information available through questioning on voir dire. Since the early 1970s, supplemental juror questionnaires have been used sporadically but with increasing frequency in both federal and state courts.[1] Many of the notable trials in the past few years have employed supplemental juror questionnaires. Examples of these trials include *In re Exxon Valdez Litigation, International Paper v. Affiliated FM Insurance Co., Mercado v. Warner-Lambert Co., Royal Palm Resort v. Mitsui Construction Co. Ltd., State of Connecticut v. Michael Skakel, United States v. Oliver North, State of California v. O.J. Simpson, United States v. Timothy McVeigh,* and *United States v. Terry Nichols.*

141

What Are Supplemental Juror Questionnaires?

Supplemental juror questionnaires are designed to elicit a variety of information from jurors. Depending on their scope, these questionnaires address the jurors' background characteristics, experiences, activities, and opinions and evaluations. For example, these questionnaires can explore the following areas:

- *Background characteristics:*
  Occupation/employment
  Education
  Marital status
  Income
- *Experiences:*
  Victimization
  Involvement in lawsuits
  Exposure to/awareness of pretrial publicity
- *Activities:*
  Hobbies and spare-time activities
  Organizational membership
- *Opinions and evaluations:*
  General views concerning the presumption of guilt/innocence
  Trust in law enforcement
  Views on causes of crime
  Views on providing monetary compensation for noneconomic damages
  Views concerning punitive damages
  Favorable/unfavorable impressions of a party or parties
  Beliefs in the guilt of a criminal defendant or liability of a civil defendant

Supplemental juror questionnaires can vary considerably in the number of questions asked and the subsequent length of the questionnaire. For example, Table 1 shows the lengths of supplemental juror questionnaires used in various criminal and civil trials.

The jurors' answers to the questions posed in the questionnaire serve as a starting point for the examination of jurors, either by the judge, the lawyers, or both. Follow-up questions may be allowed by the court to clarify answers or to pursue important areas of concern revealed by the jurors' answers. Subsequent voir dire questioning proceeds in the customary manner.

How to Use Supplemental Juror Questionnaires

There are two basic methods for employing supplemental juror questionnaires.[2] These methods differ based on whether jurors complete the questionnaires off-site before trial (off-site method) or at trial (on-site method).

OFF-SITE METHOD. One method for obtaining information requested on supplemental juror questionnaires is to mail copies of the questionnaires to

TABLE I
LENGTHS OF SUPPLEMENTAL JUROR
QUESTIONNAIRES USED IN VARIOUS CRIMINAL AND CIVIL TRIALS

	Number of Questions Asked	Pages
Type of Case		
Criminal:		
U.S. v. Oliver North	36	13
Michigan v. Jack Kevorkian	60	12
State of Connecticut v. Michael Skakel	69	16
U.S. v. Marion Barry	69	25
U.S. v. Timothy James McVeigh	158	40
U.S. v. Stacey Koon et. al.	148	52
State of California v. O.J. Simpson	303*	87
Civil:		
Mercado v. Warner-Lambert Co.	37	1
International Paper v. Affiliated FM Insurance Co.	53	11
John Doe v. Kohn et. al.	59	13
In re Exxon Valdez Litigation	82	21
Mildred Valentine v.		
Dow Corning Corporation, et. al.	96	24
Royal Palm Resort v. Mitsui Construction Co. Ltd.	91	31

* Due to misnumbering of questions, the total number of questions was 303 instead of the numbering of 294 that appears on the questionnaire.

potential jurors before the trial.[3] The court or jury administrator sends the questionnaire to potential jurors with a cover letter explaining *how* jurors are to complete and return the questionnaires and *when* the questionnaires must be returned. The questionnaires are accompanied by postage-paid, self-addressed mailers for their return. The following cover letter illustrates this approach.[4]

Questionnaires are usually mailed to jurors three to six weeks before the trial begins. Jurors return the completed questionnaires by mail to the court or, in some jurisdictions, to a printing company where the questionnaires are photocopied.

It is important to secure the completed questionnaires from as many potential jurors as possible in order to maximize the benefits obtained from this approach. Therefore, follow-up contact with potential jurors is sometimes necessary. However, follow-up procedures are inconsistently applied across jurisdictions. In some jurisdictions, jurors who fail to return their questionnaires by a specific date are contacted by the court or jury administrator in an effort to secure the completed questionnaires. In other jurisdictions, no follow up is attempted. Often in these latter jurisdictions, it is

UNITED STATES DISTRICT COURT
NORTHERN DISTRICT OF GEORGIA
2211 UNITED STATES COURTHOUSE
75 SPRING STREET, SW
ATLANTA, GEORGIA 30303-3361

LUTHER D. THOMAS   JURY & NATURALIZATION SECTION
CLERK OF COURT   404-331-6670
                                                    August 18, 1998

Dear Juror:
    You have been selected as a prospective juror in the U.S. District
Court at Atlanta, Georgia. To assist the Court in impaneling a jury on
August 31, 1998, you are requested to answer the questions on the
enclosed juror questionnaire.
    The purpose of this questionnaire is to provide information in writ-
ing to help all parties select a fair and impartial jury. Your responses to
these questions will save a great deal time for you, the judge, and the
lawyers.
    You must sign the questionnaire, and your answers are given to the
Court under the oath that precedes your signature. Do not consult with
anyone in preparing your answers. Your answers are given under oath,
so answer as completely, candidly, and accurately as possible. The information that you give in response to this questionnaire will be used by the
Court and the lawyers to select a jury.

**PLEASE COMPLETE THE QUESTIONNAIRE WITH A <u>BLACK</u>
<u>PEN</u>. DO NOT WRITE ON THE BACK OF ANY PAGE. RETURN THE
QUESTIONNAIRE BY MAILING IT IN THE ENCLOSED POSTAGE
PAID ENVELOPE FOR RECEIPT NO LATER THAN [SPECIFY DATE].**

    Should you have any further questions, do not hesitate to contact the
Jury Office at (404)331-6670.

                                                    Sincerely,

                                                    Lucy S. Moses
                                                    Jury Administrator

hoped that jurors who fail to return their questionnaires will bring the completed questionnaires with them when they come to court.
    Copies of the completed questionnaires are made available to the parties
(and the judge) at some designated date prior to trial. As we shall see later
in this chapter, this time period may range from the day of trial to one week
or more before trial.

ON-SITE METHOD. The second method of obtaining information on supplemental juror questionnaires takes place when jurors report for trial. Jurors complete the questionnaires upon their arrival for jury service, either in the jury lounge or some other appropriate setting. The completed questionnaires are then photocopied by the court for use by the parties and the judge.

The time available for attorneys to examine jurors' answers varies from a few hours to several days. For example, in the *Exxon Valdez* civil case, jurors completed the questionnaires on a Monday and returned two days later for voir dire questioning. In the *O.J. Simpson* murder trial, jurors completed the questionnaire and then returned a week later for the beginning of voir dire. In the trials of *Timothy McVeigh* and *Terry Nichols*, potential jurors reported to a rented auditorium where they completed the questionnaires and were excused for seven to ten days while the 480 to 500 questionnaires were reproduced and processed. The jurors were then contacted forty-eight hours prior to the day they were to arrive at court. However, in other cases, parties have had only a few hours at most to review the questionnaires before beginning voir dire questioning.

DECIDING WHICH METHOD TO USE. There are four major considerations in choosing either method for administering supplemental juror questionnaires or, in jurisdictions where procedures are already in place, seeking changes in the methods employed. These considerations are: (a) allowing sufficient time for review; (b) obtaining as many completed questionnaires as possible; (c) accommodating the length of the questionnaire; and (d) minimizing outside influences.

Allow sufficient time for review. It is important that the parties are allowed sufficient time to review the jurors' responses to the questionnaires. For the average-length questionnaire administered to 15 or more potential jurors, allowing only a few hours of review time will be inadequate for effective consideration of the jurors' answers. At least an overnight review of this information is necessary whether using the off-site or on-site method. When the jury venire contains large numbers of potential jurors or when there are a large number of questions contained in the supplemental juror questionnaire, additional time will be necessary.

Obtain as many completed questionnaires as possible. Unlike with the on-site method, a major concern with the off-site method is ensuring that all jurors complete the questionnaires and return them by the designated time. Maximizing the return rate for the questionnaires requires (a) specific instructions about when the completed questionnaires are due; (b) a self-addressed, postage-paid, return mailer; and (c) a follow-up strategy for dealing with jurors who fail to meet the deadline.

Ideally, the date for return of the completed questionnaires should be one to two weeks before trial (or the date when the parties will have access to the completed questionnaires). Asking the jurors to return the completed questionnaires within a short specified time upon receipt encourages them to not delay in completing (and possibly forgetting to complete or send) the questionnaire.

Sending the questionnaires out several weeks before trial gives the court sufficient time to contact those jurors who do not meet the return deadline and also allows extra time for them to subsequently return their completed questionnaires. If a follow-up procedure is not used, it will be necessary for the court to have those jurors who arrive at trial without having completed the questionnaire take the time to complete it on-site. Additional time also will have to be scheduled for the parties to receive copies of the newly completed questionnaires and review them.

Accommodate the length of the questionnaire. Supplemental juror questionnaires that range from two to twenty pages in length can be accommodated by both the off-site and on-site methods fairly easily. In the case of the off-site method, double-sided copying of the questionnaire is helpful in reducing the number of pages (and postage costs). However, the advantages of double-sided copying are often outweighed by logistical issues, i.e., jurors are more likely to inadvertently skip questions on the back sides of pages; duplication problems can arise; and the information contained on double-sided questionnaires is more difficult for lawyers to manage during questioning. Relatively lengthy questionnaires often are better suited for the on-site method. Lengthy questionnaires may make the overall process of completing and returning questionnaires by mail unwieldy. Of greater concern is the probable increase in nonreturn rates by jurors who are asked to complete a long questionnaire. A twenty- to eighty-page questionnaire can be daunting. As such, the on-site method has the advantage of providing a structured time frame for completion.

Minimize outside influences. A problem that is rarely addressed is the issue of jurors receiving assistance (or interference) in completing their questionnaires. Any interaction or assistance provided by outside individuals carries the potential for decreasing the honesty and candor of potential jurors' answers. Obviously outside influence is more likely with the off-site method, where the court's ability to control the setting and monitor potential jurors is absent. While no data exist on the frequency of interference with the off-site method, it is a potential problem nonetheless. When using the off-site method, strong cautionary instructions should accompany the questionnaire in order to minimize the occurrence of any outside influence, particularly in controversial cases where the pressures for such interference are likely to be greatest. In such cases, it may even be necessary to use the on-site method to minimize any potential for outside influence.

REQUESTING THE USE OF SUPPLEMENTAL JUROR QUESTIONNAIRES. Particularly for supplemental juror questionnaires initiated by the lawyer, it is sometimes necessary to submit a motion to the court requesting their use. If the motion is not simply a formality, it will be important to set out: (a) why a supplemental juror questionnaire is necessary in the case; (b) the possible benefits secured through the use of a supplemental juror questionnaire; (c) a proposed procedure for using supplemental juror questionnaires, if one is not in place; and (d) recommended changes in the present procedure, if necessary. Care should be taken to anticipate potential problems and make concrete suggestions on how they can be resolved.[5]

WHY USE SUPPLEMENTAL JUROR QUESTIONNAIRES? There are a number of potential benefits to using supplemental juror questionnaires, including (a) increased juror disclosure; (b) development of more effective follow-up questions; (c) ability to pre-screen jurors; (d) minimizing infection of the panel; (e) availability of greater total information; and (f) promotion of a faster jury selection.

Increased disclosure. The use of written questionnaires provides jurors with a greater sense of privacy and comfort than answering questions in open court, in front of their fellow jurors and the press. As a result, jurors are more likely to be more candid in their answers to questions in supplemental juror questionnaires than to questions posed in open court, particularly when faced with group questioning. This factor is important when considering potentially sensitive topics, such as personal experiences with alcoholism, drug abuse, mental illness, and prior sexual assault.

Increased disclosure through supplemental juror questionnaires comes at a cost. When jurors answer questions on these questionnaires, lawyers cannot observe any associated verbal and nonverbal behavior. Sometimes this trade-off is fairly negligible. Other times it can deprive lawyers of significant information. Consequently, supplemental juror questionnaires should not be considered a substitute for in-court questioning and diligent in-court follow-up of important issues.

More effective follow-up questions. Supplemental juror questionnaires can play an important role in uncovering valuable information that should be pursued during voir dire. Candid answers contained in these questionnaires typically reveal information that otherwise might not be shared in the course of voir dire questioning. For example, on the questionnaires, jurors may

---

Potential benefits of using juror questionnaires

- Increases disclosure by jurors
- Promotes development of more effective follow-up questions
- Allows for pre-screening of jurors
- Minimizes potential infection of the panel
- Provides greater total information on jurors
- Promotes a faster jury selection

admit to having been arrested in the past or having been a victim of sexual assault. However, many jurors do not provide the same information if asked on voir dire, thereby precluding the follow-up of potentially critical information.

Promoting effective follow-up questions is not restricted to the domain of sensitive topics. Even with more innocuous information, e.g., jurors' familiarity with products at issue in the litigation, the answers jurors give can serve as an important starting point for in-depth questioning.

Pre-screening of jurors. Supplemental juror questionnaires can be used as a tool to eliminate potential jurors from further consideration in the jury selection process. The court may decide *a priori* that certain answers by jurors reflect bias, conflict of interest, or taint, which would disqualify them from jury service. When jurors give these answers, the court simply removes them from further consideration. Thus, valuable time is not wasted questioning a potential juror who will not be qualified to serve.

This pre-screening capability of supplemental juror questionnaires was used by the trial judge during jury selection in *United States v. Oliver North.* In this case, jurors who had been exposed to Oliver North's immunized testimony before Congress could not serve. Three questions (Questions 30, 31, and 32, shown below) were developed to elicit information concerning the possible exposure of jurors to the immunized testimony:

30. Did you see any part of Lt. Col. North's testimony before any congressional committee over television or otherwise?

Yes _____   No _____

31. Did you read any part of any of his testimony before a congressional committee in any newspaper, magazine or book?

Yes _____   No _____

32. Did you listen over radio or otherwise to any part of any of his testimony before a congressional committee?

Yes _____   No _____

Those potential jurors who answered affirmatively to any of the above questions were removed from the jury pool. This procedure saved a considerable amount of time by eliminating many potential jurors prior to voir dire examination. For example, only 38 percent of the first 40 potential jurors who completed the questionnaire passed these screening questions. Thus, time was not wasted examining potential jurors who eventually would have to be removed for cause.

Pre-screening can be accomplished through other criteria as well. For example, employees of one of the parties may be eligible for automatic removal. Expression of bias, provided it meets the standards for a challenge for cause, is another criterion. As long as the criteria are decided upon beforehand, supplemental juror questionnaires have significant potential for streamlining the jury selection process.

Minimal infection of the panel. Whenever questioning of potential jurors occurs in the presence of other jurors, there is the potential for the answers given to infect or taint the remaining jurors present. For example, in response to questioning regarding pretrial publicity, a potential juror may answer, "I read that the defendant confessed to the crime during police questioning." The disclosure of such a fact (if this confession was inadmissible) could infect and prejudice other jurors who heard this remark. By including questions regarding pretrial publicity in the supplemental juror questionnaire, the parties and the court are alerted to possible problems. Subsequent individual questioning of potentially tainted jurors out of the presence of the other potential jurors may be in order.

A similar situation could arise in products liability cases should a potential juror reveals that his or her employer stopped using the product at issue because it was "defective." This type of statement made in open court could infect other jurors. The same information given on a supplemental juror questionnaire would infect no one and would alert the court to the possible need for private questioning of that individual.

Greater total information. Supplemental juror questionnaires provide a greater range of information to the parties at the conclusion of voir dire questioning. These questionnaires add to and enhance the information the parties can uncover during voir dire.

Faster jury selection. A final benefit of supplemental juror questionnaires is the potential for conducting voir dire more quickly. Supplemental juror questionnaires can reduce the need for repetitive questioning of jurors.[6] The judge and/or the lawyers do not need to pursue with each individual juror or panel of jurors the questions that appear on the questionnaire. As a result, valuable court time is saved and juror boredom is reduced. Questions that address the juror's educational background, work history, occupation, prior victimization, and spouse's occupation can be efficiently covered in the questionnaire, with the voir dire reserved for any necessary follow up.

Supplemental Juror Questionnaire Checklist

The following checklist illustrates the kinds of procedural information of interest when considering the use of a supplemental juror questionnaire.

SUPPLEMENTAL JUROR QUESTIONNAIRE PROCEDURE CHECKLIST

		TOPICS
Yes	*No*	
		Initial needs:
[ ]	[ ]	Has the jurisdiction used a supplemental juror questionnaire before?
[ ]	[ ]	If questionnaires have been used, are they used routinely?
[ ]	[ ]	If questionnaires are used routinely, does the court use a standard questionnaire?

Yes	No	
[ ]	[ ]	If a standard questionnaire is used, will the court allow changes to be made?
[ ]	[ ]	Is a motion required when seeking to use a supplemental juror questionnaire?
		By when does the motion need to be filed?
		_____
[ ]	[ ]	Does a copy of the desired questionnaire need to accompany the motion?
		Which method for completing the questionnaires will be used?
		[ ] Off-site method
		[ ] On-site method
[ ]	[ ]	Is it desirable to request that a different method be used contrary to the method presently in use?

When using the off-site method:

How far in advance of the trial/jury selection will the questionnaires be mailed to potential jurors?

  [ ]   6 weeks or more
  [ ]   5 weeks
  [ ]   4 weeks
  [ ]   3 weeks or less

How far in advance of the trial/jury selection will potential jurors be instructed to return the completed questionnaires?

_____

When will the parties be allowed to see the completed questionnaires?

_____

Yes	No	
[ ]	[ ]	Is there a procedure in place for the follow-up of potential jurors who fail to return questionnaires?
[ ]	[ ]	Are procedures in place for the efficient copying and distribution of the completed questionnaires?
[ ]	[ ]	Will there be sufficient time for review of the completed questionnaires prior to questioning of the potential jurors?
[ ]	[ ]	Is there a satisfactory procedure in place for processing completed questionnaires returned on the day of trial?
[ ]	[ ]	Is there a satisfactory procedure in place for having potential jurors complete questionnaires when they report for trial/jury selection, if necessary?
[ ]	[ ]	Are changes in the procedures needed to promote more effective use of the questionnaires?

When using the on-site method:

Yes	No	
[ ]	[ ]	Will all potential jurors be completing the questionnaire at the same time?
[ ]	[ ]	Is there an appropriate location/setting for all potential jurors to complete the questionnaire?
[ ]	[ ]	Are procedures in place for the efficient copying and distribution of the completed questionnaires?

[ ]   [ ]   Will there be sufficient time for review of the completed question-
                       naires prior to questioning of the potential jurors?

[ ]   [ ]   Are changes in procedures needed to promote more effective use of
                       the questionnaires?

The answers to the above questions should serve as a sound basis for securing the best possible logistics for the use of supplemental juror questionnaires. The difficult part then becomes the creation of the questionnaire itself.

Format of Juror Questionnaires

Juror questionnaires have several components: (a) introduction; (b) background information; (c) knowledge of witnesses, lawyers, and parties; (d) awareness of the case; (e) case-relevant opinions; and (f) oath or affirmation. While treated separately below, in practice these components often overlap.

The questionnaires from several trials will illustrate various points concerning juror questionnaires. Questionnaires from two prominent criminal trials will be featured, the Oklahoma City bombing trial of Timothy McVeigh and the Iran-Contra trial of former Lieutenant Colonel Oliver North. The questionnaire used in the civil trial that arose out of the Exxon Valdez oil spill will also be featured.[7]

Introduction

The introductory section of the questionnaire informs the jurors as to the purpose of the questionnaire, how the questionnaire is to be completed, and other logistical and procedural information. This section contains many of the following elements. First, jurors are sworn to give truthful answers

---

The basic elements of juror questionnaires:

- Introduction
- Background information
  - General background characteristics
  - General experiences
  - Case-related experiences
- Knowledge of witnesses, lawyers, and parties
- Awareness of the case
- Opinions and evaluations
  - General opinions
  - Case-specific opinions
  - Opinions/evaluations of parties and/or other entities
- Signature/oath affirming truthful answers

(which is followed up with the oath and juror's signature at the conclusion of the questionnaire). Second, jurors are given a brief explanation of the case or sometimes simply its name. Third, jurors are told that the purpose of the questionnaire is to expedite the jury selection process and facilitate the selection of fair and impartial jurors. Fourth, jurors are told what will happen after they complete the questionnaire and what to do if any juror wants to discuss certain questions and follow-up questions in private. Fifth, jurors are told how to complete the questionnaire. Sixth, jurors are asked not to discuss the questions or their answers with anyone. Finally, general instructions may be given to jurors concerning several issues, such as following the case in the media, not discussing the case or their answers to the questions on the juror questionnaire with anyone, and not letting anyone discuss the case in their presence.

The following introduction is from the juror questionnaire used in the Oklahoma City bombing trial of Timothy McVeigh, and it covers most of the points discussed above:

TO THE PROSPECTIVE JUROR:

The information which you give in your answers to this questionnaire will be used only by the court and the parties to select a qualified jury. After a jury has been selected, all copies of your response to this questionnaire will be returned to the Clerk of the Court and kept in confidence, under seal, not accessible to the public or the media. The attorneys are under orders to maintain the confidentiality of any information they learn in the course of reviewing this questionnaire.

Please answer each question as completely and accurately as you can. Your complete written answers will save a great deal of time for the Court, the parties and you. <u>There are no right or wrong answers to the questions</u>. In order to ensure that your answers are not influenced by the opinions of others, <u>you should fill out the questionnaire by yourself without consulting or talking with any other person</u>.

You are expected to sign your questionnaire, and your answers will have the effect of a statement given under oath to the court. What is needed is your very best, honest effort to answer the questions contained in this booklet.

If you cannot answer a question because you do not understand it, write "Do not understand" in the space after the question. If you cannot answer a question because you do not know the answer, write "Do not know" in the space after the question. If you need extra space to answer any question, please use the extra blank sheets of paper included at the end of the questionnaire. Be sure to indicate on the blank page the number of the question you are answering.

Please write or print legibly. If your answers are illegible, you may be required to re-copy your answers.

After you leave today, you may not discuss any of the questions or your answers with anyone else, including members of your immediate family. If anyone approaches you and attempts to learn about any aspect of the questionnaire, you may not answer their inquiries. If they persist, you should report this to the Court.

The sole purpose of this questionnaire is to encourage your full expression and honesty, so that all parties will have a meaningful opportunity to select a fair and impartial jury to try the issues in this case. Thank you for your full cooperation. It is of vital importance to the Court.

In comparison to the *McVeigh* questionnaire, the introduction from the *North* juror questionnaire was very brief:

You have been sworn to give true and complete answers to all questions. The information sought by this questionnaire is requested to expedite the jury selection process in this case and will be of assistance to the Court and counsel.

Please complete the questionnaire by marking the appropriate answers or by furnishing your answers or details in the spaces provided. You are not to talk with anyone else about any question or answer when completing your responses. Your answers are to be your answers, and your answers alone.

The introduction from the *Exxon* questionnaire was also brief, but it took a "bullet" approach to its instructions:

This questionnaire is designed to assist the court and the parties in the jury selection process. It is a private court document that will not be used for any other purpose. The information will not be disclosed to any unauthorized person.

INSTRUCTIONS

- Answer each question.
- If you do not understand the question, write the words "Do Not Understand."
- If you do not know the answer, write the words "Don't Know."
- Do not discuss the questions or your answers with anyone else, including other jurors.
- If anyone tries to discuss the questionnaire or the case with you, please notify the staff.
- The staff are not permitted to answer your questions about the questionnaire.
- There are no right or wrong answers. We are simply seeking information to assist the court with the jury selection process.
- Write only on the front side of the pages.

Background Information

The major goal of the juror questionnaire is to provide background information on potential jurors in a uniform manner. This background information sheds light on two important questions: Who are the potential jurors? Have the jurors had any experiences that might influence how they would view the case? This information addresses three areas: the jurors' general background characteristics, general experiences, and case-relevant experiences.

The first questions on the questionnaire gather much of this background information. The format of the questions is usually a combination of closed-ended questions (questions seeking a "yes," "no," or other set of explicit or implicit response categories) and open-ended questions (questions seeking narrative or other unguided, freely formulated answers).

GENERAL BACKGROUND CHARACTERISTICS. The initial questions on the questionnaire address basic demographic and socioeconomic characteristics of potential jurors. Relevant information would likely include:

- Name
- Location of residence
- Age/date of birth
- Employment status
- Occupation
  — Job title
  — Nature of work
  — Supervisory experience
- Educational background
  — Grade level completed
  — Field(s) of study
  — Degrees received
- Residence ownership status
- Marital status
- Spouse's employment status
- Spouse's occupation
- Names, ages, occupations of any children
- Political preference or leanings
- Membership in organizations
- Bumper stickers

GENERAL EXPERIENCES. Questions also address important general experiences that jurors may have had. Experiences such as being a victim of a crime or prior involvement as a party to a lawsuit can influence the general reactions jurors have to a specific case. This influence appears in terms of both their decision-making and their actions during deliberations. Examples of potentially important general experiences include:

- Military service
  — Branch
  — Rank
  — Type of discharge
  — Participation in military police or court-martials
- Prior crime victimization
- Contact with those falsely accused of crimes/wrongdoing

- Involvement in lawsuits
  — Claim for personal injury
  — Prior experience as a plaintiff or defendant
  — Experience as a witness
- Prior jury service
  — Type of case considered
  — Whether a verdict was reached
  — Prior experience as a foreperson on a jury
- Hobbies
- Television viewing habits
- Reading habits

CASE-RELATED EXPERIENCES. Other experiences jurors have had can be important given the circumstances of the case. Jurors may have used the product at issue in a product liability case. They may be familiar with relevant locations or driving conditions that are key aspects in litigation arising from a traffic accident. They may have been a victim of a violent crime. These experiences can have a profound influence on how jurors view the case. Case-related experiences could be in such areas as:

- Prior psychological counseling
- Prior use of a party's product or services
- Ownership of stock in a party's company
- Prior employment by a party
- Being a victim of sexual assault or spousal abuse
- Prior traffic accidents
- Unsatisfactory experiences with governmental agencies
- Unsatisfactory experiences with financial managers/stockbrokers
- Unsatisfactory experiences with law enforcement personal
- Unsatisfactory experiences with building contractors
- Unsatisfactory experiences with the medical profession

An example of questions addressing case-related experiences can be found in the *Exxon* questionnaire. The use of alcohol and the problem of alcoholism played a key role in the case. This area was subsequently addressed in a series of eight questions (questions 68 through 75). Three questions illustrate inquiries into this area:

69. Have you, any member of your family, or any close friend, ever had an alcohol or drug abuse problem? (check all that apply)

    [ ] YES—Me   [ ] YES—Household Member

    [ ] YES—Spouse   [ ] YES—Family Member

    [ ] YES—Ex-Spouse   [ ] YES—Close Friend

    [ ] NO—No One

    If yes to any of the above, in what type of treatment program (such as hospitalization, Alcoholics Anonymous, counseling, etc.) was he/she involved, if any?

Person (i.e., "Family Member," "Spouse")	Treatment

. . .

72. Have you, a family member, or a close friend ever been involved in an accident or mishap that allegedly involved a person who was under the influence of alcohol or drugs?   [   ] YES   [   ] NO

If yes, please describe the incident, who was involved, the outcome, and its effect on you: (if more than one incident, list most recent one here and others on page 20 or 21)

Description / Who was involved?
[Space for answer]

Outcome / Effect on you:
[Space for answer]

73. Have you, or to your knowledge has any member of your family, or a close friend, ever been involved in firing or disciplining a person that was allegedly under the influence of alcohol or drugs in a job-related context?
[   ] YES   [   ] NO

If yes, please describe the incident, who was involved, the outcome of the incident, and its effect on you: (if more than one incident, list most recent one here and others on page 20 or 21)

Description / Who was involved?
[Space for answer]

Outcome / Effect on you:
[Space for answer]

Knowledge of Witnesses, Lawyers, and Parties

In addition to background information, juror questionnaires investigate whether potential jurors know any of the witnesses, parties, lawyers, or party representatives. All the witnesses are listed in alphabetical order on the questionnaire without their being identified with any party. Not identifying potential witnesses with a party avoids problems that arise when jurors make inferences regarding a case based on the number of witnesses a party has or the party's failure to call a certain witness. The jurors are given an opportunity to mark the name of any witness they may know. Jurors also indicate whether they know any of the parties, lawyers, or other representative of the parties.

The *McVeigh, North,* and *Exxon* questionnaires explored whether the jurors knew any of the potential witnesses, lawyers, and parties in the cases. For example, the *McVeigh* questionnaire addresses this area through the following question:

145. During the trial, the following people may be involved or mentioned. Please look over the list and note any person you know personally or have spoken with.

Vicki Zemp Behenna
Mary Anne Castellano
Sean Connelly
Aitan Goelman
Joseph H. Hartzler
Paul J. Johns
Lynne Kubik
Larry A. Mackey
Margaret Melville
Scott Mendeloff
James Orenstein
Sherie Perez
Patrick M. Ryan
Penney Trujillo
Beth A. Wilkinson
Stephen Jones
Timothy McVeigh
Terry Lynn Nichols
Robert Nigh, Jr.
Richard Burr
Jeralyn Merritt
Robert L. Wyatt, IV
Mandy Welch
Cheryl Ramsey
Chris Tritico
Michael D. Roberts
James L. Hankins
Randall T. Coyne
Amber L. McLaughlin
Holly Hillerman
Robert J. Warren
Sam Guiberson
Maria Ryan

Please identify anyone you know or have spoken with:

_____

_____

_____

. . .

148. Do you personally know anyone who might be a witness in the trial?

                    __ Yes   __ No

   If yes, whom do you know and what is the nature of your relationship with them?

   _____

   _____

   _____

The *North* questionnaire approached this area as follows:

20. The following is a list of people whose names may come up during the trial of the case. If you personally know or have any connection (personal, business, or social) with any of these individuals, or have heard of any of them, circle the number in front of the name of that person:

   1. ABRAMS, Elliot
   2. ACHESON, Gayle
   3. ALBRIGHT, Art
   4. ALLEN, Charles
   5. ARMACOST, Michael
   6. ARMITAGE, Richard
   7. BARNES, Michael
   8. BARTLETT, Linda June
   9. BECK, Patricia
   10. BERMUDEZ, Enrique
   11. BERRY, Steven
   12. BOLAND, Edward P.
   13. BOLTON, Bobby
   14. BOONE, LaVerne
   15. BRANDELL, Nancy
   16. BULLOCK, Jeffrey
   17. BURGHARDT, Raymond
   18. BUSH, George
   19. CALERO, Adolfo

                . . .

   193. WOBENSMITH, John
   194. ZADEH, Mousalreza Abrahim
   195. ZUCKER, Willard

21. If for any reason you have an unfavorable opinion about anyone listed under question 20, put the number or numbers of such person or persons on the line below:

   _____

                . . .

26. Do you personally, or does any member of your immediate family, know or have any connection (personal, business, or social) with any attorney, employee or representative of:

   a. Office of Independent Counsel, including attorneys
   b. Lawrence E. Walsh
   c. John W. Keker
   d. Michael R. Bromwich
   e. David M. Zornow

   Yes _____ No _____

   If "yes," please specify_____

27. Do you personally, or does any member of your immediate family, know or have any connection (personal, business, or social) with any attorney, employee or representative of:

   a. Law Firm of Williams & Connolly, including attorneys
   b. Brendan V. Sullivan, Jr.
   c. Barry S. Simon
   d. Terrence O'Donnell

   Yes _____ No _____

   If "yes," please specify _____

29. Do you personally, or does any member of your immediate family, know or have any connection (personal, business, or social) with the defendant, Oliver L. North?

   Yes _____ No _____

   If "yes," please specify _____

The *Exxon* questionnaire did not explore this area beyond a single general question.

79. Do you know anyone you believe to be in any way involved in this lawsuit?

   [ ] YES   [ ] NO

   If yes, please explain:
   [Space for answer]

Awareness of the Case

In cases where there has been appreciable pretrial publicity, a section of the juror questionnaire can explore pretrial publicity-related issues. In this section, questions assess whether or not jurors have heard, read, or seen anything about the instant case, what they recall about the case, whether they have discussed the case with others, and what opinions, if any, they have formed about the parties in the case.

Again, the *McVeigh*, *North*, and *Exxon* questionnaires illustrate attempts to collect this information from jurors. For the *McVeigh* case it was important to ask questions not only concerning the jurors' awareness of the case and any opinions that were formed, but also about the potential for contacts with those involved as victims, rescuer workers, and other forms of contact with the event and its aftermath:

PUBLICITY

This case involves the bombing of the Murrah Federal Building in Oklahoma City, Oklahoma, on April 19, 1995. It is commonly called the "Oklahoma Bombing" case.

140. If you have heard of or read anything about this case, please indicate where you heard or read about it. (Check all that apply.)

T.V. News	_____
Radio News	_____
Newspaper	_____
Magazines	_____
Books	_____
Internet	_____
On-line	_____
Conversations	_____
Heard other people discussing the case	_____

141. How would you describe the amount of media coverage you have seen about this case?

_____ Very much (went out of your way to read about it and watch news accounts of it).

_____ Quite a bit (read a few articles or watched a few television specials).

_____ Not too much (just basic coverage on the nightly news or morning news).

_____ None or hardly at all (just heard about it).

. . .

146. Did you personally know anyone who was killed in the Oklahoma City bombing?

Yes _____   No _____

If yes, please explain. _____

_____

147. Do you personally know anyone who was injured in the Oklahoma City bombing?

Yes _____   No _____

If yes, please explain. _____

_____

_____

149. Did you or any member of your family or close friends assist in the rescue effort after the bombing in any way?

     Yes _____   No _____

     If yes, please explain: _____

     _____

150. Did you or any member of your family or close friends provide assistance to people participating in the rescue efforts in any way?

     Yes _____   No _____

     If yes, please explain: _____

     _____

151. Did you or any member of your family or close friends give any money, gifts in kind, or any form of assistance to victims of the bombing?

     Yes _____   No _____

     If yes, please explain: _____

     _____

152. Do you know anyone who suffered any economic loss as a result of the Oklahoma City bombing?

     Yes _____   No _____

     If yes, who was the person: _____

     _____

153. Have you visited the Murrah Building site in Oklahoma City since April 19, 1995?

     Yes _____   No _____

     If yes, please explain: _____

     _____

     _____

154. Please summarize what you have seen, read or heard about this case:

     _____

     _____

     _____

     _____

     _____

155. Have you formed any opinion about the defendant, Timothy McVeigh?

     Yes _____   No _____

If yes, what opinion(s) have you formed and on what are they based?

_____

_____

_____

_____

_____

In the *North* questionnaire, seven questions addressed pretrial publicity issues. Of particular concern were questions 30, 31, and 32, which served as the initial screening questions in the jury selection process. As discussed earlier, affirmative answers by jurors to questions 30, 31, or 32 led to their automatic exclusion. The seven questions were as follows:

19. Have you read or seen or heard anything about this case before coming to this Court?

Yes _____   No _____

. . .

28. The defendant in this case is Lt. Col. Oliver L. North. Have you read anything in newspapers or magazines, watched anything on television or heard anything on radio concerning him or regarding this case generally?

Television   Yes _____   No _____
Radio   Yes _____   No _____
Newspaper   Yes _____   No _____
Magazine   Yes _____   No _____
Book   Yes _____   No _____

30. Did you see any part of Lt. Col. North's testimony before any congressional committee over television or otherwise?

Yes _____   No _____

31. Did you read any part of any of his testimony before a congressional committee in any newspaper, magazine or book?

Yes _____   No _____

32. Did you listen over radio or otherwise to any part of any of his testimony before a congressional committee?

Yes _____   No _____

33. Have you contributed money to any organizations, signed petitions, attended any meetings or rallies supporting or opposing Oliver L. North?

Yes _____   No _____

34. Except as noted above, do you have any personal knowledge of any aspect or fact in this case so far as you know?

Yes _____   No _____

If "yes," explain briefly:
[Space for answer]

Pretrial publicity issues played a unique role in the *Exxon Valdez* case. Not only were jurors potentially exposed to massive amounts of pretrial publicity, but a considerable number of Alaskan residents participated or knew others who had participated in the oil spill cleanup efforts. In addition, a number of Alaskans filed lawsuits against Exxon Corporation for damages resulting from the oil spill. Thus, the questionnaire addressed a number of areas relating to the jurors' exposure to pretrial publicity and other "sources" of information concerning the oil spill, cleanup efforts, and damage to the spill-affected areas.

35. The grounding of the *Exxon Valdez* and resulting oil spill occurred in the early morning of March 24, 1989. How much have you heard about this incident? (please check one)

A Great Deal	Some	Very Little	Nothing at All

What were your primary sources of information regarding the event?
[Space for answer]

36. Approximately how many articles would you estimate you have read about the grounding of the *Exxon Valdez* and resulting oil spill? _____

37. Approximately how many television shows or news programs have you seen or heard regarding the grounding of the *Exxon Valdez* and resulting oil spill?

_____

. . .

39. Did you, or any close friends or relatives, personally participate in the post-spill cleanup effort?

[ ] YES   [ ] NO

If yes, please describe who participated and the nature of this participation, including whether the individuals were volunteers or hired workers:
[Space for answer]

39A. Have you attended any meetings or presentations concerning the oil spill or the cleanup?

[ ] YES   [ ] NO

If yes, please state what you remember about the time, place, and sponsor of the meeting:
[Space for answer]

40. Have you or has any close friend or relative made a claim or received payment for any damages caused by the grounding of the *Exxon Valdez* and resulting oil spill?

[ ] YES   [ ] NO

If yes, please describe the claim or complaint, and what the outcome was:
[Space for answer]

41. How closely did you follow any of the legal proceedings or trials that have already been held regarding the grounding of the *Exxon Valdez*?[8]

Very Closely	Occasional[ly]	Very Seldom	Not at All

42. Which lawsuits did you follow and what do you recall about them?

Lawsuit	What Do You Recall?

43. Have you attended any meetings or presentations at which the oil spill or cleanup efforts were discussed by a speaker or presenter? (at work, social organizations, fraternal organizations, civic or business groups, etc.)

[ ] YES   [ ] NO

If yes, please explain:
[Space for answer]

44. Have you or has anyone in your household received any type of mailing which advocated any position on the *Exxon Valdez* oil spill litigation?

[ ] YES   [ ] NO

If yes, please explain:
[Space for answer]

. . .

47. Prior to the oil spill, had you ever been to any of the areas that later were exposed to oil from the *Exxon Valdez*?

[ ] YES   [ ] NO

If yes, please name those areas:
[Space for answer]

Since the oil spill have you been to any of the areas that were exposed to oil from the *Exxon Valdez*?

[ ] YES   [ ] NO

If yes, please name those areas:
[Space for answer]

. . .

49. Have you, a family member, or a close friend, ever been involved in any of the following? (check all that apply)

	Self	Family Member	Close Friend
Sport Fishing in Prince William Sound	___	___	___
Subsistence Fishing	___	___	___
Subsistence Hunting	___	___	___
Commercial Fishing	___	___	___
Recreational Boating in Prince William Sound	___	___	___

50. Do you own land in the vicinity of Prince William Sound, Kenai Peninsula, or Kodiak Island?

   [ ] YES   [ ] NO

   If yes, please specify where:
   [Space for answer]

The questionnaire did not elicit the jurors' opinions on the negligence of either Captain Hazelwood or Exxon Corporation. However, two questions addressed opinions concerning the impact of the spill and general perceptions of some of the entities involved in the dispute. These questions were the following:

45. Do you have any opinions or feelings that the positive effects of the grounding of the *Exxon Valdez*, the resulting oil spill, and the cleanup effort which followed outweigh the negative effects?

   [ ] YES   [ ] NO

   If yes, please explain (why, where you got your information, etc.):
   [Space for answer]

46. Based on your experience and knowledge, what is your general response to each of the following types of organizations or businesses? (check the response that most closely expresses your opinion about each type of organization)

	Extremely Favorable	Somewhat Favorable	Somewhat Unfavorable	Extremely Unfavorable
Local Governments/ Municipalities	___	___	___	___
Aquaculture Organizations	___	___	___	___
Seafood Processors	___	___	___	___
Commercial Fishermen	___	___	___	___

(continued)

	Extremely Favorable	Somewhat Favorable	Somewhat Unfavorable	Extremely Unfavorable
Native Corporations	_____	_____	_____	_____
Tribal Governments	_____	_____	_____	_____
Natives	_____	_____	_____	_____
Exxon Corporation	_____	_____	_____	_____

Case-Relevant Opinions

The primary purpose of the juror questionnaire is to gather supplemental information that will serve as a starting point for voir dire questioning. However, these questionnaires may include inquiries into the jurors' opinions and beliefs that may influence their views on the case. Jurors' opinions regarding governmental "sting" operations, extramarital affairs, tort reform, compensation for pain and suffering, punitive damages, governmental officials, corporations and their activities, and the death penalty are examples of some of the areas of concern. Other opinions of interest could include whether the jurors would (a) ascribe to police officers more credibility than they would to other witnesses; (b) have difficulty judging others; (c) require a criminal defendant to prove his or her innocence; and (d) follow the judge's instructions.

Questions from the *McVeigh* juror questionnaire illustrate various case-relevant opinions, ranging from the jurors' views on the credibility of law enforcement officers and accomplices and opinions concerning the federal government, to their views on the death penalty:

110. Would you tend to believe the testimony of a state or federal law enforcement officer

_____ as much as any other witness
_____ less than most other witnesses
_____ more than most witnesses

. . .

117. What are your views about cases in which the government uses a convicted accomplice who has pled guilty and agreed to testify as a prosecution witness in the hope that he will receive a reduced sentence?

_____

_____

118. Would you tend to believe the testimony of a convicted accomplice who has pled guilty and is testifying as a prosecution witness?

_____ Believe as much as any witness
_____ Believe less than most witnesses
_____ Consider his testimony with skepticism, great care, and caution

. . .

122. How much do you respect the federal government?
(circle one number)

| Not at all | | | | Somewhat | | | | A great deal | |
| 1 | 2 | 3 | 4 | 5 | 6 | 7 | 8 | 9 | 10 |

123. What role do you think the federal government should play in people's lives?

_____

_____

_____

_____

124. How well do you think the government presently plays that role?

_____

_____

125. Do you think the federal government interferes with and is too intrusive in our daily life? (circle one number):

| Not at all | | | | Somewhat | | | | Extremely | |
| 1 | 2 | 3 | 4 | 5 | 6 | 7 | 8 | 9 | 10 |

. . .

121. The death penalty—capital punishment—is an issue on which many thoughtful citizens strongly disagree. Whether the law should provide for such punishment is a question that has been frequently debated in Congress, in state legislatures and other public forums. While the jury must, of course, follow the law as it now is and on which detailed instructions will be given if there is a guilty verdict, it is important for you to tell us what views or opinions you may have about the use of the punishment of death in criminal cases generally and without regard to the facts and circumstances that may be shown to be relevant to this particular individual defendant.

In any case in which the charge carries the possible penalties of life in prison without possibility of release, or death, the law requires that prospective jurors answer questions regarding their thoughts, feelings, and opinions on the possible penalties. This is true even though the defendant might not be guilty and, thus, the trial might not reach the penalty stage. You must not assume from any questions asked that Mr. McVeigh will be found guilty of any crime.

With these thoughts in mind, please answer the following questions:

(a) If you, individually, had the power to decide what the law should be as to capital punishment, how would you decide with respect to the following statements? (Please indicate yes or no.)

  i. A penalty of death is justified in all cases in which someone has been killed by a criminal act. ____

ii. A penalty of death is generally justified when someone has been killed by a criminal act, with very few exceptions. _____

iii. There are some cases in which the death penalty is justified but generally it is not. ____

iv. The death penalty is generally not justified but there are a few exceptions. _____

v. The death penalty is never justified. _____

(b) In your opinion, what is the best reason for <u>imposing</u> a penalty of death in a case in which someone was killed by a criminal act?

_____

_____

(c) In your opinion, what is the best reason for <u>not imposing</u> a penalty of death in a case in which someone was killed by a criminal act?

_____

_____

In the *North* questionnaire, only a few questions address case-relevant opinions:

21. If for any reason you have an unfavorable opinion about anyone listed under question 20 [potential witness list], put the number or numbers of such person or persons on the line below:

_____

25. Would your experience on any situation covered by 23 and 24, above [involvement in court proceedings, investigations, or prior jury service], affect your ability to be a fair and impartial juror in this case?

Yes _____ No _____

If "yes," explain:

_____

35. Is there anything about the subject matter of this case or the points covered in this questionnaire which creates a doubt in your mind as to whether you could be a fair, objective, and impartial juror in this particular case?

Yes _____ No _____

The *Exxon* questionnaire addressed several case-relevant opinions through the following questions:

48. Do you have any opinions one way or the other about whether environmental standards in Alaska are too high for companies which do business in Alaska?

[ ] YES   [ ] NO

If yes, please explain:
[Space for answer]

65. In some cases jurors are asked to make a determination as to whether or not punitive damages should be awarded in order to punish defendants or to deter certain conduct or behavior. Do you have any opinion opposed to that basic concept of punitive damages?

[ ] YES [ ] NO

If yes, please explain:
[Space for answer]

66. Have you heard or read anything about when or under what circumstances punitive damages should be awarded?

[ ] YES [ ] NO

a. If yes, please explain:
[Space for answer]

b. Do you have an opinion about awarding punitive damages?
[ ] YES [ ] NO

If yes, please explain, and include your source of information if possible:
[Space for answer]

67. Some groups and individuals promote the position that there are too many juries awarding too many plaintiffs' verdicts. Do you have any opinion on that subject?

[ ] YES [ ] NO

a. If yes, please explain:
[Space for answer]

b. Have you ever read, seen or heard any type of information on that subject?
[ ] YES [ ] NO

If yes, please explain:
[Space for answer]

c. Have you ever belonged to any type of group or organization which has promoted any opinion on the subject of jury verdicts?
[ ] YES [ ] NO

If yes, please explain:
[Space for answer]

81. Do you know of any reason not disclosed in your answers to these questions why you could not be a fair and impartial juror in this case?

[ ] YES [ ] NO

If yes, please explain:
[Space for answer]

On occasion, juror questionnaires include questions that address jurors' opinions of a more general nature in addition to case-relevant items. Judges may allow questioning in such areas as authoritarianism (e.g., Do you agree or disagree with the statement that obedience and respect for authority are the most important values children should learn?) and racism (e.g., How would you feel if a family member or relative married someone of a different race?).[9] When available, such information can greatly enhance the lawyer's understanding of jurors.

Designing the Questionnaire

A key to the successful use of juror questionnaires lies in the design of the questionnaire itself. Several considerations are important.[10]

Choosing the Question Format

OPEN-ENDED V. CLOSED ENDED QUESTIONS. As discussed in Chapter 4, there are two basic types of questions: open-ended and close-ended. Open-ended questions do not specify or restrict the answers to be given. Examples of these questions are: "What is your marital status?" "What is your opinion about the appropriateness of the death penalty as a punishment for premeditated murder?" "Why?" "How do you feel about providing money damages for pain and suffering?" For each of the above questions, jurors give their answers without being forced to choose from stated or implied answers.

Closed-ended questions seek to restrict the juror's answers to a few specified or implied answers. "Yes or no" type questions are the most common form of closed-ended questions, e.g., "Have you ever been a victim of a crime? [   ] Yes [   ] No" Other examples of closed-ended questions are:

What is your marital status: (check one answer)

[   ] Single, never married

[   ] Single but currently living with nonmarital mate

[   ] Currently married

[   ] Currently separated or divorced

[   ] Widowed

Please indicate whether you agree or disagree with the following statement:

The death penalty is an appropriate punishment for people who commit premeditated murder.

[   ] Agree strongly [   ] Agree somewhat

[   ] Disagree somewhat   [   ] Disagree strongly   [   ] Unsure

Advantages of open- and closed-ended questions. Each type of question possesses several advantages. The advantages to asking open-ended questions are the following. First, open-ended questions have greater potential to uncover useful information from jurors than otherwise would occur through closed-ended questions by forcing jurors to answer the questions in their own

---

Advantages of open-ended questions:

- Greater potential for uncovering information
- Provide clues into the communication skills and thought processes of jurors
- Provide a more effective basis for follow-up questions

---

words. Particularly with questions addressing the experiences and opinions of jurors, what jurors write can be very revealing. For example, asking jurors the following question could yield several answers:

> How would you feel about awarding substantial money damages to a plaintiff provided the law and the facts supported such a finding?
>
> *Answer one:*   "If the defendant was negligent, I think the plaintiff is entitled to compensation no matter what that amount would be."
>
> *Answer two:*   "I think plaintiffs are being awarded too much money from juries, but if the law says its okay then I would do it."
>
> *Answer three:*   "I really couldn't award a large amount of money. I can't see ruining the defendant to pay the plaintiff a lot of money."

Each of the above answers is slightly different and provides a glimpse into the thought processes of these jurors.

Second, open-ended questions can reveal important information in the writing of the answers beyond the actual opinions expressed by jurors. The jurors' answers reflect the jurors' communication skills and how logical and sophisticated their thinking is. This information can be important when considering the desirability of potential jurors and the likely impact they would have in deliberations.

Finally, the answers to open-ended questions can lead to more effective follow-up questions during subsequent voir dire questioning. For example, the above answers to the question concerning their feelings about awarding substantial money damages to a plaintiff would provide indications for what follow-up questions to ask. We see in answers two and three that the jurors are focusing on different issues in their opinions. Answer two focuses on the plaintiff, with a perception that plaintiffs, in general, are being awarded too much money. Answer three focuses on the impact of any award on the defendant. The different focus of these two answers provides the basis for what follow-up questions should be asked of these jurors.[11]

Closed-ended questions also have a number of advantages. First, closed-ended questions are relatively easy to answer. Jurors simply "check off" or circle the appropriate answer. Second, closed-ended questions focus jurors'

Advantages of closed-eended questions:

- Can be presented in easy-to-answer formats
- Focus the jurors' attention on the answers of interest
- Provide for quick review of jurors' answers

---

attention on what potential answers are of interest. For example, jurors can be asked:

What best describes your opinion of Acme Corporation?

[ ] Very favorable   [ ] Somewhat unfavorable

[ ] Somewhat favorable   [ ] Very unfavorable

[ ] Neutral/No opinion

By selecting among options ranging from very favorable to very unfavorable, jurors are directed to provide their impressions of Acme Corporation on the dimension of favorable/unfavorable feelings. Without these categories, jurors could have easily given their opinions of Acme Corporation as a corporate employer, possible polluter, or maker of quality products instead of the desired evaluative dimension of favorable/unfavorable feelings.

Finally, closed-ended questions are easier to review during jury selection. The answers to open-ended questions must be categorized (or coded) in some way so that jurors' answers can be evaluated. Detailed answers are read and categorized (either formally or informally) as reflecting a certain type of response, e.g., the answer reflects the belief that the defendant is guilty or liable or some variation of this type of response. Answers to closed-ended questions are categorized in advance through the selection of the possible answers available for the question.

WHEN TO USE EACH TYPE OF QUESTION. Following are several considerations for when to use open-ended and closed-ended questions.

Uncovering opinions. While both open-ended and closed-ended questions are useful in discovering what jurors believe, closed-ended questions are relatively better when the answers of interest are specific, nonsensitive, and few in number. When a fuller exploration of jurors' opinions is desired, open-ended questions are more useful.

In addition, open-ended questions can be more effective in uncovering sensitive opinions where closed-ended questions, through the presentation of a particular position, might lead jurors to answer in a less candid and more socially acceptable manner. The potential detail in the answers to open-ended questions can help to mitigate the problem of jurors being less than candid.

Recalling information. When it is important to uncover what jurors recall about an event, e.g., pretrial publicity, open-ended questions provide the most effective basis for gathering this information. "Please describe what you have heard about [the event]?" or "Please describe as fully as you can what you recall about [the event] from what you have heard, read, seen, or discussed with others?"

The potential for altering jurors' memories. Beside having jurors report on what they recall, open-ended questions minimize the chances of subtly influencing the jurors' memories or impressions concerning an event. Asking a closed-ended question directed at uncovering a specific piece of information can affect jurors' impressions of what happened. For example, asking jurors, "Have you heard anything regarding a possible confession to the crime made by the defendant?" could inadvertently taint jurors. While it would be important to know whether jurors had heard about a possible confession, asking jurors directly could leave some jurors who had not heard about any alleged confession with the impression that the defendant had confessed to the crime.

Meaningful possible answers are unwieldy or unknown. When all meaningful responses are either not known or are too unwieldy to include in a "check-off list," open-ended questions can more efficiently secure the needed information. For example, it may not be possible to anticipate all possible answers that jurors may give regarding their opinions or backgrounds. Also, it is not efficient in many situations to list all possible responses to a question. Using open-ended questions solves these problems by leaving space for jurors to fill in their answers.

Meaningful possible responses are known and few in number. When meaningful answers can be identified and are relatively few in number, closed-ended questions promote efficiency in both the answering of the questions and the evaluation of the jurors' answers. In some situations, only a few answers are of interest. Closed-ended questions provide a simple method for collecting this information by having jurors "check off" the appropriate answer.

Ease of answering. Closed-ended questions are preferable when the desired information can be easily obtained by providing the appropriate response options as compared to having jurors write out their answers.

The availability of standardized categories. Some questions, particularly concerning the jurors' beliefs and attitudes, may need jurors' answers to be restricted to standardized response options that have been developed through social science research. A common approach in opinion research is to have people indicate their degree of agreement or disagreement with certain opinion statements. The responses available may be "agree strongly," "agree somewhat," "disagree somewhat," and "disagree strongly." In these situations, use of the standard response categories is needed for appropriate comparisons with prior research.

The response categories are needed to direct possible answers. When the responses to a question may take many forms, closed-ended questions can improve the usefulness of jurors' answers by specifying appropriate possible answers.

The potential for tedium. Closed-ended questions are helpful in situations where jurors may become tired when completing a lengthy questionnaire. When jurors are tired and face numerous open-ended questions, they may choose not to fully disclose the information requested. Also, jurors may choose to avoid writing detailed answers by inaccurately saying that the answer is not applicable or that they have no opinion. Providing short answer, closed-ended questions encourages jurors to complete their questionnaires.

The need for automation. Provided the desired information can be effectively collected through closed-ended questions, the fixed format of the response categories allows for greater ease in automating the jurors' answers. This feature is desirable when the jurors' answers are being converted to computer readable data.

Phrasing of Questions

The phrasing of questions has a great impact on the usefulness of the information jurors provide. Both the phrasing of the question and any answer categories have an impact on the usefulness of the question. The following recommendations help obtain useful information from jurors.

DEVELOP NEUTRAL QUESTIONS. It is important to recognize that completing questionnaires is a social interaction. Jurors answer the questions knowing that, at a minimum, their answers will be made available to the parties and the court and, potentially, to the general public. As a result, jurors may not be candid. They may seek to answer in a manner that presents a positive public image of themselves. Careful consideration must be given to developing questions that do not lead jurors to certain answers or encourage them to respond in a socially desirable manner.

This socially desirable response bias in the questioning process can result from both the wording of the questions and the response options available. The question itself can indicate the "correct" or socially desirable answer. For example, "You would be fair and impartial, wouldn't you?" is not a neutral question. The phrasing of the question suggests to the juror what the correct answer is.

Particularly when addressing issues of the jurors' ability to follow judicial instructions and to be fair, questions can easily suggest what the "correct" answer is. For example, consider the following question.

"36. The law is that no witness is entitled to any greater or less belief solely because of his occupation or profession. Recognizing this, would you be inclined to believe a witness either more or less solely because the witness was a police officer or law enforcement?"[12]

The introductory sentence and first few words of the question tell jurors what their answers should be—which may have nothing to do with what the juror really believes. A less leading question on this issue is:

Do you believe that the testimony of a law enforcement officer is more or less likely to be truthful than testimony of a witness who is not in law enforcement?

[ ] More   [ ] Less   [ ] Equally likely[13]

The following questions are more subtle but no less problematic concerning the issue of fairness (with problematic areas shown in italics).

33. Would the fact that one of the defendants is a corporation, as opposed to an individual, interfere with your ability to give the defendants *as fair* a trial as you would any individual?

Yes _____   No _____[14]

79. Some of the evidence in this case was obtained as a result of electronic surveillance at an attorney's office. *The gathering of evidence by such procedures is lawful.* Do you have any feeling or opinion about secret electronic surveillance or secretly recorded conversations that might affect your ability to consider such evidence *fairly*?

Yes _____   No _____[15]

42. You may be called upon to sit on a jury in a criminal case in which the Government accuses someone of possessing a firearm in relation to a serious drug offense. Do you have any particularly strong feeling about either drugs or firearms that would interfere with your *ability to be fair and impartial* to both sides?

_____ Yes   _____ No [16]

The answers from which jurors must choose can also bias jurors' responses. Consider the following question:

55. Do you hold any personal opinions about the use of undercover, or "sting," operations by law enforcement agencies, in which, for example, friends or associates of a subject co-operate in monitoring the subject's activities? _____. If "yes," please check the response below which most accurately reflects your opinion.

_____ I am opposed to such methods.
_____ I favor the use of such methods.
_____ I have some reservations about the use of such methods, but realize they are sometimes necessary.

Please explain briefly, if you wish.[17]

A subtle bias was introduced in the third answer option: "I have some reservations about the use of such methods, *but realize they are sometimes necessary* [italics added]." The phrase in italics is problematic for two reasons. First, the phase ascribes a positive evaluation to the need for this activity for all jurors who have reservations. Second, this phrase precludes the identification of other potential reasons for having reservations about "stings."

As we have seen, it is important not to give jurors any clues to what might be the "fair" or "correct" answer. One way to minimize socially desirable answers is to acknowledge the legitimacy of all possible answers so that jurors are not led to a particular answer. One method to establish the legitimacy of various answers, particularly when considering various opinions, is to tell jurors prior to answering questions that there are no "right" or "wrong" answers. This instruction, often given in the introduction of the questionnaire or at the beginning of a particular section, reduces the pressure to answer in a socially desirable manner.

In addition, telling jurors through the wording of the question that any answer they choose has support within the community can establish answer legitimacy and foster truthful answers. The following two questions illustrate this approach.

116. Sexual abuse of children is a subject about which many people have differing opinions and ideas. For each of the following statements, please rate how much you agree or disagree with each:

a. Allegations of sexual abuse made by children often prove to be false.

_____ Agree strongly
_____ Agree somewhat
_____ Disagree somewhat
_____ Disagree strongly
_____ Other:_____ [18]

or

Some people believe that alcoholism is a physical disease that causes alcoholics to be unable to control their drinking. Others believe that alcoholism is simply a lack of will power and self-control on the part of the alcoholic. Which statement best describes your opinion?

[ ] Alcoholism is a physical disease that causes alcoholics to be unable to control their drinking; or

[ ] Alcoholism is simply a lack of will-power and self-control on the part of the alcoholic.

In the first question, jurors are told that people have differing opinions on the following issues. In the second question, jurors are told that some people support either of the two answers. In both questions, jurors are not given a hint as to which answer is more socially acceptable.

SEEK ALL RELEVANT INFORMATION. It is imperative that all relevant information is sought in both the phrasing of the questions and the response cate-

What to consider when phrasing questions:

- Avoid the socially desirable response bias.
- Seek all relevant information.
- Avoid mixing dimensions.
- Seek consistency in response options across questions.
- Avoid unnecessarily asymmetric categories.
- Avoid overly inclusive questions.
- Avoid multiple embedded questions.
- Avoid double-barreled questions.
- Avoid double negatives.
- Keep questions simple.
- Seek full answers.

gories provided. This is one of the most important areas in constructing questionnaires. Many times crucial information is lost at this point in the process. For example, in criminal trials, it is important to know whether potential jurors (or their family or friends) have been arrested or questioned by police in connection with a crime. Oftentimes, this topic is addressed by the following type of question:

Have you ever been charged with a felony?[19]

Unfortunately, the above question eliminates a considerable amount of potential information. Many jurors may feel that unless they have been formally charged or indicted that they need not respond affirmatively to this question. In addition, jurors may not know what constitutes a felony. As a result, the question misses certain relevant information, i.e., whether the potential juror has been questioned or arrested in connection with a crime. In addition, this question does not seek similar information about the potential jurors' family or friends (which likely would be of interest). The following question takes one possible approach to circumventing these problems:

Have you or a family member or close friend ever been questioned by the police, arrested, or charged with a crime? (Check all that apply)

	Self	Relative	Close Friend
Questioned by police	[ ]	[ ]	[ ]
Arrested	[ ]	[ ]	[ ]
Charged	[ ]	[ ]	[ ]

Beyond the scope of the question itself, it is important to select response categories that uncover all desired information. As such, the answer options presented should not preclude appropriate information. For example, consider the following question:

What is your marital status?
[   ] Single   [   ] Married   [   ] Divorced   [   ] Widowed
[   ] Living with another adult(s)[20]

This question is missing a potentially important response, i.e., being separated. As such, those potential jurors who are separated would have to decide between the options of married and divorced. Since justifications could be made for choosing either answer, there is no way to readily identify "separated" jurors.

AVOID MIXING DIMENSIONS. In many questions, response categories are intended to reflect a specific dimension such as frequency, positive/negative opinion, or guilt. When developing appropriate response categories for such questions, care should be taken not to use more than one dimension within a set of answers. Mixing dimensions can result in confusion in either the interpretation of the answers given or confusion on the part of the jurors who must answer the questions. For example, consider the responses available to the following question that appeared in one of the breast implant lawsuits:

86. In regard to having breast implants, which one of the following statements comes closest to your own personal view?

_____ There is never a good reason to alter your original body.
_____ Breast implants are acceptable only in cases of breast damage or tissue removal.
_____ I approve of people wanting to look as good as they can.
_____ It is not for me to say what someone should be allowed to do with their own body.
_____ If one elects to have surgery, any resulting consequences are his/her responsibility. [21]

The problem with the above question is that it mixes several dimensions. Acceptance and approval (although not entirely the same concept) of reasons for having breast implants (i.e., "never a good reason," "breast damage or tissue removal," and "wanting to look as good as they can") are mixed with responsibility for the procedure's outcome (i.e., "consequences are his/her responsibility"). In addition, even the "no opinion" category ("It is not for me to say what someone should be allowed to do with their own body.") mixes in a new dimension, i.e., the right to have the procedure. The reference to "what someone should be allowed to do" addresses the right to have this procedure, not approval or disapproval of the procedure. The mixing of dimensions can produce confusion in the jurors' minds and hide information from the parties as well. It is possible for some jurors to approve and other jurors to disapprove of a woman having breast implants, while still believing that the consequences of the procedure are the woman's responsibility. If the jurors focus on the approval/acceptance dimension(s), the litigants would be deprived of valuable information concerning the responsibility dimension.

SEEK CONSISTENCY IN RESPONSE OPTIONS ACROSS QUESTIONS. To complete a questionnaire in a minimal amount of time with minimal confusion, it is helpful to use the same response options for as many of the questions as is possible and desirable. Whenever potential jurors encounter different response options they must on some level stop and evaluate what these new options are. When different questions can use the same response categories without compromising the quality of the information gained, potential jurors can answer the questions more efficiently and with less possibility of confusion. For example, consider the following question.

> 67. Based upon what you have heard or read about this case, do you believe that the government's investigation was unfair in any respect?
>
> _____ Yes
> _____ No
> _____ Think so
> _____ Don't Know/No Opinion[22]

The above "think so" category appeared only once in the entire questionnaire. Not only is this option only asked once, it is ambiguous. A relevant option that could have been used is "probably" which was used in five other questions from the same questionnaire.

AVOID UNNECESSARILY ASYMMETRIC CATEGORIES. While it's sometimes desirable to minimize the number of categories from which jurors are to choose, the categories should not ignore information by using too restrictive, asymmetric categories. For example, consider the following question:

> 150. Do you think O.J. Simpson's celebrity status may make it very difficult for you to find him guilty or not guilty regardless of what the evidence shows?
>
> _____ Possibly
> _____ Probably
> _____ Probably not
> _____ Definitely not[23]

The options listed above reveal two problems. First, jurors are restricted from saying that they "definitely" think it would be difficult to find Simpson guilty or not guilty. The more balanced choices for this question are: "Definitely," "Probably," "Probably not," and "Definitely not." Second, the answers (i.e., possibly, probably, probably not, and definitely not) are not in the proper order. The logical order of the answers is: probably, possibly, probably not, definitely not. Without answers placed in a logical order, some jurors could become confused about the meaning of "possibly" and probably."

AVOID OVERLY INCLUSIVE QUESTIONS. Just as some questions can be too restrictive, others can be overly broad in their scope. Overly inclusive questions reduce the amount and quality of information provided. Consider the following question:

> Do you hold any bias or prejudicial feelings concerning companies, corporations, organizations, clubs, races, unions, religions, or other people or things?[24]

While the above question covers most of the bases for prejudice or bias (although, as discussed earlier, a socially desirable response bias has been introduced by the phrase "bias or prejudicial feelings"), its overly broad nature inhibits disclosure of the requested information. Jurors are likely to view such a question as asking whether, in general, they are prejudiced. It is unlikely that jurors will go through the process of examining their feelings regarding each of the above-referenced categories of prejudice or, for that matter, respond "yes" if they are willing to admit bias against only one of the many referenced objects of prejudice.

AVOID MULTIPLE EMBEDDED QUESTIONS. Sometimes a single question can contain a number of different requests. When this occurs, care must be taken so that information is not lost as a result of jurors inadvertently skipping parts of the question. For example, consider the following question:

> 19. Do you, to your knowledge, have any personal or family connection of any sort with the defendant Marion S. Barry, Jr.? _____. With the United States Attorney for the District of Columbia, Jay P. Stephens, or his staff, including Assistant United States Attorneys Judith Retchin and Richard Roberts? _____. With defense attorneys R. Kenneth Mundy, Reginald L. Holt, Robert W. Mance, or Karen McDonald? _____. If any answer is "yes," please explain briefly.[25]

Some jurors may overlook parts of the above question simply because of its length.

It is possible to ask for several pieces of information within a single question, provided jurors are given direction and an opportunity to answer each component of the question. When making multiple requests within a single question it is often helpful to use headings and response options to guide jurors to complete answers. The following question illustrates this approach.

> Have you or any of your family or close friends ever been employed or received any training in any local, state, or federal law enforcement agency, including but not limited to the following? (Check all that apply)

	Self	Family	Friend
Police or sheriff's department	[ ]	[ ]	[ ]
Federal Bureau of Investigation (FBI)	[ ]	[ ]	[ ]
Treasury Department	[ ]	[ ]	[ ]
Department of Alcohol, Tobacco and Firearms	[ ]	[ ]	[ ]

. . .

Military Police	[ ]	[ ]	[ ]
Internal Revenue Service (IRS)	[ ]	[ ]	[ ]
Central Intelligence Agency (CIA)	[ ]	[ ]	[ ]
Other law enforcement agency:	[ ]	[ ]	[ ]

Please explain for each checked answer: _____ "

AVOID "DOUBLE-BARRELED" QUESTIONS. A question containing two or more components that can potentially be in conflict is referred to as a double-barreled question. Such questions can produce confusion both in the jurors' understanding of what is being asked and in the interpretation of subsequent answers. Two examples of these types of questions appeared in one of the assisted suicide trials of Dr. Kevorkian.[26] The first question combines two different situations and asks for a single answer.

> 39. Do you have any philosophical, religious, political or moral beliefs against suicide for the terminally ill, who have only a short time to live, or persons in constant, severe pain that no medicine or treatment has been able to relieve?
>
> Yes ___   No ___   Uncertain ___

As can be seen, the "yes" answer is unclear. "Yes" could mean that the juror has beliefs against suicide in both scenarios, or only in the terminally ill situation, or only in the constant pain situation. Greater clarity for this issue would be gained by addressing these two situations separately or providing jurors with response categories that allow them to respond to each situation.

Consider the following similar situation:

> 37. With respect to abortion, do you consider yourself pro-choice or pro-life?
>
> Yes ___   No ___

This question may be intended to uncover whether jurors have taken a position as to being either pro-choice or pro-life. However, jurors may think that they are expected to indicate their position, yet they have no option that allows them to do so. Clarity in the question could be achieved by the following:

> Which of the following best describes your opinion on abortion. Is it:
>
> [   ] Pro-choice
> [   ] Pro-life
> [   ] Neither pro-choice or pro-life
> [   ] Undecided/no opinion

The potential for confusion inherent in double-barreled questions makes their use extremely problematic.

AVOID DOUBLE NEGATIVES. Another problem with the phrasing of questions arises when they include double negatives. Questions that use double negatives are more difficult to answer than those that employ only a single negative term. This type of question requires that jurors consider each part of the statement containing a negative term separately and then combine these components to decide what their answer should be. However, in doing so, jurors can become confused, leading to inaccuracies in their answers. An example of this type of question is the following:

> Do you disagree that a criminal defendant should not be required to prove his or her innocence?

Removing the double negative from the question makes it much easier to understand: "Do you believe that a defendant should be required to prove his or her innocence?"

KEEP QUESTIONS SIMPLE. Using simple questions is fundamental to gaining information from jurors. Complex sentence structure, technical terms, sophisticated terminology, and legalese reduce the jurors' ability to understand what is being asked of them.

SEEK FULL ANSWERS. When using closed-ended questions, it is possible to increase the usefulness of the answer by making follow-up requests. Examples of follow-up requests include "Please explain:"; "Why?"; and "What is the basis for this opinion?"

While follow-up requests are useful for obtaining a more complete understanding of important opinions held by jurors, they should not detract from the jurors' willingness to provide answers. For example, the follow-up request such as, "Please explain briefly, if you wish," may be seen by some jurors as optional. Particularly with lengthier questionnaires, explicitly giving jurors the option not to provide an explanation—when one is desired—could reduce the information gained from those questions. For example, consider the following two questions, from the criminal trials of former Washington, D.C., mayor Marion Barry and O.J. Simpson, respectively:

56. Do you have an opinion about the fairness of law enforcement agencies using concealed video and audio recording devices during the course of an undercover investigation? _____. If "yes," please check the response below which most accurately reflects your opinion.

    _____   I am opposed to the use of concealed recording devices.
    _____   I favor the use of concealed recording devices.
    _____   I have some reservations about the use of concealed recording devices, but realize they are sometimes necessary.

    Please explain briefly, if you wish.[27]

188. "Some races and/or ethnic groups tend to be more violent than others."

    _____ Strongly agree
    _____ Agree
    _____ Disagree
    _____ Strongly disagree
    _____ No opinion

    If you wish to do so, please explain your answer:
    _____ [28]

The problem in both of the above questions is that the phrase "if you wish" is used. When an answer is optional, particularly with questions that appear later in lengthy questionnaires, jurors are more likely to choose not to provide an answer. If the information is important enough to seek, then it should be asked for directly without giving jurors the option of not responding.

Designing the Questionnaire Format

As we have seen, choosing and phrasing the questions to be included on the juror questionnaire is of major importance. However, careful attention must also be paid to the format of the questionnaire itself. The format of the questionnaire should (a) set the expectations in a nonbiased manner; (b) include "set-up" questions; (c) use redundancy to avoid missing information; (d) strike a balance between open-ended and closed-ended questions; and (e) present questions in an easy-to-read format.

SETTING EXPECTATIONS. At various points in the questionnaire jurors often are given directions on what is expected of them. In the introduction to the questionnaire, jurors may be told how to physically complete the questionnaire, e.g., checking appropriate boxes and answering each question completely. This is also a time when the expectations of the jurors can be set to produce the greatest candor. Jurors should be told that their answers are to be honest, candid, and complete. In addition, telling jurors that there are no "right" or "wrong" answers reduces the pressure to answer in a socially acceptable manner.

Expectations are set not only with the tone and content of the introduction to the questionnaire, but (along with any verbal instructions given) with instructions or "hints" that may appear throughout the questionnaire. Some questionnaires contain section headings to alert jurors to the general nature of questions that follow. For example, jurors may be told that the ensuing questions deal with pretrial publicity or opinions about the death penalty. While section headings are useful, it is important to phrase them in a neutral manner. Headings such as "PERSONAL ATTITUDES AND EXPERIENCES— THE ABILITY TO BE FAIR"[29] or "XIV. ETHNIC PREJUDICE"[30] give jurors a

---

Tips for designing the questionnaire format

- Don't bias expectations.
- Include "set-up" questions.
- Use redundancy to avoid missing information.
- Balance the use of open-ended and closed-ended questions.
- Use easy-to-read layouts.

strong hint about the socially acceptable response. As such, more neutral headings, e.g., "General Opinions," are more likely to minimize the potential for biasing the expectations of jurors.

USING "SET-UP" QUESTIONS. Since juror questionnaires and voir dire questioning should always be considered as interrelated components in the jury selection process, special attention should be given to how questions in the questionnaire can be used to set up or enhance the utility of subsequent voir dire questioning. The "set-up" questions approach can be used in a number of ways. First, questions can be used as a basis for securing additional information during voir dire. Questions addressing certain backgrounds and experiences can serve as the starting point for more in-depth discussion of the juror's knowledge and beliefs concerning related topics during voir dire. For example, in an environmental pollution case, familiarity with various governmental regulations, in general, and environmental regulations, in particular, would serve as the starting point for a discussion of the juror's knowledge and views regarding the enforcement of environmental regulations.

Second, set-up questions are particularly valuable in addressing sensitive areas where jurors are likely to be reluctant to disclose information in open court. For example, jurors are more likely to respond candidly to the following questions when they are posed on a questionnaire as compared to during voir dire.

> Have you or a family member ever had occasion to seek treatment from a counselor, psychiatrist, psychologist, or other mental health professional?
>
> Yes [   ]   No [   ]

or

> Have you ever been the victim of a rape or sexual assault?
>
> Yes [   ]   No [   ]

Third, in some cases, set-up questions can act as screening questions. As discussed earlier in this chapter, in the trial of former Lt. Colonel Oliver North, three questions were asked concerning whether potential jurors were exposed to his immunized testimony before Congress. Jurors answering yes to questions 30, 31, or 32 were automatically excluded from the jury selection process, saving a considerable amount of time in the jury selection process.

Finally, set-up questions can help to remove problems of socially desirable bias in questions traditionally asked by the court. As mentioned earlier, the use of phrases such as "fair and impartial," "bias," and "Do you understand that the law is . . ." encourage ego-enhancing answers on the part of jurors. Posing the questions in written form can secure the necessary information without introducing this bias, as in the following examples.

> Do you believe that a defendant in a criminal case should testify or produce some evidence to prove that he or she is not guilty?
>
> Yes [   ]   No [   ]

or

> If your opinion of what the law should be is different from what the judge says the law is, would you tend to follow your own opinion about the law in deciding on your verdict?
>
> Yes [ ]   No [ ]   Unsure [ ][31]

Neither of the above questions interject a bias. However, when the same topics are addressed by the court, jurors can more easily be made aware of what the "correct" answers are based on how the questions are phrased. The value of asking the nonbiased question in the questionnaire is that the jurors' true beliefs are more likely to be revealed. The parties and the court still have the opportunity to follow up on the answers to determine whether some bias is present or not.

USE REDUNDANCY TO AVOID MISSING INFORMATION. To some degree, redundancy can be useful in juror questionnaires. It can serve as a reliability or consistency check on the answers of jurors. Questions answered inconsistently serve as a red flag for the parties that further follow-up and attention is needed with a given juror. For example, in the criminal trial of O.J. Simpson, several questions addressed the issue of the jurors' beliefs concerning the guilt or innocence of Mr. Simpson:

93. If you have discussed this case with friends and/or relatives, do your friends/relatives overall seem to lean toward thinking that O.J. Simpson is:

_____ Not guilty
_____ Probably not guilty
_____ Not Sure
_____ Probably guilty
_____ Guilty

138. Based upon your feelings toward O.J. Simpson, are you inclined to believe him guilty of the crimes with which he has been charged?

Yes _____   No _____

Please explain: _____

_____

139. Based upon your feelings toward O.J. Simpson, are you inclined to believe him not guilty of the crimes with which he has been charged?

Yes _____   No _____

Please explain: _____

_____

. . .

147. Does the fact that O.J. Simpson excelled at football make it unlikely in your mind that he could commit murder? Why or why not?

_____

149. Do you think you may find it more difficult to believe the evidence presented to you if it conflicts with your beliefs about O.J. Simpson? Why or why not?

_____

_____

150. Do you think O.J. Simpson's celebrity status may make it very difficult for you to find him guilty or not guilty regardless of what the evidence shows?

_____ Possibly
_____ Probably
_____ Probably not
_____ Definitely not

Please explain:

_____

_____

155. As a result of what you have seen or heard or read about this case, do you think O.J. Simpson is:

_____ Not guilty
_____ More likely not guilty than guilty
_____ More likely guilty than not guilty
_____ Guilty
_____ No opinion[32]

The above seven questions reflect efforts to address jurors' beliefs concerning the guilt of the defendant from several directions and at several different points in the questionnaire. As such, any inconsistency in the jurors' answers could be pursued to see whether the inconsistency occurred as a result of confusion, an attempt to deceive, or some other reason.

Redundancy of questioning or topic areas can also help prevent useful information from being missed in the questionnaire. This often happens when addressing the jurors' backgrounds and experiences, such as the jurors' membership or participation in organizations. Consider the following commonly asked question:

Please list organizations to which you belong or in which you participate, either now or in the past. (For example, civic, social, religious, charitable, volunteer, political, sporting, professional, business, recreational, and union membership.)

With the above question, it is possible that jurors may fail to remember or record their participation in certain organizations of particular interest to the parties given the circumstances of the case. In view of this, a conceptually redundant (but more focused) question may be added to elicit a specific response. The following illustrates this approach in the context of a criminal case.

Have you ever belonged to or donated money to a group or organization that is concerned with people accused of crimes or people in prison, such as ACLU and prison outreach?

Yes _____   No _____

If yes, which group(s):

By asking both questions, you do not exclude valuable information either as a result of jurors' failing memories (broad question) or a question's narrow focus.

However, when issues of reliability and overlooking critical information are not explicitly involved it is desirable to avoid redundancy. In lengthy questionnaires, redundancy in questions can wear jurors down, leading to decreased comprehensiveness and candor in their answers to subsequent questions. In addition, the redundancy exhibited in the Simpson criminal questionnaire may be a luxury not available in cases where limits are placed on the length or content of questionnaires.

BALANCING OPEN-ENDED AND CLOSED-ENDED QUESTIONS. Earlier in this chapter, we considered the relative merits of the use of open-ended as compared to closed-ended questions. The practicalities of designing the overall format of the questionnaire require that a balance often must be struck between the greater information potential contained in open-ended questions and the efficiencies available through closed-ended questions. In general, a questionnaire will contain a majority of closed-ended questions, with open-ended questions being saved for circumstances where they are more efficient in eliciting desired information. A key factor to remember with open-ended questions is juror tedium. Particularly with lengthy questionnaires, using many open-ended questions can result in jurors becoming fatigued, which in turn can result in less willingness on the part of jurors to provide complete and candid answers to all questions. This situation is made even worse when a number of important open-ended questions appear near the end of the questionnaire. Thus, the number and placement of open-ended questions should be carefully balanced.

USING AN EASY-TO-READ FORMAT. The layout of the questionnaire can foster or hinder its full and efficient completion. The layout of the questionnaire should enhance the jurors' abilities to read and answer questions. Sufficient space to completely answer questions is crucial. Insufficient space can result in truncated answers or skipped questions. When space is not available for all possible answers, extra sheets of paper should be attached to the questionnaire with instructions for their use. Backs of pages should not be used because of the potential loss of this information during the duplication and distribution process. In addition, using multiple embedded questions or packing questions together without sufficient spacing between them can also lead to jurors becoming frustrated or inadvertently skipping entire questions or some of their components.

Maximizing the Utility of Restricted-Length Questionnaires

In most cases, the length of the questionnaire is a matter of concern. When space is at a premium, efficient design of the questionnaire is paramount. The court may place limits on the number of questions or pages allowed, necessitating adjustments in what is asked and how. Several approaches are useful.

AVOID DUPLICATING INFORMATION. Obtain information from sources other than the juror questionnaire, when possible. For example, a potential juror's occupation, marital status, current address, involvement in prior lawsuits, or prior victimization may be available from qualification questionnaires, and as such, it need not be repeatedly solicited. However, make sure that critical information is correct and current.[33]

DESIGN QUESTIONS THAT MINIMIZE SPACE REQUIREMENTS. Use open-ended questions to save valuable space. Consider the following two approaches to gathering information on a juror's educational background:

34. (a) How far did you go in school? (Without mentioning name of school(s)

    [   ] Elementary School   [   ] Junior High School

    [   ] Some High School   [   ] High School complete
                                                           or equivalency

    [   ] Technical, Vocational, or
           Business school

List area[s] of training and degrees, if any:

_____

_____

    [   ] Some College/Community college

    [   ] College complete

    [   ] List fields of study and degree(s), if any:

_____

_____

    [   ] Post graduate work

List fields of study and degree(s), if any:

_____   34

6. How far did you go in school?_____

    If schooling beyond high school, please list:

    Areas studied: _____Degrees: _____   35

The latter of the two approaches uses a series of open-ended questions to uncover a juror's educational background at a substantial savings of valuable space.

SET PRIORITIES FOR DESIRED INFORMATION. Establish priorities for crucial information when questionnaire space is limited. Consider what can be obtained during voir dire questioning when setting priorities. Information best obtained during voir dire questioning should not take up valuable space on the questionnaire. While shorter questionnaires tend to focus on the general backgrounds and experiences of jurors, specific items of information, particularly if they are of a sensitive nature (e.g., treatment by mental health professionals or unpleasant experiences with law enforcement), rise in priority for the limited space available.

Questions concerning the jurors' opinions are generally saved for use in voir dire when space is an issue. However, inclusion of opinion questions in restricted-length questionnaires is appropriate when (a) only a few opinion questions are needed to identify critical jurors (e.g., important opinion questions as revealed by jury research or past experience); (b) the trial judge will allow the question to be better phrased in a questionnaire (e.g., an open-ended question) as compared to during voir dire questioning; or (c) jurors are more likely to candidly answer sensitive questions in the questionnaire than in an open court examination.

Managing the Information

One of the difficulties in using juror questionnaires, particularly lengthy ones, is that they can be bulky and awkward to handle in court. This problem is heightened when the questioning of jurors occurs in a group setting where the lawyer must examine several questionnaires at a time. The common practice of using Post-It Notes or highlighters to mark critical information is often defeated when notes fall off or highlighted answers are overlooked in the process of shuffling papers.

Steps can be taken to reduce the information the juror questionnaire contains to a more easily managed form. One way is to create a juror summary form on which desired information from the juror questionnaire is recorded in a standardized manner. This form is usually one or two pages long, depending on the size and complexity of the juror questionnaire from which it is drawn.[36]

Table 2 is an example of a juror summary form that was used in *United States v. Kristen Gilbert*, a death penalty case tried in Massachusetts. This form uses a checklist approach (with comments) to reduce information contained on a fifteen-page, fifty-one-question juror questionnaire to fit on one legal-size sheet.[37] The form relies heavily on space-saving features of check boxes to record "yes/no" responses (i.e., Y[ ] N[ ]) or other aspects of the juror's answer, along with blanks to record the comments jurors made to open-ended questions. Relevant question numbers are designated with a "< >" for ease of identification. The first part of the form contains basic information on

TABLE 2
U.S. v. Gilbert Juror Summary Form
JUROR # _____   Decision: _____

<1>Name _____ Age _____ Sex _____ Race_____ Address: _____

<2>Hardship? Y[ ] N[ ] <3>Reason: _____

<4> Yrs. @ residence _____ <10 yrs: where? _____

<5>Education/training _____ Area: _____

<6>Employment: _____

<6><retired/unempl./change>Past jobs:_____ <7>**Supervise?** Y[ ] N[ ] #: _____

<8>**Training:** [ ]Accounting [ ]Law [ ]Security/PI [ ]Medicine/nursing [ ]Psychology/Counseling [ ]Criminal Justice
[ ]Education [ ]Chemistry/pharmacology Describe: _____

<9>Marital status: _____ <10>Spouse's job: _____

  Sp-Employer: _____ Sp-Educ: _____

<11>Kids? Y[ ] N[ ]_____
_____

<12>**Wrk/vol.: Medical facility?** Y[ ] N[ ] _____

<13>**Military?** Y[ ] N[ ] _____ Branch:_____ **Combat?** Y[ ] N[ ]

<14>**Treatment @ VA?** Y[ ] N[ ]_____ **Op:**_____

<15>**Heart/lung/diabetes probs?** Condition _____ Treatment _____

<16> **Law enforce/security?** Y[ ] N[ ] _____

<17>**Wrk. gov't.?** Y[ ] N[ ] _____

<18>**Concerns w/cops' test.?** _____ <19>**Concern if Def. not testify?** _____

<20>**Wrk. w/Rx?** Y[ ] N[ ]_____ Discuss? _____

<21>**Familiar** w/ [ ]epi [ ]potassium [ ]insulin [ ]captopril [ ]nifedipine [ ]ketamine _____

<22>**Orgs w/in10 yrs.:** _____ <23>**Reform orgs?** _____

<24>**Lawsuit?**Y[ ] N[ ] Circumstances: _____

<25>**News Source** _____<26> **Mags/newspapers:** _____

<27> **Local TV?** Y[ ] N[ ] _____

<28>**Op:Prosecutors?** _____ <29>**Op:Defense?** _____

<30>**Contacts w/VAMC?** _____ <31>**Visit VAMC?**_____

<32>**Jury service:** _____ <33>**Grand?** _____

<34>**Affect service?** _____ <35>**Criminal case?**_____

<36>**Victim?** _____ <37>**ICU?**_____ Op: _____

<38>**Serious injury/death: crime/negl.?** _____

<39>a. **PTP Heard?** Y[ ] N[ ] b. **How much?**_____ c. **Follow?**_____ d. **How heard?** _____
   e.**What:** _____
   f. **Opinion:** _____
   g. **Op: Gilbert:**_____ h. **Expressed Op:** _____

<40>**Not approp. to serve?** Y[ ] N[ ]_____ <41>**Dif. judge?** _____

<42>**Op: Death Penalty?** _____

<43>**Changed:** _____ <44>**DP: Never impose?** Y[ ] N[ ] _____

<45>**DP: intent. = death:**_____ <46>**DP:2 = death** _____

<47>**DP: support use:** [ ]more [ ]same [ ] less _____

<48>**DP/victim orgs?**_____ <49>**Problems?** _____

<50>**Stress?**_____ <51>**Other issues/concerns?** _____

Other comments: _____

Death penalty: _____ (Pro/soft/anti)   Nondeath rating: _____

Overall Rating: _____ (1 = very Neg.; 5 = very Pos.)   Leadership: _____ (1 = Very Weak; 5 = Very Strong) the juror, e.g., name, sex, race, age, education, and occupation. The second section converts numerous general and case-specific experiences into identifying phrases with check boxes and space for associated comments, if necessary. The third section addresses the critical opinions asked for in the questionnaire. Information on the jurors' opinions of prosecutors and defense attorneys (Q28 and Q29), exposure to pretrial publicity and its resulting influence (Q39a-h), and opinions concerning the death penalty (Q42–Q47) can be found here.

The final section of the form contains evaluations of the juror based on the full juror questionnaire and, if desired, the answers to voir dire questions. These evaluations consist of a rating of the juror in terms of (a) death penalty views ("pro/soft/anti"); (b) nondeath penalty orientation (i.e., the rating of pro-prosecution to pro-defense leanings not related to the death penalty); (c) overall rating of juror favorability (1 "very negative" to 5 "very positive"); and (d) the leadership potential of the juror (1 "very weak" to 5 "very strong"). The final decision on what to do with the juror ("decision") is located at the upper right-hand corner of the rating form.

It is useful to highlight valuable or key information on the juror summary form to further enhance the utility of this information. Highlighting can be done by printing the relevant questions on the form in bold print (as was done in Table 2) or manually highlighting answers as they are recorded on the form.[38]

Computer-Assisted Processing

When time and resources permit, the jurors' answers to the questionnaires may be transferred from the juror questionnaires to a computer storage system. There are several benefits to storing the data for jurors on a computer.

First, the information can be structured so that only what is important is printed on the form. Additional information is still accessible, however, and can be retrieved/printed at any time.

Second, the computer can print forms that contain a summary section consisting of answers of concern or "red flags" for each juror. For example, when certain information is of concern (e.g., certain occupations, prior experiences, or opinions), placing a section at the end of the juror summary form listing any red flag responses for each of the jurors ensures that key information is not overlooked.

Third, a computer storage system is very efficient at retrieving and processing information on large numbers of jurors. A rapid examination can be made of the distribution of jurors in the trial venire based on any stored characteristic. For example, if one wants to know the distribution in the trial venire of males, victims of crime, important opinions, various leadership ratings, or favorability scores, or some combination of relevant characteristics, the computer need only be instructed to produce this information.

Fourth, printing the order in which jurors will be considered along with important information associated with these jurors can lead to the more effective exercise of peremptory challenges. A listing of the key characteristics of jurors in a hypothetical trial venire is illustrated below. Such a list presents a clearer picture of the best strategy for exercising peremptory challenges in light of the impact of removing any particular juror.

JUROR LISTING

#	Name	Sex	Age	Occupation	Rating	Leadership
12	Bill Smith	M	36	Carpenter	4	3
39	Jane Shifflet	F	22	Secretary	2	2
07	Willie Brown	M	65	Retired teacher	1	5
25	Susan Jones	F	47	Psychologist	5	5

Finally, it is relatively easy to compare individual jurors to the results of any jury studies conducted in the case. In many cases, jury research studies, such as juror profile surveys and, in some cases, small-group research (e.g., focus groups and trial simulations), can provide information on the profiles of favorable and unfavorable jurors. These profiles are often in the form of mathematical equations. Computers can easily calculate the favorability of jurors when such profiles are available. This information is extremely useful in trial jurisdictions where the exercise of the peremptory challenges occurs without the benefit of questioning the jurors who will replace the excluded jurors.

NOTES

1. For other discussions of juror questionnaires, *see* THE JURY 1987: TECHNIQUES FOR THE TRIAL LAWYER, Litigation and Administrative Practice Series (1987); BLUE & SAGINAW, JURY SELECTION: STRATEGY AND SCIENCE (1990); and BONORA, KRAUSS & ROUNDTREE, JURYWORK: SYSTEMATIC TECHNIQUES (1999). A number of jurisdictions have recommended the use of juror questionnaires as part of recent efforts to improve jury trials. Examples of these jurisdictions include state courts in Arizona, California, Colorado, Florida, Maryland, New York, along with the District of Columbia. See also a discussion of the desirability of using juror questionnaires in MURPHY, HANNAFORD, LOVELAND & MUNSTERMAN, MANAGING NOTORIOUS TRIALS (1998).

2. It is important to distinguish between qualification questionnaires, which are sent out by the court to establish the jury pool, and "nonqualification" or supplemental juror questionnaires, which are designed to provide additional information to that provided on the qualification questionnaire. It should be noted that some courts routinely send out supplemental juror questionnaires on their own initiative. However, these latter questionnaires are often general in nature and not designed to meet the needs of a specific case. Whether the supplemental juror questionnaire originates from the court or from the parties in a given case, the comments apply to both. However, we will be focusing our attention on those supplemental juror questionnaires that are at least partly under the control of the parties.

3. In some jurisdictions, requests for using juror questions must be made sufficiently far in advance for the trial judge to issue an order for their use (accompanied by the questionnaire) six weeks or more before the issuing date of the jury summons. Therefore, advance planning and familiarity with local rules are necessary.

4. This cover letter was used for the juror questionnaire in United States v. Bobby Johnson and Larry Hunt.

5. Appendix 1 contains the motion for improvements in voir dire procedures, including the use of a juror questionnaire, submitted by the defense in Commonwealth of Virginia v. John Allen Muhammad, Criminal Case 54362–54365. For an excellent discussion of juror questionnaires and sample motions in support of their use, *see* BONORA, KRAUSS & ROUNDTREE, JURYWORK: SYSTEMATIC TECHNIQUES (1999).

6. It should be noted that when voir dire questioning is brief and, overall, jury selection is conducted within a short time span to begin with, using a juror questionnaire likely would not lead to appreciable time savings.

7. Many of the examples used in the following sections are drawn from questionnaires appearing in the Appendix IV companion CD. *See* this appendix for the full text of the questionnaires used in these examples and for additional questionnaires.

8. There are some problems with the wording of question 41 and its response categories. First, this question asks how closely the jurors followed "any" of the legal proceedings or trials, but jurors are given only one set of responses to cover the multiple events. Second, the response categories are supposed to address the dimension of how "closely" they followed these events. However, these categories reflect a mixture of two dimensions; closeness and frequency, e.g., "very closely" versus "occasional[ly]" and "very seldom." This question would benefit from addressing the level of attention paid to the legal proceedings in general and choosing a single dimension for the response categories.

9. The 52-page juror questionnaire used in the federal civil rights trial of the four policemen accused of violating the civil rights of Rodney King included a number of such general opinion questions. *See* United States v. Stacy Koon, Laurence Powell, Timothy Wind, & Theodore Briseno, No. CR 92 686 JGD (C.D. Cal. 1993).

10. Ideally, all parties and the judge should contribute to the construction of a juror questionnaire. While there are occasions where one party proposes a questionnaire that the judge adopts, input from all parties is necessary to ensure that all parties benefit from the questionnaire. The parties should work together to produce a mutually agreeable questionnaire for review and approval by the judge. Given the judge's final authority over the content of the questionnaire, it is useful to develop questions that meet the needs of the parties and are also likely to meet with the judge's approval.

11. It is important to realize that jurors who gave answers one and two could both have responded "no" to the standard close-ended question, "Would you have any reservations in awarding substantial monetary damages to the plaintiff, provided the law and the facts supported such a finding?" However, their answers to the open-ended question shows that these jurors do not hold the same opinion.

12. This question appeared in the juror questionnaire used in United States v. Anthony Salerno et al., which appeared in THE JURY 1987: *Techniques For the Trial Lawyer*, Litigation and Administrative Practice Series.

13. This question appeared in the questionnaire used in United States v. Gold Unlimited, et al., Civil Action No. 4:95-CV-57-R.

14. This question appeared in the juror questionnaire used in Doe v. Kohn Nast, Re: 93-4510 (United States District Court for the Eastern District of Pennsylvania).

15. This question appeared in the juror questionnaire used in United States v. John Stanfa et al., Criminal No. 94-127 (United States District Court for the Eastern District of Pennsylvania).

16. This question appeared in the juror questionnaires sent out by the Federal District Court for District of South Carolina in 1995.

17. This question appeared in the juror questionnaire used in United States v. Marion S. Barry Jr., Criminal No. 90-0068 (United States District Court for the District of Columbia).

18. This question appeared in the juror questionnaire used in the first trial of People of California v. Erik G. Menendez and Joseph L. Menendez, Case No. BA068880.

19. This question appeared in the questionnaire used in United States of America v. Jean Claude Oscar, et. al., Criminal No. 2:93cr131 (United States District Court for the Eastern District of Virginia).

20. This question appeared in the juror questionnaire used in People of Michigan v. Dr. Jack Kevorkian, 93-10158.

21. This question appeared in the juror questionnaire used in Mildred Valentine v. Dow Corning Corporation, et al., Case No. 943437.

22. This question appeared in the juror questionnaire used in People of California v. Heidi Fleiss, Case No. BA083380.

23. This question appeared in the juror questionnaire used in People of California v. O.J. Simpson, Case No. BA097211.

24. This question appeared in a juror questionnaire used in the Northern District of Oklahoma (1995).

25. This question appeared in the *Barry* juror questionnaire, *supra* note 17.

26. *See Kevorkian, supra* note 20.

27. This question appeared in the *Barry* juror questionnaire, *supra* note 17.

28. This question appeared in the *Simpson* juror questionnaire, *supra* note 23.

29. This section heading appeared in the juror questionnaire used in *Salerno et al, supra* note 12. Italics not in the original.

30. This section heading appeared in the juror questionnaire used in People of Tennessee v. Courtney B. Mathews, Docket No. 33791.

31. This latter question appeared in the juror questionnaire used in United States v. Bobby Johnson and Larry Glen Hunt, Crim. No. 1:97-CR-426. Less than one-half (48 percent) of the sixty-one potential jurors said they would follow the law (i.e., answered "no"), with 52 percent of the potential jurors answering that they would follow their own opinion or were unsure of what they would do in this situation.

32. These questions appeared in the *Simpson* juror questionnaire, *supra* note 23.

33. It should be noted that occupations or employment status can change between the time when the qualification questionnaire was completed and the trial date. As such, it is helpful to ask at the beginning of oral voir dire whether there are any changes to the information provided on the qualification questionnaires.

34. This question appeared in the *Stanfa* questionnaire, *supra* note 15.

35. This question appeared in the questionnaire used in United States v. Hollis Earl Roberts, No. CR 95-35-S.

36. The topic of summary juror forms in the context of information gathered during voir dire questioning will be considered in Chapter 8.

37. As juror questionnaires become longer and more complex, juror summary forms become extremely valuable in managing the information contained on these questionnaires.

38. Sometimes certain information, e.g., the race of the juror, should not be included on the summary juror form. This is the case when by including such information the lawyer invites the suspicion of discriminatory use of peremptory challenges. For a discussion of the topic of the discriminatory use of peremptory challenges, *see* Chapter 9.

CHAPTER 8

Evaluating Potential Jurors

Objectives

- To examine the various sources of information relevant to jury selection.
- To understand how individual jurors act on a jury.
- To examine methods of efficient recordkeeping.
- To develop systematic methods for evaluating jurors.

The task of selecting a jury requires that lawyers evaluate potential jurors and decide how to exercise peremptory challenges and challenges for cause. This chapter focuses on the evaluation of potential jurors. The successful accomplishment of this task requires collecting information on potential jurors, understanding how potential jurors will act in deliberations, and integrating this knowledge to produce a final evaluation for each potential juror.

Collecting Information on Potential Jurors

There are two major sources of information regarding potential jurors: (a) information gathered prior to trial and (b) information that surfaces during the voir dire phase of trial.

Pretrial Information

So far, the focus of this book has been on the voir dire process to the exclusion of what lawyers may find out about potential jurors before trial. Arriving at the overall evaluation of potential jurors, however, requires consideration of all information pertaining to them. Two sources of information are available in the pretrial stage: juror investigations and social science research methods. The fundamental difference between these two sources of information lies in the relationship of the information to specific jurors. Juror investigations gather information concerning the potential jurors themselves. Social science

---

Sources of pretrial information on potential jurors:

- Juror investigations
  - Private investigations
  - Public records
  - Juror "drive-bys"
  - Information searches on Internet
  - Community networks
- Social science methods
  - Focus groups
  - Trial simulations
  - Community surveys

---

research methods consider opinions, beliefs, and background characteristics of people in the trial community to predict the desirability of potential jurors.

JUROR INVESTIGATIONS. In most jurisdictions, lists of potential jurors, or what are termed the trial venires, are available from the court from twenty-four hours to several weeks in advance of trial. The information available on these lists may be of a limited nature, such as the names and addresses of the potential jurors, or the lists may contain more detailed information, such as the ages, occupations, marital status, and any prior jury service of these jurors.

Armed with the information from the jury list, lawyers can acquire more information about the potential jurors. This information comes from a variety of sources: private investigators, public records, juror "drive-bys," information searches on the Internet, and community networks.[1]

Sometimes lawyers hire private investigators to collect background information on potential jurors. Private investigators may speak with individuals who know the potential jurors, either directly or indirectly. In addition, investigators often examine public records and drive by the homes of jurors looking for information with which to evaluate potential jurors. A summary of this information is given to the lawyers for use at trial.

Whether through the use of private investigators or other personnel, lawyers also can examine the information available in public records regarding potential jurors. These records may include civil and criminal records, motor vehicle records, property tax rolls, and political party registration. The information acquired from these records can be very valuable. For example, knowing whether or not the defendant hospital has sued a potential juror for failure to pay hospital bills is important in a medical negligence suit. The hospital that has sued a potential juror is probably facing a potentially hostile or unsympathetic juror.

Juror drive-bys can be a source of information. In this approach, lawyers, or others, drive to the residences of jurors. They take notes regarding the jurors' homes and sometimes take photographs of relevant aspects of the surroundings. Attention is paid to such considerations as the value associated with the residence (wealth), the condition and "neatness" of the residence, the visible possessions of the jurors or their family members (e.g., toys indicating the presence and ages of any children), and the presence of any indicators of the jurors' social and political views (e.g., signs or bumper stickers supporting political candidates or causes). This information adds to what is already known about the potential jurors and serves to round out the picture.

A relatively new arrival on the scene of juror investigations is the use of the Internet. Popular search engines such as "Google.com" can rapidly search the Internet for references to potential jurors' names (e.g., in connection with writing letters to the editor, receiving awards, or having personal websites). While the likelihood of individual jurors being identified in such searches is still rare, this resource may prove increasingly useful as more and more information is placed in public areas on the Internet.

The last source of information obtained through juror investigations involves the use of what are termed "community networks." A community network relies on the establishment of a collection or network of individuals who represent the different segments of the trial community. When the names of potential jurors become known, members of the network are contacted to see if they know the potential jurors or have access to information from other people who may know these jurors. This information is then pooled and made available to lawyers when considering each juror. Key to the effectiveness of this approach is the development of contact people from many different segments of the trial community, not just the friends and associates of the lawyers.

Caution: Information from community networks is particularly susceptible to the unreliability and personal biases of the people who provide this information.

The subjective nature of much of the information at issue presents problems of unreliability in using community networks. Often network members provide such comments regarding the desirability of potential jurors as "This would be a great juror" or "Don't take this juror." However, these observations may be wrong. To minimize the risks inherent in these subjective evaluations, it is important to elicit the underlying reasons for the comment so that lawyers can judge for themselves the accuracy of the evaluations in light of their intimate knowledge of the case.

SOCIAL SCIENCE RESEARCH METHODS. Two basic research methods develop information for use in evaluating potential jurors prior to trial: opinion polling and small group research.

For more than thirty years, social scientists have been using survey methods to develop profiles of who would make desirable and undesirable jurors.[2] To develop juror profiles, social scientists conduct surveys or opinion polls in the trial jurisdiction. These surveys elicit the opinions and views of jury-qualified people (who are not the members of the trial venire) along with information on their backgrounds and past experiences. The profiles of desirable and undesirable jurors emerge by examining the relationships between jurors' opinions and background characteristics. In short, polling techniques determine which characteristics of potential jurors (profiles) predict important beliefs or opinions, such as opinions concerning the guilt or liability of the defendant. At trial, lawyers use these profiles to evaluate the desirability of potential jurors.

The second source of pretrial information results from pretrial studies of community members' reactions to the case or litigation using small group research techniques. Two prominent techniques are focus groups and trial simulations.[3] Both techniques bring together small groups of jury-equivalent people who consider issues relevant to the case. In general, focus groups concentrate on the discussion of issues raised in the litigation. Trial simulations attempt to more closely approximate the experience actual jurors receive in trials by presenting information in a trial format, including deliberations.

Both trial simulations and focus groups primarily investigate trial issues and potential jury verdicts. However, some of these studies have sufficient numbers of "jurors" who participate so that it is possible to detect differences in verdict preferences based on the backgrounds and opinions of the participants. Like surveys, this information forms the basis for profiles of desirable and undesirable jurors. At trial, lawyers use these profiles in much the same way as those resulting from juror surveys.

Trial Information

The second major source of information on potential jurors comes from what lawyers uncover about potential jurors during the jury selection process. This information, drawn from juror questionnaires and the results of the voir dire questioning process, reveals the opinions, emotions, background characteristics, and past experiences of potential jurors based on their answers and their verbal and nonverbal communication. As such, these topics have been the focus of previous chapters. However, we have yet to consider an important piece of the puzzle of jury selection: How will these jurors act on a jury?

The Jury as a Group

So far our attention has been on the jurors as individuals—their desirability in terms of their opinions, values, and experiences. To complete the evaluations of potential jurors, however, it is necessary to consider each individual in the context of the final jury. Two aspects of how jurors act on a jury are of interest: individual participation and group dynamics.

Individual Participation

An important quality of juries should be kept in mind: Juries are temporary groups. Jurors are assigned the task of participating in a jury in order to render a decision concerning a dispute between litigants. However, the lifetime of a jury is only as long as it takes to complete its task (or to declare itself unable to do so). Generally, this is a matter of a few days or weeks. The short-term nature of juries and the fact that the jurors are assigned to juries produces a situation where what jurors bring with them to the task plays an important role in how they participate.

LEADERSHIP POTENTIAL. A major consideration in evaluating potential jurors is the influence that various members of the jury will have on the deliberation process. Much of this attention is on identifying potential leaders on the jury. One of the key leaders on the jury is the foreperson. This individual can exercise a great deal of control over the jury's actions. The foreperson can direct the order of the discussion, balloting, and, through his or her leadership position, exert persuasive pressures on members of the jury. But the question is, "Who is likely to be elected foreperson?" Forepersons tend to be those jurors who have been on juries before, come from higher-status occupations, have experiences that are relevant to the task (e.g., mechanical engineers in patent cases), and are more assertive during voir dire (e.g., exhibit stronger responses and/or talk more). In addition, potential jurors who are accustomed to leading others or giving directions to others in their daily lives (e.g., through their occupations or personal activities) are likely to assume a leadership role on the jury.

Beyond being elected foreperson, which jurors are likely to be more influential or possible leaders on the jury? Obviously, those jurors who would tend to be elected foreperson are also more persuasive on juries, e.g., jurors having higher-status occupations, task-relevant experiences, and assertive personalities. In addition, the educational experiences of jurors play a role in their participation in jury deliberations. Jurors with greater educational experience participate more in deliberations, have a greater understanding of the judge's instructions, and generally are more persuasive than less educated jurors. Jurors with higher incomes—typically related to a higher level of educational experience and higher occupational status—also tend to participate

---

Considering jurors in the context of the jury:

- Individual participation
  - Leadership potential
  - Individual differences in amount and nature of participation
- Group dynamics
  - Subgroup formation
  - Cohesion
  - Majority influence
  - Stages of deliberations

more in deliberations and are more persuasive. In general, the persuasive jurors are confident and talkative. They can persuade less confident and less articulate jurors through verbal pressure to modify their positions.[4]

DIFFERENCES IN PARTICIPATION. Bonora, Krauss & Roundtree have suggested a five-category model to represent the participation of jurors.[5] The categories are as follows: (a) leaders, (b) followers, (c) fillers, (d) negotiators, and (e) holdouts. Leaders are those jurors who either directly or indirectly use their abilities, skills, and power to affect the verdict chosen by influencing the other jurors' opinions and/or the decision process used to reach a verdict. These jurors tend to be talkative, direct, and assertive in social situations (including voir dire questioning). In addition, influence or leadership can also arise through the social skills of jurors. These "social" leaders act through friendliness, humor, kindness, and courtesy. Noticing which jurors appear to take the lead in initiating conversations, bring other jurors into conversations, and in other ways develop rapport with their fellow jurors provides clues as to social leaders. As mentioned earlier, clues to leadership potential on the jury are high social status (associated with occupation, income, and education), leadership experience through jobs or activities, articulateness, confidence and assertiveness, analytic ability, and prior relevant experience (e.g., having served on a jury before).

Followers, on the other hand, are the "supporters" on the jury. They are more passive than leaders, yet still reach their own conclusions. However, these jurors are less self-assured and are susceptible to influence by the leaders. Jurors in occupations characterized by their carrying out the orders of others are likely candidates for followers.

Fillers are those jurors who are not assertive in any way on the jury. They lack the confidence and in some cases the intellectual ability to understand the case or judicial instructions. They are the least active of the jury members and have difficulty in deliberations. During voir dire, these jurors are the silent members of the panel, speaking only when spoken to and often unsure of their answers (e.g., "I don't know"). Passivity and sometimes subservience characterize their nonverbal behavior. The occupations of these jurors reflect an absence of developed verbal skills. As the label implies, fillers play a negligible role in the deliberation process.

The fourth category of jurors, negotiators, are the mediators on the jury. They tend to facilitate compromise and the easing of tensions. These jurors can be, and often are, leaders on the jury. The skills necessary to bring about group consensus (such as articulateness and the ability to bring out all viewpoints) are also the skills that promote leadership. Jurors with occupations that rely on their interpersonal skills in forming group consensus—not autocratic decisions—are likely candidates for negotiators. Discussing with jurors their role in decision-making at their workplace can reveal valuable clues to potential negotiators.

The final category is the holdout juror. While rare on juries (as evidenced by the infrequency of hung juries), holdouts are characterized by nonconformity, opinionatedness, and stubbornness. In many cases, these jurors reject authority and leadership by others. They exhibit opinionated views, a lack of sensitivity to the opinions of others, and little need for social approval. It should be kept in mind, however, that true "holdouts" are rare and can favor either side in the dispute. They are not always holdouts for the criminal defendants—hence they are not necessarily rebellious against authority.

Group Dynamics

While we speak of a jury as a single group, it is important to realize that a jury starts out as a collection of individuals. It evolves into a collection of subgroups that usually, but not always, coalesce into a single group identity. During the deliberations, the jurors' activities usually follow several stages and exhibit characteristic influences of group processes. Anticipating the dynamics of the deliberation process is a necessary step in evaluating jurors and in effective jury selection. Below we consider several aspects of jury group dynamics: subgroup formation, cohesion, majority influence, and stages of deliberations.

SUBGROUP FORMATION. The formation of subgroups in a jury often starts while the jury is being selected. It can be observed when jurors associate with one another at breaks during jury selection and talk together while they are sitting in the jury box. As the trial progresses, subgroups emerge when jurors have lunch together and mill around together during breaks. Subgroups form as a result of recognized commonalities among jurors. These commonalities may be in terms of physical characteristics, social status, recreational activities and hobbies, past experiences, general interests, geographical location, or opinions and values. For example, race and gender are powerful indicators of initial subgroup formation. As jurors get to know each other, commonality of interests and opinions (particularly as they relate to the jurors' opinions concerning the case) gain an important role in the evolution of subgroups.

Understanding how subgroups form is important for two major reasons: the majority's influence on minorities and the influence of the voir dire in subgroup formation. As we shall see later, the majority on the jury plays a key role in the eventual verdict that the jury reaches. Knowing which jurors will tend to come together in subgroups offers the opportunity to shape the majority on the final jury. Identifying potential subgroups also enables the lawyer to consider jurors who would serve as links between various subgroups. These individuals often share characteristics with more than one subgroup, e.g., gender or occupation. As discussed above, mediators often serve as a link between subgroups because of their ability to bring consensus out of divergent perspectives and opinions. Since a unanimous or a particular majority verdict is often desired, it is necessary to consider individuals who could act as go-betweens or links that can bring one or more subgroups together, thus arriving at a majority faction in the jury.

The voir dire process itself can play a significant role in the development of subgroups. The questioning of potential jurors reveals their interests, opinions, and occupations, as well as other information that can serve as the basis for commonalities between jurors and the formation of subgroups. Lawyers can shape the formation of subgroups by highlighting to various jurors their commonalities with other jurors (e.g., "Mr. Smith, I see that you agree with Mr. Jones on this issue," or "Ms. Schifflet, I see that you and Mr. Jenkins both gave money to MADD"). Through such highlighting statements (or simply pursuing selected questions), jurors can be encouraged (but not forced) to form subgroups based on certain commonalities.

COHESION. The cohesiveness of the jury plays a role in its ability to reach a consensus on a verdict. Jurors who work together well are more likely to be able to reach consensus. Thus, fostering cohesion will facilitate a unanimous verdict. Cohesion stems from the abilities of jurors to blend their personalities in order to work together. However, outside forces also can influence cohesion. One of these forces is the power of suggestion. If jurors are told that they will be able to work well together, they are more likely to do so. For example, telling jurors that they all have common sense or some other characteristic (e.g., respect for one another's opinions) that will enable them to work well together will lead to greater group cohesiveness. This power of suggestion is reinforced when the lawyers highlight the kinds of commonalities at issue.

MAJORITY INFLUENCE. The powerful influence that a majority exerts on minorities in groups is well documented. In juries, as in other groups, the majority can exert a great deal of pressure on minority members to conform to the majority's position. This is particularly the case when the minority is one juror. In general, a simple majority of jurors who initially favor acquittal will foreshadow an acquittal. In criminal cases, however, convictions often require an initial preference for conviction of over two-thirds of the jurors. The question arises as to what type of influence majorities exert. Whether majority or otherwise, there are two types of influence that appear in groups: informational influence and normative influence. Jurors can influence each other by providing information (e.g., recalling items of evidence or parts of judicial instructions) to the decision-making process—what is called *informational influence*. In addition, jurors can lead another juror to conform to the majority by giving their opinions, thereby indicating a majority consensus for the desired position—what is termed *normative influence*. In general, informational as compared to normative influence tends to exert a stronger impact on verdicts. However, both of these influences are present and tend to be intertwined in the interactions of jurors.[6]

STAGES OF DELIBERATIONS. While it may not seem so on the surface, jury deliberations tend to follow a pattern that consists of four phases.[7] The first phase of deliberations is the *orientation* phase. At this stage jurors define the task they face, elect a foreperson, and provide their tentative positions or views on "what happened." The deliberations proceed to the open *conflict* phase. Since the jurors have revealed their opinions and positions and are now aware of those who oppose them or have competing "stories" for what happened, they direct their comments to the jurors in opposition. This phase is characterized by a rigidity in opinions stated (or the correctness of the "stories" proposed to account for the evidence and legal instructions) aimed at changing the minds of the opposition jurors.

Conflict resolution is the third phase of deliberations. If the jury is going to arrive at consensus on a verdict, jurors begin to identify the potential verdicts or stories for what happened that are likely to lead to agreement. The comments of jurors shift to more flexible statements. There is a lessening of the rigidity that characterized their previous statements along with greater movement toward the most acceptable verdict choice. Finally, should the jury reach a verdict (or if animosity in a hung jury is not too great), deliberations enter the *reconciliation* phase. The jurors express mutual support and group solidarity while attempting to heal the wounds produced by the conflict.

Integrating Information: The Final Evaluation of Jurors

When it comes to jury selection, it is crucial to consider all potential jurors in a systematic fashion. Fundamental to this approach is accurate recordkeeping.

Recording Information

In evaluating jurors it is necessary to gather all relevant information available and condense it into something usable. This requires generating records for each potential juror that contain the desired information. As discussed earlier, information may be available in addition to what surfaces during voir dire. If so, the final records for jurors will include this additional information. Often such "extra" voir dire information is kept on separate sheets attached to the jurors' records.

Three approaches to recording information on potential jurors are the jury box form, the individual form, and the individual checklist. While these approaches will be discussed separately, in many instances a combination of these forms is used in jury selection.

JURY BOX FORM. The jury box form is a record sheet that corresponds to the physical layout of the jury box or panel. Key to this approach is that the form reflects the view that the lawyer has in questioning the jurors. For example, if questioning occurs using a panel of six, twelve, or fourteen potential jurors, the form should visually represent the respective array of jurors. Table 1 is a full-page form for a panel of twelve jurors. In those cases where key information is to be asked of all jurors (e.g., views on pain and suffering or the defendant not testifying), it is possible to place codes for these areas on the original forms. Having such forms with critical areas already noted allows for easy and simple recording of this information for all jurors. The use of multiple forms allows lawyers to maintain the integrity of the relative positions of jurors in the jury box during the removal and replacement process in jury selection. In addition, Post-it Notes or some other small, self-adhesive note pad may be used to record information on replacement jurors in their appropriate location in the juror box.

An important feature of the jury box form is that it minimizes the likelihood that information pertaining to one juror is mistakenly assigned to another juror. The juror who is speaking (or several jurors raising their hands) is simply matched up with the appropriate place on the jury box form. This form also allows for quick notations of interactions among jurors (e.g., juror 1 and juror 2 sharing a joke together or a friendly interaction), thus providing information on potential group development. In addition, the jury box gives a picture of the composition of the jury at a glance.

INDIVIDUAL JUROR FORM. A second approach to recording information on jurors is the individual juror form. As the name implies, the individual form contains only information relevant to a specific juror. Table 2 illustrates the type of information contained on this type of form.

The individual form contains several types of information regarding the potential juror. The initial part of the form provides certain basic background information on the juror (e.g., name, seat number, sex, age, race, and occupation). The second part of the form provides space for any additional relevant background information on the juror. This section could just as easily provide reference to specific background characteristics of importance, as shown by the information in parentheses.

The third section of the form considers critical opinions the juror reveals during voir dire questioning. Again, space could be provided for these opinions and/or reference could be made to specific opinions, as shown by the information in parentheses. The fourth section contains the overall ratings of the juror's nonverbal communication. This section isolates the juror's reactions to questioning by the lawyers and the judge. In addition, a comment section provides any elaboration on these ratings that is necessary. If more in-depth analysis of the nonverbal communication is of interest, the user can expand this section to include various verbal and nonverbal behaviors or cues.

The fifth section provides for the overall evaluations of the juror. This section includes the rating of his or her leadership potential and the final favorability rating, along with the decision regarding the use of a peremptory challenge. The final section contains space for any additional comments. Such comments may include tactical observations and observations concerning emerging group dynamics relevant to this juror, among other comments.

The major value of the individual form is the greater amount of information it contains. One of the problems with the jury box form is that during lengthy voir dire, the form becomes crowded with notations and is somewhat unwieldy. The individual form stores more information. This form is particularly useful when individual sequestered voir dire is undertaken.

TABLE I
SAMPLE JURY BOX FORM
JURY

7.	8.	9.	10.	11.	12.
1.	2.	3.	4.	5.	6.

CHALLENGES: _____   NUMBER USED: _____
OPPONENT'S CHALLENGES: _____   NUMBER USED : _____

However, it becomes more difficult to record information on the individual forms when several jurors are providing information at one time, as in the group questioning format.

INDIVIDUAL CHECKLISTS. The third approach involves the use of checklists. This approach involves developing a list of potentially relevant characteristics of jurors. The relevant information pertaining to each juror is subsequently

TABLE 2
SAMPLE INDIVIDUAL JUROR FORM

NAME: _____ JUROR SEAT #: _____

ADDRESS: _____ SEX: _____ RACE: _____

AGE: _____ MARITAL STATUS: _____ OCCUPATION: _____

EDUCATION: _____ TRAINING/STUDY: _____

ADDITIONAL BACKGROUND:

(VICTIM OF CRIME): _____

(PRIOR DEFENDANT): _____

CRITICAL OPINIONS:

(AUTHORITARIANISM): _____

(DAMAGES SCALE): _____

OVERALL NONVERBAL COMMUNICATION:

PLAINTIFF: POS. [ ]   NEUTRAL [ ]   NEG. [ ]   COMMENTS _____

DEFENDANT: POS. [ ]   NEUTRAL [ ]   NEG. [ ]   COMMENTS _____

JUDGE: POS. [ ]   NEUTRAL [ ]   NEG. [ ]   COMMENTS _____

OVERALL SCORES:

LEADERSHIP: 1. [ ] VERY STRONG   3. [ ] SOMEWHAT WEAK

                      2. [ ] SOMEWHAT STRONG   4. [ ] VERY WEAK

RATING: 1. [ ] VERY POSITIVE   4. [ ] SOMEWHAT NEGATIVE

                      2. [ ] SOMEWHAT POSITIVE   5. [ ] VERY NEGATIVE

                      3. [ ] NEUTRAL

DECISION: [ ] DEFINITELY REJECT   [ ] REJECT IF POSSIBLE   [ ] ACCEPT

ADDITIONAL COMMENTS:

_____

_____

TABLE 3
SAMPLE ITEMS FOR JUROR CHECKLIST

YES	N/A	NO	
[ ]	[ ]	[ ]	Is the juror employed?
[ ]	[ ]	[ ]	Is the juror or immediate family employed in the insurance profession?
[ ]	[ ]	[ ]	Has the juror ever studied law?
[ ]	[ ]	[ ]	Any contacts in law enforcement?
[ ]	[ ]	[ ]	Ever been a defendant in a civil suit?

checked off as it is revealed on voir dire. Table 3 illustrates a few of the items that may appear on a checklist.

Checklists may serve an evaluative function as well. The checklist in Table 4 includes a rating system for jurors (e.g., checking "positive [+]," "neutral [0]," "negative [–]," or "unknown [x]" in response to an item) in addition to the traditional checklist.[8] When using the checklist as a rating form, the overall evaluation score for the potential juror results from combining the various ratings in some manner. Often the overall score reflects the simple addition of the various scales, with negative values assigned to negative ratings.

The checklist approach has two major advantages. First, checklists provide an easy method for recording information on potential jurors. Second, checklists provide a quick visual summary of this information.

There are, however, several disadvantages in the use of checklists. First, as with the individual juror form, group questioning of jurors makes the use of such forms unwieldy. Second, when using checklists with rating systems, combining the numerous ratings is problematic. Simply adding all the ratings together is inappropriate, because obviously not all characteristics are equally important. For example, is it equally informative that a juror receives a negative rating on "body language" while at the same time receiving a positive rating on "education"? In addition, it is highly unlikely that all of the many characteristics comprising the final rating are important in the final positive, neutral, or negative status of a juror. Using the checklist approach as a rating system requires that attention be paid to which characteristics are relevant and the relative importance of these characteristics.

CHOOSING A RATING FORM. In deciding on a method of recording information on jurors it is important to use the approach that best suits the needs of the voir dire situation. In group voir dire, some variation of the jury box form is preferable. When jurors are questioned individually or in groups of two or three, the individual form or the checklist form may be the most efficient way to gather detailed information. During lengthy voir dire questioning in a group setting, using a jury box form in conjunction with a checklist or individual form may prove the best method for keeping track of information on potential jurors.

TABLE 4
SAMPLE ITEMS FOR AN EVALUATIVE JUROR CHECKLIST

RATING:

YES	NA	NO		
[ ]	[ ]	[ ]		Is the juror employed?
[ ]	[ ]	[ ]		Is the juror or immediate family employed in the insurance profession?
[ ]	[ ]	[ ]		Has the juror ever studied law?
[ ]	[ ]	[ ]		Any contacts in law enforcement?
[ ]	[ ]	[ ]		Education beyond high school

. . . .

"+"	"0"	"-"	"x"	
[ ]	[ ]	[ ]	[ ]	Belief regarding limits on monetary awards
[ ]	[ ]	[ ]	[ ]	Views on punitive damages

. . . .

[ ]	[ ]	[ ]	[ ]	Overall, nonverbal communication

OVERALL SCORES:

LEADERSHIP: 1. [ ] VERY STRONG   3. [ ] SOMEWHAT WEAK
             2. [ ] SOMEWHAT STRONG   4. [ ] VERY WEAK

RATING: 1. [ ] VERY POSITIVE   4. [ ] SOMEWHAT NEGATIVE
             2. [ ] SOMEWHAT POSITIVE   5. [ ] VERY NEGATIVE
             3. [ ] NEUTRAL

DECISION: [ ] DEFINITELY REJECT   [ ] REJECT IF POSSIBLE   [ ] ACCEPT

ADDITIONAL COMMENTS:

_____

_____

No matter what form is eventually chosen, maintaining detailed notes on potential jurors is important in the evaluation of jurors and the subsequent effectiveness of jury selection. If jury selection occurs over the course of several days or longer, there will be a tendency to remember more information about the jurors questioned later than about jurors encountered earlier in the voir dire process. Keeping detailed records helps to minimize any problems in selective memory. In addition, overall evaluations of jurors may change as a function of the distribution of favorable and unfavorable jurors in the jury pool. It is a fact of life that some jurors look relatively better or worse after later jurors express their opinions. Thus, in practice, overall rating systems may not be as absolute as we would like. Practice in using rating scales and keeping detailed records will minimize any rating scale shifts.

Finally, as will be discussed in the next chapter, the *Batson* line of cases[9] concerning the nondiscriminatory use of peremptory challenges places a premium on documenting the reasons for the exercise of peremptory chal-

---

Keys to effectively evaluating jurors:

■ Choose an appropriate form for recording information on jurors

— Jury box form
— Individual juror form
— Individual checklist

■ Make systematic evaluations of all jurors

— Develop critical rating dimensions.
— Be sure to rate jurors on their potential leadership/dominance.
— Include overall favorability and leadership/dominance scores in the final ratings.

---

lenges. Careful note taking concerning the jurors' opinions, nonverbal behaviors, and backgrounds is necessary to successfully defend against a *Batson* challenge.

Systematic Evaluation: Assigning Values to Jurors

At the completion of voir dire, it is necessary to evaluate the potential jurors based on the information available. This information comes from many sources: opinions jurors express on voir dire, their verbal and nonverbal communication, their background characteristics and experiences, and their likely group leadership/dominance. Assigning values to jurors often takes two (or more) steps: rating the juror on important characteristics or dimensions and creating a final overall rating of favorability.

RATING JURORS. In considering how to rate potential jurors it is first necessary to determine the areas of concern in the case and what the favorable or unfavorable characteristics are. The case analysis conducted in preparation for voir dire provides a good idea of what is important to know about the jurors, e.g., their opinions, personal experiences, background characteristics, and leadership potential.

The next step is to distinguish between jurors based on the characteristics of interest, e.g., opinions on the death penalty or willingness to award damages. One method is to establish a rating system or scale for evaluating these critical characteristics that is agreed upon by those who will evaluate potential jurors. The rating scale provides either a numerical value or a label reflecting the evaluation of jurors on a particular characteristic. Evaluations of jurors are frequently made on a simple three-point scale (e.g., positive, neutral, and negative) or a four- or five-point scale, where "1" represents the lowest or the most positive value and "4" or "5" the highest or most negative value on the characteristics of interest. An example of a five-point scale reflecting the overall favorability of jurors would be "1" strongly favors the client, "2" leans in favor of the client, "3" is neutral, "4" leans in favor of the opposition, and "5" strongly favors the opposition.

A five-point scale is useful in many instances, particularly when overall ratings are being made. The neutral position ("3") allows for greater discrimination between jurors and reflects the potentially true state of mind of the juror.[10] For example, a five-point rating scale for the jurors' views on the death penalty would be as follows:

1. Favors the use of the death penalty under all conditions.
2. Favors the use of the death penalty under limited circumstances.
3. Does not favor or oppose the death penalty.
4. Opposes the use of the death penalty, but would consider it under certain circumstances.
5. Opposes the use of the death penalty under all circumstances.

The above system could be applied to any major opinion of interest, e.g., monetary damages, support for the legal rights of criminal defendants, belief in the infallibility of the United States Patent Office, trust in corporations, and views on the effects of oil spills. A question or series of questions are developed that allow jurors to be placed into one of the categories. Even when a numerical system is not used, establishing the appropriate opinion categories will help to focus attention on which opinions are desirable and which are undesirable.

When rating jurors it is important to assign scale values as soon as possible. The best time to make the rating is during or right after the questioning of the juror. If it is not feasible to make immediate ratings, rate the jurors at the next recess or other appropriate break. Practice prior to trial in making ratings will increase both the speed and the reliability of the evaluations made in the courtroom.

For jury selections that last more than one day, review the evaluations and ratings of jurors over the course of the process. During the evenings, address the ratings of each juror under consideration. Seek consensus on the final evaluations of each juror when more than one person is rating jurors. When consensus is not possible, additional information should be sought concerning the potential jurors at issue during subsequent voir dire questioning in order to achieve agreement on their ultimate desirability.

Sometimes there is a temptation to treat "good" jurors in a superficial manner when discussing the desirability of potential jurors. However, it can be a mistake to ignore good jurors. Jurors can start out appearing to be favorable to the client (perhaps because of some desired background characteristic or personal experience) only to reveal undesirable qualities upon closer scrutiny. By determining both good and bad points of all jurors, overlooked areas of inquiry surface along with a total picture of the jurors' desirability. Thorough questioning of the jurors will also yield benefits in developing examples for later use at trial that communicate desired points, e.g., examples or analogies from business, school, or household settings.

Finally, in the process of reaching consensus, there is often a need to put the information that lawyers have recorded on potential jurors in more manageable form—on index cards, for example. However, care is needed in reducing information on potential jurors so that nothing of value is lost. Decide what information is important and be sure it stays with the ratings of potential jurors.

MAKING THE FINAL RATING. Once ratings of the information on potential jurors have been made, it is necessary to combine these ratings into a single rating or set of ratings that will serve as an indicator of the party's preference for the potential juror. For example, in many personal injury cases, the juror's (a) willingness to award damages, (b) preference for equity, (c) views on the responsibility accorded the defendant for the actions at issue, (d) nonverbal communication, and (e) important personal experiences (e.g., prior involvement in lawsuits) will need to be combined into an overall preference rating for the juror. These considerations may be in addition to any survey-based profiles of favorable and unfavorable jurors.

In most cases, the evaluations of jurors involve the subjective weighting of the value given to each characteristic. For example, when the plaintiff's case is strong on liability, the dimension of willingness to award damages may be assigned more importance (greater weight) than the dimension of liability. When empirical studies are available (e.g., trial simulations, focus groups, or archival data), the results of these studies may indicate the relative importance of the various characteristics.

The final ratings themselves should contain enough diversity to allow for discrimination between jurors. A five-point scale reflecting the intuitive dimension of favorability to the client is often useful. This scale would be set up as follows:

[   ] 1. Very favorable/positive (pro-client)
[   ] 2. Somewhat favorable/positive (leaning toward client's position)
[   ] 3. Neutral (not leaning either way)
[   ] 4. Somewhat unfavorable/negative (leaning toward the opposition's position)
[   ] 5. Very unfavorable/negative (pro-opponent)

Assigning a score from 1 to 5 generally offers enough spread between values to allow adequate discrimination between jurors. For those who are less comfortable using numerical scales, it would be just as easy to rate jurors on an analogous plus/minus system:

[   ] + + Very favorable/positive
[   ] + Somewhat favorable/positive
[   ] 0 Neutral
[   ] - Somewhat unfavorable/negative
[   ] - - Very unfavorable/negative

In addition to the juror's overall rating of favorability it is necessary to consider how dominant the potential juror will be on the jury. For this, a number of factors are of interest:

- The juror's assertiveness during voir dire
- The juror's self-confidence and strength reflected in his or her non-verbal communication
- Any leadership of other jurors the juror exhibits during breaks
- The differential treatment accorded the juror by other jurors
- The presence of social status, educational background, or occupational indicators of leadership

These observations form the basis for evaluations of dominance/leadership. Since finer points of discrimination on leadership are not usually necessary, a four-point dominance scale is usually sufficient. Such a scale would be set up as follows:

[   ] 1. Very dominant (likely leader)

[   ] 2. Somewhat dominant (influential but not a leader)

[   ] 3. Somewhat submissive (follower)

[   ] 4. Very submissive (nonparticipant)

The reason for separate ratings on favorability and dominance/leadership is that the favorability of potential jurors is independent of how much influence they will exert during the course of jury deliberations. Having both ratings gives a more complete picture of whom to reject. For example, a potential juror who is very unfavorable (scores a "5" or "− −" on the favorability scale) and also is very dominant (scores a "1" on dominance/leadership) would rate the higher priority for rejection than a potential juror who also is very unfavorable yet is submissive (scores a "4" or "5" on the dominance/leadership scale).

Employing ratings of leadership in this manner also facilitates the consideration of group dynamics in the decision to accept or reject jurors. In some cases, it is desirable to include dominant yet somewhat unfavorable jurors on the jury (provided the case is strong). This is particularly true when there is a possibility that a dominant, very unfavorable juror might enter the jury because of an insufficient number of peremptory challenges. This circumstance also can arise in those situations where making a decision in favor of the client requires jurors to go against popular opinion.

When time permits (e.g., during lunch breaks or overnight recesses), it is helpful to develop a visual representation of the jurors under consideration. One such approach involves placing the jurors' names along with their ratings and other important information on index cards. These cards are ordered from least favorable to most favorable on a bulletin board or table based on the ratings of these jurors. This method enables lawyers to see at a glance the relative favorability of numerous potential jurors. In addition, it provides an easy method to discriminate between potential jurors who fall into the same category. The following chart illustrates this approach. The numbers in parentheses reflect the juror's favorability rating followed by their dominance rating as may be found in the struck jury method.[11]

Potential Juror Favorability Ratings

Very Favorable	Somewhat Favorable	Neutral	Somewhat Unfavorable	Very Unfavorable
Juror 2 (1/1)	Juror 6 (2/3)	Juror 3 (3/3)	Juror 1 (4/4)	Juror 5 (5/2)
Juror 8 (1/3)	Juror 7 (2/2)	Juror 4 (3/4)	Juror 11 (4/2)	Juror 12 (5/1)
Juror 19 (1/2)	Juror 14 (2/3)	Juror 9 (3/2)	Juror 18 (4/1)	
Juror 20 (2/1)	Juror 10 (3/2)	Juror 13 (3/4)		
	Juror 15 (3/2)	Juror 16 (3/3)		
	Juror 17 (3/3)			

As can be seen in the chart above, not everyone within a category is equally desirable. This becomes important when considering whom to reject within a given category and there are not sufficient peremptory challenges to reject all jurors from the category. Using the chart, when three peremptory challenges are available, the most likely candidates for removal are juror 12 [5/1], juror 5 [5/2], and juror 18 [4/1].

One final point remains in developing ratings of the desirability of potential jurors. It is important not to settle for oversimplified statements of desirability and undesirability, e.g., "No way can we take this guy." It is necessary to have comparable information for all jurors. Particularly in longer jury selections, where people tend to remember general assertions and forget the underlying reasons for these opinions, complete information on all jurors is crucial to effective jury selection.

NOTES

1. It is important to recognize the legal limits of investigating jurors. Contact with potential jurors is strictly forbidden. However, the appropriateness of contact with the family members of jurors or their associates can vary between trial jurisdictions. Anyone who pursues juror background investigations should make sure that all relevant personnel are aware of what is permitted in their trial jurisdiction. In addition, the sponsor of juror investigations also needs to weigh the advantages of collecting certain types of information (e.g., comments from neighbors or employers) with the disadvantages of the investigations becoming known to individual jurors. Alienating potential jurors through background investigations gone astray can have some very negative consequences for the lawyer.

2. For a discussion of the use of surveys in jury selection, *see* FREDERICK, THE PSY-CHOLOGY OF THE AMERICAN JURY (1987), Frederick, *Using Juror Surveys to Solve Problems at Trial*, FOR THE DEFENSE 8 (Aug. 1987), and Frederick, *Social Science Involvement in Voir Dire: Preliminary Data on the Effectiveness of "Scientific Jury Selection,"* 2 BEHAV. SCI. & L. 1 (1985).

3. *See* Frederick, *Searching for Rocks in the Channel: Pretesting Your Case Before Trial*, FOR THE DEFENSE 26 (Apr. 1990), and FREDERICK, THE PSYCHOLOGY OF THE AMERICAN JURY (1987).

4. *See* HASTIE, PENROD, & PENNINGTON, INSIDE THE JURY (1983). It is also the case that jurors who sit at the ends of the tables in the jury deliberation rooms are more likely to be elected foreperson. This position is likely to combine factors such as location and the fact that those who are leaders are likely to choose these positions.

5. *See* BONORA, KRAUSS & ROUNDTREE, JURYWORK: SYSTEMATIC TECHNIQUES (1999). In some jurisdictions, a designated seat in the jury box determines who will be assigned the role of foreperson. In these jurisdictions, the importance of the role of foreperson is likely reduced but not necessarily eliminated.

6. As an example of the power of normative influence, consider the following exchange between a judge and a juror during the post-verdict polling of a jury that had found the defendant guilty.

COURT: Ms. Moore, the question that was asked—we read off the three verdicts. The question was asked to you, was this then, meaning when you were back in the jury room and signed the verdict forms, was that then and is this now your verdict on all three charges?

JUROR MOORE: I mean, I just voted with the rest of the people. I wanted to vote no.

COURT: Do you agree with the verdict forms as tendered and read by the clerk?

JUROR MOORE: Do I agree with them?

COURT: Yes.

JUROR MOORE: No, but I just voted with everybody else.

COURT: Did anybody force you or coerce you into signing?

JUROR MOORE: No. It was—I wasn't the only one that voted that way. We just voted for everybody else's sake.

7. *See* FREDERICK (1987), *supra* note 3, for a further discussion and citations.

8. For a more complete checklist, *see* BROVINS & OEHMKE, THE TRIAL PRACTICE GUIDE: STRATEGIES, SYSTEMS, AND PROCEDURES FOR THE ATTORNEY (1992).

9. *See* Batson v. Kentucky, 476 U.S. 79 (1986); Hernandez v. New York, 500 U.S. 352 (1991); and J.E.B. v. Alabama *ex rel.* T.B., 511 U.S. 127 (1994).

10. A five-point scale is often preferred to a four-point scale. A four-point scale can force the rating of a juror into an artificial position of either favoring or not favoring the party. In addition, lumping "neutral" and "leaning" jurors together can have unfortunate consequences. If one is not careful, a peremptory challenge inadvertently may remove a neutral juror while allowing a leaning juror to remain.

11. In the sequential method of jury selection the jurors under consideration at any one time may be as few as one to as many as twelve to fourteen jurors or more. Using such a visual ranking approach in this method during a recess is often not practical or useful.

CHAPTER 9

Selecting the Jury

Objectives

- To consider bases for challenges for cause.
- To examine the use of peremptory challenges in light of nondiscriminatory use requirements.
- To examine strategies for exercising peremptory challenges based on the structure of the jury selection process.

Contrary to what the name implies, jury selection is actually a filtering process of juror rejection. Potential jurors are removed from consideration based on the evaluations made by the respective parties and the judge. Those potential jurors who remain after this filtering process, depending on the jury selection environment, serve as the jury. Evaluation of jurors was the focus of the previous chapter. This chapter focuses on the process of removing jurors that results in the final jury. As such, consideration is given to preparing for jury selection, understanding how to prevent jurors from serving on the jury, and developing strategies for exercising peremptory challenges.

Preparing for Jury Selection

Fundamental to effective jury selection is knowing exactly how jurors will be selected at trial. This requires becoming familiar before the trial begins with the jury selection procedures and traditions the trial judge employs. Not only is this information necessary to effectively operate within the system, but it will identify procedures or areas that need to be improved, e.g., the need for individual questioning concerning specific topic areas. Addressing with the judge any areas of concern in the jury selection process prior to trial will help in improving the voir dire conditions.[1]

Using a checklist approach in reviewing jury selection and voir dire procedures will ensure an understanding of what lawyers will face and what needs to be done to get the most out of voir dire. The following checklist illustrates the kinds of information of interest.

JURY SELECTION AND VOIR DIRE PROCEDURE CHECKLIST

Topics

Yes	No	Request	
			Juror questionnaires
[ ]	[ ]	[ ]	Will juror questionnaires be used?
[ ]	[ ]	[ ]	Will jurors complete the questionnaire prior to their arrival at trial?
[ ]	[ ]	[ ]	Will jurors complete the questionnaire at trial?
[ ]	[ ]	[ ]	Will there be sufficient time to review the jurors' responses prior to examining the jurors (e.g., recess, overnight, or extended period of time)?
[ ]	[ ]	[ ]	Will lawyers be allowed to ask follow-up questions based on the jurors' answers on the questionnaire?
[ ]	[ ]	[ ]	Will the answers on the questionnaire be used as a screening device to remove certain jurors prior to voir dire (e.g., hardship or bias issues)?
			Voir dire questioning: Who will ask the questions? What will be the format for questioning?
[ ]	[ ]	[ ]	Will the trial judge conduct a preliminary examination of jurors?
[ ]	[ ]	[ ]	Will the trial judge conduct all questioning?
[ ]	[ ]	[ ]	Will questioning be allowed by parties?
[ ]	[ ]	[ ]	Will jurors be questioned in a group setting?
[ ]	[ ]	[ ]	Will individual questioning by lawyers (either in general or for specific content areas) be allowed?
[ ]	[ ]	[ ]	Will potential jurors be sitting in the spectators' section while awaiting their examination?
[ ]	[ ]	[ ]	Will individual questioning on potentially sensitive areas be conducted outside the presence of other jurors (e.g., in the judge's chambers)?
[ ]	[ ]	[ ]	Are procedures in place to prevent the tainting of jurors as a result of hearing comments made by other jurors (e.g., nonpanel members being absent from the courtroom or sequestering all but the individual juror being questioned)?
[ ]	[ ]	[ ]	Will open-ended questions be allowed?
[ ]	[ ]	[ ]	Will special topic areas (e.g., racism, pretrial publicity, and relevant experiences) be addressed?
			Jury selection procedures: How will challenges for cause be addressed and what method for exercising peremptory challenges will be used?
[ ]	[ ]	[ ]	Will challenges for cause be addressed when examining the juror in question?

Yes	No	Request	
[ ]	[ ]	[ ]	Will challenges for cause be addressed at the conclusion of the party's questioning of the panel?
[ ]	[ ]	[ ]	Will challenges for cause be made outside the presence of the juror in question or other jurors (e.g., at the bench)?
[ ]	[ ]	[ ]	Will there be a reasonable time period during which to consider the exercise of peremptory challenges (e.g., a brief recess or break)?
[ ]	[ ]	[ ]	Can peremptory challenges not used during the selection of the trial jury be added to those available for the selection of alternate jurors?
[ ]	[ ]	[ ]	Will a struck jury method be used?
[ ]	[ ]	[ ]	Will peremptory challenges be exercised simultaneously (blind strikes)?
[ ]	[ ]	[ ]	Will each party be allowed (or required) to exercise more than one challenge at a time?
[ ]	[ ]	[ ]	Will a party be allowed to pass on the exercise of a peremptory challenge and still be able to use that challenge and others should additional rounds be necessary? (i.e., can peremptory challenges be saved for later use?)
[ ]	[ ]	[ ]	Will replacement jurors for those struck take the seats of stricken jurors?
[ ]	[ ]	[ ]	Will the trial jury reflect the nonstricken jurors in order of their appearance in questioning?
[ ]	[ ]	[ ]	Will a sequential jury method be used?
[ ]	[ ]	[ ]	Will peremptory challenges be exercised on an individual or per-panel basis?
[ ]	[ ]	[ ]	Will "back strikes" be allowed (striking previously passed jurors)?
[ ]	[ ]	[ ]	Will the questioning of jurors and the exercise of peremptory challenges always follow the same party order?
[ ]	[ ]	[ ]	Will replacement jurors take the seats of stricken jurors?
[ ]	[ ]	[ ]	Will replacement jurors for those stricken for cause be seated immediately?

Knowing your environment: a key to preparing for jury selection

- Will a juror questionnaire be used?
- Who will ask the questions and under what format?
- What are the procedures for raising challenges for cause and exercising peremptory challenges?

Additional questions:

- What is the size of the trial jury?
- How many alternates will be chosen?
- What is the size of the panels used in group questioning?
- How many peremptory challenges will each party have?
- How many peremptory challenges are allocated for the selection of alternates?
- Is there a need for additional peremptory challenges?
- Will certain parties share challenges and, if so, in what manner?
- How will juror hardship issues be addressed and what would be the possible grounds for hardship?
- How long will the trial be expected to last?
- Once the trial commences, should it be necessary to excuse jurors, in what order will alternates replace these jurors?
- If a jury selection expert is used, will this person be allowed to sit with the lawyer during jury selection?

Preventing Jurors from Serving on the Jury

Armed with a thorough understanding of the jury selection environment, attention shifts to the task of removing potential jurors. Jurors can be removed in one of two ways: through challenges for cause and through peremptory challenges.

Challenges for Cause

Challenges for cause were briefly considered in Chapter 4 in the context of the style of questioning used to secure such a challenge.[2] Challenges for cause are those challenges within the discretion of the trial court that seek to remove potential jurors for failure to meet statutory qualifications for jury service or because of bias or prejudice. This bias or prejudice may be of an inferred or actual nature. For example, when a potential juror reports having a business relationship with one of the parties, being a blood relative of a party, or having a pecuniary interest in the outcome of the case, the court may infer that the juror could not be fair and impartial. While there are a number of circumstances from which bias may be inferred, generally speaking these "grounds" are set forth in the controlling statutes.

Bases for challenges for cause:

- Failure of the juror to meet statutory requirements.
- Inferred bias or prejudice on the part of the juror.
- Actual bias or prejudice exhibited by the juror.

Actual bias, on the other hand, centers on statements the potential juror makes during voir dire that reflect bias against a party or an inability of the juror to discharge his or her duty. For example, potential jurors who say they believe the defendant is guilty or liable and that they will not base their decision on the facts and the law as presented in court will be removed for cause.

Great deference has been paid to jurors' assertions on whether they can be fair. Trial courts are reluctant to remove a potential juror who expresses a prejudicial sentiment (e.g., "I think the defendant is guilty") yet later claims to be fair and impartial. The Supreme Court[3] has expressed great reluctance to second-guess the trial courts in this matter, ruling that jurors' affirmations of fairness are sufficient to render a challenge for cause unnecessary.[4]

Challenges for cause are unlimited in number, but they are limited in their scope. In practice, challenges for cause are granted infrequently. Success in securing these challenges requires careful attention to laying the foundation concerning bias or prejudice. In most cases, the court entertains challenges for cause as circumstances arise, although some courts consider these challenges at the end of the questioning of a group of jurors. Ideally, challenges for cause should be made outside the presence of the potential jurors so that the jurors under consideration are less likely to take offense at these challenges. When peremptory challenges are at a premium (or exhausted), care should be taken in pursuing challenges for cause. You do not want to alienate a potential juror whom you cannot remove with a peremptory challenge if the court rejects the motion for a challenge for cause.[5]

Peremptory Challenges

The second way to remove a potential juror is through the peremptory challenge. Peremptory challenges are a statute-specified number of strikes that lawyers can exercise against potential jurors.

STATUS OF PEREMPTORY CHALLENGES. Peremptory challenges have been under increased scrutiny since *Batson v. Kentucky*.[6] In *Batson*, the Supreme Court ruled that the prosecution's use of its peremptory challenges to exclude jurors on the basis of race (i.e., challenging African-American jurors) violated the equal protection clause of the Fourteenth Amendment. The Court set out a three-step procedure for determining whether peremptory challenges were exercised in a discriminatory manner. First, the defendant must establish a prima facie case of purposeful racial discrimination in the prosecutor's use of peremptory challenges. To establish a prima facie case, the defendant must show (a) that the juror is a member of a cognizable racial group, (b) that the prosecutor has exercised peremptory challenges against venire members of the defendant's race, and (c) in combination with the above factors, any other relevant circumstances that raise the inference of purposeful discrimination.[7] These latter relevant circumstances include any "pattern" of exercising peremptory challenges against African Americans or the prosecutor's questions and statements made during voir dire examination that would support or refute an inference of discriminatory intent.[8]

Second, once the defendant makes a prima facie case for purposeful discrimination the burden shifts to the prosecutor, who must present race-neutral explanations for the exercise of peremptory challenges. While these explanations need not rise to the level of a challenge for cause, they cannot be simple assertions of intuition, possible shared-race partiality, or affirmations of good faith by the prosecutor.[9] The third step is the determination by the trial court, in light of the prosecutor's stated reasons, that the peremptory challenges at issue were a result of purposeful discrimination.

Since *Batson*, a series of decisions have established that (a) the defendant need not be of the same race as the juror;[10] (b) criminal defense lawyers cannot exercise peremptory challenges in a discriminatory manner, e.g., against African-American jurors;[11] (c) peremptory challenges may not be used in a discriminatory manner in civil trials;[12] and (d) peremptory challenges may not be used in a discriminatory manner against Latinos[13] and Hispanics.[14] Some lower courts have extended the bar to discriminatory use of peremptory challenges to whites.[15] Significantly, the Supreme Court has ruled that the equal protection clause of the Fourteenth Amendment protects jurors, not simply the parties, from discrimination in jury selection.[16]

The Supreme Court extended its consideration of peremptory challenges to the area of gender in *J.E.B. v. Alabama ex rel. T.B.*[17] It ruled that the equal protection clause prohibits the discriminatory use of peremptory challenges based solely on the gender of jurors, or on the assumption that an individual juror would be biased in a particular case because the juror happened to be a man or a woman.

Under *Batson* and *J.E.B.*, once a party exercises its challenges against members of a specific race or Hispanic origin or gender, the opposing party must raise an objection establishing a prima facie case of discriminatory intent before the jury is empaneled and the jury venire is dismissed and the trial begins. While a "pattern" of exercising peremptory challenges is useful in establishing a prima facie case of discriminatory intent, it may not always be necessary. Removal of a single juror through impermissible reasons is unconstitutional.[18]

After a prima facie case is made, the original party is afforded the opportunity to explain its use of peremptory challenges in a nondiscriminatory manner. This explanation does not have to reflect the level of bias necessary for a challenge for cause. It simply must be based on a characteristic other than the juror's race, Hispanic origin, or gender that is not merely a pretext for such a discrimination-based challenge.

In practice, the standards to which the explanations are applied resulting from *Batson* and *J.E.B.* challenges are somewhat unclear. The courts appear willing to recognize the use of peremptory challenges on the basis of the opinions expressed by jurors, and challenges based on occupational status, background, lifestyle, or nonverbal communication of the juror may be acceptable. However, while a juror's inability to look at the lawyer or hesitancy in answering questions may be a sufficiently (race-) neutral explanation for the lawyer's exercise of a peremptory challenge,[19] an unarticulated "feeling" based on the demeanor of the juror may not.[20]

Key to the success of neutral or nonpretextual explanations for the exercise of peremptory challenges given by the original party is whether the trial judge believes them. When the trial court makes a finding of fact regarding the discriminatory use of peremptory challenges, appellate courts are extremely reluctant to set this determination aside.[21]

In addition to the explanations offered, some courts have looked at the behavior of the parties for indications of discriminatory intent. Unequal treatment of jurors in terms of both the questioning process and the use of similar information from jurors of different races (or genders) was viewed as reflecting discriminatory intent.[22] Thus, consistency in the information sought (i.e., seeking similar information from all jurors) and in the rationale for striking jurors (e.g., striking jurors of all races or genders with certain occupations) is important. Finally, at least one court has ruled that if a policy adopted by a party across cases serves to exclude certain occupations or lifestyles, then discriminatory intent is absent.[23]

What is clear from these rulings is that peremptory challenges cannot be exercised in a discriminatory manner based on race, Hispanic origin, or gender. The ability to articulate specific nonpretextual or neutral reasons for exercising peremptory challenges is the key to successfully avoiding a *Batson* or *J.E.B.* challenge. While some commentators have said that these decisions have sounded the death knell for the peremptory challenge, the reports of its death may be premature. As discussed in Chapter 2, stereotyping such as that addressed in *Batson* and *J.E.B.* is often employed in the absence of more useful information on jurors (e.g., their opinions and experiences). Lawyers must now seek more information and employ more sophisticated rationales for the exercise of peremptory challenges. Shifting away from stereotypes will require greater consideration of the jurors' opinions, beliefs, and experiences. Both the majority and the dissenting opinions in *J.E.B.* point to properly conducted voir dire as the tool with which lawyers can gather the information needed so that it becomes unnecessary to rely on gross stereotypes in the exercise of peremptory challenges.

Considerations when exercising peremptory challenges:

- Challenges must not be based on the juror's race, Hispanic origin, or gender.
- Vary the exercise strategy to account for the jury selection method (i.e., sequential v. struck jury methods).
- Consider the impact that the local trial practice and procedures will have on exercise strategies.

Conducting Jury Selection in Light of Batson and J.E.B.

In any court case, and particularly in those cases where issues of discriminatory use of peremptory challenges may arise, it is important to maximize the information gained through voir dire. As stressed in earlier chapters, capitalizing on the fundamentals of conducting effective voir dire is essential to this task. The key points will be reiterated here.

ASK ABOUT THE JURORS' OPINIONS AND EXPERIENCES. Jurors' experiences and opinions are better predictors of juror desirability than mere stereotypes. It is important to ask questions that will uncover relevant experiences and opinions of jurors. For example, in excessive force cases, questions that address prior experiences with discrimination, being stopped by police without a reason, knowledge of friends or acquaintances who have been injured while in police custody, and being a victim of a crime are often relevant. Also potentially relevant are the jurors' views on the likelihood that law enforcement officers would use excessive force and their views on the use of force by law enforcement officers.

In some cases, the pursuit of relevant information requires going beyond what normally occurs in the trial jurisdiction. When this situation arises, it is necessary to seek from the court greater latitude in the questioning process in general or greater latitude in specific areas to obtain the relevant information.

TAKE ADVANTAGE OF OPEN-ENDED QUESTIONS. When addressing important issues in voir dire, ask questions that require jurors to express their opinions in their own words where possible. Open-ended questions, e.g., "What do you think about . . .?" or "Tell me about your experiences with (police officers)," force jurors to reveal more about their opinions and thought processes than standard closed-ended questions.

UTILIZE GOOD VOIR DIRE SKILLS. Utilize skills that enhance the jurors' willingness to disclose information about their experiences and opinions. Be supportive and empathetic during voir dire. Do not "interrogate" jurors. Be attentive and show jurors that their answers are important. Also, jurors can be encouraged to tell more about themselves and their opinions through modeling, self-disclosure, and providing positive reinforcement for open and honest answers, e.g., "Thank you," "That's interesting," or "I appreciate your candor."

PURSUE QUESTIONS IN A CONSISTENT MANNER. To be most effective in jury selection, it is important to gather information in a consistent fashion from all jurors. Sometimes questioning of certain jurors is shortened because it is assumed that these jurors will be removed peremptorily in the absence of grounds for challenges for cause. This practice can be self-defeating. Some jurors who were initially thought to be "bad" later are discovered to be acceptable or even "good" based on their past experiences or opinions. For example, in a death penalty case arising out of an armed robbery where the defense was focusing on penalty issues rather than guilt, a potential juror said she would have a bias against the defendant because her husband had recently been shot during an armed robbery. While initially undesirable for the defense, her desirability abruptly changed when she later disclosed that she would not impose the death penalty in a case of armed robbery.

Inconsistent questioning of jurors is a particularly unwise practice in trials where *Batson* and *J.E.B.* issues may arise. Failure to treat jurors of different critical groups, e.g., race, equally in the questioning process can lead to the inference of discriminatory intent in the subsequent exercise of peremptory challenges.

KEEP GOOD RECORDS. Valuable support for the removal of jurors is available by noting specific answers given or reactions exhibited by these jurors during voir dire questioning. To this end, good recordkeeping is important so that these observations are available for later use in providing nondiscriminatory explanations for the peremptory challenges exercised.

DO NOT HIGHLIGHT RACE OR GENDER IN THE RECORDS. Recording the jurors' race and gender is often useful in helping to prevent confusion when trying to remember which jurors said what. However, highlighting the race or gender of jurors in the records kept on them can lead to an inference of discriminatory intent. For this reason it is desirable to at least avoid highlighting these characteristics and, in some cases, to consider not recording this information at all.

ARTICULATE SPECIFIC REASONS FOR CHALLENGES. While the explanations for using peremptory challenges need not rise to the level of bias needed for a challenge for cause, these explanations must be clear, reasonably specific, and legitimate. Vague references to "not feeling comfortable" with a juror are likely to be viewed as inappropriate. Explanations should be based on more objective information, e.g., stated opinions or experiences, when available, that lead to an inference of the presence of some degree of bias. In presenting these explanations, capitalize on several features of the juror's answers, experiences, or behaviors to paint a total picture of the basis for the peremptory challenge.

When relying on observations of the jurors' verbal and nonverbal behavior, place these observations into context for the judge as part of the explanation for a peremptory challenge. For example, remind the judge that a juror reacted in an undesirable manner by folding his or her arms or turning away, frowning, and avoiding eye contact when considering the topic of the presumption of innocence or the liability of the defendant.

In the previous chapter we presented methods for evaluating jurors. *Batson* and *J.E.B.* argue for more systematic evaluation and decision-making regarding peremptory challenges. It is no longer sufficient to rely on the simple reaction of "I don't like this juror." It is necessary to ask oneself, "What is it about the juror's answers, demeanor, background, or experiences that I don't like or that makes me feel uncomfortable?" The answer to this question forces a decision-making process more in line with *Batson* and *J.E.B.*, even if the decision appears at first to be based on a "gut" reaction. Asking this type of question also keeps in mind what information is needed to go beyond the use of stereotypes.

BE CONSISTENT. Being consistent in the manner in which peremptory challenges are exercised can go a long way in supporting explanations of nondiscriminatory intent. For example, excluding all jurors of a certain occupation no matter what their race or gender would substantially benefit an explanation of nondiscriminatory intent. As the Court suggested in *J.E.B.*, as long as the stated reason for the peremptory challenge is not a pretext, exclusion of jurors based on an occupation or experience that is predominantly associated with a particular gender, e.g., having military experience or being a nurse, may not be unconstitutional.

While consistency is desirable, it is not always possible. Just as stereotypes applied to gender and race will be overly broad, so are stereotypes applied to such factors as occupations. Not all members of a given occupation may be undesirable. When this situation arises, it is necessary to point out reasons why a potential juror was not removed by a peremptory challenge while other jurors with the same occupation were removed. The key issue again is pretext. The differentiating reason(s) for accepting the potential juror while removing others having the same occupation must be non-pretextual and brought to the court's attention.

Strategies for Exercising Peremptory Challenges

The strategies for the exercise of peremptory challenges are affected by the method used for these challenges (i.e., the sequential versus the struck method) and the practices of the trial jurisdiction. In deciding to strike any potential juror the key is: *know the jury selection environment*. Key questions are the following:

- Does the jurisdiction allow back strikes?
- Are peremptory challenges exercised simultaneously or sequentially?
- When potential jurors are excused, what happens with replacement jurors?
- Do replacement jurors take the seats occupied by the excused juror or do jurors simply slide up in the seating order?
- How are alternates chosen?
- Can an exercise of a peremptory challenge be passed up without losing it?
- Must all of the allotted peremptory challenges be used?
- Does the trial jurisdiction operate under the sequential method or the struck jury method?

The answers to these questions and others raised in the jury selection and voir dire procedure checklist presented earlier will affect the strategy for striking jurors.

Sequential Method

In Chapter 1, a distinction was drawn between two general jury selection methods, the sequential and the struck methods. The sequential method uses a rotating method of questioning and challenging jurors. Usually, the questioning of jurors occurs in a group format by one party with the exercise of any challenges prior to the examination of the jurors by the remaining party. When an individual questioning method is used under this system, the questioning and exercise of any challenges are conducted with one juror at a time.

Under the sequential method, a basic strategy of jury selection is to remove first any potential jurors who may qualify for a challenge for cause. After the removal of any potential jurors for cause, the least desired jurors are struck first. When the court does not require that peremptory challenges be exercised at one time, removing the worst one or two potential jurors and seeing who replaces them is helpful in determining whether additional members of the original panel need to be removed. For example, suppose a party has six peremptory challenges and is questioning a panel of twelve potential jurors. If three in the panel are on the higher range of undesirability, the two worst jurors could be removed and their replacements questioned. This questioning may reveal that the replacement jurors are desirable. If this is the case, the third member of the original three undesirable jurors may be removed. However, if the two replacement jurors are worse than the third original juror, then the replacements should be removed and the original juror retained.

The uncertainty surrounding replacement jurors inherent in the sequential method requires the exercise of peremptory challenges in anticipation of what kinds of jurors will fill the empty seats. In essence, lawyers must anticipate what the probabilities are that an even less desirable juror will replace the stricken juror. Where possible, lawyers should take advantage of the opportunities to know who is in the jury venire. When information exists concerning the potential jurors who will replace jurors who are struck, the probabilities of having undesirable jurors enter the panel can be determined. For example, if the replacement pool contains ten jurors, two of whom are expected to be undesirable, the probabilities of either of those jurors entering the panel are two in ten, or 20 percent, provided the replacements are randomly selected from the replacement pool. If only three replacement jurors remain in the pool, two of whom are undesirable, the probabilities are 67 percent that an undesirable juror will enter the panel, assuming the use of random selection methods. Obviously, depending on the number of peremptory challenges available, the decision to exercise a peremptory challenge would be different in these two situations. Calculating the probabilities in this manner gives a clearer picture of what to do.

Information on the jury venire can come from several sources. First, the jury list can provide clues to the composition of the entire jury venire. Second, the clerk of court may be able to provide a list of the order in which replacement jurors will appear (provided replacement jurors are not randomly drawn as each seat becomes vacant). Knowing the order can greatly affect decisions regarding the exercise of peremptory challenges.

Third, if jury selection occurs over an extended period of time, the answers given by the jurors can be used as an estimate of the distribution of opinions in the jury venire. Fluctuations due to random selection will occur in the appearance of desirable or undesirable jurors. However, if the majority of jurors exhibit desirable or undesirable opinions in the initial stages of the selection process, this can be used (absent other information) as a guide to what to expect from replacement jurors.

Finally, when juror questionnaires are used, the information contained on these questionnaires can provide a valuable estimate of the distribution of jurors in the jury venire. In the 1975 criminal trial of Joan Little for the murder of a jailer, the defense team used a juror questionnaire to determine the distribution of desirable and undesirable jurors in the venire. In this case, jurors were sequestered and examined individually under the sequential method, thus maximizing the uncertainty surrounding replacement jurors. Armed with survey-based profiles and using the juror questionnaires available for small groups of potential jurors at a time, the defense team was able to predict the distribution of desirable and undesirable jurors for each group. With this knowledge, it was possible to be more selective in the use of peremptory challenges. If the distribution looked good, then the defense could be more discriminating in who was passed. If the group looked bad, then challenges could be saved for the worst of the group.

Two final points remain concerning the exercise of peremptory challenges using the sequential method. First, the last challenge always should be exercised with great caution. If the last challenge is used and an even less desirable juror enters the jury, the only way to remove the replacement juror is through a challenge for cause. Second, notwithstanding the previous statement, if an unacceptable juror enters the box, he or she must be dealt with either through a peremptory challenge, a challenge for cause, or rehabilitation/education. An unacceptable juror by definition should not be allowed to remain on the panel. Sometimes it is necessary to accept an undesirable juror on the panel because the probabilities are relatively high that a less desirable juror will enter. However, a juror who is, in total, unacceptable at the conclusion of questioning should be removed.

Struck Method

The struck method varies from the sequential method in that the questioning of all the jurors by the parties and the exercise of any challenges for cause occur before either party has to exercise its peremptory challenges. Under this system, the only uncertainty is against whom the opposing party will exercise its peremptory challenges.

When exercising peremptory challenges under the struck method, there are several important considerations. First, if the trial jurisdiction uses a simultaneous or "blind" strike method of exercising peremptory challenges (where the parties simultaneously exercise all strikes at one time), it is important to remove the least desirable jurors in order of their rankings.

Second, the order in which potential jurors are removed becomes critical when exercising strikes in some alternating fashion. In most cases, the best strategy is to rank-order the least desirable jurors in terms of which jurors should be removed by a peremptory challenge. The list should always include more jurors than the number of peremptory challenges available. Sometimes the opposing party will remove one of the targeted potential jurors. With this ranking in mind, remove jurors in order of their "obviousness" as being undesirable. That is, remove first those jurors whom the opponent will assume are going to be removed. Employing this strategy makes it possible to capitalize on a situation where the opponent removes one of the targeted jurors who is less obviously undesirable. The opponent's mistake frees up a peremptory challenge thereby allowing for the removal of an additional undesirable juror from the hit list.

Using the example discussed in Chapter 8, following is the ranking of the least desirable potential jurors with their desirability ratings in parentheses:

Juror 12 (5/1)

Juror 5 (5/2)

Juror 18 (4/1)

Juror 11 (4/2)

Juror 1 (4/4)

Using this list and the three peremptory challenges available, the top three least desirable jurors will be struck. If the opponent strikes one of the top three, the next least desirable juror becomes eligible for removal.

Third, it is helpful to take the jury list of qualified jurors (i.e., those who have been questioned by the parties and not removed for cause) and highlight those potential jurors appearing on the least desirable list (with their associated ranking). This makes it easy to see how the jury is evolving as the strikes are exercised, and there is little likelihood that an undesirable juror will be overlooked.

Fourth, pay attention to the implication of using and not using (passing) peremptory challenges. Since the jury is usually composed of the first number of jurors equal to the jury size (e.g., six, seven, or twelve) who are not stricken, the focus should be on who enters the jury when jurors are struck. Focusing too heavily on the top of the list of jurors may allow an undesirable juror to make the cut as the final juror. It does not matter whether a juror is number 1 or number 12, they all sit on the same twelve-person jury.

Fifth, it is important to consider how the exercise of peremptory challenges by both parties will affect the possible juries that would result. Sometimes the favorability of the jury as a whole would be increased by altering the original strategy for exercising peremptory challenges as a response to whom the opponent removes. For example, it may be desirable to change later peremptory challenge decisions to compensate for the lack of certain groups on the jury (e.g., females or males, minorities, or those with certain educational backgrounds). Such decisions may even involve "passing" on a round of peremptory challenges. Considering the possible juries in advance enables a more effective fashioning of the best jury available under the circumstances.

Sixth, alternates on the jury are also important. In a system where a challenge can be passed (or even saved), the choice of when to pass can have substantial consequences. For example, consider a situation where the jury has been selected and now two alternates are needed. Each side has one challenge per alternate juror slot. The following are the six potential jurors under consideration with their desirability ratings in parentheses:

Alt 1 (3)   Alt 2 (3)   Alt 3 (1)   Alt 4 (5)   Alt 5 (3)
Alt 6 (5)

The first three are considered for alternate juror slot number one. The opposing lawyer chooses to remove Alt 3. Should a peremptory challenge be used? No. Not removing either Alt 1 or Alt 2 ensures that the two alternate jurors will each have a desirability score of no better (or worse) than 3. If a challenge is exercised, it will ensure that the second alternate will have a score of 5. That is, when either Alt 1 or Alt 2 (each with a score of 3) is removed, the remaining alternate takes the first alternate juror's slot. However, this results in two potential alternate jurors with scores of 5 and only one challenge to use against them. The opponent will remove Alt 5 (3) and the final alternate juror's slot will be filled by a juror with a score of 5, the least desirable score.

Seven, a variation of the struck method can include an element of the sequential method, thus potentially producing a change in strategy. This variation occurs after all the needed jurors are qualified and jurors are randomly drawn to fill the needed seats (jurors plus alternates) in the jury box. The parties begin exercising peremptory challenges in rounds with empty seats being filled by random selection of the replacement jurors and each party is presented with a full and passed jury. The importance of this variation lies in the decision-making process as the rounds unfold. Knowing the distribution of the desirable/undesirable potential replacement jurors sometimes leads to a situation where it is better not to remove a juror and accept the panel as it is than to continue the process and possibly end up with a less favorable jury. Advance consideration of this issue is needed to help identify this situation and act on it when it arises. In addition, it is helpful to graphically portray the total distribution of jurors before strikes are exercised. A visual representation of the qualified jurors enables the lawyer to track what happens to jurors and, as a result, see when it may be better to end the selection process. Particularly when the overall pool of qualified jurors is unfavorable, knowing that the distribution of replacement jurors has become even more adversely skewed and an insufficient number of peremptory challenges remain with which to address the situation, settling for the jury as it stands in the process becomes the more desirable choice.

Finally, as with the sequential method, the evolving nature of the jury (and alternates) remains the most important concern in selecting a jury. The basic question in any jury selection is, given the composition of the jury, is it acceptable to the client's cause to allow a given potential juror on the jury? If the answer is no, all steps should be taken to remove the potential juror.

NOTES

1. *See* the discussion in Chapter 5 concerning improving voir dire procedures.

2. *See* Babcock, *Voir Dire: Preserving "Its Wonderful Power,"* 27 STAN. L. REV. 545–65 (1975), and FREDERICK, THE PSYCHOLOGY OF THE AMERICAN JURY (1987).

3. Mu'Min v. Virginia, 111 S. Ct. 1899 (1991).

4. However, *see* discussions of problems with juror candor and honesty in Chapter 2 and Chapter 5 that indicate that judges should not rely totally on the jurors' assurances of impartiality.

5. In the struck system, sometimes a few jurors beyond the necessary number of jurors are screened or qualified before peremptory challenges are exercised. In this situation, it is often useful to renew challenges for cause against jurors that were denied earlier by the judge. Judges have been known to grant some of these challenges, particularly with "close call" jurors, when extra qualified jurors are readily available.

6. Batson v. Kentucky, 476 U.S. 79 (1986).

7. *Supra* note 6, at 87–88.

8. *Supra* note 6, at 88.

9. *Supra* note 6, at 88.

10. Powers v. Ohio, 499 U.S. 400 (1991).

11. State v. McCollum, 112 S. Ct. 2348 (1992).

12. Edmonson v. Leesville Concrete Co., 111 S. Ct. 2077 (1991).

13. Hernandez v. New York, 500 U.S. 352 (1991).

14. Allen v. Hardy, 478 U.S. 255, 259 (1986).

15. *See* Brown v. Neurodiagnostic Assocs., P.C., District of Columbia Superior Court, No. 90-CA-4171 (1992), where plaintiff used all his peremptory challenges to excuse white potential jurors, and State v. Knox, La. Sup. Ct., No. 91-KK-1906, 61 U.S.L.W. 2369 (1992), where an African-American defendant exercised its challenges against white potential jurors.

16. *Supra* note 10.

17. J.E.B. v. Alabama *ex rel.* T.B., 511 U.S. 127 (1994).

18. *See J.E.B, id.* at 142 n.13. *See also* Cadwell v. Maloney 159 F.3d 639 (1st Cir. 1998), Coulter v. Gilmore 155 F.3d 912 (7th Cir. 1998), United States v. Hernandez-Herrera, 273 F.3d 1213 (9th Cir. 2001), United States v. Bishop, 959 F.2d 820, 827 (9th Cir. 1992), United States v. Lorenzo, 995 F.2d 1448 (9th Cir. 1993), and United States v. Horsley, 864 F.2d 1543, 1546 (11th Cir. 1989).

19. *See* People v. Mack, 128 Ill. 2d 231, 538 N.E. 2d 1107 (1989) and United States v. Cartlidge, 808 F.2d 1064 (1987). However, for a different view of lack of eye contact, *see* Wright v. State, 586 So. 2d 1024 (Fla. 1991).

20. *Wright, id.,* where the juror's lack of eye contact makes the prosecutor feel uncomfortable.

21. *Supra* note 13.

22. *See Brown, supra* note 15.

23. Wylie v. Vaughn, 773 F. Supp. 775 (E.D. Pa. 1991).

Motion for Suggested Voir Dire Procedures and Request for Expert Help in Jury Selection in *Commonwealth of Virginia v. John Allen Muhammad*

VIRGINIA:

IN THE CIRCUIT COURT FOR PRINCE WILLIAM COUNTY

COMMONWEALTH OF VIRGINIA   :
                                  :
          -vs.-   :   Criminal Case 54362
                                  :   54363
JOHN ALLEN MUHAMMAD   :   54364
          ACCUSED   :   54365

DEFENDANT'S SUGGESTIONS REGARDING VOIR DIRE
AND REQUEST FOR EXPERT HELP WITH JURY SELECTION

John Allen Muhammad, by counsel, hereby moves the Court concerning the

conduct of jury selection which will allow counsel to make meaningful use of strikes for

cause and preemptory challenges.[1] Counsel also requests funds to hire a jury consultant.[2]

PREFACE

A defendant, of course, has a constitutional right to an impartial jury. Turner v.

Murray, 476 U.S. 28 (1986). Just as clearly, the right to an impartial jury extends to the

sentencing phase of a capital case. Morgan v. Illinois, 504 U.S. 719 (1992). The key to

effectuating this right is an adequate voir dire:

---

[1] Counsel previously made some of these suggestions as part of Mr. Muhammad's motion
seeking a lengthy juror questionnaire. While the court rejected the proposed
questionnaire, it does not appear that the court ruled on counsel's suggestions regarding
jury selection, some on which are renewed herein.

[2] In support of these requests we have attached as an exhibit the affidavit of Dr. Jeffery
Thomas Frederick, the Director of Jury Research Services for the National Legal
Research Group, Inc., in Charlottesville, Virginia, along with a copy of Dr. Frederick's
c.v. We incorporate in this Motion the points Dr. Frederick details in his affidavit
concerning the difficulties facing the court and counsel in selecting a jury in a case such
as this one, which is not only a death penalty case, but one which has received
unrelenting national attention and one in which the alleged crimes include multiple
murders committed as part of a scheme, allegedly, to terrorize the population at large.

Part of a defendant's right to an impartial jury is an adequate voir dire to identify unqualified jurors. "Voir dire plays a critical function in assuring the criminal defendant that his [constitutional] right to an impartial jury will be honored. Without an adequate voir dire the trial judge's responsibility to remove prospective jurors who will not be able impartially to follow the judge's instructions and evaluate the evidence cannot be fulfilled." Hence, "the exercise of [the trial court's] discretion, and the restriction upon inquiries at the request of counsel, [are] subject to the essential demands of fairness." (citations omitted).

Morgan v. Illinois, 504 U.S. at 729-30. If there is *reasonable doubt* about the ability of a juror to give the accused a fair trial, that doubt is sufficient to require his exclusion, "[f]or . . . it is not only important that justice should be impartially administered, but it should also flow through channels as free from suspicion as possible." David v. Commonwealth, 26 Va. App. 77, 80 (emphasis added), quoting Breeden v. Commonwealth, 217 Va. 297, 298 (1976).

As lawyers and judges familiar with the trial of capital cases know, extracting reliable information regarding a potential juror's views on the death penalty is a delicate operation requiring a searching inquiry. "Given the important, delicate and complex nature of the death qualification process, there can be no substitute for thorough and searching inquiry...." State v. Williams, 550 A.2d 1172, 1182 (New Jersey, 1988). It is widely acknowledged that, with many jurors, initial responses to death-qualifying questions cannot be taken at face value. See Gray v. Mississippi, 481 U.S. 648, 662-663 (1987) ("[D]espite their initial responses, the venire members might have clarified their positions upon further questioning and revealed that their concerns about the death penalty were weaker than they originally stated. It might have become clear that they could set aside their scruples and serves as jurors.") The Court in Wainwright v. Witt,

2

469 U.S. 423, 425 (1985), recognized that a searching inquiry is often necessary before jurors can be excluded on the basis of moral, philosophical or practical reservations regarding a particular punishment. "[T]here veniremen may not know how they will react when faced with imposing the death sentence, or may be unable to articulate, or may wish to hide their true feelings." It is required that counsel explore the answers given by a potential juror without accepting at face value what may appear to be a claim of neutrality, or a claim of ability to follow the court's instructions.[3] By statute, Virginia recognizes the importance of lawyer-conducted voir dire. Code of Virginia Section 8.01-358 and 19.2-260 (guarantying right to counsel-conducted voir dire). See also the Affidavit of Dr. Frederick at pages 11 through 14.

The need for a searching inquiry, at least as far as views on the death penalty are concerned, has been heightened as a result of the critical caselaw concerning exclusion of jurors from a death penalty jury. Adams v. Texas, 448 U.S. 38 (1980), as interpreted in Wainwright v. Witt, supra, modified the stringent "automatic" and "unmistakably clear" standard that must be met before a juror's punishment views could result in disqualification from service in a capital case. Compare Witherspoon v. Illinois, 391 U.S. 510, 520 n. 9, 522 n. 21 (1968) with Adams v. Texas, 448 U.S. 38, 45 (1980) (before a cause challenge is granted, the juror's punishment views must "prevent or substantially impair the performance of his duties as a juror ... ") and Wainwright v. Witt, 469 U.S. at 424 ("standard is whether the jurors views would 'prevent or substantially

_____

[3] "As with any other trial situation where an adversary wishes to exclude a juror because of bias, then, it is the adversary seeking exclusion who must determine, through questioning, that the potential juror lacks impartiality." Wainwright v. Witt, supra, 469 U.S. at 423; "We note in addition that respondent's counsel chose not to question Colby himself . . . . This questioning might have resolved any perceived ambiguities in the questions . . . ." Id. at 434.

3

impair the performance of his duties as a juror . . . .'"). Because it is reversible error to exclude someone who has strong views either for or against the death penalty, but who will not automatically impose it or exclude it, Gray v. Mississippi, 481 U.S. 648 (1987) (exclusion of juror for cause in capital prosecution when juror was not irrevocably committed to vote against death penalty regardless of the facts and circumstances of the case was reversible constitutional error not subject to harmless error review); David v. Commonwealth, supra, 26 Va. App. at 79, the need for detailed questioning to unearth the limits of a venire member's true feelings is crucial. Improper removal of just one juror will cause a reversal. Davis v. Georgia, 429 U.S. 122 (1976); David v. Commonwealth, 26 Va. App. at 80.

Questioning about death penalty views extends beyond simply whether the prospective juror is for or against the death penalty. It applies as well to *all* aspects of death penalty law. A juror, for example, who says that he would not automatically impose a death sentence may believe nevertheless that mitigating evidence, or certain categories of it, will not ever allow him to impose a sentence of life without parole. Likewise, a juror may believe that once the state has proven an aggravating circumstance, death will always be appropriate. And, a juror may believe that death is always appropriate where aggravating circumstances are found and no mitigating evidence is presented.[4]

---

[4] As Dr. Frederick recounts in his affidavit, a large percentage of jurors may hold misconceptions about legal principals. Dr. Frederick describes his recent survey in the Norfolk Division of the Eastern District of Virginia (of which Virginia Beach comprises approximately 37% of the jurisdiction), in which he discovered that, of the jury-qualified respondents in the survey, 20% believed that if the prosecution goes to the trouble of bringing someone to trial, the person is probably guilty; 42% believe that defendants in criminal trials should have to prove that they are innocent; and 24% believe that a

The seating of such jurors is improper because the constitution gives a defendant the right to rely on any mitigating circumstance in order to avoid the death sentence. Lockett v. Ohio, 438 U.S. 586 (1978) ("[I]n all but the rarest kind of capital cases [a sentencing authority may not] be precluded from considering, as a mitigating factor, any aspect of a defendant's character or record ... as a basis for a sentence less than death."); Buchanan v. Angelone, 522 U.S. 269 (1998) (Chief Justice Rehnquist writing that: "In the [penalty phase], our cases have established that the sentencer may not be precluded from considering any constitutionally relevant mitigating evidence."); Morgan, 504 U.S. at 7, n. 3 (Scalia, J., dissenting). "Presumably, under today's decision a juror who thinks a 'bad childhood' is never mitigating must also be excluded."

It is no answer to say that a juror's statement that he or she will follow the court's instructions ends the matter. The court's instructions at the end of the case will do nothing to alert counsel and the court that such jurors are even sitting on the panel. The instructions do not inform the jurors that they must be open to considering mitigating evidence. Even if such instructions are given, they come too late, for a juror who believes that mitigation is never sufficient to spare a life may not be able to follow such an instruction. The time to find out if the jurors are willing to consider mitigating evidence, and all classes of it, is at the outset. The same is true for all the categories of questions we propose to propound to the venire (effect of race, effect of the nature of the alleged offenses, effect of pre-trial publicity, etc.).

---

defendant in a criminal trial who does not testify is probably guilty. Frederick Affidavit at p. 8.

With these thoughts in mind, we respectfully make the following suggestions for the conduct of voir dire.

Individual Voir Dire

We ask that voir dire be individual, particularly with regard to certain of the suggested topics, such as publicity, fear and predetermined views about the defendant, but particularly concerning views on the death penalty. There is abundant precedent for individual voir dire on death in recent federal cases (United States v. Wills, United States v. Regan, United States v. Lentz, all from the United States District Court for the Eastern District of Virginia). Counsel is aware of at least one death penalty case from Prince William County in which jurors were first questioned as a group, then brought before the court in groups of two for further voir dire on the issues of pre-trial publicity, the existence of any bias or prejudice, the formation of an opinion as to guilt, willingness to base a verdict solely on the law and the evidence, and attitudes towards the death penalty. LaVasseur v. Commonwealth, 225 Va. 564 (1983).

Individual voir dire will ensure that the jury panel is not tainted by the opinions of jurors whose views ultimately call for their disqualification. This is a very real danger, for example, where one juror is asked to describe the publicity he has heard about the case. Reciting what has been heard spreads that news to others who may not have heard it. Likewise, where a juror reveals that his entire family lived in fear during the shootings charged in these cases, those listening are likely to be influenced concerning whether or not the population at large was intimidated (having heard a fellow citizen assert that fact), an issue they will be called upon to determine at trial. And, where a potential juror hears another declare that the death penalty is the only appropriate sentence in the case, that

6

may well have an effect on how the hearing juror determines what society requires in the way of punishment should there be a conviction. Group voir dire also may prevent a juror from forthrightly volunteering what he or she may believe to be an embarrassing opinion. While all these considerations come into play in a regular case, that this is a death penalty case, and one which has received enormous press coverage and engendered such strong feelings, requires that extra care be taken.

In further support of this request we refer the court to pages 10 – 14 of the Frederick Affidavit.

Additional Preemptory Strikes

We request that the court consider allowing counsel more than the mandated four preemptory strikes currently allowed. Given the great publicity in the case and given the very strong feelings aroused, it is very likely that even though the court may find jurors who meet the various tests established above, the majority of them will be leaning towards conviction and a sentence of death. If that is apparent from voir dire, the fifth and sixth amendments to the United States constitution require additional strikes.

Proposed Procedure

We suggest that 15 jurors be instructed to appear at court each morning, and 15 each afternoon. The court has previously indicated that it would consider having the jurors fill out a brief juror questionnaire at the time they appeared, which would then be given to counsel to use in voir dire. Arrangements would have to be made for copying of those questionnaires so that they could be distributed to the court and all counsel. The court and counsel would then conduct voir dire. Strikes for cause would be exercised immediately. When the total number of qualified jurors reaches the number needed for

7

both sides to exercise their preemptory challenges and still seat a jury of 12, plus alternates, at which point voir dire would end.

Juror Questionnaire.

Counsel has prepared a short juror questionnaire which has been forwarded to the Commonwealth's Attorney. We will work with the Commonwealth's Attorney to see if we can jointly propose a questionnaire to the court.

Jury Consultant

To aid counsel with jury selection in this case, we also seek funds to hire Jeffery Frederick, the Director of the Jury Research Services for the National Legal Research Group, Inc., of Charlottesville, Virginia. Dr. Frederick's c.v. is attached as an exhibit to this pleading. The need for expert help is evident from what is discussed above, including the nature of the charges, the extreme publicity, the strongly held opinions in the community, and the fear engendered in the community over the course of the shootings.

As outlined by Dr. Frederick in his affidavit, he has been hired by both the defense and the prosecution. He has personally been hired by the prosecution in the cases of United States v. Leo Felton and Erica Chase (conspiracy to commit terrorism); United States v. Kristin Gilbert (death penalty case); United States v. Oliver North, and United States v. Admiral John Poindexter. He has also assisted states prosecutors in Connecticut, and also in Virginia (Commonwealth v. Glenn Barker). He lists 41 other state cases in which jury consultants have been employed. See Frederick affidavit at pages 16 through 19. Dr. Frederick would aid with the preparation for voir dire, with advising on voir dire in court, and by helping the defense exercise strikes.

8

239

Respectfully Submitted,

JOHN ALLEN MUHAMMAD
By Counsel

Counsel for the Accused:

Jonathan Shapiro by MC.

Jonathan Shapiro
Law Office of Jonathan Shapiro, P.C.
910 King Street
Alexandria, Virginia   22314
(703) 684-1700

Peter D. Greenspun
Greenspun and Mann, P.C.
10605 Judicial Drive
Suite A-5
Fairfax, Virginia   22030-5167
(703) 352-0100

Certificate of Service

I hereby certify that a true copy of the foregoing Motion was hand delivered, this
6 day of August, 2003, to Paul B. Ebert, Commonwealth's Attorney for Prince William
County, and to James A. Willett and Richard A. Conway, Assistant Commonwealth's
Attorneys.

Jonathan Shapiro

9

240

NATIONAL LEGAL RESEARCH GROUP, INC.
Serving the Legal Profession since 1969

2421 IVY ROAD, POST OFFICE BOX 7187
CHARLOTTESVILLE, VIRGINIA 22906–7187
800-727-6574 Fax 434-817-6570
e-mail: research@nlrg.com • web: www.nlrg.com

AFFIDAVIT OF JEFFREY THOMAS FREDERICK, Ph.D.

1.   I am Jeffrey Thomas Frederick, Ph.D., and a copy of my curriculum vitae is attached to this Affidavit.

2.   I currently serve as the Director of Jury Research Services for the National Legal Research Group, Inc., in Charlottesville, Virginia, and have held that position since 1985. I am also a member of the American Society of Trial Consultants (ASTC), a former member of the ASTC Board of Directors (2000-2003), Chair of the Sub-Committee on Jury Selection Standards and Practice Guidelines for ASTC, and a member of the American Psychology/Law Society (Division 41) of the American Psychological Association. I have also taught courses addressing issues concerning the jury system and jury selection at Towson University, University of Virginia School of Law, and the University of Virginia Department of Psychology.

3.   Over the past 28 years, I have conducted research and published articles addressing juror/jury behavior and jury selection, in particular. Also, I have authored two books on the topic: *Mastering Voir Dire and Jury Selection: Gaining an Edge in Selecting and Questioning a Jury*, Chicago, Illinois: American Bar Association Press (1995) and *The Psychology of the American Jury*, Charlottesville, Virginia: The Michie Company (1987).

1

LEGAL RESEARCH, ANALYSIS, AND ADVOCACY FOR ATTORNEYS

4.   I have lectured in the area of jury research, jury selection, and jury trials extensively, including programs for the United States Department of Justice, the American Bar Association, the American Psychological Association, and the American Society of Trial Consultants.

5.   In addition, I have lectured and published scholarly articles on the subject of jury selection and voir dire, venue, and the use of juror questionnaires, including their use in capital cases. These lectures include programs on jury selection and procedures for improving juror disclosure in capital cases for both government and criminal defense training seminars. I have also assisted both the Department of Justice and criminal defendants in death penalty cases. Recent federal death penalty cases in which I have consulted include *United States v. Coleman Leake Johnson Jr.* (Virginia: Defense), *United States v. Christopher Wills* (Virginia: Defense), *United States v. Aaron Haynes* (Tennessee: Defense), and *United States v. Kristen Gilbert* (Massachusetts: Prosecution).

6.   I have been qualified as an expert witness in jury issues and jury behavior in both State and Federal Courts in Virginia.

7.   Since 1975, I have assisted attorneys in the criminal area (both defense and prosecution) and the civil area (both plaintiff and defense). Our firm has provided assistance in juror profile surveys, venue surveys, focus groups, trial simulations, voir dire question and supplemental juror questionnaire development, physical evidence evaluation, case presentation evaluation, witness preparation, in-court evaluation of jurors' verbal and nonverbal communication, trial observation of jurors, and post-trial interviews of jurors. I have assisted attorneys in hundreds of cases over the past 28 years.

2

242

8.   In light of my experience and expertise in jury selection in general and capital cases in particular, the defense attorneys for John Allen Muhammad have asked me to provide this affidavit in support of the court-appointment of a trial consultant to assist the defense and in support for improved jury selection procedures.

9.   Challenges faced in jury selection. Several challenges facing the defense in this case in terms of jury selection are noteworthy (a) the importance and impact of pretrial publicity, (b) death penalty beliefs and issues, (c) relevant experiences and opinions of jurors, and (d) factors inhibiting juror candor and disclosure.

10.   The importance and impact of pretrial publicity. The trial of *Commonwealth of Virginia v. John Allen Muhammed* offers a tremendous challenge in selecting a fair and impartial jury. A good first step was taken in securing a fair trial by moving the trial out of Prince William County. However, with the regional and national publicity concerning this case that has already occurred and is likely to occur in the future, many jurors can be expected to have a great deal of "knowledge" of the case and to have formed opinions concerning the guilt or innocence of the defendant and what an appropriate punishment should be if he is found guilty. In fact, a recent online article appearing in the *Virginia Pilot* (July 17, 2003) lists Websites containing court documents on both sniper suspect cases and describes the City of Virginia Beach's plan to post a Website concerning this case (although it is unclear if this Website will only contain logistical/tourist information or more case relevant information or links to Websites containing such information). Further complicating the situation is the connection between the two defendants who, while being tried separately, are inextricable

3

interwinded.   The coverage of the overall "D.C. sniper case" links the two suspects, John

Allen Muhammad and Lee Boyd Malvo, with many incriminating statements attributed to

Malvo.   Thus, bias-producing information (e.g., admissions or statements reflecting lack

of remorse) concerning one defendant is easily imputed to the other defendant.   Inquiry

into jurors' awareness of pretrial publicity and the impact on their decisions raises a

considerable challenge to uncovering jurors who can keep an open mind concerning this

case.

      11.   Social science research indicates that jurors are not passive recorders of

information presented at trial, but they are active information processors.[1]   In order to

process information presented in their lives and at trial, jurors construct "stories" for what

happened.   The "stories" that jurors build are not limited to trial information but are

influenced by the information, experiences, and opinions jurors bring with them to trial.

One of the most influential sources of pretrial information and opinions is pretrial

publicity.   Social science research on pretrial publicity has shown that it does influence

jurors' decisionmaking.[2]   However, research also shows that jurors often do not recognize

---

[1]Pennington &Hastie, *Explaining the Evidence: Tests of the Story Model for Juror Decision Making*, 62 Journal of Personality and Social Psychology 189 (1982); Hastie, Penrod & Pennington, *Inside the Jury*, Cambridge, Ma.: Harvard University Press (1983).

[2]Moran & Cutler, *The Impact of Prejudicial Pretrial Publicity*, 21 Journal of Applied Social Psychology 345 (1991); Studebaker & Penrod, *Pretrial Publicity: The Media, the Law and Common Sense*, 3 Psychology, Public Policy and the Law 428 (1997); Sue, Smith & Gilbert, *Biasing Effects of Pretrial Publicity on Judicial Decisions*, 2 Journal of Criminal Justice 163 (1974); and Vidmar, *Case Studies of Pre- and Midtrial Prejudice in Criminal and Civil Litigation*, 26 Law and Human Behavior 73 (2002).

4

and/or admit bias produced by pretrial publicity. One study[3] found that only 26% of those jurors exposed to damaging pretrial publicity recognized their biases, while the remaining supposedly "neutral" jurors who were exposed to damaging pretrial publicity still convicted the defendant at a 2-to-1 rate as compared to jurors not exposed to such publicity. Later studies have supported this finding.[4] Similar results concerning the "hollowness" of assertions by respondents that they can be "fair and impartial" have been found in surveys and public opinion polling.[5] Thus, the impact of pretrial publicity on jurors will continue to be a difficult problem in this case.

      12.   <u>Death penalty beliefs and issues</u>. Beyond the issues surrounding pretrial publicity, this case offers additional challenges arising from the sensitive issues that need to be addressed during the jury selection process. Paramount among these issues is that the defendant faces the ultimate punishment as a potential verdict in this case. Death penalty opinions will play a key role in this case, both directly and indirectly. Social science research has shown that (a) death-qualified jurors are more prone to convict[6] and

---

     [3]Sue Smith & Pedroza *Authoritarianism, Pretrial Publicity and Awareness of Bias in Simulated Jurors*, 37 Psychological Reports 1299 (1975).

     [4]Ogloff & Vidmar, *The Impact of Pretrial Publicity on Jurors: A Study to Compare the Relative Effects of Television and Print Media in a Child Sex Abuse Case*, 18 Law and Human Behavior 507 (1994).

     [5] Vidmar, *supra* note 9. Surveys conducted by our firm have repeatedly found that jurors' claims of impartiality are not related to their views as to the guilt or innocence of the defendant.

     [6]*See* Cowan, Thompson, & Ellsworth, *The Effects of Death Qualification on Jurors' Predisposition to Convict and on the Quality of Deliberations*, 8 Law and Human Behavior 53 (1984) and Moran & Comfort, *Neither "Tentative" nor "Fragmentary": Verdict Preference of Impaneled Felony Jurors as a Function of Attitude Toward Capital Punishment*, 71 Journal of Applied Psychology 146 (1986).

5

hold more anti-civil libertarian beliefs concerning presumption of innocence and burden

of proof[7]; (b) the death qualification process increases perceptions of guilt and the

appropriateness of the death penalty[8]; (c) many jurors in capital cases have a

misunderstanding about their role as sentencers and believe that the death penalty is

mandatory for most murders[9] regardless of the law and evidence in mitigation; and (d)

death-qualified jurors are more likely to endorse aggravating circumstances, with

excludable jurors being more likely to endorse nonstatutory mitigators.[10]

13.   For many jurors, beliefs concerning the death penalty are deeply held

beliefs resulting from childhood, religious and moral upbringing, and personal

experiences. Jurors often enter the courtroom with strong and fixed opinions about the

death penalty which, as reflected in the above research, can have a profound impact on

how they view the defendant, their support for legal principles, and their view of the

appropriateness of the implementation of the death penalty. It is only through in-depth

---

[7]*See* Fitzgerald & Ellsworth, *Due Process v. Crime Control: Death Qualification and Jury Attitudes*, 8 Law and Human Behavior 31 (1984).

[8]*See* Haney, *On the Selection of Capital Juries: The Biasing Effects of Death Qualification*, 8 Law and Human Behavior 121 (1984) and Haney, *Examining Death Qualification: Further Analysis of the Process Effect*, 8 Law and Human Behavior 133 (1984).

[9]*See* Bowers, Sandys & Steiner, *Foreclosing Impartiality in Capital Sentencing: Jurors Predispositions, Attitudes and Premature Decision-making*, 83 Cornell Law Review 1476 (1998).

[10]*See* Butler & Moran, *The Role of Death Qualification in Venireperson's Evaluations of Aggravating and Mitigating Circumstances in Capital Trials*, 16 Law and Human Behavior 175 (2002). Earlier research found that excludable jurors are more receptive to mitigating than aggravating circumstances (under Witherspoon v. Illinois, 1968*). See* Luginbuhl & Middendorf, *Death Penalty Beliefs and Jurors' Responses to Aggravating and Mitigating Circumstances in Capital Trials*, 12 Law and Human Behavior 263 (1988).

6

questioning and exploration of the jurors' views on the death penalty that both the defense and the prosecution can uncover what is needed to pursue challenges for cause and to intelligently exercise peremptory challenges. This questioning will need to address religious and moral views on the death penalty and life imprisonment without parole; the unique circumstances of this case (e.g., the defendant being charged with terrorism, the number of victims, past–and potentially future–statements made by the co-defendant, alleged national scope of the "shooting spree," and views concerning why the trial was moved to this community and resulting discussions within this community); and views concerning aggravating and mitigation factors, among other issues in order to determine whether jurors will be able to keep an open mind and fulfill the legal requirements for jury service in a case that potentially involves the imposition of the death penalty.

14.   Relevant experiences and opinions of jurors. In addition to pretrial publicity and the death penalty issues, it will be necessary to explore a number of sensitive opinions and experiences of jurors relevant to this case. These additional opinions and experiences include, but are not limited to, exploration of the jurors' views on legal principles (e.g., presumption of innocence and the defendant's right not to testify), identification with the victims of the sniper shootings, and exposure to victimization, among other issues.

15.   The importance of such inquiries is revealed in a survey of jury-qualified residents of the Norfolk Division of the Fourth Federal Judicial District of Virginia conducted in April of this year under my direction and previously reported in support of a change of venue motion in *United States v. Sa'ad El-Amin.* Significant minorities of

7

residents who are qualified for federal jury service in the Norfolk jurisdiction (of which Virginia Beach comprises approximately 37% of the jurisdiction) hold beliefs contrary to established legal principles. Of the jury-qualified respondents in the survey (a) 20% believe that if the prosecution goes to the trouble of bringing someone to trial, the person is probably guilty; (b) 42% believe that defendants in criminal trials should have to prove that they are innocent; and (c) 24% believe that a defendant in a criminal trial who does not testify is probably guilty. This research is supported by other survey studies conducted by our firm and by other researchers which reveal large minorities of jury-qualified individuals holding beliefs contrary to legal principles.[11]

16.   Factors inhibiting juror candor and disclosure. Major hurdles facing the defense are also present in the jury selection setting and voir dire procedures. As I noted in my book, *Mastering Voir Dire and Jury Selection,*[12] the jury selection setting contains many features that serve as obstacles to an effective and informative voir dire. These factors are:

> *Formal setting.* The formal physical environment of the courtroom and the behavior and roles of the court personnel can intimidate many jurors, thus inhibiting their full participation in voir dire.

---

[11]Yankelovich, Skelley & White, *The Public Image of the Courts: A National Survey of the General Public, Judges, Lawyers and Community Leaders* (1978) (available at the National Center for State Courts, Williamsburg, Va.); *see also* Bonora, Krauss & Roundtree, *JuryWork: Systematic Techniques*, St. Paul, Minn.: The West Group (1999); and Frederick, *The Psychology of the American Jury*, Charlottesville, Va: The Michie Company (1987).

[12]Frederick, *Mastering Voir Dire and Jury Selection: Gaining an Edge in Questioning and Selecting a Jury*, pp.71-72,Chicago, Il.: American Bar Association Press (1995).

8

Subordinate position. Jurors are reluctant to be candid because they are in a subordinate position, not allowed to speak unless they have been given permission to do so.

Brief examination. The short duration of the questioning of any individual jurors minimizes their openness.

Public disclosures. The answers that jurors give (some of which may concern very personal information) usually are made in open court, which lessens their willingness to answer honestly.

Evaluation apprehension. Jurors are often reluctant to answer candidly because of their concerns over what others might think of them.

Group questioning. The fact that the questioning of jurors often occurs in groups ranging from several jurors to twenty or more jurors leads to conformity to the opinions and behaviors expressed in these groups.

17. In addition to, and in conjunction with, issues of the setting and format of voir dire procedures, as was discussed in terms of pretrial publicity, the ability to recognize and/or acknowledge bias is a difficult task for jurors. Additional research supports the problematic nature of relying on jurors' assertions of fairness as true indicators of impartiality. Empirical studies have demonstrated (a) the inability of people to accurately report or "know" factors influencing their decisions,[13] (b) juror lack of

---

[13]Nisbett & Wilson, *Telling More than We Can Know: Verbal Reports on Mental Process*, 84 Psychological Review 231 (1977).

9

candor during the voir dire process,[14] and (c) concerns over evaluations (often referred to the "socially desirable response bias") inhibiting candor and honesty.[15]

18. Potential remedies. While it is indeed a thorny task to ferret out bias through the voir dire and jury selection process, there are procedures and approaches that help. These approaches include (a) individual sequestered voir dire, (b) in-depth questioning by attorneys, (c) the use of supplemental juror questionnaires, and (d) the appointment of a trial consultant.

19. Individual sequestered voir dire. One of the first steps to increasing juror candor and honesty is to conduct individual sequestered voir dire. As noted above, there is great pressure to provide socially desirable or acceptable answers when questioned in a group setting. As such, jurors are less likely to be as candid and forthcoming as necessary to uncover the various forms of bias as are likely to exist in this case. Research has demonstrated the superiority of the individual sequestered method in eliciting bias in capital cases.[16]

---

[14]Broeder, *Voir Dire Examinations: An Empirical Study*, 38 Southern California Law Review 503 (1965); Mize, *On Better Jury Selection: Spotting Unfavorable Jurors Before They Enter the Jury Room*, 36 Court Review 10 (1999); Seltzer, Ventuti & Lopes, *Juror Honesty During Voir Dire*, 19 Journal of Criminal Justice 451; and Vidmar, *supra* note 9.

[15]*See* Marshall & Smith, *The Effects of Demand Characteristics, Evaluation Anxiety, and Expectancy on Juror Honesty During Voir Dire*, 120 The Journal of Psychology 205 (1986). *See generally* Chaikin & Derlega, *Self-Disclosure*, Contemporary Topics in Social Psychology (Thibaut and Carson eds,. 1976) and Suggs & Sales, *Juror Self-disclosure in Voir Dire: A Social Science Analysis*, 56 Indiana Law Journal 245 (1981).

[16]Nietzel & Dillehay, *The Effects of Voir Dire Procedures in Capital Murder Trials*, 6 Law and Human Behavior 1 (1982) and Nietzel, Dillehay & Himelein, *Effects of Voir Dire Variations in Capital Trials: A Replication and Extension*, 5 Behavioral Sciences and the Law 467 (1987).

10

20.   Not only will there be a greater likelihood of juror candor, but there will be less chance for jurors' remarks to "taint" other jurors. Individual sequestered voir dire removes the risk of jurors being influenced by statements made by other jurors as can occur during group voir dire.

21.   Individual sequestered voir dire also reduces conformity pressures experienced by jurors during voir dire.[17] Jurors exposed to the responses of their fellow jurors–or lack thereof–can feel pressure to respond in a similar manner, thus conforming to the "normative" values or behavior of the group. Such conformity can result in decreased candor and even lack of participation in the voir dire process.

22.   <u>In-depth questioning by attorneys.</u> A related concern is the need for in-depth questioning of jurors by the attorneys for the prosecution and defense.[18] Research indicates that expansive voir dire yields greater revelations of juror bias.[19] In addition, research has shown that in-depth attorney-conducted voir dire combined with individual sequestered voir dire elicits greater admissions of bias on the part of jurors.[20] In-depth or

---

[17]*See* Frederick, *The Psychology of the American Jury*, Charlottesville, Va.: Michie Company (1987).

[18]I recognize that the court already may be planning to allow in-depth questioning by the attorneys. However, I have included this discussion because of the importance of this feature of jury selection, particularly in this case.

[19]Moran, Cutler & Loftus, *Jury Selection in Major Controlled Substance Trials: The Need for Extended Voir Dire*, 3 Forensics Reports 331 (1990).

[20]Johnson & Haney, *Felony Voir Dire: An Exploratory Study of its Content and Effect*, 18 Law and Human Behavior 309 (1994). An example of this occurred in a recent death penalty case in which I was involved in state court in Florida. In this case, the judge asked several questions of jurors in an individual sequestered format concerning their opinions on the death penalty prior to additional questioning by the parties. Eventually, eleven potential jurors were removed for cause after being identified as not being able to follow the law

11

expansive questioning in terms of the nature of the questions asked and the breadth of topics considered leads to a greater likelihood that attorneys will uncover areas of the jurors' experiences or opinions that reveal possible bias (whether or not this is sufficient to be considered for a challenge for cause). There are numerous topics that are relevant in this case, including pretrial publicity (see above), the complex issues concerning the death penalty (see above), support for legal principles (see above), involvement with the war effort and antiterrorism efforts (given that one of the charges involves terrorism), fear of the defendant and/or jury service, among others, that need to be addressed with jurors. It is through in-depth voir dire questioning and the use of a comprehensive supplemental juror questionnaire that underlying biases arising from these areas will have the greatest chance of discovery by the parties in such a unique case as this.

23.   In-depth questioning by the parties is facilitated by the use of open-ended questions. Open-ended questions serve a vital role in fostering juror disclosure. Open-ended questions are questions that do not restrict the responses or answers of jurors. Open-ended questions such as, "What have you read or heard about the case? or "What

---

concerning the death penalty. Of these potential jurors, five (45%) were identified through the questioning by the judge, while the remaining six potential jurors (55%) were only later identified as a result of questioning by the parties. Further, the six potential jurors who made it through the judge's questioning were later removed for cause based on either (a) the view that the death penalty was the only acceptable punishment for premeditated murder, or (b) the unwillingness to consider mitigation factors in their decisions on the appropriate punishment. This finding highlights the need for in-depth questioning by all participants in the voir dire process. In addition, it shows a potential disadvantage encountered by defendants in death penalty cases. The latter jurors who were removed were the types of anti-defendant biased jurors who need to be identified through in-depth questioning and removed in a death penalty case. *State v. Jerry Layne Rogers*, CR No. 83-1440-CF (Fla. 2002).

12

are your impressions of the guilt or innocence of the defendant based on what you have read or heard about this case?" or "I see that you answered in your questionnaire that you would want to impose the death penalty for someone convicted of murder because of the cost of keeping someone in prison. What did you mean by this?" require jurors to put their thoughts, opinions, and feelings into their own words. As a result, the parties and the judge have a better opportunity to understand what jurors really think or feel. In both juror questionnaires and voir dire, open-ended questions provide greater insight into the beliefs and thought processes of jurors. Closed-ended questions often take a "yes" or "no" format or restrict the response options in other ways. These questions are more susceptible to clues as to what the "correct" or socially desirable answer is and, when submitted in a group questioning format, are more susceptible to conformity pressures. In addition, when phrases are included in closed-ended questions such as "The law requires . . .", "Do you hold any bias . . ." or "Do you understand that . . . ," the potential for candid and honest responses is severely compromised.

24.   In-depth voir dire and open-ended questions also help to attack the "minimization effect." Jurors often seek to minimize the extremity of their opinions and their exposure to and the impact of pretrial publicity.[21] It is my experience that it is relatively common for jurors to say that they have heard "a little" or "not much" or "*just* what was in the media*" about a case, only later to recount a great deal of information that they have gleaned from media reports. Only through careful, in-depth questioning and the use of open-ended questions with follow-up prompts (e.g., Do you recall anything

---

[21]Vidmar, *supra* note 9.

13

else?") will attorneys and the court stand the best chance of uncovering the full extent of the jurors' knowledge, experiences, and opinions as they relate to this case.

25. **The use of supplemental juror questionnaires.** Based on a discussion with defense attorney Jon Shaprio, it appears that the Court is willing to utilize a supplemental juror questionnaire in this case. A key feature of supplemental juror questionnaires is that in addition to their value in securing information in a time-efficient manner, they also promote juror candor. As would be expected based on the research on factors inhibiting juror candor and what is reflected in the answers to questionnaires I have used in the past, jurors are more likely to be candid about their opinions and experiences in the privacy of completing a well-constructed juror questionnaire than in answering questions in open court. Thus, the supplemental juror questionnaire would play a key role in addressing sensitive areas (e.g., prior crime victimization or exposure to law enforcement and the criminal justice system) and important opinions (e.g., views on the death penalty and perceptions of the guilt or innocence of the defendant) in this case.

26. **The illusion of tension between the supplemental juror questionnaire and the need to observe jurors.** A concern that is often raised with supplemental juror questionnaires is the inability to observe the demeanor and actions of jurors during questioning into critical areas. While it is important to observe jurors during the voir dire process, as noted above, reliance on the jurors' affirmations of impartiality and candor during voir dire is problematic. Fortunately, it is not necessary to rely exclusively on either approach. A well-designed supplemental juror questionnaire addressing important backgrounds, experiences, and opinion issues with jurors does not preclude addressing

14

254

these topics during voir dire. In fact, supplemental juror questionnaires are just what their name implies. They are a supplement to the voir dire process. These questionnaires can uncover opinions and experiences of jurors that need to be further addressed in voir dire where the parties and the judge can observe the demeanor of the jurors. In this role, supplemental juror questionnaires serve to enhance the jury selection process, enabling the parties to uncover potential grounds for challenges for cause and to more intelligently exercise their peremptory challenges.

27. The appointment of a trial consultant. Jury selection in death penalty cases is not the same as other criminal cases. Voir dire questioning is necessarily more in-depth and emotional reactions of jurors given the life and death issues involved in death penalty cases are more intense. Even among death penalty cases in Virginia (and across the nation), this case is fairly unique. The media focus on the events surrounding this case has been and, as trial approaches, will continue to be intense. The defendants are alleged to have killed 10 people in the Washington D.C. area in a shooting spree that grabbed the nation's attention in October 2002 (with additional investigations concerning the defendant's alleged links to more deaths across the nation). Statements have appeared in the media that attribute Defendant Malvo as having admitted to participation in the shootings and as reflecting a lack of remorse and even pride in the shootings. The defendant is charged with committing an act of terrorism, at the same time that this country has committed substantial resources in its war against terrorists and terrorism.

28. A trial consultant with extensive death penalty experience and experience in highly publicized cases would be a valuable and necessary addition to the defense team.

15

A trial consultant with death penalty experience would assist in the development of a supplemental juror questionnaire and the analysis of the completed questionnaires, development of voir dire questions and potential follow-up questions, incourt evaluation of jurors and the suggestion of follow-up questions during jury selection, and the evaluation of persuasion issues as they relate to this case.

29.   Trial consultants have provided assistance in a number of highly publicized death penalty cases, including the *United States v. Timothy McVeigh* (for both the prosecution and defense), *United States v. Theodor Kaczynski* (defense), *United States v. Kristen Gilbert* (for both the prosecution and defense) and *South Carolina v. Susan Smith* (defense) cases. In the past three years, I have been appointed by the Court to assist the defense in two federal death penalty cases in Virginia (*United States v. Coleman Johnson* and *United States v. Christopher Wills*) and one death penalty case in Tennessee *(United States v. Aaron Haynes)*. Also, I have been a member of the defense team in *United States v. Zacarias Moussaoui* and recently assisted the defense in *State of Florida v. Jerry Lane Rogers* (death penalty case). The defense is not alone in recognizing the need for a trial consultant in significant trials. I have assisted federal prosecutors in, among other cases, *United States v. Leo Felton and Erica Chase* (conspiracy to commit terrorism), *United States v. Kristen Gilbert* (death penalty case), *United States v. Oliver North* and *United States v. Admiral John Poindexter*. In addition, I have assisted state prosecutors in *State of Connecticut v. Michael Skakel* (murder) and *Commonwealth of Virginia v. Glenn Barker* (murder).

16

30.   An informal survey of a few trial consultants who have assisted in court-appointed capital cases conducted by Margie Fargo, President of Jury Services Inc. of the National Capital Area, yielded court appointments in the following capital cases in Alabama, the District of Columbia, Florida, Georgia, Maryland, North Carolina, South Carolina, Tennessee, and Virginia:[22]

U.S. v. Aaron Haynes, USDC W.D. Tennessee (Memphis, 2003)

U.S. v. Kevin Gray et al., USDC DC (Washington, D.C., 2002)

U.S. v. Tommy Edelin et al., USDC DC (Washington, D.C., 2001)

U.S. v. Christopher Wills, USDC E.D. Virginia (Alexandria, 2001)

U.S. v. Coleman Johnson, USDC W.D. Virginia (Charlottesville, 2001)

Tennessee v. Antonio Carpenter (Fayette County, 2000)

U.S. v. Carl Cooper, USDC DC (Washington, D.C., 2000)

North Carolina v. Harrison (Transylvania County, 2000)

North Carolina v. Fisher (Halifax County, 2000)

North Carolina v. Holmes (Johnston County, 2000)

U.S. v. Antonio Carpenter, USDC W.D. Tennessee (Memphis, 2000)

Tennessee v. Paul Dennis Reid, Jr. (Davidson County, 1999 & 2000)

North Carolina v. Mealy (Onslow County, 1999)

North Carolina v. Fletcher (Rutherford County, re-sentencing hearing, 1999)

---

[22]This survey does not reflect all the death penalty cases in which a trial consultant was court-appointed in these states. This list also does not include death penalty cases where the public defender's office or some other resource retained the services of a trial consultant. For example, I worked with the public defender's office in *Commonwealth of Virginia v. Christopher Goins* and with private defense counsel in *North Carolina v. Joan Little*.

17

North Carolina v. Wiley (New Hanover County, 1999)

North Carolina v. Alan Gell (Bertie County, 1998)

Tennessee v. Paul Dennis Reid, Jr. (Montgomery County, 1998)

South Carolina v. Jeffrey Motts (Spartanburg County, 1997)

U. S. v. Donny Cable, et al., USDC M.D. Tennessee (Nashville, 1997)

North Carolina v. James Burmeister (Cumberland County, 1997)

North Carolina v. Smith (venue changed to Pitt Co., 1997)

North Carolina v. Archie Billings (Caswell County, 1996)

Tennessee v. James H. Dellinger, Gary Sutton (Blount County, 1996)

Tennessee v. Courtney Mathews (Montgomery County, 1996)

North Carolina v. Daniel Green (Roberson County, 1996)

North Carolina v. James Thomas Jordon (Mecklenburg County, 1996)

North Carolina v. Wendall Williamson (Orange County, 1995)

North Carolina v. Lockleer (Roberson County, 1995)

North Carolina v. Hunt (Roberson County, 1994)

North Carolina v. John Clark (Roberson County, 1994)

Florida v. Fred Riley (Palm Beach County, 1994; April & June trials)

Georgia v. Ahmond Dunnigan (Fulton County, 1993)

Alabama v. Walter Moody (Jefferson County, 1993)

Tennessee v. Joe T. Baker (Sumner & Montgomery Counties, 1991 & 1993)

Georgia v. John Hightower (Morgan County, 1988)

Commonwealth of Virginia v. John Robinson (City of Alexandria, 1988)

18

Florida v. Robin Scott (Palm Beach County, 1986)

Florida v. Ronald Meunier, (Broward County, 1980)

North Carolina v. Alonzo Powell (Cumberland County,1979)

North Carolina v. Norris Taylor (venue changed to New Hanover Co., 1979)

North Carolina v. Steven Silhan (venue changed to Columbus, Co., 1979)

31.   It is my opinion that the above outlined procedures and approaches are
necessary in order for the defense to intelligently exercise its peremptory challenges and
for the defendant to receive a fair trial.

EXECUTED UNDER PAINS AND PENALTIES OF PERJURY

Date: _7/25/03_

_____

Jeffrey Thomas Frederick, Ph.D.

19

259

VITA

Name	Jeffrey Thomas Frederick, Ph.D.
Address	1326 Allister Greene Charlottesville, VA 22901
Occupation	Director, Jury Research Services National Legal Research Group, Inc. 2421 Ivy Road, Charlottesville, Virginia 22903

Office Phone	(800) 727-6574	Local (804) 817-6574
Home Phone	(804) 978-7329	
Date of Birth	February 14, 1952	Marital Status: Married (1 child)

EDUCATIONAL BACKGROUND

North Carolina State University   1980   Ph.D.   Social Psychology
Raleigh, North Carolina   (Minor: Sociology)

North Carolina State University   1979   M.S.   Social Psychology

Pacific Lutheran University   1974   B.S.   Psychology
Tacoma, Washington

PROFESSIONAL EXPERIENCE

1985-present Director, Jury Research Services, National Legal Research Group, Charlottesville, Virginia 22901

1982-85 Director, Jury Research Services, 1433 Westwood Road, Charlottesville, Virginia 22901

1975-present Assistance has been provided in hundreds of cases. I have utilized a full spectrum of jury research techniques on a case by case basis. These techniques include: juror/community surveys, juror tracking studies, venue surveys, focus groups, trial simulations, physical evidence evaluation, case presentation evaluation, *voir dire* question and supplemental juror questionnaire development, witness preparation, in-court evaluation of jurors' verbal and nonverbal communication, trial observation of jurors, and post-trial interviews of jurors. I have personal experience in every phase of employing these techniques. I have also provided expert testimony through affidavits and at trial.

TEACHING

Psychology

1981-82	Assistant Professor	Department of Psychology University of Virginia
1976	Instructor	North Carolina State University (Social Psychology)
1976	Instructor	North Carolina State University (Introductory Psychology)

Mass Communication

2000-2002	Faculty	Towson State University (Jury Behavior: Comm 612)

Law

1995-97	Faculty	National College of District Attorneys
1989	Faculty	Trial Advocacy Institute Law School, University of Virginia
1988	Faculty	Trial Advocacy Institute Law School, University of Virginia
1983	Lecturer	Federal Executive Institute Charlottesville, Virginia
1979-82	Lecturer	School of Law University of Virginia
1982	Faculty	American Law Institute-American Bar Association Program on Civil Trial Practice, Madison, Wisconsin
1982	Faculty	Trial Advocacy Institute Law School, University of Virginia
1981	Lecturer	Masters Program for Appellate Court Judges Law School, University of Virginia
1979	Faculty	American Law Institute-American Bar Association Program on Trial Evidence in Federal and State Courts, Madison, Wisconsin

Sociology

1983	Visiting Assistant Professor	Department of Sociology University of Virginia

RESEARCH

1980-81	Research Associate	Tayloe Murphy Institute, Darden Graduate School of Business. Responsible for data management and analyses and manuscript preparation for NIMH grant, #AG01522-22, concerning the status of elderly ethnic groups in the U. S. Project involved analysis of large data files from the 1960 and 1970 U.S. Censuses (318,000 and 250,000 cases, respectively) utilizing regression, logistic regression, and path analysis.
1979-80	Research Assistant	Tayloe Murphy Institute, Darden Graduate School of Business. Responsible for data analysis for NIMH grant concerning the status of the ethnic elderly.
1977-78	Survey Director	H.E.W. # 1 R18 MH28990-01. Responsible for development, implementation, and data analyses of periodic surveys assessing the effectiveness of a publicity (attitude change) campaign concerning the crime of rape.

MEMBERSHIP IN PROFESSIONAL ORGANIZATIONS

American Psychological Association
American Psychology/Law Society
American Society of Trial Consultants (Member: Board of Directors)

EDITOR

Jury Research Update

HONORS

Who's Who in American Colleges and Universities 1974

PUBLICATIONS (BOOKS)

Frederick, J. *Mastering Voir Dire and Jury Selection: Gaining an Edge in Questioning and Selecting a Jury*. Chicago, Illinois: American Bar Association Press, 1995.

Frederick, J. *The Psychology of the American Jury*. Charlottesville, Virginia: The Michie Company, 1987.

PUBLICATIONS (JOURNALS)

Frederick, J. (1999) Understanding and Identifying Juror Bias. *The Journal*, Summer, *11*, 3, 2-10.

Frederick, J. (1997) Effective voir dire. *The Compleat Lawyer*, Summer, 26-30.

Frederick, J. (1996) Persuasion at trial: Opening statements. *Defense Practice Notebook*, 1, 76-78.

Frederick, J. (1996). Searching for rocks in the channel: Pretesting your case before trial. *Defense Practice Notebook*, 1, 65-68.

Frederick, J. (1996) How to increase juror participation and candor in restricted *voir dire* settings. *The Journal*, Summer, 8-13.

Frederick, J. (1991) Persuasion at trial: Opening statements. *For The Defense*, March, 27-29.

Frederick, J. (1990). Searching for rocks in the channel: Pretesting your case before trial. *For The Defense*, April, 26-29.

Frederick, J. (1990). Jurors' verbal and nonverbal communication: What attorneys should look for during jury selection. *Virginia Lawyer*, November, *39*, 24-27.

Frederick, J. (1988). Effective *voir dire*: From the mouths of jurors. *Trial*, August, 66-70.

Frederick, J. (1988). *Voir dire* and peremptory challenges. *Case & Comment*, January-February, *93*, 18-24.

Frederick, J. (1987). Using juror surveys to solve problems at trial. *For The Defense*, August, 8-12.

Frederick, J. (1985). Social science involvement in *voir dire*: Preliminary data on the effectiveness of "scientific jury selection." *Behavioral Sciences and the Law*, *2*, 1-20.

Frederick, J. (1984). Four ways to use a litigation psychologist in jury trials. *The Florida Bar Journal*, *10*, 633-637.

Frederick, J. (1984). Social science assistance for the civil trial lawyer: New tools for old problems. *Trial Lawyers Section Newsletter-The Florida Bar*, *10*, 3, 1-5.

Frederick, J. (1983). Social science and the civil jury trial. *Trial Briefs*, *14*, 26-27.

Frederick, J. (1978). Jury behavior: A psychologist examines jury selection. *Ohio Northern Law Review, 5,* 571-585.

McConahay, J., Mullin C., & Frederick, J. (1977). The uses of social science in trials with political and racial overtones: The trial of Joan Little. *Law and Contemporary Problems, 41,* 205-229.

Frederick, J. & Luginbuhl, J. (1977). Factors which influence decisions reached by jurors: Focus on rape. *Bulletin of the North Carolina Psychological Association, 1,* 20-25.

Humor

Frederick, J. & Hildreth, J. (1978). The last chance journal. *The Worm Runner's Digest, 20,* 76-78.

INVITED COLLOQUIA

Frederick, J.T. The Psychologist as jury trial consultant: practical, empirical, and ethical issues. Presented at North Carolina State University, 1993.

Frederick, J.T. Contemporary approaches in litigation: Social science techniques applied to trial practice. Presented at the University of Virginia School of Law, 1984.

Frederick, J.T. Scientific jury selection: Legal, psychological, and ethical issues. Presented at Dickerson College, 1983.

Frederick, J.T. The use of the social scientist in jury selection. Presented at the University of Virginia School of Law, 1978.

Frederick, J.T. The use of a predictive hybrid additive-interactive model in jury selection. Presented at Duke University, 1975.

PRESENTATIONS AT PROFESSIONAL MEETINGS

Frederick, J.T. Jury selection in wrongful death cases. Presented at the Virginia Association of Defense Attorneys, Williamsburg, Virginia, October 3, 2002.

Frederick, J.T. Jury selection standards: Results of an online poll of the ASTC membership. Presented at the American Society of Trial Consultants annual meeting, Denver, Colorado, June 8, 2002.

Frederick, J.T. Trial lawyer's toolbox: Improving jury selection through small group research and juror profile surveys. Presented at Institute of Continuing Legal Education in Georgia, Atlanta, Georgia, March 14, 2002.

Frederick, J.T. Picking the juries of today: The marriage of new techniques and traditional approaches. Presented at the Virginia Association of Defense Attorneys, Norfolk, Virginia, October 4, 2001.

Frederick, J.T. The fundamentals of persuasive opening statements and closing arguments. Presented at the Federal American Inns of Court, Washington, D.C., September 19, 2001.

Frederick, J.T. and Groot, R. Juror surveys and questionnaires. Presented at Defending a Capital Case in Virginia XIII, Washington and Lee School of Law, Lexington, Virginia, March 30, 2001.

Frederick, J.T. Understanding the jury–New tools in trial consulting. Presented at Virginia State Bar Young Lawyers Conference, Charlottesville, Virginia, March 9, 2001.

Being more effective in Voir Dire. Inns of Court, Charlottesville, Virginia, February 15, 2001.

Frederick, J.T. Overcoming juror bias. Presented at the Advanced Auto Practice Conference for the Virginia Trial Lawyers Association. Charlottesville, Virginia, July 14, 2000.

Frederick, J.T. Lawyer advertising: Who's paying the price? Presented at Litigation Section Board of Governors Section Workshop Program for the Virginia State Bar Association Annual Meeting. Virginia Beach, Virginia, June 18, 1999.

Frederick, J.T. Creating a graduate certificate program in litigation consulting. Panel discussant at the National Communication Association Convention. New York, New York, November 22, 1998.

Frederick, J.T. Jury selection in prosecutions involving scientific evidence. Presented at the Northeast Environmental Enforcement Project Conference. Charlottesville, Virginia, November 17, 1998.

Frederick, J.T. The psychology of the American jury, part 2: Persuasion at trial-- from opening statements to closing arguments. Presented at the State Bar of New Mexico Annual Convention, Carlsbad, New Mexico, September 26, 1998.

Frederick, J.T. The psychology of the American jury, part 1: How to be more effective in jury selection and voir dire. Presented at the State Bar of New Mexico Annual Convention, Carlsbad, New Mexico, September 25, 1998.

Frederick, J.T. Jury selection in capital cases: A jury consultant's perspective. Presented at the Association of Government Attorneys in Capital Litigation Convention. San Antonio, Texas, July 31, 1997.

Frederick, J.T. Understanding the mindsets of jurors: The key to jury selection. Presented at the Duquesne University Law School Continuing Legal Education Program. Pittsburgh, Pennsylvania, July 17, 1997.

Frederick, J.T. Voir dire and jury selection: Practical insights regarding information gathering. Presented at the American Society of Trial Consultants Convention. St. Petersburg, Florida, May 16, 1997.

Frederick, J.T. Juror perception research. Defense Counsel Symposium sponsored by the Virginia Insurance Reciprocal. Wintergreen, Virginia, May 9, 1997.

Frederick, J.T. Mastering *voir dire* and jury selection. Presented at the American Bar Association Annual Convention. Orlando, Florida, August 2, 1996.

Frederick, J.T. Advanced jury selection and persuasion. Presented to Pennsylvania District Attorneys Association, Philadelphia, Pennsylvania, February 14, 1996.

Frederick, J.T. *Voir dire* and jury psychology. Presented to Louisiana District Attorneys Association, Lafayette, Louisiana, November 29, 1995.

Frederick, J.T. Jury selection for the general practitioner. Workshop provided at the American Bar Association Annual Convention, New Orleans, August 9, 1994.

Frederick, J.T. Trying patent cases before juries. Paper presented at the Patent Club of Washington, D.C., Washington, D.C., January 21, 1993.

Frederick, J.T. Jury persuasion. Paper presented at the Virginia Association of Defense Attorneys Annual Convention, Williamsburg, Virginia, September, 1991.

Frederick, J.T. Getting the most out of jury selection. Paper presented at the New Mexico State Bar Annual Convention, Albuquerque, New Mexico, September, 1991.

Frederick, J.T. Persuasion at trial. Paper presented at the Maryland State's Attorneys' Association Winter Conference, Champion, Pennsylvania, January 1989.

Frederick, J.T. Using focus groups, trial simulations, and surveys to prepare for trial. Paper presented at the Virginia Association of Defense Attorneys Annual Convention, Charlottesville, Virginia, October 1988.

Frederick, J.T. Preparing to win: Techniques used by jury consultants. Paper presented at the Richmond Association of Legal Assistants, Richmond Virginia, March 1988.

Frederick, J.T. How jurors decide sexual assault cases. Workshop presented at the Virginia Department of Health Conference on Acquaintance Sexual Assault, Charlottesville, Virginia, September 1987.

Frederick, J.T. Jury studies in tobacco cases. Paper presented at the Second National Conference on Tobacco Products Liability, Boston, Massachusetts, January 1986.

Frederick, J.T. & Walker, L. Scientific selection of the jury. Paper presented at the District of Columbia Judicial Conference, Washington, D.C., June 1983.

Frederick, J.T. Jury behavior: Equity considerations in student and juror decisions. Paper presented at the annual meeting of the American Psychology Law Society, Cambridge, Massachusetts, October 1981.

Frederick, J.T. The use of social science methodology and quantitative analysis in the courts: New perspectives on jury selection. Paper presented at the annual meeting of the Florida State Bar Association, Orlando, Florida, 1981.

Frederick, J.T. Social science methods and jury selection: A practitioner's view. Paper presented as part of symposium entitled *Social science and jury selection: Psychological and legal perspectives* at the annual meeting of the American Psychological Association Convention, Los Angeles, California, 1981.

Frederick, J.T. The social scientist as an advocate's aide. Paper presented at the annual meeting of the Florida Defense Lawyer's Association, Amelia Island, Florida, September 1981.

Spar, M., Martin, J., Serow, W. & Frederick, J. Economic status of the European ethnic elderly. Paper presented at the Missouri Gerontology Institute Economics of Aging Conference, St. Louis, Missouri, April 1981.

Frederick, J., Spar, M., Martin, J. & Serow, W. Determinants of labor force participation for the white ethnic elderly. Presented at the Southwestern Sociological Association Convention, Dallas, Texas, 1981.

Spar, M., Martin, J., Serow, W. & Frederick, J. Income characteristics of the European ethnic elderly: 1960-1970. Paper presented at the Southern Regional Demographers Group, October 1980.

Frederick, J. How a social scientist does jury selection. Presented to the Charlottesville-Albemarle Bar Association, 1979.

Luginbuhl, J. & Frederick, J. A methodological review of rape research. Paper presented as part of the Symposium on Rape Research at the American Psychological Association Convention, Toronto, Canada, 1978.

Frederick, J. The effects of decision alternatives available, participants' respectability, and sex of subject on decisions reached by simulated juror: A comparison between two populations. Paper presented at the Southeastern Psychological Association Convention, Atlanta, Georgia, 1978.

Frederick, J., Luginbuhl, J. & Cowgell, V. The reactions of simulated jurors to the crime of rape: A review. Paper presented at the Southeastern Psychological Association Convention, Hollywood, Florida, 1977.

Frederick, J. & Luginbuhl, J. The accused rapist: Influence of penalty options and respectability. Paper presented at the American Psychological Association Convention, Washington, D.C., 1976.

SEMINARS (GOVERNMENT)

Fundamentals of persuasive opening statements and closing arguments. Presented at the United States Attorney's Office Retreat (California), San Francisco, California, April 18, 2002.

Everything you wanted to know about trial consultants . . . Presented at the United States Attorney's Office Conference (Massachusetts), Boston, Massachusetts, January 10, 2002.

How to be more effective in jury selection and voir dire. Presented to the Florida Prosecuting Attorneys Association, Marco Island, Florida, July 10, 2001.

Selecting the jury you want. Presented at the Advanced Seminar for Environmental Crimes at the National Advocacy Center, Columbia, South Carolina, May 12, 2000.

How to be more effective in jury selection and voir dire. Presented at the United States Attorney's Office Conference (Georgia), Atlanta, Georgia, March 5, 1998.

Jury selection in trials involving scientific evidence. Presented at the Department of Justice Environmental Crimes Division Meeting in Denver, Colorado, March 26, 1998.

How trial consultants can assist in antitrust litigation. Presented at the Department of Justice Antitrust Division Meeting, Chicago, Illinois, September 17, 1997.

Understanding the mindsets jurors. Program provided for the Strategic Criminal Litigation Course for the National College of District Attorneys, Chicago, Illinois, April 14, 1997.

The psychology of jury trials. Presented to the Office of State's Attorneys' Coordinator, Baltimore, Maryland, April 10, 1997.

Juror learning and retention problems during the prolonged, technical trial. Program provided for the Complex Litigation Course for the National College of District Attorneys, San Diego, California, December 2, 1996.

Structuring the effective juror questionnaire for the long term or sequestered jury. Program provided for the Complex Litigation Course for the National College of District Attorneys, San Diego, California, December 1, 1996.

Advanced jury selection and persuasion techniques. Two-hour training program provided for Advanced Criminal Advocacy Training Seminar for the Office of Legal Education, Executive Office for United States Attorneys, Washington, D.C., August 6, 1996.

Advanced jury selection and persuasion techniques. Two-hour training program provided for Advanced Criminal Advocacy Training Seminar for the Office of Legal Education, Executive Office for United States Attorneys, Washington, D.C., March 6, 1996.

Mastering *voir dire* and jury selection. Presented at Litigation and Training Seminar. Sponsored by the United States Attorney for the Southern District of Alabama, Mobile, Alabama, November 28, 1995.

Gut v. science in jury selection. Presented at the Late Twentieth Century Criminal Lawyering Conference. Sponsored by the United States Attorney for the Eastern District of Pennsylvania, Philadelphia, Pennsylvania, August, 1995.

The art and science of jury selection. Two-hour training program provided for Advanced Criminal Advocacy Training Seminar for the Office of Legal Education, Executive Office for United States Attorneys, Washington, D.C., July 19, 1995.

Voir dire and jury selection strategies. District-wide CLE Seminar, United States Attorney's Office for the Eastern District of Virginia, Richmond, Virginia, June 19, 1995

Jury issues: The psychology of persuasion at trial. One-hour training program provided for the Affirmative Civil Enforcement Seminar for the Office of Legal Education, Executive Office for United States Attorneys, Milwaukee, Wisconsin, June 14, 1995.

The art and science of jury selection. Two-hour training program provided for the Complex Prosecutions and Advanced Grand Jury Seminar for the Office of Legal Education, Executive Office for United States Attorneys, Portland, Oregon, May 11, 1995.

Voir dire from the expert's point of view. One-hour training program provided for the Capital Litigation in the Federal Courts Seminar for the Office of Legal Education, Executive Office for United States Attorneys, Dallas, Texas, May 3, 1995.

Jury selection: Approaches and techniques. Two-hour training program provided for the Advanced Training Program for the United States Attorney's Office for the District of Columbia, Airlie, Virginia, April 27, 1995.

The mindset and dynamics of the jury. Program provided for the Strategic Criminal Litigation Course for the National College of District Attorneys, Santa Fe, New Mexico, February 27, 1995.

The science of jury selection. Two-hour training program provided for the Complex Prosecutions and Advanced Grand Jury Seminar for the Office of Legal Education, Executive Office for United States Attorneys, Kansas City, Missouri, February 15, 1995.

Getting the most out of jury selection: The art and science of jury selection. Three-hour training seminar provided to the Advanced Criminal Advocacy Training program for the Office of Legal Education, Executive Office for United States Attorneys, Washington, D.C., January 10, 1995.

The science of jury selection. Two-hour training seminar provided for the Complex Prosecutions and Advanced Grand Jury Seminar for the Office of Legal Education, Executive Office for United States Attorneys, Orlando, Florida, October 28, 1994.

Taking a byte out of crime: Explaining computer science testimony to jurors. Three-hour training seminar provided to the Federal Bureau of Investigation, Quantico, Virginia, October 25, 1994.

Jury selection and communication skills. Three-hour training seminar provided to the Advanced Criminal Advocacy Training program for the Office of Legal Education, Executive Office for United States Attorneys, Washington, D.C., August 5, 1994.

The psychology of jury persuasion II: Voir dire and jury selection in criminal cases. Two-hour training seminar provided to the Criminal Division, Department of Justice, January 19, 1994.

The psychology of jury persuasion I: Pretrial research and trial techniques. Three-hour training seminar provided to the Criminal Division, Department of Justice, December 14, 1993.

Persuasive opening statements and closing arguments: The Exxon Valdez case revisited. Two-hour training seminar provided to the Department of Environmental Crimes, Department of Justice, December 8, 1992.

The psychology of jury selection and *voir dire*. Paper presented at the Virginia's Office of Attorney General training seminar, November 5, 1992.

Trial persuasion and jury selection. Three-hour training seminar provided to the United States Attorney's Office (Alabama). Mobile, Alabama, October 23, 1992.

SEMINARS (NONGOVERNMENT)

Jury selection techniques and strategies in medical malpractice litigation. Presented to the First Annual ProAd Claims/Legal Retreat, Richmond, Virginia, November 6, 1999.

The psychology of the American jury: How to be more effective in jury selection, voir dire, and communication. Presented at the Richmond Bar Association Meeting, Richmond, Virginia, December 10, 1998.

The psychology of persuasion: Themes in medical negligence cases. Presented at the Trial Lawyers Association of Metropolitan Washington, D.C. Conference, Washington, D.C., October 23, 1998.

How to be more effective in jury selection. Inns of Court, Norfolk, Virginia, October 15, 1997.

Picking Jurors: Getting to know them before its too late. Richmond Bar Association, Richmond, Virginia, February 27, 1996.

Pretesting your case through small group research. Inns of Court, Richmond, Virginia, January 1995.

Stereotypes and jury selection: Life after *Batson* and *J.E.B.* Inns of Court, Norfolk, Virginia, October 1994.

What litigation psychologists have to offer plaintiff's attorneys. Virginia Trial Lawyers Seminars on Tort Litigation, McClean, Richmond, Norfolk, and Roanoke, Virginia, April 1990.

Overview of jury research techniques: The techniques employed and what they buy you. Paper presented at the Academy of Florida Trial Lawyers' Jury Study Seminars, Orlando and Ft. Lauderdale, February 1989.

Voir dire and jury selection. Paper presented at the Criminal Law Seminar sponsored by the Virginia State Bar, Fredericksburg and Williamsburg 1989.

The use of social science techniques in trial advocacy. Paper presented at the Institute of Trial Advocacy, School of Law, University of Virginia, Charlottesville, Virginia, January 1989.

Voir dire and jury selection. Papers presented at the Virginia Trial Lawyers Seminars on the Trial of a Personal Injury Action in Virginia, McClean, Richmond, Norfolk, and Roanoke, Virginia, November 1987.

Testing your case before trial: The use of trial simulations. Papers presented at the Virginia Trial Lawyers Seminars on the Trial of a Personal Injury Action in Virginia, McClean, Richmond, Norfolk, and Roanoke, Virginia, November 1987.

Using surveys in litigation. Paper presented at the Virginia Trial Lawyers Seminars on the Trial of a Personal Injury Action in Virginia, McClean, Richmond, Norfolk, and Roanoke, Virginia, November 1987.

Improving *voir dire* skills. Paper presented at the Oregon Trial Lawyers Association's Advanced Seminar on *Voir Dire* in Civil and Criminal Cases, Portland, Oregon, May 1987.

Trial simulations: Testing your case before trial. Paper presented at the Oregon Trial Lawyers Association's Advanced Seminar on *Voir Dire* in Civil and Criminal Cases, Portland, Oregon, May 1987.

The use of surveys in litigation. Paper presented at the Oregon Trial Lawyers Association's Advanced Seminar on *Voir Dire* in Civil and Criminal Cases, Portland, Oregon, May 1987.

Using trial simulations and surveys to enhance trial presentations. Paper presented at the Louisiana Trial Lawyers Association's Seminar on Trial Strategies, Lafayette, Louisiana, March 1987.

The use of psychological services in contemporary litigation. Paper presented at the Virginia Association of Women Trial Attorneys, Charlottesville, Virginia, March 1986.

Pre-trying one's cases: The mock jury approach to obtaining more favorable jury verdicts. Paper presented at the North Carolina Academy of Trial Lawyers' Annual Seminar, Myrtle Beach, South Carolina, June 1985.

New tools of the trade: Social science techniques applied to contemporary litigation. Paper presented at the North Carolina Academy of Trial Lawyers' Patron's Round Table Seminar, Emerald Island, North Carolina, May 1985.

Social science assistance in *Shell Oil Co. v. Newport News Shipbuilding Co.*: A model for contemporary corporate litigation. Paper presented at the Tenneco Oil Company Senior Counsel's Meeting, Houston, Texas, March 1985.

CONTINUING LEGAL EDUCATION (CLE) PROGRAMS

Sponsor

2000-   Accredited on-line CLE programs for use on the Internet.

1992-94   Accredited continuing legal education programs in Virginia and Florida on the psychology of jury trials.

Programs

The psychology of jury trials. Four-hour CLE program presented in Richmond, Tysons Corner, and Norfolk, Virginia, 1992.

The psychology of jury selection and persuasion. Five-hour CLE program co-sponsored with the Institute for Continuing Education in Georgia, Atlanta and Savannah, Georgia, September 1992.

The psychology of jury trials. Five-hour CLE program presented in Richmond, Tysons Corner, Norfolk, and Roanoke, Virginia, 1991.

The jury--skills and psychology. Six-hour CLE program presented to the Vermont Bar Association, Burlington, Vermont, November, 1991.

Jury selection and persuasion. Five-hour CLE program co-sponsored with the Institute for Continuing Education in Georgia, Atlanta and Savannah, Georgia, September 1988.

APPENDIX II

Sample Opinion Questions for Selected Criminal Voir Dire Topics

This appendix addresses selected opinion topics that are of interest in jury selection in many criminal trials. Most of the questions are presented in a closed-ended format. The designations "P" and "D" indicate questions more likely to be asked by the prosecution and by the defense, respectively.

Presumption of Innocence

[D] Do you believe that if the prosecution goes to the trouble of bringing someone to trial, the person is probably guilty?

[D] If you had to vote right now, how would you vote? [Do you realize that the defendant is not guilty?]

[D] How did you feel when you heard that [name of defendant] was arrested for this crime?

[D] Did you have the feeling that the authorities had arrested the right person?

[D] Do you believe that sometimes innocent people are convicted of crimes they did not commit?

Burden of Proof

[P] As a representative of the people of this [country/state/locality], it is my duty to provide evidence that will convince you that the defendant committed the crimes charged. Do you understand that this is my duty, not the defendant's, and that I take this duty seriously?

[D] In our system of justice, the prosecution has the burden to prove each element of a crime beyond a reasonable doubt. That is, it is the prosecution's duty to prove to you beyond a reasonable doubt that the defendant committed the crime charged. Would you have any trouble holding the prosecution to this burden?

[D] Do you believe that defendants in criminal trials should have to prove that they are innocent?

[D] How would you feel if the defense did not present any evidence at all?

[D] Would you tend to hold it against the defendant should the defense present no evidence at all? That is, would you tend to think the defendant was guilty?

[D] Would you expect the defense to prove the prosecution wrong?

Circumstantial Evidence

[P] In a trial, there are two ways to prove a particular fact. The first way is by direct evidence, evidence that by itself proves a fact, e.g., an eyewitness's statements or someone's fingerprints on an object. The second way to prove a particular fact is by circumstantial evidence. Circumstantial evidence involves a collection of facts that lead you to conclude that another fact occurred, e.g., if you wake up one morning and snow is on the ground, where previously no snow had been, you would conclude that it snowed sometime during the night. Now, in this case, there will not be any direct evidence that the defendant murdered the victim; the case relies on circumstantial evidence. Would you tell me how you feel about considering only circumstantial evidence in deciding whether the defendant murdered the victim?

[P] Do you think that circumstantial evidence is somehow inferior or weak evidence?

[P] If we provided circumstantial evidence that led you to conclude beyond a reasonable doubt that the defendant was guilty, would you have any reservations in returning a guilty verdict based on circumstantial evidence?

[P] Would you have reservations in convicting a defendant of a serious crime such as murder without such evidence as DNA, fingerprints, or an eyewitness?

[D] The prosecution in this case will likely bring in circumstantial evidence and try to convince you that, taken together, this evidence proves beyond a reasonable doubt [the defendant's] guilt. Now, let's consider circumstantial evidence for a minute, because sometimes it can appear stronger than it really is. Suppose you round the corner of a building and see someone injured on the ground. Next to the victim is a man holding a stick bending over him. Now, many people's first impression likely would be "Look, there is the attacker standing right next to his victim." However, can you imagine other explanations for the man to be found holding the stick? [For example, the man just arrived on the scene and picked up the stick.]

Or, in the snowfall scenario described by the prosecutor, would the presence of a snow-making machine nearby affect your confidence in the initial conclusion that it snowed overnight?

[D] Do you understand that circumstantial evidence must be viewed with great caution because it has the potential to give false impressions?

Standard of Proof

[P] As the prosecutor in this case, I have the duty of proving beyond a reasonable doubt that the defendant is guilty of [the crimes charged]. Now, many of you have heard the phrase "beyond a reasonable doubt" before—perhaps on television or in your reading about courtroom events. This is the standard of proof used in criminal trials. As the phrase implies, it is a reasonable standard. It is reasonable—based on our common sense—that we remove any serious, well-founded doubt that you may have about the defendant's guilt. And this we will do. However, I should remind you that the standard is not "beyond an unreasonable doubt." As the judge will instruct you later, we do not have to remove all possible—and trivial—doubt, but only any substantial or serious doubt. Would you have any reservations in returning a guilty verdict if we met this standard?

[P] If you served on the jury in this case, would you have any reservations in returning a verdict of guilty against the defendant if the evidence proved beyond a reasonable doubt that the defendant was guilty of first-degree murder?

[P] If you served as a juror, you would be required to judge the defendant and return a verdict of guilty if the evidence proved beyond a reasonable doubt that the defendant is guilty. Would you have any reservations in returning a guilty verdict if the evidence proved the defendant to be guilty? How would you feel about returning a guilty verdict?

[P] In your mind, is there a difference between being absolutely 100 percent certain as compared to believing beyond a reasonable doubt that the defendant committed the crime?

What does the phrase "beyond a reasonable doubt" mean to you?

[D] Let us take a few minutes and talk about an important concept in American criminal law, that is, the prosecution's having to prove that the defendant is guilty beyond a reasonable doubt. This is an important test. In fact, this is the highest standard in the American judicial system. In a civil case, the plaintiff must prove his case by a preponderance of the evidence. This is a mild standard compared to what you will be deciding in this trial. Beyond a reasonable doubt means beyond *all* reasonable doubt. You must be certain that the defendant is guilty of the crime charged before you consider convicting the defendant. In coming to your decision, you must apply this standard to each element of the charge. And if the prosecution has not proved each element beyond all reasonable doubt, then it is your duty to return a not guilty verdict. Do you believe that you would do that in deciding this case with your fellow jurors?

[D] If you served as a juror in this case, would you have any reservations in returning a not guilty verdict if the prosecution failed to prove beyond a reasonable doubt that [the defendant] committed the crimes charged?

[D] Would you feel that in not returning a conviction your job was somehow incomplete or a failure?

Pretrial Publicity

Have you heard anything on the radio or seen anything in the newspaper, on television, or the Internet, or had discussions with friends or coworkers concerning this case [be explicit with the case description]?

Tell me a little about what you recall from what you heard, saw, or discussed.

What went through your mind when you read/heard/saw reports concerning [the event in question and subsequent events/reports]?

What did you think about the defendant when you read/heard/saw these reports?

Before coming to court today, what were your thoughts about the case or [the defendant]?

Based upon what you have heard and discussed with your friends and coworkers, have you formed any impressions of what happened?

What are these impressions?

[D]   What do you see when you look at the defendant right now?

Defendant Not Taking the Stand

[P]   According to the law, the defendant does not have to testify. However, should he/she decide to do so, you are to judge his/her credibility in the same way as you would that of other witnesses. That is, you need to consider what he/she has to gain, his/her demeanor, and whether his/her story makes sense. Would you have any reservations in doing this should the defendant testify?

[D]   Do you believe that a criminal defendant should be required to testify in his/her own defense?

[D]   Do you think that defendants in criminal trials who do not testify in their own defense are probably guilty?

[D]   Would you expect that someone accused of a crime would naturally want to tell his/her side of the story?

[D]   What would your impression be of defendants who do not testify in their own defense?

[D]   How would you feel about a defendant who chooses not to take the stand at trial?

[D]   If [the defendant] does not take the stand, do you feel that this would indicate to you that he/she is probably guilty?

[D]   Could you find [the defendant] not guilty of [the crime(s) charged] if he/she does not take the stand to tell his/her side of the story?

[D]   Would you tend to feel that he/she was trying to hide something?

[D]   Would a defendant not taking the stand be, in your mind, a point in favor of the prosecution?

Racism[1]

What does the phrase "racial prejudice" mean to you?

When you hear the phrase "racial discrimination," what does it mean to you?

How do you feel about interracial marriage?

Do you think that blacks [other racial or ethnic group] are more likely to commit crimes than whites? Why?

Do you think that policemen are more likely to use force in apprehending black [other racial or ethnic group] people than white people? Why?

Do you think that whites are being discriminated against in job hiring or promotions as a result of affirmative action?

What are your feelings about affirmative action programs?

Do you think that racial prejudice is a problem of the past or do you think it is still present today? How so?

Behavior of Defendant/Witnesses
(primarily defense-oriented questions)
Lifestyle

The evidence may show that [the defendant or witness] was what is called a homeless person. What are your feelings about people who are homeless?

Have you ever seen our city's homeless people who live near [certain sections of the area]?

How did you feel when you saw them?

What went through your mind when you saw them?

Why do you think that homeless people are without homes?

Would the fact that someone is homeless make his/her testimony less credible than that of other people?

Would you base your decision on the credibility of a witness's testimony on what he/she says on the witness stand and not on the fact that he/she is homeless?

There will be evidence that [the defendant] was attending a party at which drugs were used. Would the fact that he/she was at this party lead you believe that he/she must have done something wrong?

Would you tend to assume that he/she must be guilty?

Alcoholism/Drug Addiction

Do you drink any alcoholic beverages on occasion?

Do you have any religious or moral beliefs against the drinking of alcoholic beverages?

Do you have any negative impression of those who choose to drink alcoholic beverages?

Do you think that it is possible that consuming alcohol [drugs] can impair one's thinking?

Do you think that it is possible for someone to consume enough alcohol [drugs] that he/she does not know what he/she is doing?

Do you think that heavy drinking [drug use] over a number of years can cause brain damage?

Do you believe that people may use alcohol [drugs] as an excuse for not being responsible for their behavior?

Do you think that as long as someone who is severely inebriated has not passed out or is still conscious he/she knows (or should know) what he/she is doing?

Do you think it is likely that heavy drinking [drug use] can cause someone to act irrationally?

Do you think that heavy drinking [drug use] can make someone do things that he/she did not really want to do?

Do you believe that alcohol only releases inhibitions and does not really cause irrational behavior?

Do you think it is impossible for someone to drink so much alcohol that he/she does not know what he/she is doing?

Do you believe that signs of physical impairment (e.g., lack of coordination or slurring of speech) are the only ways to tell if someone's thought processes have been affected by the consumption of alcohol [drugs]? What would be some other ways?

Do you believe that alcoholism [drug dependency/addiction] is a physical disease that causes alcoholics [drug addicts] to be unable to control their drinking [drug use], or do you believe that alcoholism [drug dependency/addiction] is simply a lack of willpower and self-control on the part of the alcoholic [drug addict]?

Do you believe that heavy drinking [drug use] on the part of an alcoholic [someone addicted to drugs] over a number of years can reduce his/her capacity to think clearly?

Do you believe that an individual who drinks [uses drugs], no matter what the circumstances, should be responsible for his/her actions?

Do you think that an alcoholic [someone who is addicted to drugs] should be responsible for his/her actions when he/she is severely inebriated?

Immunity/Special Treatment

[D] Do you believe that criminals might lie in order to get a better deal (or a reduced prison sentence) from the government?

[D] How do you feel about witnesses who testify as a result of receiving money or special treatment by the government in terms of their willingness to tell the truth?

[D] Do you feel that the government would not bring in a witness unless what he/she had to say was the truth?

[P] What are your views on the credibility of criminals who testify against a defendant in exchange for immunity or possible special treatment from the government?

Criminals/Informants Inducing Others to Commit Crimes

[P] How do you feel about law enforcement agencies using informants to uncover criminal activity in our community?

[P] Informants are the ones closest to the crime and often have firsthand knowledge about what goes on. Obviously, police officers in uniform are not likely to be around when certain crimes are committed. Would the fact that certain evidence in this case will come from such informants disqualify this evidence in your mind simply because the witness was an informant?

[P] Do you believe that just because someone has been involved in criminal activity he/she should not be believed when he/she tells about the criminal activity of others?

[D] Do you believe that criminals might try to pressure someone into illegal activity if it meant more money being paid to these criminals or less jail time for them?

[D] Do you believe that if criminals are paid money or receive preferential treatment there is an incentive for them to tell the police what the police want to hear?

Conduct of Lawyers
Objections

During the course of trial, there will be times when I will raise objections over procedural matters and the court will determine whether these objections are valid. This is part of my job. Would you have any concerns about these objections?

Would you feel that what would have been said is deserving of your attention?

Would you be able to simply decide this case on what is said on the stand and not on any speculation about why an objection was raised?

Rigorous Cross-Examination

During the course of the testimony of witnesses brought by [the opposing party], I will have an opportunity to question the witnesses to bring out information from them that I think you should know. Sometimes, it is necessary to be fairly forceful. I will try at all times to be courteous to these witnesses, but I may have to be forceful. Would the fact that I question a witness in a forceful manner cause you any concern in this case?

Witness Credibility

Do you believe that when someone may benefit from the outcome of this trial this fact should be considered in evaluating this person's willingness to tell the truth?

What do you consider to be important factors in determining whether a person is telling the truth on the stand?

Would you consider the demeanor of the witness in evaluating whether he/she is telling the truth?

Would you be willing to consider what witnesses might gain as a result of their testimony in determining their truthfulness?

Expert Witnesses: Mental Health Professionals

What are your impressions of the ability of people trained in the field of mental health to understand the human mind?

Do you believe that people would be a lot better off if they simply took responsibility for their actions instead of seeking counseling from psychologists or psychiatrists?

Do you have any feeling that opinions rendered by individuals trained in the field of mental health are just subjective speculations and not deserving of serious consideration?

Would you tend to discount what a psychologist/psychiatrist would have to say as compared to a surgeon or someone who can point to a broken bone and say, "That's a broken bone"?

Multiple Defendants

[D]   There are several defendants in this case. Would the fact that there is more than one defendant lead you to believe that they all must be guilty of something?

[D]   Would the presence of multiple defendants lead you to believe that if one defendant is guilty they all must be guilty?

[D]   Have you heard the phrase "guilt by association"? What does that phrase mean to you?

[D]   Would you be able to consider only the evidence pertaining to a given defendant and not tend to consider all the evidence as applying to all the defendants?

[D]   Do you feel that you will be able to consider each defendant separately and require the prosecutor to prove beyond a reasonable doubt that any individual defendant is guilty of a crime?

Multiple Charges

[D]   In this case, the defendant faces [number] charges in this indictment. Would the fact that he/she faces [number] charges tend to form the impression in your mind that he/she is really some kind of criminal?

[D]   Would the fact that he/she faces a number of charges lead you to believe that he/she must be guilty of something?

[D]   The prosecutor held up a copy of the indictment of [the defendant] and it is pretty thick. Would the fact that this indictment is [number] pages long and contains [number] charges give you the impression that [the defendant] must have done something wrong?

Death Penalty

[Explain that killing in self-defense and accidental killings are not to be considered in the discussion.]

What are your views on the death penalty as a punishment for those convicted of premeditated murder?

Do you have any religious, moral, ethical, or philosophical beliefs that lead you to support or oppose the death penalty?

What factors would be important to you in deciding whether or not a person should receive a death sentence?

[D]   Do you favor the death penalty for anyone who deliberately kills another person?

[D]   Are you in favor of the death penalty for [specify appropriate case, e.g., premeditated murder]?

(If in favor of the death penalty) Can you tell me why you favor the death penalty?

[D]   (If favor the death penalty) What are the main reasons for why you support the death penalty?

[D]   Do you consider yourself to be a strong supporter of the death penalty for [premeditated murder]?

[D]   For what crimes do you believe the death penalty is an appropriate punishment?

[D]   Under what circumstances do you consider the death penalty to be an appropriate punishment?

[D]   If a person is convicted of first-degree murder, do you feel that he/she should receive the death penalty?

[D]   Do you believe in an "eye-for-an-eye" in cases of [premeditated murder]—that is, [if a person premeditates the killing of another person], he/she should pay for it with his/her life?

[D]   Do you believe that everyone who [commits a premeditated murder], no matter what the circumstances, should be sentenced to death?

[D]   If you were convinced beyond a reasonable doubt that the defendant was guilty of first-degree murder, would the defense have to convince you that he/she should not receive the death penalty?

[D]   Do you feel it is best to sentence someone to death rather than risk any possible danger to others?

[D]   Do you feel that if someone takes a life through intentional murder, that person should forfeit his life?

[D]   Do you believe a sentence of death is the only appropriate sentence if someone is convicted of intentional murder?

[D]   Do you believe that it is better to sentence someone to death rather than put him/her in prison for the rest of his/her life?

[D]   Do you believe that a life sentence is not a severe enough punishment for someone convicted of intentional murder?

[D]   Do you think that it would be difficult for you to *realistically* consider life imprisonment without release for someone convicted of premeditated murder?

[D]   Do you feel that mitigating factors, e.g., childhood abuse or drug addiction, are merely excuses and not legitimate considerations in deciding whether someone convicted of capital murder should receive life imprisonment without release versus death?

[D]   Can you imagine any situation where the crime is so horrendous that you would feel the death penalty is appropriate? If you found the crime to be severe enough that you felt the death penalty was appropriate, would you be able to consider both the death penalty and life imprisonment without release in deciding what the appropriate punishment should be?

[P]   (If against the death penalty) Can you tell me why you do not favor the use of the death penalty as a punishment for premeditated murder?

[P]   Could you return a verdict of death if you found by the evidence and the law that there were one or more aggravating circumstances *and* these circumstances are not outweighed by any mitigating circumstances?

[P] Would you have any reservations in returning a verdict of death should you find that one or more aggravating circumstances exist *and* that any mitigating circumstances found to exist did not outweigh the aggravating circumstances?

[P] Would you have any reservations in returning a verdict of death if you found one or more aggravating circumstances to exist *and* the defendant did not prove that *any* mitigating circumstances were present?

[P] Are your opinions about the death penalty such that they would prevent or substantially impair your ability to discharge your duty as a juror to consider either (a) the guilt or innocence of the defendant, or (b) all the appropriate punishments should the defendant be found guilty?

[P] The [State/Commonwealth/United States] is seeking the death penalty against the defendant in this case. That means that should you find the defendant guilty of [premeditated murder], you must decide whether the defendant should be sentenced to death or sentenced to life imprisonment without possibility of parole. Voting to sentence someone to death—to execute the defendant—is obviously a very serious decision. Do you feel that you would have any reservations in being able to make such a decision in this case?

[P] Each juror must sign the verdict form that sentences the defendant in this case. Would you have any reservations in personally signing a verdict form that would mean the defendant would be executed?

[P] This is the time to tell us if you have any reservations or concerns. You can take a minute to think about it if you like and tell me if you would have any reservations whatsoever in sentencing the defendant to death if you felt that the aggravating factors outweighed the mitigating factors.

Actions by Law Enforcement Personnel/Investigation Techniques

[P] How do you feel about the use of sting operations to catch those involved in criminal activity?

[P] During this trial, you will hear testimony from a police officer who went undercover to gather evidence in this case. Do you have any personal views concerning this type of activity that would give you any reservations in accepting this testimony simply because it was gathered in an undercover operation?

[D] Do you think that it is more important for police to seek the truth than simply to try to convict a defendant?

[D] Do you think that a police officer would try to prevent the defense from collecting valuable evidence in order to hinder the defendant's case?

Have you ever seen an incident where police officers used force to arrest or otherwise detain someone?

What were your impressions of the police officer(s) involved?

[P] Do you have any concerns about whether it is fair to prosecute or punish a police officer charged with using too much force to make an arrest?

[D] Would the fact that a police officer hit someone with a nightstick lead you to believe that excessive force was used?

[D] Would you consider the total circumstances of the situation in determining whether the actions of the police officer were appropriate?

[D] Would the fact that the person arrested had been struck approximately [number of times] times indicate to you that excessive force was used?

[D] In considering whether a police officer is guilty of using excessive force, what factors do you think would be important to know?

Eyewitness Testimony

[P] In this case, we will present several eyewitnesses who will describe for you exactly what they saw that day. Do you have any feelings about testimony by eyewitnesses that would make it difficult for you to properly consider their testimony given under oath?

[D] Do you believe that under certain circumstances an eyewitness's memory for what happened might not be accurate? Can you tell me what you think might be some of the circumstances where an eyewitness might make an honest mistake in what he/she remembers about what happened?

Testimony by Law Enforcement Officers

[D] Would you believe the word of a policeman over that of other witnesses?

[D] Do you believe that some police officers might lie or hide the truth when it comes to their testimony in court?

Would you tend to give more weight, about the same weight, or less weight to the testimony of police officers as compared to other witnesses?

Evidence at Issue

[P] There will be tape recordings introduced at trial that reflect the conversations of the defendant in this case (concerning a particular aspect of this case). How do you feel about using tape recordings of conversations in a trial like this?

[P] Would you have any reservations in considering this evidence in arriving at a decision concerning the guilt or innocence of the defendant?

[P] How do you feel about the use of concealed videotape and audiotape recordings in undercover investigations of criminal activity?

[D] There will be audiotapes presented by the prosecution allegedly indicating some criminal activity on the part of [the defendant]. If you served as a juror, would you be able to listen carefully and consider exactly what was said on these tapes and not simply accept the prosecutor's explanation of what the conversation was about?

Criminal Justice Issues

[D] In your opinion, what are the major causes of crime?

[D] How do you feel about the way the criminal justice system is working in the United States?

[D] In general, what are your impressions of the way police and other law enforcement agencies conduct criminal investigations?

[D] Which of the objectives—punishment, rehabilitation, or public safety—do you feel is the most important consideration in sentencing those convicted of violent crimes?

[D] Do you feel that the criminal justice system treats criminals too harshly, about right, or too leniently?

[D] Do you believe that the law does too much to protect the rights of criminal defendants and not enough to protect the rights of crime victims and their families?

[D] Do you feel that people who are wealthy are held less responsible for their actions than the average person?

Closing Questions

[D] Would you feel that it is important that you stand by your opinion? Why is that?

[D] If you served on the jury and your fellow jurors were unable to agree on the verdict—what we call a hung jury—how would you feel about that?

[D] Would you feel a sense of failure or incompleteness in not being able to agree on a verdict?

[D] Would you feel as though you hadn't done your job as a juror?

[D] If you believed by what you heard and saw in court that the prosecution had failed to prove beyond a reasonable doubt that [the defendant] was guilty, would you be willing to stand by your decision no matter whether other jurors felt a different way?

[D] If you are selected to serve as a juror on this case, would you be concerned about reactions to the verdict by anyone?

[P] The verdict of guilty requires a unanimous decision among the jurors. If you served as a juror in this case, would you be willing to go over the evidence in the case, listen to your fellow jurors' views, and work with them toward a unanimous decision in this case?

[P] Do you have any religious, moral, or ethical beliefs that would make it difficult for you to sit in judgment of another person in a criminal trial?

Do you believe that if the law as the judge gives it to you at the end of this case goes against your personal views of what the decision should be, you would tend to base your verdict on your personal views of the case?

Since I may not have asked the kind of question—perhaps about some past experience or certain beliefs that you hold—that would have raised a question in your mind, let me ask this. If you were at either one of these tables, would there be any reason why you would not want yourself as a juror in this case? That is, at this time, would you feel uncomfortable being at either table and having someone like yourself as a juror?

NOTES

1. Some of these questions are drawn from BONORA, KRAUSS & ROUNDTREE, JURYWORK: SYSTEMATIC TECHNIQUES (1999).

APPENDIX III

Sample Opinion Questions for Selected Civil Voir Dire Topics

This appendix addresses selected opinion topics that are of interest in jury selection in many civil trials. Most of the questions are presented in a closed-ended format. The designations "P" and "D" indicate questions more likely to be asked by the plaintiff and by the defense, respectively.

Victim Compensation

[P] Do you believe that victims should be compensated to the full extent the law will allow?

[P] How do you feel about the law that provides for monetary compensation for victims of another's negligence?

[P] Through monetary compensation the law seeks to make the victim "whole." That is, the law seeks to compensate the victim for his/her suffering. This may be economic loss, loss of physical abilities, and/or other kinds of losses. Would you have any reservations in awarding monetary damages for these types of losses in rendering your verdict?

[P] Do you believe that every effort should be made to compensate victims of another's negligence?

[P] How important do you believe it is that victims are compensated when they have been injured through the negligence of others?

[D] Do you believe that all injured people deserve to be compensated, even if that means that a defendant who is not negligent pays the award?

[D] How do you think you would feel if you found that the defendant was not negligent and, therefore, the plaintiff was not entitled to any compensation whatsoever from the defendant?

Corporate Responsibility

[P] According to the law, a corporation is responsible for the actions of its employees while they are on the job. If we show that the injury to [the plaintiff] was the result of the negligent actions of the defendant, would you have any reservations in awarding damages to [the plaintiff]?

[P]   Do you have any reservations or concerns with the law that holds a corporation responsible for the actions of its employees?

[P]   Would you have any reservations in holding [the defendant] responsible for any negligent actions of its employees?

Tort Reform/Lawsuit Crisis

Have you heard, seen, or read anything about what has been called the "lawsuit crisis" (or money awards by juries)? What do you think about this?

How do you feel about lawsuits in general?

Do you feel that jury awards are becoming too high?

Do you feel that there are too many lawsuits?

Do you feel that people today are too eager to file lawsuits?

Do you feel that people nowadays are too quick to sue others?

[P]   Do you feel that most people who sue others have legitimate grievances?

[P]   Do you feel that the laws should be changed to make it harder to sue corporations?

[P]   Do you support legislative efforts to place caps on the amount of money juries can award?

Medical Negligence Issues

Lawsuits Against Doctors

How do you feel about patients suing their doctors?

[P]   Do you believe that patients should have a right to sue doctors for negligent treatment?

[D]   Do you believe that just because a patient is injured the doctor is negligent?

[D]   Do you believe that when something goes wrong it must be the doctor's fault?

[P]   Do you have any reservations concerning lawsuits against doctors?

[P]   Do you believe that doctors can be negligent in the treatment of their patients?

[P]   Do you believe that patients should bear the consequences of their doctor's negligence?

[P]   Do you believe that a doctor should be held liable if he/she routinely performs operations that should not be performed, even though the doctor "believes" the operations are appropriate?

[P]   Do you believe that a doctor should be responsible for the consequences of his/her failure to perform appropriate medical tests?

[P]   Do you believe that just because a doctor does not intend to hurt his/her patient he/she should not be responsible for any negligent actions on his/her part?

[P]   Do you believe that even if the treatment a doctor gives is below the standard of care (or what competent doctors should do) the doctor *should not* be held liable for any injury resulting from his/her treatment?

[P]   Sometimes bad things happen through no fault of those involved. However, do you believe that when doctors are negligent they should be responsible for their negligence?

[D]   Do you feel that it is up to doctors to prevent all harm to their patients?

[D]   Do you feel that a bad outcome in a medical situation can occur without nurses or doctors being at fault?

[D]   Do you feel that just because someone dies in the hospital, the doctor or nurses must have done something wrong?

[D]   Do you feel that if the patient is not at fault for a serious complication arising from surgery, it must be the fault of the medical personnel who treated the patient?

[D]   Do you feel that mistakes can be made in nursing care and this does not automatically mean that these actions caused the problems encountered by the patient?

Patient and Doctor Responsibilities

[P]   Do you believe that doctors should make sure that their patients understand all the consequences of an operation or treatment plan prior to proceeding with the operation or treatment? [Or is it enough that the patient decides to go through with it?]

[P]   Do you believe that it is a doctor's duty to perform the necessary tests to ensure that selected treatments or operations are appropriate for his/her patients?

[P]   Do you think that doctors should be responsible for the treatment of their patients?

[P]   Do you think that it is the patient's responsibility to know what is best for him/her?

[P]   Do you believe that patients have a right to expect quality care from their doctors?

[P]   Would you have any reservations in returning a verdict in favor of the plaintiff in a case involving the doctor's failure to diagnose a serious illness?

[P]   Would you have any reservations in filing a lawsuit against a doctor or other medical personnel if you felt that you were hurt as a result of their negligence?

[D]   How do you feel about a situation where a patient withholds information from his doctor?

[D]   Do you believe that patients should not withhold important information from their doctors?

[D]   Do you believe that not only the doctor but the patient also is responsible for the success of his/her treatment?

[D]   Do you feel that even though a patient has signed a consent form recognizing the risks of certain complications, if one of these complications occurs it still should be the doctor's or hospital's fault?

Credibility

[P]   Do you believe that a doctor is more credible than other people just because he/she is a doctor?

[D]   Do you feel that you really can't believe the testimony of doctors/nurses when they are accused of negligence?

Other Medical Issues

[P]   Do you trust the doctors you have seen to provide the appropriate medical attention that you need?

[P] Do you believe that a patient has a right to expect to receive appropriate treatment from doctors?

[P] Do you understand that patients are in the position of having to trust doctors to do what is right?

[P] Do you believe that some patients may not receive proper medical treatment when seen by a doctor?

[P] Do you believe that a doctor would knowingly perform unnecessary surgery or operations?

[P] Do you believe that doctors are concerned only with helping others and are not concerned with making money?

[D] Do you believe that when it comes to hospital records or charts, if the doctors or nurses do not record an action in the paperwork, they probably didn't do it?

Alcohol-Related Accidents

[P] Do you believe that when someone drinks and chooses to drive he/she should be sure that his/her driving will be unaffected?

[P] What are your impressions of the effect of alcohol on one's driving ability?

[P] There may be evidence that the defendant was drinking prior to his/her driving that [evening]. Do you believe that alcohol can impair driving abilities (e.g., reaction times) even if one is not legally intoxicated?

[P] Do you believe that it is the driver's responsibility to make sure he/she is in a condition to drive safely?

[D] How do you feel about someone who has a few drinks and drives his/her car, provided he/she is not drunk?

[D] Do you think it is improper to drink and then drive a motor vehicle?

[D] Do you understand it is not against the law to do so?

[D] Would you feel that with any amount of drinking, a driver would be necessarily impaired?

[D] Would you feel that if the evidence showed that the defendant had a drink or two sometime before the accident you would expect the defense to prove that the defendant was not impaired?

Negligence

[P] During the course of this trial, you will hear several important legal terms. One such term is "negligence." Negligence is simply the lack of "ordinary (reasonable) care." It is the failure to do what a reasonably careful and prudent person would have done or the doing of something that a reasonably careful and prudent person would not have done. In this case the ordinary care standard applies to what a reasonably careful and prudent [doctor/driver] would have done in this situation. Would you have any reservations in applying this standard of care to [the defendant's] actions?

[P] Do you believe that the defendant would have to intend to harm the plaintiff in order for him/her to be negligent instead of the defendant not acting with the proper care given the circumstances?

[P] Would you have any difficulty in finding the defendant negligent if he/she did not intend to hurt the plaintiff?

[D] Would you have any reservations in rendering a verdict in favor of the defendant, if the plaintiff failed to prove that the defendant was negligent [liable]?

Plaintiff's Standard of Proof

[P] Do you believe that 51% is too low a standard for plaintiffs in (personal injury) cases?

[P] Do you believe that 51% is too low a standard in cases involving a potential verdict in the millions of dollars?

[P] Would you have any reservations in deciding a case against the defendant if the plaintiff showed that it was more likely than not that the defendant was negligent?

[P] Would you feel that given the size of the damages in the case something more than a preponderance of the evidence would be needed in order for them to find in favor of the plaintiff?

Presumption of Liability

[D] Do you believe that given the fact that [the defendant's car struck and killed the plaintiff] [the defendant's name] is in some way liable?

[D] Do you feel that he/she must have done something wrong?

Law Enforcement Actions

[P] Do you believe that law enforcement personnel should not be sued for their actions while they are on the job?

[P] How do you feel about lawsuits against law enforcement personnel?

[P] Would you have any reservations in finding the defendant liable, provided the evidence and law support such a finding, simply because he/she is a [law enforcement officer, state trooper, or policeman]?

[P] Would you have any reservations in awarding substantial damages against the defendant simply because he/she is a [law enforcement officer, state trooper, or policeman]?

[P] Would you tend to give the defendant's testimony greater weight as compared to other witnesses simply because he/she is a [law enforcement officer, state trooper, or policeman]?

[P] Do any of you believe that when police officers are pursuing someone for speeding, they are not responsible for their actions?

Wrongful Death

[P] This lawsuit involves seeking monetary damages from the defendant for the loss of a life, the life of [the plaintiff]. How do you feel about providing monetary damages for the death of a family member?

[P] How do you feel about providing monetary damages for the death of someone caused by the negligence of others?

[P]   Do you believe that money can't bring a person back, so why try?

[P]   Do you believe that it is important to provide such compensation?

[P]   Do you believe that lawsuits for the death of someone are not appropriate?

[P]   Do you believe that monetary damages are not appropriate when it involves the death of someone?

[P]   Do you feel that since you really cannot compensate someone for the loss of a loved one such compensation should not be given?

[P]   Do you believe that since money won't bring back people who have been killed [in traffic accidents or other relevant situation], lawsuits of this type should be limited to economic losses, such as lost income?

[P]   Do you think that because of the difficulty in coming to a figure for damages only a token amount should be awarded?

[D]   Now, the plaintiffs' lawyer, [name], mentioned the heartache that family members suffer when someone in the family dies. Do you believe that when a family member dies [in a traffic accident], the plaintiffs deserve monetary compensation?

[D]   Do you believe that the family deserves monetary compensation simply because they have chosen to bring this lawsuit?

Contributory Negligence

[D]   According to the law, if a plaintiff acted in a manner that contributed to his/her own injury, he/she is not entitled to compensation. This is what is referred to as contributory negligence. If you found that the plaintiff did contribute to his/her own injury by [specify reasons], would you be willing to return a verdict against the plaintiff?

[D]   According to the law, if the plaintiff, [name], was in any way responsible for what happened to him/her that day, then he/she is what the law calls "contributorily negligent." That is, if he/she contributed to his/her injury by any of his/her actions or lack of actions that day, then he/she is contributorily negligent. Now, in this case, we contend that the evidence will show that the plaintiff was contributorily negligent because [specify reasons]. Would you have any reservations in finding the plaintiff contributorily negligent if you found that it was more likely than not that his/her actions were a cause of his/her injuries that day?

[D]   The law says that if the plaintiff is contributorily negligent, he/she is not allowed to receive any monetary damages. Would you have any reservations in finding the plaintiff contributorily negligent if it meant his/her not being allowed any monetary damages?

[D]   Would you have any reservations in turning to the plaintiff and saying that you find him/her contributorily negligent?

Damages

Compensatory Damages

[P]   When it comes to awarding money in a lawsuit, which do you think is worse: to award too little money to an injured party OR to award too much money to an injured party?

[P] When it comes to including money in your verdict, which do you think is worse: to include too little money for an injured party OR to include too much money for the injured party?[1]

[P] In your role as a juror, should you find that the defendant is liable (was negligent) would you award the full amount of damages allowed by law? Would you have any reservations in doing so?

[P] If you were a juror, would you have any negative feelings about returning a multi-million dollar verdict if the evidence warrants such a verdict?

[P] What problems would you have in returning a multi-million dollar verdict?

[P] According to law . . . (describe elements). Some of these damages we usually do not think of in monetary terms. Would you give careful consideration to [pain and suffering or other factors] and assign a dollar figure for each of these factors if the evidence supported such a finding? Would you have any reservations/any hesitation in doing so?

[P] Would you have any reservations in awarding damages for [the pain and suffering of the plaintiff]?

[P] Do you believe that these elements (list relevant elements) are any less important than damages for the loss of income or other monetary damages?

[P] Would you have any reservations in awarding substantial monetary damages?

[P] Some people would have a problem awarding millions of dollars in a civil lawsuit simply because it seems like a large sum of money. Do you feel this way?

[D] Would you have any reservations in awarding no monetary damages, that is, a verdict of zero dollars to the plaintiffs, if they failed to prove all aspects of their case under the laws of [this state]?

[D] Would the fact that the plaintiff has claimed [X million dollars: amount from pleading] in damages produce in your mind an impression that the plaintiff deserves [X million] dollars?

[D] Does this fact lead you to believe that the plaintiff deserves at least some money?

[D] Do you believe that just because someone is injured he/she should receive some compensation?

[D] Do you believe that just because someone files a lawsuit they deserve something?

[D] Do you feel that, should damages be awarded, these damages should reflect a logical analysis of the case based on the instructions as given by the judge?

[D] Do you have any concerns that your emotions may influence you in considering the amount of money, if any, that should be awarded in this case?

[D] Do you feel that it is important that if the defendant is not negligent, then the plaintiff should not receive any monetary award?

---

[1]For an excellent discussion of the virtues of not using the word "award" in voir dire (and throughout the trial) by plaintiffs, *see* Ball, David Ball on Damages: A Plaintiff's Attorney's Guide for Personal Injury and Wrongful Death Cases (2001). While using the term "award" is contrary to the positioning of the plaintiff's case, our research has shown that voir dire questions that use "award" detect differences between those jurors who have problems with "awarding" plaintiffs large sums of money and those jurors who do not. It remains to be seen whether such differences in phrasing produce any differences in the ability to detect anti-plaintiff jurors during voir dire.

[D] Would you have any reservations in awarding no monetary damages to the plaintiff if the evidence supported such a finding? That is, no matter how much sympathy you may have for him/her and his/her family, would you have any reservations in returning a verdict of no money damages?

[D] Do you believe that given the fact that [defendant] is a corporation, it should pay for the injuries to the plaintiff no matter what the evidence shows?

[D] Do you believe that given the fact that the defendant is a large corporation, it should pay for the injuries to the plaintiff regardless of whether or not the defendant was negligent?

[D] The plaintiff has asked for [X million dollars]. Do you feel that it would be easier for you to award monetary damages to the plaintiff when the defendant is a corporation than when the defendant is a person?

[D] Do you feel that justice would be done if you found that the defendant is not negligent and, hence, that the plaintiff is not entitled to money damages?

[D] Do you feel, for whatever reason, that a money award for any emotional suffering of someone (for "x") should necessarily be a large sum of money?

[D] Do you feel that given your views about life, you would tend to initially accept the damages figures (for "x") claimed by the plaintiff as being appropriate?

[D] Do you believe that it would take a little more evidence to render a verdict against a person than to return a verdict against a corporation like [defendant]?

[D] Based on what you know at this time, do you think that the defendant should be punished for what happened to the plaintiff?

Award Cap

[P] Would the fact that the damages in this case could run as high as [amount] dollars produce any hesitation in your mind in returning an award in this amount?

[P] Do you believe that an award of [amount] would simply not be justified under any circumstances—even if the facts in the case supported such a finding?

Mitigation of Damages (Defense)

[D] According to the law, individuals have a duty to mitigate or minimize the injury they receive. In this case that means [describe circumstances (e.g., failure to wear safety equipment)] constitutes the failure to mitigate damages. If the plaintiff failed to mitigate his/her damages, the law says that he/she is not entitled to compensation for any injury that would not have occurred if [specify appropriate behavior that should have occurred]. Should you serve on the jury in this case and find that the plaintiff failed to [specify appropriate behavior] would you have any reservations in reducing any award, if we are liable, by the amount that reflects this difference in injury?

[D] Tell me what you think about someone's failure to [specify appropriate behavior] in this situation.

Punitive Damages

[P] [Definition of punitive damages.] Would you have any reservations in awarding punitive damages against the defendant if the evidence and law supported such a finding?

[P] How do you feel about awards that are designed to punish corporations for wrongdoing?

[P] Do you feel that punitive damages should not be used to punish corporations for wrongdoing?

[P] Do you believe that corporations should not be punished through punitive damage awards when [specify circumstances (e.g., employees ignore safety regulations)], no matter what the circumstances?

[P] Do you feel that punitive damages do more harm than good?

[P] Would you have any reservations in returning a verdict of substantial punitive damages if the law and the facts supported such a finding?

[P] Do you feel that punitive damages serve a valuable role in punishing corporations for wrongdoing?

[P] Would the fact that it would take a large award to make a corporation the size of [the defendant] take notice and prevent future injuries cause you any reservations in awarding punitive damages?

[P] Would you be willing to return a verdict for substantial punitive damages if the evidence and law supported a finding of punitive damages?

[D] Do you feel that just because the plaintiff makes a claim for punitive damages, they are appropriate in this case?

[D] Based on what you know, do you have any feeling that the defendant should be punished for what happened?

[D] If you felt that the defendant did not act [relate definition of punitive damages to situation], would you have any reservations in not returning punitive damages?

Sympathy

[P] The judge will instruct you that you should not base your decision on liability of the defendant on sympathy. The plaintiff [plaintiff's family] has not come here today seeking sympathy. However, when you consider the issue of damages you will need to come to grips with exactly what has happened—how this tragedy has changed his/her life. If you served as a member of this jury would you be able to consider this and not "close your eyes" to these facts?

Would you have any reservations doing so?

[D] This is a case in which we all feel great sympathy for the plaintiffs. However, the judge will instruct you that you are not to base your decision in this case on sympathy. If you served as a member of this jury would you be able to set all sympathy aside and decide this case on the facts and law presented in this trial?

Would you have any reservations in doing so?

[D] Have there been times in your life when you have had to make decisions you knew would disappoint someone, e.g., on the job or with family or friends?

How did you handle those situations?

[D] In this case, you will be asked to make a decision that will disappoint the plaintiff. That is, we maintain that the defendant is not liable. Would you have any hesitation in returning a verdict in favor of the defendant when it results in disappointing the plaintiff?

[D] Do you think that making one side or the other happy in this situation is how this case should be decided?

[D] Could you have sympathy for [the plaintiff or his/her family] and still understand that his/her own actions were a cause of his/her injury (death)?

[D] If you are a juror in this case, the judge will instruct you that your decision is not supposed to be based on sympathy for one party or the other. Would you have any reservations in deciding this case strictly on the evidence and the law in this case and not on any sympathy you may feel for either party?

Multiple Plaintiffs (Defense)
Liability

There are [number] plaintiffs in this trial. Would that fact indicate to you that this case is more important than if there was only one plaintiff?

Do you feel that given the number of plaintiffs the defendant must be liable?

With [number] plaintiffs, each of the plaintiffs' cases must be considered on its own. Would you have any reservations in considering each plaintiff separately in arriving at your decision in this case?

Contributory Negligence

According to the law, if a plaintiff contributes in any way to his/her injury, he/she is not entitled to recover any damages. If you found that any or all of the plaintiffs were contributorily negligent, would you have any reservations in returning a verdict of no monetary damages for each of those plaintiffs?

In considering the [number] plaintiffs, would you have any problem with treating each plaintiff separately in recognizing how his/her actions may have contributed to his/her injury?

Do you feel that by raising this fact we are trying to put the blame where it doesn't belong? That is, these people have been injured and it just isn't right to say they may have contributed to their own injury?

Separate Damages

In this case there are [number] plaintiffs. The extent of injury is different for each one. Would you be willing to consider each plaintiff separately in deciding what damages, if any, are appropriate for each plaintiff?

If you considered one, two, or all of the plaintiffs as not entitled to damages from the defendant, would you be able to return a verdict of no damages for these plaintiffs?

Would you have any reservations in doing this?

Contract Disputes

Could you tell me a little about your views on the responsibilities of the parties who sign contracts?

What do you think are some of the obligations or duties of those who sign a contract?

Do you believe that when someone signs a contract they should live up to the agreement?

Do you believe that when corporations sign a contract they should live up to the agreement also?

Have you heard the expression "A person's word is their bond"? What does this expression mean to you?

Sometimes companies or individuals may make a verbal contract or agreement. Tell me a little about what you think about verbal contracts.

Do you believe that verbal contracts are any less valid than written contracts?

Would you have any reservations in holding the parties to their verbal commitments?

Do you believe that if a company has any questions about the terms or tasks involved in a contract it should ask about these items before signing the contract?

Do you believe that in making bids for a contract a company should make sure it is clear on exactly what needs to be done before submitting a bid?

If you find that both parties signed the contract, would you have any problems in making both of the parties live by the contract terms?

Would it make any difference to you that it would cost one party money to live up to the contract terms?

[P] Do you believe that parties should follow the contract terms no matter what the consequences?

[P] Do you feel that there are any situations where a party should not be required to fulfill the terms of a contract? What would be examples of those situations?

How do you feel about the parties living by the terms of the contract they signed?

Would the fact that one party must pay additional money to meet the terms of the contract be a good excuse for not following the contract?

[D] Do you feel that lawsuits should not be used by businesses as a way to make up for money lost through bad business decisions?

Which do you feel is more important—the intent of the parties when they signed the contract or the actual wording of the contract that the parties signed?

[P] *[After defining fiduciary duty]* How important do you feel it is that when a party has a fiduciary duty to another it avoids even the appearance of acting for its own benefit?

[P] Do you feel that fairness and honesty have different meanings when you are dealing with business investments as compared to individual relationships?

Patent Disputes

[P] Do you feel that it is not fair to sue a business for infringement of a patent when it did not know the patent existed?

[P] Do you feel that if a business does not know about a patented (product or process) and develops a similar (product or process) on its own, it should not have to pay any royalties to the patent holder?

Overall, do you have any reason to believe that researchers at the United States Patent and Trade Office *do/do not* adequately investigate applications made for patents?

[D] Do you feel that the USPO can make mistakes by granting a patent when it should not do so?

[D] Do you feel that the process by which one is granted a patent is generally fool-proof?

Do you feel that big corporations would deliberately infringe on a patent in order to avoid paying royalties?

Do you feel that when big corporations are accused of infringing on a patent they would say anything to avoid paying legitimate royalties?

Do you feel that companies should not be allowed to reverse engineer a competitor's product to see how it works?

Do you feel that reverse engineering plays a valuable role in keeping businesses competitive?

Product Liability

What is your opinion of [relevant industry or company]?

[P] What do you feel are the responsibilities of a manufacturer concerning the safety of those using its products?

[P] Do you feel that too often companies put profits over the safety of their products?

[P] Do you feel that [relevant industry/manufacturers] would delay in employing safety measures in their products in order to make greater profits?

[P] Do you feel that makers of [product/industry] need to do more to make their products safe?

[P] Do you feel that most big corporations are greedy (untrustworthy)?

[P] Do you feel that if people smoke, even if they quit, they should not complain if they have medical problems later in life?

[P] Do you feel that lawsuits against [industry/manufacturer] alleging defective products serve to make these products safer?

[P] Do you feel that warning labels on products are ineffective because people generally ignore them anyway?

[P] How important are safety issues for you when buying a [certain product]?

[D] Do you feel that lawsuits against manufacturers needlessly drive up the prices of their products?

[D] Do you feel that lawsuits against manufacturers of medical products make it harder for patients to get needed medical care?

[D] Do you feel that it is simply not possible to prevent all injuries from the misuse of a product?

[D] What do you feel are the responsibilities of consumers for the safe use of a product?

[D] What do you feel are the responsibilities of workers concerning the safe use of potentially dangerous equipment?

In terms of government safety regulations in [a given area/industry], do you feel that safety regulations for this industry are too strict, about right, or not strict enough?

Do you consider yourself to be very cautious when personal safety is involved?

[P] When buying a vehicle, would you say that for you safety is very important, somewhat important, or not as important as other factors?

Do you feel that workers should not sue for injuries on the job when they did not follow safety rules?

Do you feel that most accidents occurring in the workplace are the result of carelessness on the part of the workers?

Toxic Tort

[P]   How concerned are you with the issue of toxins in the environment?

[P]   Do you believe that toxins in the environment is an important problem?

[P]   Do you believe that chemicals in our food and environment are a major cause of illness or cancer?

In terms of government environmental regulations in [a given area/industry], do you feel that environmental regulations for this industry are too strict, about right, or not strict enough?

[P]   Do you feel that the government is doing enough to protect our environment from pollution?

[P]   Do you feel that if a manufacturer's use of chemicals harms the health of workers or other citizens, it should be responsible for paying for the consequences no matter what the cost?

Multi-Vehicle Accidents

[D]   Do you believe that when there is a large multi-vehicle accident, everyone is partially at fault?

[P]   Some people believe that when a *driver* on the highway hits *another vehicle* which has stopped or slowed down during bad weather conditions the *driver* is at fault for not leaving sufficient distance to stop or avoid an accident. Others believe that the *driver* is not at fault because bad weather simply can cause accidents to happen. How do you feel about this? [Or] Which view is closer to your own: the *driver* is at fault for not leaving sufficient distance to stop or avoid an accident OR the *driver* is not at fault because bad weather simply can cause accidents to happen?

[P]   How concerned are you with personal safety when driving on the highway or Interstate?

[D]   Do you believe that bad traffic accidents can happen with no one being at fault?

[P]   Do you believe that it is reasonable to expect drivers to be in control at all times while driving on Interstate highways?

[P]   Do you believe that tractor-trailer drivers often drive too fast for road conditions?

Conduct of Lawyers
Objections

During the course of trial, there will be times when I will raise objections over procedural matters and the court will determine whether these objections are valid. This is part of my job. Would you have any concerns about these objections?

Would you feel that what would have been said is deserving of your attention?

Would you be able to simply decide this case on what is said on the stand and not on any speculation about why an objection was raised?

Rigorous Cross-Examination

During the course of the testimony of witnesses brought by the [opposing party], I will have an opportunity to question the witnesses to bring out information from them that I think you should know about. Sometimes, it is necessary to be fairly forceful. I will try at all times to be courteous to these witnesses, but I may have to be forceful. Would the fact that I question a witness in a forceful manner cause you any concern in this case?

Closing Questions

Do you have any religious, moral, or ethical beliefs that would make it difficult for you to decide this case in favor of either party?

[P] Do you have any religious, moral, or ethical beliefs that someone should not sue another person?

Do you believe that if the law as the judge gives it to you at the end of this case goes against your personal views of what the decision should be, you would tend to base your verdict on your personal views of the case?

[D] The defense presents its case last, after all the evidence is presented by the plaintiff. Would you have any problem in waiting to make up your mind until the defense has had a chance to present its case?

[D] Would you wait until after the defense presented its case and you have heard the judge's instructions on the law before making up your mind?

[D] Do you think that it would be important to wait until the end of the case before you make up your mind? Why is that?

[D] Would you expect the defense to prove the plaintiff wrong—that is, you would not require the plaintiff to prove its own case?

[D] If you believed by what you heard and saw in court that the plaintiff had failed to prove by a preponderance of the evidence that [the defendant] was negligent, would you be willing to stand by your decision no matter how the other jurors felt?

[D] Would you feel that it is important that you stand by your opinion? Why is that?

Since I may not have asked the kind of question—perhaps about some past experience or certain beliefs that you hold—that would have raised a question in your mind, let me ask this. If you were seated at either one of these tables, would there be any reason why you would not want yourself as a juror in this case? That is, at this time, would you feel uncomfortable being at either table and having someone like yourself as a juror?

As you sit right now, do the plaintiff and the defendant start out even, or do you feel one starts out a little ahead of the other?

At this time, do you feel because of your experiences and beliefs that in your mind the plaintiff [defendant] starts out this case a little ahead of the defendant [plaintiff]?

As it stands now, how many of you feel that you would tend to lean a little in favor of the plaintiff [defendant]?

This is a very serious case. Do you feel that there is any reason whatsoever that you could not be fair to both sides in this case?

APPENDIX IV

List of Juror Questionnaires

Criminal Trials

Armed Robbery

U.S. v. Aaron Haynes, United States District Court, Western Division of Tennessee, Cr. No. 01-20247. (see below)

Wisconsin v. James H. Oswald, Waukesha Co. Circuit Court: Case No. 94-CF-0228. (see below)

Wisconsin v. Theodore W. Oswald, Waukesha Co. Circuit Court: Case No. 94-CF-0227. (see below)

Bribes/Illegal Gratuities/Perjury

U.S. v. Alfonzo Espy, United States District Court for the District of Columbia, Cr. No. 97-0335 (RMU).

U.S. v. Oliver North, United States District Court for the District of Columbia, Cr. No. 88-0080. (Iran Contra)

Grand Larceny

New York v. Dennis Kozlowski and Mark Swartz, Indictment Number 5259/02. (Tyco)

Medicaid Fraud

U.S. v. Bobby Johnson and Larry Hunt, United States District Court for the Northern District of Georgia. Cr. No. 1:97-CR-426. (Superseding)

Murder (Noncapital)

California v. Robert Blake, Case No. LA040377. (February 2004)

California v. Robert Blake, Case No. LA040377. (November 2004)

California v. O.J. Simpson, Case No. BA 097 211.

Commonwealth of Virginia v. Andrew Alston, Cr. Case No. 04-02.

Connecticut v. Michael Skakel, FST-CR00-135792 T.

Michigan v. Jack Kevorkian, 93-10158.

North Carolina v. Michael Peterson, File No. 01-CRS 24821.

North Carolina v. Rae Lamar Wiggins (Rae Carruth), Case No. 99-CRS-46567-69.

Texas v. Robert Durst, Case No. 04-CR-0323.

Wisconsin v. James H. Oswald, Waukesha Co. Circuit Court: Case No. 94-CF-0228.

Wisconsin v. Theodore W. Oswald, Waukesha Co. Circuit Court: Case No. 94-CF-0227.

Murder (Capital)

California v. Erik and Joseph Menendez, Case No. BA068880.

California v. Scott Peterson, Stanislaus Co. Superior Court, No. 1056770. (Laci Peterson murder)

California v. David Westerfield, San Diego County Superior Court, No. SCD165805. (Danielle van Dam murder)

Florida v. Jerry Layne Rogers, Criminal Division, Case No. 83-1440-CF.

New Jersey v. Fred Neulander, Indictment No. 1993-06-00, Camden County.

Tennessee v. Courtney Mathews, Case No. 01-5-01-9511-22-00219, Montgomery County District 19. (Taco Bell murders)

U.S. v. Shawn Breeden et al., United States District Court, Western Division of Virginia, Cr. No. 3:03CR000013-001.

U.S. v. Emile Dixon, United States District Court, Eastern District of New York, CR01-389.

U.S. v. Tommy Edelin et al., United States District Court, District of Columbia, Case No. 98-264.

U.S. v. Kristen Gilbert, United States District Court, Western Division of Massachusetts, 96CR30054–MAP. (Veteran's Hospital murders)

U.S. v. Kevin Gray et al., United States District Court, District of Columbia, Case No. 00-157.

U.S. v. Aaron Haynes, United States District Court, Western Division of Tennessee, Cr. No. 01-20247-D.

U.S. v. Coleman Johnson, Jr. (#1) United States District Court, Western Division of Virginia, Cr. No. 3:00CR00026.

U.S. v. Coleman Johnson, Jr. (#2) United States District Court, Western Division of Virginia, Cr. No. 3:00CR00026.

U. S. v. Theodore John Kaczynski, United States District Court, Eastern District of California, CR-S-96-259 (GEB). (Unabomber case)

U.S. v. Timothy McVeigh, United States District Court, District of Colorado, Cr. Action No. 96-CR-68-M. (Oklahoma City Bombing)

U.S. v. Jean Claude Oscar et al., United States District Court, Eastern Division of Virginia, Cr. No. 2:93CR131.

U.S. v. Julio Otero and Felix Ortiz-Velez, a/k/a "Bori", Case No. 3:CR-96-005.

U.S. v. Darrell David Rice, United States District Court, Western Division of Virginia, Cr. No. 02-CR-26-ALL.

U.S. v. Gary Sampson, United States District Court, Eastern Division of Massachusetts, Case No. 02CR10384.

U.S. v. Christopher Wills, United States District Court, Eastern Division of Virginia, Cr. No. 99-396-A.

Commonwealth of Virginia v. Charles Riner, Cr. Case No. F00-39.

Commonwealth of Virginia v. John Allen Muhammad, Cr. Case No. CR54362-65. (D.C. sniper case)

Negligent Homicide

People v. Frank Ronald Castro, Guam Superior Ct., Cr. Case No. CF 0324-98.

Obstruction of Justice

U.S. v. Arthur Andersen, United States District Court for the Southern District of Texas, Cr. No. H-02-121. (Enron scandal)

Organized Crime/RICO/Narcotics

U.S. v. Joseph Anemone, United States District Court for the Eastern District of New York, 01CR0056(CBA).

U.S. v. Liborio Bellomo et al., United States District Court for the Eastern District of New York, 02CR140(ILG).

U.S. v. C. Eugene DeFries, United States District Court for the District of Columbia, Cr. No. 93-117.

U.S. v. Alberto Figueroa et al., United States District Court for the Eastern District of New York, 00CR778(RJD).

U.S. v. Peter Gotti et al., United States District Court for the Eastern District of New York, 02 CR 606 (FB).

U.S. v. Mark Hoyle et al., United States District Court for the District of Columbia, Cr. No. 92-0284.

U.S. v. John Stanfa et al., United States District Court for the Eastern District of Pennsylvania, Cr. No. 94-127.

Possession of a Controlled Substance/Drug Trafficking

U.S. v. Marion Barry, United States District Court for the District of Columbia, Cr. No. 90-0068.

U.S. v. Manuel Noriega, United States District Court for the Southern District of Florida, Case No. 88-79-CR-HOEVELER.

Pandering

California v. Heidi Fleiss, Los Angeles Superior Court, Case No. BA083380.

Securities Fraud

U. S. v. Martin Grass, Franklin Brown, & Franklyn Bergonzi, United States District Court for the Middle District of Pennsylvania Case No's: CR. 1CR02-146-01, CR. 1CR02-146-02, CR. 1CR02-146-03. (Rite Aid)

Sexual Assault

Colorado v. Kobe Bryant, Eagle County District Court, Case No. 03CR204-Division G.

U.S. v. Hollis Earl Roberts, United States District Court for the Eastern District of Oklahoma, Case No. CR 95-35-S.

Wisconsin v. Mark W. Chmura, Waukesha Co. Circuit Court: Case No. 00-CF-427.

Terrorism

U.S. v. Usama Bin Laden et al., United States District Court for the Southern District of New York, S(7) 98 Cr. 1023(LBS). (Embassy bombing)

U.S. v. Leo Felton and Erica Chase, United States District Court, Eastern Division of Massachusetts, Cr. No. 1:01CR 10198-NG. (Domestic terrorism)

U.S. v. Abdel Rahman et al., United States District Court for the Southern District of New York, No. S9 93 Cr. 181(MBM). (2nd World Trade Center bombing).

Violation of Civil Rights

U.S. v. Lemrick Nelson, United States District Court for the Eastern District of New York, 94CR823(FB).

Civil Trials

Antitrust

In Re Visa Check/Mastermoney Antitrust Litigation. United States District Court for the Eastern District of New York, Case No. CV-96-5238 (JG) (2003).

Bad Faith

International Paper Co. v. Affiliate FM Insurance Cos., Superior Court, San Francisco, No 974350. (2001)

International Paper Co. & Masonite Corp. v. Affiliated FM Insurance Co., Superior Court, San Francisco, No. 974350. (2003)

Breach of Contract

Royal Palm Resort v. Mitsui Construction Co. Ltd., et al., Guam Superior Ct., No. CV1885-93.

Environmental Damage: Oil Spill

In re: Exxon Valdez, United States District Court for Alaska, No. A89-0095-CV(HRH). (Exxon Valdez oil spill)

Fraud/RICO

U.S. v. Gold Unlimited et al., United States District Court for the Western District of Kentucky, Civil Action No. 4:95-CV-57-R.

Palimony

Greenlin v. Neves, Orange County Superior Court, Case No. 00CC01135.

Products Liability

Lowery v. Peabody International Corporation et al., Circuit Court of Etowah County, CV-91-153-WHR

Mercado v. Warner-Lambert Co., Harris Co., Texas, Dist. Ct. No. 2000-42692.

Mildred Valentine v. Dow Corning Corporation et al., County of San Francisco Superior Court, Case No. 943437.

Romo v. Ford Motor Company, Stanislaus County Superior Court, Case No. 82318.

Texas v. American Tobacco Company, et al., United States District Court for the Eastern District of Texas, Civil No. 5:96-CV-91.

Sexual Assault

Mary M. v. T.G.I.Fridays, Orange County Superior Court, Case No. 00CC12460.

Qui Tam

U.S. ex rel Bortner v. Philips Electronics North America Corporation et al., United States District Court for the Eastern District of Texas, No. 1:95CV363.

Wrongful Termination

Doe v. Kohn Nash, United States District Court for the Eastern District of Pennsylvania, No. 93-4510. (AIDS Discrimination)

INDEX